Architecture of Glasgow

Andor Gomme & David Walker

Completely revised edition

Lund Humphries · London
in association with the Glasgow booksellers John Smith & Son

Copyright © 1968, 1987 A. H. Gomme & D. M. Walker

First edition 1968
Second, revised, edition 1987

Published by Lund Humphries Publishers Ltd
16 Pembridge Road, London W11

Made and printed in Great Britain by
The Bath Press, Bath

Maps by John Flower

Gomme, Andor
    Architecture of Glasgow.—2nd rev. ed.
    1. Architecture—Scotland—Glasgow
    (Strathclyde) 2. Glasgow (Strathclyde)—
    Buildings, structures, etc.
    I. Title II. Walker, David, 1933–
    720'.9414143   NA981.G55
ISBN 0-85331-504-3
ISBN 0-85331-472-1 Pbk

Illustration acknowledgements:
T. & R. Annan: 36, 70, 163, 180, 197
The Architect's Journal: 82, 83, 92, 100, 101, 212
The Architectural Review: 103, 187
Bryan & Shear: 198
Building Pictures (M. Anne Dick): 51, 57, 60, 62–5, 71–2, 74–5, 90,
97–9, 112–14, 117, 119–20, 123–4, 165, 169, 172, 181, 184, 195, 203,
206, 217, 222, 229, 238–9, 241
D. C. Buwalda: 141
Commercial Union Assurance Group: 186
Hugh C. Ferguson: 196
Glasgow Herald: 160
Glasgow Museums Service: 28
Glasgow School of Art: 198–201
A. H. Gomme: 2, 35, 42, 80, 138, 155, 159, 175, 177, 188, 192, 205,
211, 248–58, 260, 262–5, cover
Douglas Scott: 85, 185, 193
Scottish Art Review and Isabel Mackintosh: 208–10, 214
Scottish Field: 50, 173
Scottish National Monuments Record: 18–20, 26, 31, 48, 55, 58, 66–7,
79, 95, 105–6, 127, 131–2, 134–7, 143, 151–3, 156, 158, 161–2, 176,
183, 204, 218, 259
Scottish National Monuments Record and the University of
Strathclyde: 22, 29, 37, 40, 45–6, 49, 73, 107, 122, 125, 129, 133, 140,
235
The late D. L. Stewart: 33
Studio Seven: 179
Thomson, McCrea and Sanders: 261
University of Glasgow: 111, 138–9, 144, 202, 216, 223
D. M. Walker: 47, 93, 110, 128
Watson, Salmond & Gray: 174
D. W. Wrightson: 30, 32, 41, 43, 52–4, 59, 61, 68–9, 76–8, 81, 84,
86–9, 91, 94, 96, 108–9, 115–16, 118, 121, 142, 145–6, 148, 150, 154,
157, 164, 166–8, 170–1, 178, 182, 190–1, 194, 207, 213, 215, 219,
224–8, 231–4, 236–7, 240, 242–7

Jacket/cover illustration: Municipal Chambers (175). Frontispiece:
Stirling's Library (former Royal Exchange, 222), view from North
Court.

In memory of
Arnold Wycombe Gomme and Ian Gordon Lindsay

The publishers acknowledge subsidy from the Scottish
Arts Council towards the publication of this volume.

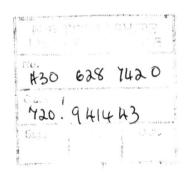

Contents

Nikolaus Pevsner **Foreword**

Sir John Summerson, we are told, is working on a book on Victorian London, as a sequel to his Georgian London. That is as it should be; for if one tries to divide the architectural interest of London into parts, one third, this is my opinion, would be of before the Restoration, one third of 1660 to 1820, and one third of 1820 and after. Try to do the same dividing for Glasgow and Edinburgh, for Liverpool and Manchester, for Bristol, for Leeds and Bradford – what would the resulting percentages be? In all these cases bar one or two the weight of importance on the Victorian and Edwardian Age would be even heavier. Yet what books have we to do justice to the Victorian and Edwardian styles in the major British cities? There is Dr Quentin Hughes's admirable *Seaport*, his account of the architectural character and the buildings of Liverpool (London 1964), and that is all. Manchester has the late Cecil Stewart's *The Stones of Manchester*, published as long ago as 1956 and now the much briefer, amply illustrated *Manchester Buildings* (Architecture North West, London and Manchester 1968), Newcastle has L. Wilkes and G. Dodds: *Tyneside Classical* (London 1964) and Bruce Allsop's *Historic Architecture of Newcastle* (Newcastle 1967), Edinburgh has Ian Lindsay's *Georgian Edinburgh* (Edinburgh 1958) and the larger A. J. Youngson: *The Making of Classical Edinburgh* (Edinburgh 1966). There is also Walter Ison's admirable *The Georgian Buildings of Bristol* (London 1952), and that is about all. I am trying in my *Buildings of England* to do justice to Victorian architecture, but I have of course neither enough space nor enough illustrations – nor alas enough information. For work on local books, journals, newspapers and photographs has only begun. Historians of the type and calibre of Asa Briggs pursue it, but historians of architecture lag behind. Examples of what ought to be done and how it ought to be done are Dr J. N. Tarn's still unpublished thesis *Housing in Urban Areas, 1840–1914* (Ph.D. Thesis Cambridge 1962) and Mr Reece Winstone's collections of photographs of Bristol (by now eleven slim volumes, and a twelfth in production, reaching from the 1850s to today). The first incidentally, as far as I am aware, to have treated the Victorian years in architecture with full appreciation and the care taken over the buildings of the preceding centuries were the late Kay Fisker and Mr Knud Milich in their big beautiful book on the architecture of Copenhagen of between 1850 and 1950 (*Danske Arkitekturstrømninger, 1850–1950*, Copenhagen 1951). But while British sightseers are ready to grant the Copenhagen town hall the status of a monument as valuable as any of earlier ages, how few realize that the Manchester and Leeds town halls are as outstanding architecturally as any building of their dates anywhere in Europe or America, and how few would even consider taking a day off to wander sightseeing through Glasgow.

They will, many of them, one may hope, in future. For Dr Gomme's book does fully what Dr Hughes's had done for Liverpool. He has all the qualities needed to put Glasgow at last on the architectural map. He writes extremely well, he describes buildings accurately, never skimping a tricky detail, and he analyses them with sensitivity, and together with Mr Walker he has done the research painstakingly before sitting down to write. And the research must have caused pains indeed, as shows in a remark of Dr Gomme's which deserves to be pulled out of the modest obscurity of a footnote into the concentrated light of this foreword. Here it is, taken from p.93: 'The main architects of the mid-nineteenth century in Glasgow formed so many partnerships with one another and moreover shared so few names that there has understandably been much confusion. There were at least seven Thomsons (only two of them related), five Hamiltons (father and son, and father and two sons, unconnected either with one another or with the Edinburgh architect), two Bairds (unrelated), five Wilsons (father, son and three others), as well as a Wylson and (from London) a Willson, and two quite distinct firms of Baird and Thomson (with no overlapping, though to add to the confusion Alexander Thomson worked at different times with both Bairds). Moreover both Bairds were John, two of the Wilsons were Charles, two of the Thomsons James; and to cap it all there is an Alexander George Thomson who is nothing to do with either Alexander or George Thomson.'

Mentioning Alexander Thomson, better known as Greek Thomson, shows that it would not be true to say that nineteenth-century Glasgow was before Dr Gomme entirely off the architectural map. Greek Thomson can be called a national figure in British architecture, and Mackintosh in this year of the centenary of his birth an international figure in architecture. Dr Gomme is briefer on the latter than on the former, taking into consideration no doubt the existence of Professor Howarth's comprehensive volume (London 1952) and what has been written by others. For Greek Thomson his chapter is of the greatest value, not least because it establishes that Greek Thomson is not all that Greek. His stature grows as one tries to see his various endeavours as part of one, personally still mysterious, personality: the faith in the neo-Greek of Schinkel, the sympathy with ancient Egypt, the insistence on square pillars instead of columns, that is the rigidly rectangular instead of the rounded, the delight in picturesque composition on the small scale of the Italianate villa and on the huge scale of the churches, and the fascination with all but continuous glazing behind, and independent of, the solid stone screens which form the fronts.

But if Greek Thomson was more Thomson than Greek, Glasgow architects and patrons in his time and even after his death were – this no one can deny – more Grecian in their sympathies than those of any other city. Churches such as James Sellars's Kelvingrove parish church of 1879 and Hugh Barclay's St George's in the Fields of 1886 will be mis-dated on a scale of about sixty years by any unwarned passer-by, and James Miller in the nineteen-twenties and thirties is a continuation of a Glasgow tradition rather than a re-revival inspired by the New York of McKim, Mead & White.

On McKim, Mead & White we have a publication of four folio volumes (New York 1915), but who has ever heard of James Miller, Hugh Barclay, and James Sellars? The fact is that, while by now names such as Soane, Barry, Butterfield, Street, Waterhouse, and Aston Webb may be said to belong to general education, the designers of a number of nationally very remarkable Glasgow buildings are unknown even to educated Glaswegians. This applies to David Hamilton in spite of his Royal Exchange of 1839, to Charles Wilson in spite of his somewhat nightmarish but for the visual scene immensely important Free Church College of 1856 and his beautiful Queen's Rooms of

1857, to John Baird's Jamaica Street warehouse of 1855, all iron and glass, to J. T. Rochead's Grosvenor Terrace of 1855, to Alexander Kirkland in spite of his sumptuously Venetian 37 Miller Street of 1854, to David Rhind's Commercial Bank of 1857, a masterpiece of original composing with Cinquecento elements, to James Sellars's mighty, neo-Greek St Andrew's Halls of 1873 and the Barony Church of 1886 by J. A. Campbell and/or J. J. Burnet.

J. J. Burnet – for Londoners Sir John Burnet – is the most mysterious of all. He would certainly deserve a monograph, though he had none of the intensity of Mackintosh or the power of Thomson. How could a man develop from a Beaux-Arts training in Paris to the bold and wholly convincing angular neo-Baroque of the narrow front of the Athenaeum Theatre of 1891 and end with the calm and competent classical Edward VII's Galleries of the British Museum on the one hand and with the 'Early Modern' Kodak Building in London and the Wallace Scott tailoring factory at Cathcart on the other? Or do all these buildings represent different men in one liberally run office?

The Wallace Scott factory, so Dr Gomme tells us, has 'recently been disgracefully mutilated', and the record of Glasgow in the cause of the preservation of her best buildings is indeed black. It is true, Thomson's Queen's Park Church was a war casualty, and it is also true that money has been voted to reinstate Thomson's Caledonia Road Church after the fire of 1965 and money is being spent on converting the gutted St Andrew's Halls – the fire took place in 1962 – into an extension of the Mitchell Library, but when at last will Mackintosh's Ingram Street Tearooms be restored and reconstructed? This seems to me the next and a foremost duty. And what of the other menaced buildings mentioned throughout Dr Gomme's text, and what of the many shop-fronts doing terrible damage to good buildings? Dr Gomme does not mince his words; his text is full of 'peculiarly callous', 'horribly mutilated', 'nasty mess', and of 'lamentables' and 'disgracefuls', and he needs all the backing he can get from readers of his book. The Adams' Assembly Rooms are gone, the Adams' Infirmary is gone, the wings of the Justiciary Court are gone, and James Adams' College Houses are now in danger from the ring road.

Dr Gomme's last chapter does not refer to the ring road specifically, but as it deals entirely with Glasgow's townscape the dangers to the visual scene of the city of the ring road as now projected are implied. Dr Gomme's treatment of the city's character and what visually constitutes it reveals him as a critic as sensitive and as sound as the other chapters reveal him in the role of the architectural historian. May the men and women of the city's council and committees ponder every word of this chapter. The chapter and indeed the whole book are an eleventh-hour warning.

Preface to the Second Edition

Sir Nikolaus Pevsner, in his exceptionally generous foreword, calls this book an eleventh-hour warning. Many would say that since it was first published in 1968 the twelfth has struck and seen Glasgow laid in ruins. We ourselves spoke then of how the city had been and still was being terribly mauled: in view of what has happened since one might wonder what we were fussing over. The record of destruction has been terrible, almost as if our book were the signal for the passing of the old Glasgow – the reports of which, living at a distance in England, I found so painful that it was a decade before I could bring myself to come back, when there was talk of a new edition and it was time to look again and see what now needed to be said. I think I was fortunate in the way I happened to see Glasgow again – arriving from Edinburgh at Queen Street (having passed near enough to Barmulloch to see the towers) and taking a bus to Kelvin Bridge. After such a ride nothing could be worse: it took me through the nearest comprehensive development area to the centre of the city, part of an architectural disaster area which stretches from where St George's Cross used to be through Cowcaddens to the top of Buchanan Street and then eastwards to the cathedral and beyond. What caused this disaster? Firstly the unassimilable road itself: an urban motorway *must* split the town apart; for buildings on a scale proportional to it can only dwarf human beings, who remain the same size however their creations grow bigger or smaller; and buildings proportioned to *them* cannot possibly relate to one another across two hundred yards of road purposely built to have no contact with them. (Much of this particular stretch is on stilts and consequently a further visual barrier.) But huge as was the swathe of destruction which cut through the city in advance of the motorway, that destruction was much larger whose aim was to clear what were thought to be unregenerable slums and stigmata on the public face of Glasgow, and to make room for whole provinces of flatted blocks none of which has the slightest pretension to artistic merit and which in no way make a truly urban landscape: they are simply a priced-down offshore version of the megalomaniac insensitivity of Le Corbusier's fifty-year-old visions of the city of the future.

As I rode westwards and found that Great Western Road was still there, the old – the real – Glasgow suddenly came into its own, and with much more force than I had known it to do before: as if it were something new (and perhaps with my eyes arrested by the effect of recent cleaning) I realized afresh the virtue of all the varied projections on the fairly commonplace tenements making up many Glasgow streets, which give a sense of such alert busy life to an otherwise humdrum scene. By contrast hardly a new block in the city has realized the significance of these variations in texture, which, small as they often are, create the wonderfully richly modelled Glasgow streetscape. Concrete balconies hung out here and there on isolated twenty-storey slabs are in this respect of no use at all, make no contribution (any more than do the endless pre-cast honeycomb grids of Anderston Cross) to the tactile fabric in which the surface itself has depth created by frequent, but not monotonously repeated, recessions and projections of detail – so easy, indeed inevitable, on classical buildings with their necessary cornices, sills, columns, pilasters and pediments, but assembled in innumerable ways by the architects and builders of the nineteenth century often in forms that were only vestigially classical or not classical at all.[1]

For those who appreciate the virtues of a truly urban, indeed metropolitan, environment, the rehousing of Glasgow could not have come at a worse moment than one when architects and local government officials thought only in terms of huge insulated buildings, when point-blocks appeared to councillors the country over to be the sign of a city in step with the modern world, and even quite small towns went up their fifteen storeys.[2] Such blocks do not create an urban environment, nor were they intended to. They stand, each one alone, enisled in a sea of emptiness, mammoths loose in a landscape otherwise featureless because dwarfed by the objects placed upon it.

But the loss of so much of the overall fabric of the city – most especially in the inner residential areas – is only one aspect of the assault that Glasgow has suffered during the last two decades. There are indeed successes of conservation to record. At least the magnificent façade of St Andrew's Halls survived the fire of 1962 and subsequent threats of total site-clearance and has been cleaned and rehabilitated to give magisterial authority to the Mitchell Library; Grosvenor Terrace, half-destroyed after fire in 1978, is once again a complete façade, though the new half is built of synthetic materials; new interiors have likewise ensured the outward survival of the New Club and the Stock Exchange; Queen's Cross church is safe in the hands of the Charles Rennie Mackintosh Society; Elgin Place has been reprieved from a fifteen-year-old sentence of death to become a disco-restaurant; and St Andrew's is fully restored. None of this would have happened without prodigious efforts from campaigners who believe in Glasgow, and they have alas been defeated more often than they have won. In the text, buildings destroyed since 1968, and in the gazatteer all demolished buildings, are marked by an obituary dagger; but a few of the worst losses must be recorded with proper prominence here (in chronological order of building): Spreull's Land, Trongate (p.53); James Adam's College houses (p.62, **40**); Houldsworth's Mill (p.106, **81**); half the north side of George Square (p.56, **34**); Abbotsford Place and all the surrounding streets (p.73, **52**); 37–51 Miller Street (p.111, **85**); almost all (and certainly all the best) of Greek Thomson's tenements (p.141 etc., **118**); Randolph & Elder's engine factory (p.107, **82**); the Dunlop Street section of the Buck's Head (p.143, **121**); St Enoch station (p.107, **89**); and perhaps worst of all two of J. J. Burnet's most assured achievements, McGeoch's (p.205, **185**) and the Alhambra Theatre (p.266, **259**). Churches, as everywhere, have been particularly at risk: among others Gorbals, Greyfriars, Barony Free and Park have gone (though Park's tower was suffered to stay on the grounds – a remarkable thing in Glasgow – of its contribution to the townscape); Langside Hill, Cowcaddens, Townhead, Tolcross and St George's-in-the-Fields have a less than certain future; St Andrew's-by-the-Green, no longer doomed by the ring road, has been cleaned but is nevertheless derelict; and – incredible anywhere else – the remains of Thomson's Caledonia Road, never safeguarded since the fire, have been once again under official threat, have been further vandalized, and nothing is done to protect what the fire-raisers and vandals have left.

The pace and scale of destruction have been the more lamentable in view of the plain evidence of an extraordinary revival of interest in Glasgow. In the last few years this has made its way into the heart of the city; and here, happily, we can move again to the positive. To go back in the golden warmth of the summer of 1984 was a delight and a revelation: the city gleams. That, despite the terrible losses, so much even now remains is to the credit of the creative energy of the nineteenth century; that it looks now so well is to that of Glaswegians of the present day who, having done so much that we have been forced to deplore, are now, publicly and privately, making prodigious efforts to realize the physical splendour of their city. Not all the restoration has been sensitive enough; but buildings whose excellence one could only guess at through the grime shine for all to see; quantities of others unregarded before reveal themselves as rich and rewarding elements in the enthralling various Glasgow scene, their modelling appreciable because now the light can cast shadows on to the pale buff or pink of their stone. Colour is an aspect of Glasgow as it cannot have been for the last hundred years: the lovely honey-coloured sandstone was already beginning to show when we wrote in the 1960s; an equally beautiful pearly grey we knew nothing of, and the pink – a newcomer to the city in the 1880s – only as something irregularly dingy with a most depressing effect on those buildings which then appeared to suffer from it.[3] But now Glasgow is really colourful; and the great work goes on: scaffolding is everywhere, signifying no longer the destructive impetus of the 1970s but cleaning and restoration, perhaps most encouragingly the refurbishing of redundant warehouses as housing: Albion Buildings, Ingram Street, 101–23 Candleriggs and 61–81 Miller Street are now complete, the last ingeniously re-using a glazed internal court for access; Virginia Court is on the way. The same spirit is behind the pedestrianization – still sporadic and on a small scale – which has added so much to the enjoyment, especially of Buchanan Street, which one no longer has to take on trust as one of the great streets of Europe: not only can one stroll at large and at ease and stop to admire where one wants; but the setting, now an outdoor room for trees and sculpture, has been immeasurably improved.[4]

There has been a wealth of new writing. Simply among those specifically concerned with the city and its architects, we have had Dr. McFadzean's *Thomson* (1979) and new editions of Howarth (1977) and Macleod (1983) on *Mackintosh*; John R. Hume's *Industrial Archaeology of Glasgow* (1974) opened up a vast range of buildings and their history which we scarcely touched upon; Andrew Gibb's *Making of a City* (1983) has a wealth of geographical and social history which – in time – would have made our architectural judgements much more secure; Michael Donnelly has written a 'preliminary study' of *Glasgow Stained Glass* (1981), Colin Johnston and Mr Hume a very full one of *Glasgow Stations* (1979); the indefatigable Frank Worsdall gave us his full-length study of *Tenements* (1979), his angry *City that Disappeared* (1981) and most recently a record of survival in *Victorian City* (1982); *Glasgow at a Glance* has always been in demand (a further revised edition has appeared); and we ourselves have been gratified by frequent requests to know when we should again be in print.

Here, then, we are. In the interests of economy the original text has been reprinted by photo-lithography with only minimal amendment; but it has been possible to include new photographs to show buildings without their funereal coats and to insert a number of corrections and some additional material into the marginal notes as well as at the ends of two chapters: where these are of substance they are distinguished by square brackets. A new chapter has been added, containing lengthier second thoughts and an exploration of buildings which, through lack of knowledge or sympathy, were ignored before. The gazetteer has been entirely reset, the maps redrawn and the architects' biographies revised as far as space would allow.[5]

Sadly our obituary cannot be confined to buildings. From among those, the generous gift of whose knowledge benefited our first edition so much, we have to record the loss first of all of A. G. Lochhead, to whom we and all Glaswegians will always owe an immeasurable debt: he it was who first discovered what it is to know the fabric of the city in depth, and it is particularly grievous that his last months were saddened by the loss of so much that he cared for. No less to be regretted are the deaths of Andrew McLaren Young, Alex Smellie, W. J. Smith, John Watson, Alex Wright, and of course Sir Nikolaus Pevsner. To compensate us, the work of revision has been made easier and more rewarding by the helpful observations of many friends. We have to thank

Richard Chafee, R. N. Millar and H. S. Stevenson for pointing out errors, and Ian Campbell, Michael Donnelly, John R. Hume, David McLees, Raymond O'Donnell and Joe Rock for important new information derived from their own researches. Judith Anderson, Ranald McInnes, Aonghus McKechnie and Mark Watson all contributed to the gazetteer. Ian Gow and, as before, Catherine Cruft have also helped in numerous ways, as have Roger Billcliffe and Juliet Kinchin. We have been once again fortunate enough to find sponsors whose generous help has enabled us to keep the price of this new edition within bounds. Our special thanks therefore first to the Scottish Arts Council both for a most munificent subsidy and for the wholehearted support which lies behind it; second (but only in time) to John Smith & Sons, and in particular Robert Clow, for so enthusiastically joining in the publishing venture and encouraging us to include many new images of the rejuvenated city. Most of all, our personal thanks go to Anne Riches, whose patient searches among records in and out of Glasgow and discoveries among the streets and buildings of the city have revealed a vast deal hitherto unknown to us, which she passed on without reserve: in particular her studies of the RIBA nomination papers have thrown a new light on to the architectural families of the late nineteenth century, on apprenticeships and assistantships, and on the Glasgow presence at the Ecole des Beaux-Arts. This second edition is inscribed to her with our ever-grateful thanks.

(1984–6)

[1] Well, there *are* a few encouraging signs, a few new buildings really incorporating into their own design an awareness of this peculiarly Glaswegian surface-in-depth: there are for example the tenements in and near Woodside Road, St George's (where the architects have had the foresight even to tone the brick to match the colour of red sandstone), and in the city the Scottish Amicable Life in St Vincent Street, and a few others: see pp.273–6 below.
[2] Tamworth in Staffordshire is a pathetic example, like a corner shop dressed up to pretend it's a supermarket. With the completion in 1967 of the 31-storey Red Road flats in Barmulloch, Glasgow had the dubious distinction of owning the highest reinforced-concrete domestic structures in Europe:

their subsequent reputation is not one that the city will want to be reminded of. Since about the mid 1970s the evidence of the psychological and social damage done by forcing people to live in high-rise flats in vast areas of nothing else has been so unmistakable that the blanket elimination and rebuilding of whole sections of the city has been abandoned; and with the setting up, first of all, of the Glasgow Eastern Area Renewal project in 1976, comprehensive redevelopment has put on new clothes and opened a new approach to what we now learn to call 'recovery areas'. (See Andrew Gibb, *Glasgow: the Making of a City* (1983), pp.169ff.)
[3] Here and there, where an uncleaned and a cleaned tenement stand side by side, one can

see immediately how the architecture is lessened by dirt: in Highburgh Road for example.
[4] Thanks to Glasgow's system of back lanes pedestrianization should present fewer traffic problems than in most English cities.
[5] One major remaining lacuna we are regretfully conscious of – the lack of any proper consideration of architectural sculpture. Glasgow sculpture deserves a monograph to itself: for the moment all we can do is to point to the brief but mouth-watering summaries in Benedict Read, *Victorian Sculpture* (1982) – see especially pp.117f, 188f, 230f, 330f, 365ff – and in Susan Beattie, *The New Sculpture* (1983), pp.90ff and 219ff.

Preface to the First Edition

Glasgow has had a bad press. For this it has itself partly to blame. The city seems to have been proud enough of itself until the first world war, but now its own people look on it with a good deal more of affection than of respect, and there are still, alas, many (in or out of authority) whose attitude to the fabric of their city can be summarized in the generalization that if it's in Glasgow it's bad. When, in 1950, my father wrote an article in the *Glasgow Herald*, stressing the urban virtues of the city – though, as it seems to me now, making excessively mild claims – this seemed to be a daring or at least paradoxical thing to do. Even more recently, Mr J. M. Reid's book, which is also not extravagant in its praise, appears to have been largely passed off as a harmless aberration. As to Glasgow's popular reputation outside, this is too widespread and too ill-informed to need further attention.[1]

The most serious consequence of this attitude is that Glasgow has been, and still is being, terribly mauled. Luckily the process has not yet gone as far as in many English cities; luckily too the bomb-damage, with one unhappy exception, was slight. There is still a chance of saving not only the best of the individual buildings (of which there are very many), but also the tough, sturdy and amazingly inventive architectural character of the city as a whole. And there are signs of a new waking up to a new attitude. At present nineteenth-century architecture is getting more respectful and more serious critical attention than at any time since it arrived: indeed the nineteenth century may in some parts be said to be definitely *in*. It is urgent that Glasgow take advantage of this new climate of feeling. For Glasgow, as we know it, is essentially a Victorian city.

Yet here again we are up against a difficulty, though, properly seen, the difficulty springs from the most interesting and important characteristic of nineteenth-century Glasgow: its architects were almost entirely regional, even local. It is no use coming to Glasgow for buildings by the well-known Victorians: there is half a church by Bodley, two by Emmett,[2] and a sketch by Pugin; Scott has two large buildings (neither among his best), Barry, Carpenter, Butterfield, Street, Pearson and Shaw none at all. Even Edinburgh architects did comparatively little in Glasgow: the Adams put up a few buildings, most of which have disappeared; and from the nineteenth century there are important works by Archibald Elliot and David Rhind, with some good terraces by George Smith, and, later, work by R. R. Anderson and J. M. Dick Peddie. Correspondingly, the Glasgow architects kept almost entirely to Glasgow (there was ample work for them there), with the very unfortunate result that neither they nor their buildings are known outside to any but a few specialists.[3] Of the major Glasgow architects of the nineteenth century – Stark, Hamilton, Baird, Wilson, Kirkland, Rochead, Thomson, Honeyman, Sellars, the two Burnets – only Thomson, and perhaps the younger Burnet, are more than names to most people. Hamilton may possibly be remembered as one of the runners-up in the competition for Westminster Palace: he is dismissed in a phrase by Professor Hitchcock, our greatest authority on Victorian architecture, who does not even mention Wilson, one of the most interesting of all the architects of the mid-century.

But not only is Glasgow one of the few cities in Britain which can claim a very strong local tradition in architecture, developing almost independently of the rest of the country: it also has a recognizable local style. And this style is in important ways different from any of the several styles which occupied the Victorian architectural stage in England. To receive the best of what Glasgow has to offer, one must be prepared to abandon preconceptions formed by acquaintance with other cities. How important this is we may learn once again from Professor Hitchcock, who denies Glasgow 'much good urbanism' in the first half of the nineteenth century, and by implication in the rest of the century too.[4] What this seems to mean is less that Professor Hitchcock has not really looked than that he has come from Edinburgh looking for more examples of what is done so supremely well there. And of course it is not to be found. But Glasgow's 'urbanism', is, I think, just as good as Edinburgh's – it is simply very different. If Glasgow is the Victorian city *par excellence* (its only possible rival is Liverpool), it must be recognized that one Victorian characteristic that it possesses pre-eminently is independence of spirit. If we are genuinely open to the possibilities of new architectural experience we ought to welcome this, rather than sadly accept it is a necessary but unfortunate condition of finding something to enjoy. To adapt a phrase of Lawrence's, all rules of construction hold good only for cities which are copies of other cities. A town which is not a copy of other towns has its own construction, and what an imitator calls faults, I call characteristics. It is an essential lesson, not only with regard to Glasgow, but for all places which seek to be themselves.

The aim of this book, therefore, is to draw attention to characteristics. It grew out of an article (which was never published) on Glasgow in the nineteenth century, into a booklet, and finally, when it seemed proper to include as much information of general interest as possible, into the present book. At first it was to appear over my name alone. But during the writing of it, I became so indebted to Mr Walker's immense and always increasing fund of knowledge and to his scrupulous reading and re-reading of the manuscripts that the only right way to acknowledge his share in the book is the one that has now been adopted. (This has the further advantage that I no longer have to make constant and repetitive reference to him in the footnotes.) Nevertheless it should perhaps be explained that the actual writing has been my responsibility, though I have absorbed many happy phrases from my colleague. The opinions and evaluations expressed represent, I think, a genuine consensus between us, arrived at, often, after much discussion, though there probably remain occasional cases of difference with which we have not thought fit to worry the reader. We have retained the first person singular, which I had used from the start, as demonstrating a personal approach for which the plural seemed pompous.

All lovers of Glasgow must be permanently indebted to the patient work of Mr A. G. Lochhead, who was the first to assemble a scientific collection of information about the city and its architects, which he has gone on refining ever since and which has been incorporated into the list, prepared for the Department of Health for Scotland (now the Scottish Development Department), of buildings of architectural and historic interest. The list was kindly made available to me in its provisional form by the Glasgow Corporation Planning Department; and I have also been able to use the second (though still not statutory) edition. Mr Reid's little book (*Glasgow*, Batsford, 1956) has been a constant stimulus, and I have quarried it extensively for historical material: it deserved to be much better known. Other recent books that I have found specially useful have been *Old Glasgow*, by the late I. G. Lindsay and Ronald Cant (Oliver & Boyd, 1947), *The Architecture of Scottish Post-Reformation Churches*, by George Hay (Clarendon Press, 1957), and lately *Glasgow*

at a Glance (Collins, 1965), a very handy collection of photographs and sprightly captions, edited by Andrew McLaren Young and A. M. Doak. We have been given valuable help, advice and encouragement by Mr Jack Coia, Mr John Harris, the late A. D. Hislop, Miss Elizabeth Jack, Mr G. L. Jarvis, the late I. G. Lindsay, Professor McLaren Young, Dr C. A. R. Radford, Mr J. W. Sim, Mr Alex Smellie, Professor W. J. Smith, Sir John Summerson, Mr John Watson and Mr Alex Wright.

We owe a special debt to Professor Pevsner for writing the foreword, and even more for being so constantly enthusiastic during the preparation of material and the writing of the book, particularly during periods when it seemed never likely to appear at all. Equally valuable have been the encouragement and stimulus given to me by Mr John Taylor of the publishing side of Lund Humphries. Rarely can an author have enjoyed the co-operation of a more eager, more helpful or more ingenious publisher. One of the greatest of his services was to introduce me to Mr David Wrightson, who has specially taken nearly half the photographs used in the book: not only is Mr Wrightson a first-class architectural photographer, he has an uncannily acute eye for the townscape and individual quality of a city. I had to do no more than point to a building for him immediately to discover the viewpoint, the lighting and the treatment which would do it most justice or render its character most vividly; and on more than one occasion his camera has actually made new discoveries about the Glasgow scene. Most of the other photographs came from the Scottish National Buildings Record, and I should like specially to thank Miss Catherine Cruft for her patient unearthing of those which would be of use to me. But many are by photographers in Glasgow, who have most generously allowed me to reproduce their work for a nominal fee and on occasion waived this altogether. Such kindness has been of inestimable help in the creation of a book the expense of which has been a constant problem to the publishers and ourselves. The problem would not have been solved without the timely and generous help of the Universities of Keele and Glasgow, each of which has made a most handsome grant towards the cost of production.

To all of these and to many others I owe an immense debt of gratitude. My prime source of encouragement throughout has, however, been my wife, who has not only borne with admirable good humour the domestic confusion without which, it seems, I cannot contrive to work, but has herself done most of the typing and worked with me on the preparation of the manuscript and above all on the preliminary work of studying buildings, photographs and drawings. She spent long hours tramping the streets of Glasgow, looking for interesting and less interesting buildings; and without the excellence of her taste and the precision of her judgement, I should have made far more blunders than I have.

Andor Gomme
Church Lawton, December 1965–April 1967

[1] As early as 1855, Glasgow architects complained of the slighting and contemptuous treatment they were given in London journals.
[2] Emmett also produced plans for the Royal Faculty of Procurators; but it was the local Charles Wilson who got the job, see p.121.
[3] Even Mackintosh, renowned though he was on the Continent, built nothing of importance outside Glasgow and its immediate neighbourhood. He is the only Glasgow architect who has so far been made the subject of a full-length study.

Chapter 1   The Medieval City

Note: Bold figure references in the text relate to the illustrations.

The authenticated history of Glasgow cannot properly be said to begin until the Middle Ages. Its origins, several hundred years earlier, are still largely a matter of legend and speculation. Nevertheless a number of well-established facts attach to these; and it is unlikely that the legends are entirely fictitious. A fort, 450 feet by 430, just on the present northern boundary of the city was excavated in 1912-14 at Balmuildy; there is no evidence of any other Roman settlement in the area, which was briefly and precariously held. But Glasgow stands just inside the western end of the Antonine Wall, and a Roman road forded the Clyde at or near the site of the Old Glasgow Bridge. Nothing now seems recoverable from the troubled times that followed the abandonment of the Antonine Wall in about 190.

At the beginning of the fifth century St Ninian returned to Scotland from Rome and began his missionary work. Though he is most commonly associated with the extreme south-west, he travelled and preached over a great part of modern Scotland. Conversion seems to have been fairly widespread in the lower part of Strathclyde, and St Ninian founded a cemetery at the point where the old Roman road crossed the glen of the Molendinar burn about a mile north of the ford over the Clyde. St Ninian probably died in about 430: so the site of Glasgow Cathedral was Christian for 100 years before it began its familiar association with St Mungo. St Mungo (whose alternative name of St Kentigern is regarded as more correct but has failed to win popular appeal) is supposed to have been the son of St Thenew, who was miraculously saved from death when she was thrown from Traprain Law by her father, the King of Lothian, after she had been found to be with child. (St Thenew once gave her name to one of Glasgow's main streets; strangely transformed, it survives in the centre of the city as St Enoch.) The child was apparently born and brought up on the north coast of the Firth of Forth, though his supposed connexion with the famous missionary St Serf is now discredited. Towards the middle of the sixth century Mungo moved westwards; and the story tells that near Stirling he met an aged and holy Christian named Fergus, who asked that when he died his body should be placed on a cart drawn by two untamed bulls and should be buried where they rested.[1] They stopped at St Ninian's graveyard; and here not only was Fergus buried, but St Mungo himself settled and founded a religious community. The site was called Cleschu or Glaschu, which is said to mean 'dear community', the *cara familia* of Mungo himself. [1a]

The King of Strathclyde chose Mungo as bishop – a term which must obviously be treated generously, though it is attested by Welsh documents which refer to him as the 'bishop of Garthmwl'. Some time later there was a pagan reaction under a king named Morken, whose relatives after his death forced Mungo to leave Strathclyde. He took refuge with St David in South Wales and later founded the monastery of St Asaph. At the Battle of Ardderyd in 573, the Christians in Strathclyde triumphed under King Rhydderch, and Mungo was recalled. After living for a time in Dumfriesshire he returned to Glasgow, whose ecclesiastical authority was thus re-asserted.

[1] Cf. J. M. Reid's *Glasgow*, pp.19–20, for the story told in more picturesque detail.
[1a] Alternatively 'Glascu' means the glas (or church) of Cu[notegernus], the Celtic form of Kentigern.

At the time of St Mungo's death (in about 590), Glasgow cannot have been more than a village; but its church continued to be a centre of religious life in the west country until Strathclyde was absorbed into the growing kingdom of Scotland. The great architect of the medieval union of the country was David I, who sought to modernize and civilize Scotland in the European way. Abbeys and bishoprics were the crucial mainstays of this new civilization, and David's first object was the reorganizing of the Church, but in independence of the Archbishop of York, who had claimed authority over the Church in Scotland. The mark of his success came in 1110 when, without reference to York, David's tutor John Achaius was consecrated Bishop of Glasgow directly by the Pope.[2]

So Glasgow became the bishop's town; and for the next 450 years this is what it remained, save that in 1488 it gained the added dignity of an arch-bishopric. It was not until well after the Reformation that the town became a Royal Burgh, but as early as 1176 William the Lion granted to Bishop Jocelin the right to establish a burgh in Glasgow with all the privileges of a royal burgh, a grant which was later solemnly confirmed by Pope Alexander III, who took the city under his protection.[3] The first cathedral of which we have any record had, however, been built many years earlier: it was begun by Achaius and consecrated in 1136. It stood above the tomb of St Mungo, perhaps on the site of Mungo's own church. From this moment the shape of the medieval town was settled: it must grow from the cathedral on its hill south-westwards to the ford across the Clyde at a place called the Stock-well, where the first stone bridge was later built (in 1345). It was not until the late eighteenth century that the sloping ridge joining cathedral and river crossing was seriously challenged as the principal axis of the city. As Glasgow grew steadily, though not fast, to a town of some size and commercial importance, so the area round the Cross gained in relative significance. It was at this point, where the land flattens out, a quarter of a mile north of the Clyde that a crossing over the glen of the Molendinar was easy; and here was the natural place for the main cross street which linked with the road from Edinburgh. So the Cross and the site of the main markets were estab-lished where the Cross still is, at the junction of Hiegait, Gallowgait, Walkergait (the modern Saltmarket) and St Thenew's Gait (now Trongate). Oddly enough Briggait (Bridgegate) did not reach the Cross directly, but ran nearly along its present line joining the bridge to the foot of Walkergait (probably to avoid danger of flooding). So the centre of business was at the other end of the town from the cathedral; but both spiritual and temporal power remained where they had always been. For the bishop was not only the bishop but a great feudal lord, whose power was marked by the size, if rather less impressively by the dignity, of his palace.[3a]

Of medieval Glasgow nothing now remains above ground apart from the cathedral and one house. The Reformation got rid of a good deal (the cathe-dral itself being, it seems, only just saved, and of course at the expense of being turned into a Protestant church, in fact into three Protestant churches, so that, after being known as the Hie Kirk for 200 years, it regained its title only by Presbyterian courtesy): there was a series of disastrous fires; the archbishop's palace became a quarry; and the cavalier Victorians eliminated almost everything that was left. Most of the old buildings that remained in High Street disappeared in the 1880s in the carnage that followed the

[2] It was not, however, until 1188 that Bishop Jocelin won a decision from Rome that the Scottish bishops were directly dependent on the Holy See.
[3] See Reid, *op. cit.*, p.29.
[3a] Recent research shows the need to modify this account: as late as the Reformation the ecclesiastical nucleus was physically separate from the burgh centred on the Cross, whence growth was northward *toward* the cathedral. See Gibb, *Glasgow – the Making of a City*, pp.14ff.

University's move to Gilmorehill. It is said that the railway company who bought the College site would have kept the old façade; but it went during road widening, when John Carrick built here and in Saltmarket for the rather unhappily named City Improvement Trust. (The quadrant below Cathedral Square was done in the early 1900s, by Frank Burnet, also for the Trust.) So the old city was got rid of by municipal design. The approximate ground plan, however, remains (though somewhat regularized and revised in the eighteenth and nineteenth centuries), together with some street names; and surviving drawings which have been adapted and absorbed into many later books make it possible to get some idea of the city in the late Middle Ages.

The area to the south-west of the cathedral must have been nearly an ecclesiastical enclave, 1. Immediately west of the cathedral was the palace or castle of the bishops and, later, archbishops, occupying an irregular hexagon about 180 feet wide and rather more than 300 feet long. The hexagon was haphazardly filled with buildings, chief of which was the 'palace' itself, or Great Hall, built by the resplendent John Cameron (bishop 1426–46), a large oblong tower house of a type familiar in later medieval Scottish castles. It was three or four storeys high, with a corbelled parapet, saddle-back roof and slightly higher extension at one end; the windows seem to have been very small. James Beaton (archbishop 1508–22) surrounded the castle grounds with a substantial ashlar wall about 15 or 20 feet high, crenellated and reinforced with circular bastions, and incorporating and enlarging a tower, built by Cameron at the south-west corner, into a pele, five storeys high, again with corbelled and crenellated parapet and saddle-back roof. Gavin Dunbar (1524–47) completed the work with a large and clumsy gate-house at the south-east corner. This was a plain rectangle with cylindrical corner turrets on the outer angles, crenellated, with a simple ridge-roof and crow-stepped gables. It had a single arched entrance. The whole castle, which had been badly treated at the Reformation, was restored by Archbishop Spottiswoode in 1611, but it was again in ruins when Defoe visited Glasgow in 1689. It was given by the magistrates as a quarry in 1755 and the last traces disappeared in 1789 to make way for Adam's Royal Infirmary.[4]

Most of the streets surrounding the castle became filled with the prebendary manses of the cathedral canons. Bishop Cameron increased the chapter from six to thirty-two, and obliged the canons to live near the cathedral. So Drygate, Rotten Row, Kirk Street and Castle Street were lined with their houses (and gardens and orchards), of which Provand's Lordship is the only remainder, **2.** Provand's Lordship was the manse of the prebendary of Barlanark, who was also known as Lord of Provan. (Provan apparently comes from the Latin *prebenda*; so the name may be merely an alternative version of the ecclesiastical title. James IV is said to have been Lord of Provan when he became an honorary canon of the cathedral.) The house is no doubt fairly typical, though possibly larger than most, for part of it may have housed some of the inmates of the adjoining St Nicholas's Hospital. Provand's Lordship was built in about 1471. It is a good example of a late medieval town house of medium size – of three storeys with attics, built of undressed stone. The front to Castle Street is plain, of three bays with regularly spaced windows which are doubtless an eighteenth-century alteration of a more

2. Provand's Lordship (1470). The back view showing the additions of 1671.

[4] It was, however, still reasonably complete when Thomas Hearne drew it in the spring of 1782.

random arrangement: perhaps the top windows originally broke through a lower eave-line into characteristic half-dormers. The end elevations both have crow-stepped gables. The back is perhaps closer to the original appearance of the building, though the wings in their present form seem to be as late as 1670 (see the date incised on a skewput). There are three crow-stepped gables, all of different sizes, and a fourth which is now no more than the base of a (later) chimney. The windows are irregularly spaced and of various sizes. The most noteworthy internal feature is the very fine stone newel stair of remarkable width. Most of the rooms have heavily timbered ceilings, the beams rough-cut. The floors and glazing are modern. 4a

Early drawings suggest that many of the houses in High Street must have been of this type, **3**, though many, especially in the lower part of the town, were of wood, at least on the upper storeys. Two of these survived in Saltmarket until quite late in the nineteenth century; and there is of course an unusually large and splendid example in Huntly House, Canongate, Edinburgh. The Glasgow tenements never grew to the height of the stone ones in Edinburgh: the city was much smaller and less pressed for space, and three storeys seems to have been the normal maximum, though certainly there were a good many smaller houses. Drygate in particular was evidently much less regular than Kirk Street and High Street, with many cottages, most of them thatched. A single-storey house, known for some reason as Lord Darnley's Cottage, stood with others on an island site immediately south of the palace, between Drygate and Kirk Street. Probably there were many like it. A few aristocratic families had houses in the town of the same general type as the manses: indeed, after the Reformation the manses of the prebendaries of Peebles and Eaglesham were absorbed into a house built by the Duke of Montrose. His house was larger, but hardly grander, than any of the others. (Nor indeed was the University, which left a rather meagre building in Rotten Row for a tenement on the site of its later buildings, and did not receive its distinctive appearance until the seventeenth century.)

The cathedral represents everything that the old city was not: a coherent, unified design of great regularity – indeed severity – in its outward form. Only at the west end did it have an appearance of less than perfect organization; and the Victorians saw to that too. Yet for all this unity, the cathedral as we have it represents the work of at least four, possibly five, periods; and the building history is less simple than it appears at first.

The see was, as we have seen, established (or re-established) by David I in about 1110, and John Achaius appointed to the bishopric. His church was consecrated in 1136, and burnt down about 1190; no visible sign now remains. Some evidence mentioned by Billings[5] suggests that whatever stone parts there were may have affinities with Kelso, another of David's foundations, though Glasgow was clearly not on the same grand scale.

Rebuilding seems to have gone ahead very fast, for by 1197 enough was standing for reconsecration. The bishop at this time was Jocelin, and his 5a church, clearly more ambitious than its predecessor, is something of a puzzle. Most of the evidence disappeared at the time of the complete rebuilding which apparently began in the 1230s and resulted eventually in the church we now have. But John Honeyman[6] showed that the south-west compartment of the lower church and, perhaps more importantly, a good deal of the lower walls of the nave can hardly be later than c.1200. The square bases of the

4a Recent renovation has cleared away the grime, but the details are now more unreliable than ever.
5 *Antiquities of Scotland*, Vol.3.
5a In fact Jocelin had already been architecturally active by 1181, when he was described as 'gloriously enlarging the cathedral' (Fawcett, *Glasgow Cathedral*, 1985, p.25); so the burnt church was at least in part his work.
6 *The Book of Glasgow Cathedral*, ed. George Eyre-Todd (1898).
[T. L. Watson took a different view of the evidence from the crypt, holding that the surviving twelfth-century shaft is not in its original place (see *The Double Choir of Glasgow Cathedral*, 2nd edn., pp.27ff). His reasoning has been (implicitly) refuted by Dr. Fawcett (*op. cit.*, pp.9, 25).]

outer vaulting shafts in the nave aisles, and the keel moulding of the shafts themselves, are of a type older than anything in the chancel. (Billings also observes[7] that the lower part of the west end is the oldest part now standing.) Yet the main structure of the nave has commonly been agreed to date from, at the earliest, the end of the thirteenth century; and it has therefore been assumed that the rebuilding of the nave stopped at a fairly early stage and was not resumed for the best part of a century.

Meanwhile the entire east end, both the lower church and the chancel, were started afresh by Bishop William de Bondington, who began work in about 1233. In 1242 a provincial council at Perth passed a canon promoting the building of the cathedral: indulgences were available to contributors to the work. There is good reason to suppose that the east end was substantially finished by Bondington's death in 1258.

Here, then, we have two known rebuildings whose chronology provides a number of puzzles. In the first place, there is the great and unusual speed with which Jocelin's church was built, particularly since Achaius's may not have been destroyed until as late as 1192. In the second, there is the remarkable fact of apparently two rebuildings within fifty years with no evidence of any further destruction by fire or collapse. Thirdly, there is the problem that Bishop Bondington apparently found a cathedral with chancel and without

[7] *Antiquities of Scotland*, Vol.3.
The evidence for Jocelin's church has recently been re-assessed by C. A. R. Radford and E. L. G. Stones in an extremely interesting article to which reference is made below (*The Antiquaries' Journal*, vol.xliv, pt.ii, 1964).
[Their account was later published in a handbook (H.M.S.O. 1970). The benches on which the aisle shafts stand are a developed version of the fragment surviving in the crypt.]

3. High Street in the seventeenth century. (From 'Glasghu Facies')

nave, yet instead of completing the nave, left that and built the east end all over again. (If it is suggested that the 'false' start on the nave belonged to the second, Bondingtonian, rebuilding but was abandoned in favour of work on the chancel, we should have to account for why it was abandoned; and further we must account for a rebuilding which – apparently intended to be complete – began with the nave rather than, as commonly, with the liturgically more important east end.) There is the further complication of the difference between the windows in the north and south aisles of the nave. Those in the south aisle must be of *c*.1300; those in the north look much earlier. They are a slight refinement on a type used largely in the crypt[8] and, with modifications, in the chancel. But the chronology of Scottish Gothic is so odd and irregular that these windows are not beyond doubt earlier than those of the nave clerestory; they cannot possibly belong to Jocelin's time, and the solution normally proposed is that they are part of a continuation of Bondington's work immediately after the completion of the east end, a continuation which for some reason – perhaps to concentrate on the crossing and tower – was then abandoned and left unfinished until the end of the thirteenth century. (It has been pointed out to me that it would be natural in Glasgow to build the north wall first both for protection against wind and to allow the sun to shine on work in progress. The south wall of the crypt would be completed last; for, left open, it gave the most convenient access for materials and scaffolding at the lowest part of the site.)

It might seem initially that a plausible way to account for this confused building history would be to assume that the fire of 1190 or thereabouts destroyed the nave of Achaius's church but only damaged the chancel. Jocelin's work was then to restore, rather than totally rebuild, the chancel – something which could reasonably easily be achieved in the five or six years at his disposal before the consecration in 1197. He then began to build the nave anew, but for some reason – shortage of money, plague, the wars with England – was prevented from going very far. Bishop Bondington was evidently a man with high ideas for his church. Even so, the obvious thing in the circumstances would have been to complete the nave first and then think about rebuilding the restored chancel on a more lavish scale. It could then be suggested that Jocelin's restoration was inadequate, that the chancel had in fact been so weakened by the fire that an entire reconstruction was necessary, a view which might account for the appeal for money some time *after* Bondington set to work. The chancel then being the more urgent, it was taken down and rebuilt to an entirely fresh design, the nave being again put off until later.

This account, however, would presuppose that the conception of the lower church belonged to the old cathedral of Achaius and was only modified under Jocelin; and this, we can be morally certain, may be ruled out. Glasgow was admittedly an important see; yet comparison with contemporary cathedrals in Celtic Britain makes it extremely unlikely that Achaius's building could have been anything like ambitious enough to include an elaborate two-storeyed east end. (Radford and Stones[9] conjecture a smallish [8a] cruciform building without aisles, similar to the twelfth-century cathedral of Bangor, occupying the flatter ground covered by part of the present nave and crossing.) The whole conception of the double church at the east end is therefore Jocelin's, and we can assume that this work (of which a fragment remains at the south-west corner of the crypt) was substantially complete

[8] As has often been pointed out, the Glasgow 'crypt' is not a true crypt, since it is wholly above ground. But it seemed pedantic to insist on 'lower church', and so I use the more familiar, if not wholly accurate, word.

[8a] It has been suggested that, once a ceremonial burying of St Mungo had taken place, his remains are unlikely to have been moved and that the present site of the tomb must have been within Achaius' church and *a fortiori* within Jocelin's. But there are recorded instances of such removals, the most famous being that of St Swithin at Winchester.

[9] See Radford & Stones, *op. cit.* pp.230–2 [handbook, p.12].

by the consecration in 1197. What form the remainder of the plan took is still largely a matter of conjecture. The solution proposed by Honeyman was that Jocelin adapted a favourite Scottish plan (cf. Elgin) of a square east end in which the chancel extends one or two bays east of the aisles. He argued that if the south-west bay of the crypt marks in fact the east end of the south aisle of Jocelin's church, then a chancel two bays longer would in fact include St Mungo's shrine, which would be under a high altar placed at the extreme east end, again a common practice in the twelfth century. On this assumption, Jocelin planned (and partly built) a church with nave of eight bays, chancel of four, probably no transepts, and aisles stopping two bays short of the east end. The crypt would only have had three bays, with single bay 'aisles' which would have been little more than ways into the area of the shrine. Radford and Stones have, however, shown that the remaining twelfth-century column was in a central position, showing that the east wall of the south aisle had at least two bays, which would imply either double aisles (most unlikely at such a date) or, as they persuasively argue, an east end which closely resembled the still existing and exactly contemporary design of Rochester, which has an eastern transept at both upper and lower levels: the remaining column therefore appears to be part of the east wall of the eastern transept.[10] It should be stressed that the conception of the lower church is in part the result of conditions imposed by the awkward lie of the land, which made normal transepts difficult and a large eastern extension impossible: the number of chapels needed by the chapter could therefore not be included at ground level, and so the huge crypt contains these as well as (originally) the shrine.

There remains the problem of the nave. If Bondington really found a church with a complete, albeit relatively modest, east end and a nave that had barely been begun, it is certainly odd that he should have once again rebuilt the crypt and chancel and allowed the completion of the nave to wait still longer. But Bondington was not appointed to the see until 1233, and Jocelin had died in 1199. In between there were four bishops, and surviving records are silent about any building going on in these thirty-four years. The times were admittedly disturbed, but it seems unlikely that almost nothing was done to carry on Jocelin's energetic work. Radford and Stones, therefore, take the heroic line of supposing that the western half of the cathedral was in fact completed in the first quarter of the thirteenth century, and that the nave was subsequently gutted in the early fourteenth, new arcades inserted and the upper parts of the outer walls rebuilt as we now have them.[11]

That there is no record of a thirteenth-century nave or of fourteenth-century demolitions is clearly inconclusive. But this account still leaves one major problem. Though it has been everywhere agreed that the nave as we have it must be early fourteenth-century, it is exceptionally conservative for that date. Apart from the windows in the south aisle and the tracery in the triforium arches, one may guess that it is not so very different from what the thirteenth-century nave might have been. And if that had existed, what would have been the point in pulling it down seventy or so years later to build something so old-fashioned? The parallel that Radford and Stones draw with the rebuilding of Exeter is in truth not very close: the Norman nave of Exeter was gutted so that it could be rebuilt in the very up-to-date style of the newly built chancel; and when Winchester nave was likewise modernized, it was done with no stylistic regard for anything that had gone before.

[10] *Ibid*. pp.228–31 [handbook, p.13]. [This view has been confirmed and illustrated by Dr Fawcett (*op, cit*., p.26): in order to incorporate the tomb his reconstructions include a central projection eastward of the transept.]

[11] *Ibid*. pp.227–8 [handbook, pp.14ff].

There remains another possibility – that, despite all evidence to the contrary, the present nave is in essence not fourteenth-century at all. What, after all, is this evidence? Principally that the columns of the nave have a smaller and simpler section than those of the chancel, with keel-moulded shafts and moulded capitals; and that the south-aisle windows and triforium tracery are of second pointed character. But it is quite conceivable that all these details are in fact alterations to an existing structure rather than part of a complete rebuilding. (Even at Winchester the fifteenth-century columns of the nave are in fact existing twelfth-century columns refined and sculpted to Perpendicular forms.) MacGibbon and Ross[12] point out that the arch-mouldings of the rather crude triforium openings are clumsily connected to the shafted jambs which run up into the clerestory – an awkwardness which could be explained by the jambs never being intended to accommodate the triforium arches which were inserted much later. Moreover a notable characteristic of the nave has not yet been mentioned – namely that its columns are much closer together than those of the chancel: the two arms of the church are of almost equal length, yet the nave has eight bays, the chancel only five. Arcades of the fourteenth century, in Scotland as in England, tend to have distinctly wider bays than those of the thirteenth; yet the nave bays are narrower than those of the mid-thirteenth century chancel: the natural assumption is that they are older. Was it then that the fourteenth-century rebuilding used the foundations of early columns as an economy (and as a further saving of money even re-used the old wall-shafts)? Why should it have? The whole assumption of the fourteenth-century *rebuilding* (rather than alteration) must be of something whole-hearted and complete. And this seems to be contradicted by the visible evidence of the structure that we have.[13] So, as things now stand, the simplest explanation is that the Decorated details result from a recutting of the doubt-less rather plain columns of the early thirteenth-century arcade, a refenestration which for some reason got no farther than the south aisle, and a none too skilful insertion of geometrical tracery into the triforium. [13a]

The rest of the building history is comparatively straightforward. The transepts, crossing, and tower can be presumed to follow immediately after the chancel – say in the 1260s – for in 1270 the chapter got permission to cut timber at Luss for a steeple. The wood was, according to Edward I, turned by the bishop (Robert Wishart) to military uses at the siege of Kirkintilloch; so the spire was probably not finished until after the War of Independence. It was struck by lightning in 1387. The opportunity was then taken to increase the height of the tower (which previously may not have been much higher than the ridge of the roofs), and the present stone spire was built during the first third of the fifteenth century. At about the same time the chapter-house, most of whose lower storey is contemporary with Bishop Bondington's rebuilding of the chancel and crypt, was completed with another vaulted room above, called the sacristy. The first meeting of the chapter of the University apparently took place in the chapter-house in 1451.

In 1484 the so-called Blacader (or Fergus) Aisle was attached to the south of the south transept, perhaps on the foundations of an earlier chapel. It was evidently intended as the undercroft of a much larger transept, which would presumably have been as high as the rest of the church. In its incomplete state it is difficult to realize the Blacader Aisle as a part of the main fabric of the cathedral. [13b]

[12] MacGibbon and Ross, *Ecclesiastical Architecture of Scotland*, vol.ii, p.189.
[13] The narrowness of the bays in the nave would, on the fourteenth-century assumption, be explained by the desire to re-use the old aisle walls, which would otherwise have had to be largely scrapped. But the nearly total rebuilding proposed would surely not have damaged its ultimate effect for such an economy? At Exeter no more than the lowest courses of the walls seem to have been re-used intact, and the early vaulting shafts were dressed off. Dr. Radford, who kindly read this account in manuscript, has allowed me to say that he now thinks 'gutted' too strong a word, and that the cores of the arcade may well be thirteenth-century. He agrees that the comparison with Exeter does not fully explain matters.
[13a] See further note 13d below.
[13b] Dr Fawcett (p.5) has shown that the shell of the Blacader aisle was almost certainly built c.1240, though it was not vaulted until the fifteenth century. The intention to go above crypt level had clearly been abandoned by c.1270 when the lower-level south transept windows were made.

The cathedral was in considerable danger from enthusiastic reformers towards the end of the sixteenth century, and did indeed have the lead stripped from its roofs, as well as losing most of its altars and statuary. Further destruction was halted by the Glaswegians themselves, led either by the Trades or by 'a very actively Protestant provost'. The building was restored and rearranged as three Protestant churches – one each in nave, chancel and crypt – with pews (and later galleries – now removed) in the chancel. At some later date both nave and chancel were ceiled with plaster, painted to imitate a ribbed vault in the manner of the nave of Paisley Abbey. The ceilings, which had dilapidated, were replaced in 1914 by the present exposed oak roofs, which follow the lines of the originals. The coloured bosses in the chancel were carved in oak taken from the old roof. (The work was carried out by the Office of Works under the supervision of W. T. Oldrieve, then government architect for Scotland.) In 1846–8 the two west towers (described below) were pulled down on aesthetic grounds and the present west front concocted by Robert Mathieson. The destruction was widely regretted at the time and has been almost universally condemned since. 13c 13d

Glasgow Cathedral is the second largest Gothic church in Scotland. Only St Andrews was larger – in its original form more than 100 feet longer.[14]

[13e] The real perpetrator of this *malfaisance*, as of other mid-century interference, was Edward Blore, Mathieson acting as executant.
[13d] Further study prompts the following observations: (*a*) there is reason to think that considerable building went on under Bishop Walter (1207–32): this could well have included the continuation of the nave begun by Jocelin. (*b*) By *c*.1260 the processional west door and the great west window were complete (the latter was fussed up but not essentially changed in 1848), suggesting that construction of the nave was, if not complete, at an advanced stage. (*c*) Unless there are continuous stone sleepers beneath the nave arcades, entirely new foundations would have been needed for arcades with bays of different span from the old; if money were not plentiful following the great operations of the east end, economy could well have dictated the re-use of old foundations and vaulting shafts even if no parts of early arcades were incorporated. (*d*) The sub-bases of the nave columns have a characteristic cavetto moulding first introduced in the crypt, and the capitals are a development of those used on the crossing piers, earlier on the easternmost columns of the chancel arcade and earliest of all in the crypt. The completion of the nave is therefore to be seen as a continuation of Bondington's work rather than a fresh beginning, and to be attributed to the last third of the thirteenth century, though the triforium tracery must be a later intrusion not calculated for in the original design of the upper storeys. Jocelin's nave settled the dimensions of the present one; the fourteenth-century notion can be ruled out.
[14] Perhaps Kelso was also larger, but it seems impossible now to reconstruct the church at all accurately.

4. The Cathedral from the south-east. (From R. W. Billings's 'Antiquities of Scotland')

Yet it is not a large building by European standards. Its total length of 285 feet is not very much over half that of Ely or Winchester; its height (59 feet) and width (63 feet) are a good deal less than half those of Amiens. Furthermore its floor area is proportionately smaller yet, for the 'transepts' do not extend laterally beyond the aisles. Glasgow is about the same size as Bristol or St David's, quite a lot smaller than Exeter or Gloucester, and very much smaller than York. It is, nevertheless, a building of great dignity and distinction.

The church looks at its best from the south-east, **4**: the dramatic fall in the land and the consequent greater height of the building from the ground supplies the vertical balance which has been missing from the west end since the loss of the towers. There is a massive strength in the eastern parts of the crypt and chancel and in the chapter-house. Moreover the great width of the two-storeyed east end, which unites the vertical accents of the buttresses into a composition which is essentially horizontal, gives an admirable feeling of stability to the whole structure. From the west on the other hand, the exceptional shortness of the transepts is much more obvious and suggests a building a little too high for its width – a somewhat restless effect increased by the coarse and feeble nineteenth-century work at the west end.

The whole of the eastern half of the cathedral was designed as a unit. Structurally the relation of chancel to crypt is simple. The columns of the chancel arcade must naturally stand above those of the principal arcade of the crypt, though this of course cannot be appreciated directly. The outer walls of the chancel aisles are the upward extension of those of the crypt; the principal buttresses are also continuous. The external appearance of the east end therefore is of the narrower and shorter upper storeys of the chancel standing on an immense two-storey plinth. But these parts belong together intimately: the unity is achieved principally through the careful repetition of details (in particular the shapes of the windows), and through the exact proportioning of the upper and lower parts one to the other. It can best be appreciated on the eastern face itself. This is, in its lower storeys, of four bays, the two in the middle corresponding to the central member of the chancel, the outer ones to the aisles of chancel and crypt. Each bay has two lancets at each level. The four pairs in the eastern face of the chancel are identical – very sharply pointed with attached shafts on the jambs, under a continuous hood-mould following the shapes of the windows. At crypt level the windows are similar, though each lancet has double shafting; and in the two narrower middle bays, the lancets are smaller and each pair linked under a single pointed arch-moulding. The narrowing here gives visual expression to the inward thrust of the buttresses, which are heavy, chamfered at the upper level, their water-tables receding into a corbelled parapet from which water-spouts jut out in the shape of boars' heads (the pattern is carried round the whole cathedral, though most of the heads are restorations). There are set-back buttresses at the south-east angle, while those at the north-east are absorbed into the chapter-house.

Above, well back from the east wall of the 'plinth', is the gable of the chancel itself. Between clasping buttresses is a single design of four extremely slender, high, sharply pointed lancets, with very deep mouldings, each lancet having its own pair of shafts. Until the middle of the nineteenth century the unity of this great four-fold window (a unity made more difficult to achieve by the even number of lancets) was emphasized in a dramatic way: the wall, whose thickness the deep reveals of the lancets draw attention to, was recessed immediately above the window, thus revealing an upper face like a water-table to the hood-mould, which, following the pattern of those on the lower storeys, marked with unusual emphasis the lateral unity of the window. Nineteenth-century restorations, however, eliminated this set-back, replaced the small, square window in the apex by a larger vesical (or lozenge-shaped) one, added a heavy coping to the gable, and pinnacles above the buttresses. The total effect has thus been greatly coarsened, and the impact and coherence of the window itself much reduced.

On its north and south faces the chancel gains in importance at the expense of the crypt, so that one has more the impression of unusually high aisles to the chancel than of a two-storeyed building. For the windows of the crypt are here only single lancets, while above them the chancel aisle windows have grown to fill the entire width of the bay in a single design. These windows are irregular. On the south side, the second from the west has a geometrical design of circles above lancets which looks *c*.1280. The third, fourth and fifth are much more primitive, in a crude form of plate tracery, each one consisting of three lancets divided by thick mullions, with quatrefoils punched into the spandrels, an arched hood-mould round each set of three. The westernmost one is somewhere in between the two types, still having thick mullions but also some attempt to bring the upper part into

5. Billings's drawing of the Cathedral from the south, showing the north-west tower after the demolition of the consistory house.

a unity. The two eastern bays, i.e., the south flank of the 'lady chapel',[15] have windows with plain Y-tracery. (On the north side of the chancel, the windows are equally ill-arranged, and one or two are very crudely designed: all these make a curious contrast with the exceptional refinement of the east front.) Plain buttresses stand between the bays and a heavier one with cutback at the end of the chancel proper. The clerestory is simple and effective: three lancets per bay under the usual corbelled parapet. The buttresses at this stage are elementary – little more than slight thickenings of the wall: there can never have been any intention of vaulting the main part of the chancel.

At crypt level each of the principal bays is subdivided by a single-storey buttress, corresponding to the shafting of the vault, which has twice as many bays as that of the chancel aisles above. It thus has a sturdy, somewhat utilitarian appearance, lightened by the rather awkwardly placed, though extremely elegant doorway. Here the space between two buttresses has been bridged by an arch and roofed to form a shallow porch, the columns of the arch being cut out of the buttresses themselves. The faces of the buttresses have shallow blank arches cut into them, very narrow and pointed, with single shafts and stiff-leaf capitals. The porch has a simple quadripartite vault, the doorway itself triple shafts and mouldings.

Of the exterior of the nave as it is now, there is less to be said, **5**. It carries on the general pattern of the eastern parts without of course any crypt. It is of eight bays, the aisle windows on each side being identical: on the north, three-light Y-tracery, similar to, but more refined than, that of the south wall of the chancel; on the south, a straightforward piece of Decorated design with three trefoils arranged in a triangle over three lancets. The third bay from the west on the south side has the main door, quite a small one: the jambs have four shafts, seeming to grow out of the thickness of the wall, with fillets in the diagonals, the arch itself being simply but richly moulded. Above this is a window in the form of a spherical triangle, containing a circle with six trefoils inside – a variant on the remaining windows: the effect is somewhat crowded. The buttresses on either side of the door have niches near the top with corbels supported on grotesques. The clerestory is almost as simple as that of the chancel. Here, each bay contains two windows, each with Y-tracery: again the effect is of a virtually continuous band of windows.

It is difficult to speak sympathetically of the west end in its present shape. The great west window, which dates from the restoration in the middle of the nineteenth century, is a feeble affair compared with that at the east end. It has two pairs of tall, cusped lancet-lights, each pair topped with a quatrefoil in a circle, and a largish wheel window above with cusped spokes: its general effect is distinctly emasculated. The stepped lancets in the half-gables [15a] of the aisles and the windows with Y-tracery underneath are also recent. So again are the crude buttresses and pinnacles, which are poorly related both to the west and to the north and south façades. Only the west door, with its double opening, remains much as when designed, though it too has been heavily restored. The doorway is very richly moulded, with five orders to the main arch and two more to each subsidiary one. The doors themselves are square-headed; and each has a tympanum with a three-light blank arcade, two cusped arches with a tall, narrow one between, miniature triple-shafts in between each pair. In the spandrel under the point of the principal arch is another blank arch, cusped, with a quatrefoil in a circle each side. All this is of the greatest delicacy and must belong to the middle of the thirteenth century.

[15] It is not clear whether this name for the eastern ambulatory and its chapels has any foundation in ancient use – it appears in Billings, and (perhaps following him) in Burnet's article on Glasgow in the Architectural Publication Society's *Dictionary*. In the fifteenth century the eastern space housed at least three separate chapels.
[It is now known that the lady chapel occupied the easternmost bay of the crypt proper, not of the chancel.]
[15a] The original west window (see fig.6) was of similar form but much more robust appearance. See n.13d above.

Until 1846 two towers flanked the west front, of very different size and character, **6**. At the south-west corner was the so-called consistory house, a four-storey pele with saddle-back roof, which came about halfway up the nave gable. It had small windows, lancets on the lower floors, mere square holes on the upper, and was heavily buttressed. The north-west tower was taller and slenderer, with a pyramidal cap, a little like the north-west tower of Dunfermline Abbey. It had evidently long been felt that the west front of the cathedral was not all it should be. Certainly its old appearance was somewhat incongruous, and the size of the consistory house may have given the end of the church itself a somewhat pinched look. In the early nineteenth century schemes were prepared for regularizing the design. 'In the year 1833, public attention was called to Glasgow Cathedral by Archibald M'Lellan, Esq., who, at his own cost, produced an extended Essay, urging the necessity of restoration. His work was the precursor of a committee having the then Lord Provost at the head, with Dr Cleland as Secretary, and the author of the preceding movement appearing modestly at the tail. This movement produced a second work, in which appeared restored elevations with two elaborately ornamented western Towers, **7**. A large fund was raised, a government grant secured for those restored designs by Mr Graham of Edinburgh, and – what followed all the enthusiasm of the Committee? A

6. (left) The west front of the Cathedral in 1835. (From Cleland's 'Proposals')
7. (right) The west front of the Cathedral as it would have been after the 1835 proposals. Only the central doorway is original (Cleland).

change of architects, and the utter disappearance of the feature it was their main object to preserve'.[16] The consistory house was the first to go; and the other soon followed because it was rather plain and 'looked odd'. Yet Billings's (admittedly not quite accurate) drawing suggests that the single tower provided just the vertical accent that the west front now badly needs.

The transepts were also restored in the nineteenth century. (Since they extended no farther than the outer walls of the aisles, the plan of the cathedral remains rectangular, not cruciform – a feature also found at Jedburgh.) The large window in the south transept is mainly Victorian in appearance. Previously there was a simpler geometrical design of three circles over five lancets, characteristic of the early Decorated period. The transom a third of the way up was, however, there before the restoration: it may have been inserted as a strengthener after the window was first built. The present one is a somewhat confused accumulation of detail. The window in the north transept is less sophisticated and relies on the simple Y-tracery used in the east and west transept windows: it may well be a good copy of the original. This transept also has the curious feature of an octagonal stair turret at its north-west corner, which cuts the easternmost window of the nave in two. It gets slimmer near the top and ends in the inevitable pinnacle.

The crossing tower is fairly squat and was probably squatter, like those

[16] Billings, *op. cit.*
[Although nominally by Gillespie Graham, these towers were evidently designed by George Meikle Kemp, then a freelance architectural assistant in Edinburgh, more usually associated with William Burn (see Lindsay, *Cathedrals of Scotland*, 1926, p.154). This is confirmed in a MS note by Kemp's friend David Cousin, to which Mr. John Dunbar has kindly drawn our attention. The basic conception is that of Kemp's Scott monument in Edinburgh.]

8. The Cathedral from the south west with the 1835 proposals for the west front and transepts (cf. 5) (Cleland).

of the Benedictine monasteries. It has composite windows of four lancets on each side and a parapet pierced with quatrefoils and crocketed pinnacles at the corners. The octagonal spire is also stocky, in three stages, divided again by pierced parapets. There are lucarnes at each stage and on the lowest pinnacles as well. These are all elaborately crocketed, and the lucarnes show the only example in the main structure of the cathedral of ogee work. [16a] All rather florid, as Billings complains, but it livens up an otherwise almost stunted spire.

Of buildings outside the main rectangle of the church, the Blacader aisle makes almost no external impact – obviously unfinished and contradicting, with its low flat top, the general lines of the cathedral. The chapter house is another matter. Its massive, heavily buttressed shape adds greatly to the impression of solidity and strength at the east end, while its slender and finely made lancets continue the eloquent horizontal lines of the east face of the church proper. The lower storey – the chapter house itself – is mostly early thirteenth-century, the upper storey mid-fifteenth. Yet the designer of the late work has carefully respected – indeed copied – that of his predecessor. Only at the top does he let fling a bit, with his double-corbelled parapet, his saddle-back roof with crow-stepped gables, his buttresses with their switchback water-tables.

9. Cathedral plan at ground level (MacGibbon and Ross).

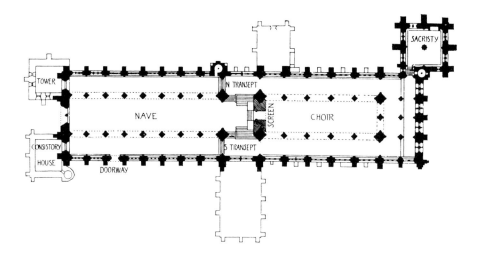

Discounting for the moment the Blacader aisle, the interior is almost entirely the work of two periods, **9**. The eastern half is Bishop Bondington's work of the mid-thirteenth century, the western is, as we have seen, either the continuation of this, in the same spirit but with variations, up to half a century later, or the somewhat altered form of a continuation of Jocelin's work. The chancel is the best piece of high Gothic architecture in Scotland, both unusually rich in detail and exceptionally unified, **10**. It is of five bays, with a two-bay extension where the aisles are returned round the east end of the presbytery as an ambulatory with chapels (the 'lady chapel'). The eastern ambulatory is a rarity in Britain, especially combined with a rectangular east end: other surviving examples are at Exeter, Romsey (Hants) and Dore (Herefs).

The main arcade stands on clustered columns about 4 feet square with a lavish display of attached shafts and mouldings; some capitals have lively

16a In the normal sense of the word: see below n.21c.

stiff-leaf design, others more naturalistic foliage, sometimes arranged in flower shapes round the capitals, sometimes collected in little clusters like poppy-heads. The arches are equally richly moulded. The triforium has two arches to each bay, again richly moulded with pairs of attached shafts in the jambs and rounded capitals. Each arch is further subdivided into two cusped openings, the smaller arches standing on clustered columns of their own. In the spandrels are circles containing quatrefoils punched through the wall in the manner of plate tracery. The clerestory has a passageway, with an interior arcade corresponding with the frames of the windows outside. It has, therefore, three openings per bay, with pointed, moulded arches on shafted columns; at each end of each bay is a very narrow, recessed blank panel with sharply pointed top, again on its own shafts – evidence of the architect's desire to have as little inert wall as possible. The clerestory passage is vaulted with tiny transverse barrel vaults, three per bay, a neat and endearing feature. Vaulting shafts run up from the capitals of the main arcade with stiff-leaf collars at the level of the triforium sill. The absence of clerestory buttressing shows that vaulting of the chancel was never seriously considered: the main point of the shafts must have been to increase the effect of height, already marked by the 1–2–3 rhythm as one ascends each bay to the top.

16b

10. The chancel looking east; as drawn by Billings in 1845.
The engraving incorrectly shows four arches in the clerestorey to every bay of the main arcade or every two of the triforium: the rationalistic Billings could only divide by two. There are in fact three, or five including the narrow flanking archlets.

16b Perhaps in a building of the very moderate height and width of Glasgow, flying buttresses would not after all have been needed (cf. Salisbury), though a thirteenth-century mason would probably have provided them if a high vault was intended.

The main impression of height comes, however, from the east end. Here the arcade continues across the end of the presbytery (the columns at the corners are particularly massive and particularly lavish). In order to keep the arcade continuous at the same level, it was necessary to divide the span with a central column – 'not a pleasing feature', as MacGibbon and Ross primly observe. (It is found also at Exeter, and at Roslyn, a church whose general shape owes much to Glasgow. A feature of Glasgow's central column is the reduction in width brought about by not carrying the outermost shafts down to the ground but supporting them on corbels just below the capital: a slight added springiness is gained by this device.) Certainly it looks awkward with an altar or communion table immediately in front of it.[17] Yet a view of the wall as a whole does not suggest an uncomfortable duality. For the great window above is the unifying and dominant feature of the whole. Now we see the reason for four lights in this window instead of the usual three or five: for two of the slender lancets stand over each bay of the east arcade. It was ingenious and correct of the designer to realize that four equal openings were needed here. A single one was at that time thought impossible to construct safely on this scale, two would have emphasized too strongly the division below (cf. the west window of Paisley Abbey), three would have set up an uncomfortable tension, five would have been too crowded. As with the clerestory, the external divisions between the lights are repeated inside. Clusters of very slender shafts, three per column, run the full height of the mullions, with stiff-leaf capitals and moulded collars at an at first sight arbitrary level, where in fact exterior and interior mullions brace one another. A further unifying factor is the exceptionally delicate decoration below the window in the spandrel of the eastern arcade: a tiny blank arcade of three bays with cusped arches on triplicated columns under a fivefold hood-mould. High above in the central spandrel of the window (impossible to see without a powerful torch) is another decoration, of two blank 'dagger'-motifs divided by a column: if this is part of the original work, it is an exceptionally early appearance of the motif, which is characteristic of tracery in England from the early fourteenth century. The roof of the chancel is a beautiful timber barrel vault, decorated with a geometrical pattern of 'ribs' running longitudinally, transversely and diagonally.

17a

The chancel aisles have quadripartite stone vaults with both longitudinal and transverse ridge-ribs added. Those of the north aisle are of an earlier type than the south. The wall-shafts are triplicated, with moulded capitals and bases standing on a continuous stone bench. The eastern ambulatory with its chapels forms a single space, four bays by two, with a row of free-standing columns, slightly nearer to the east wall than to the eastern columns of the chancel. These columns are slenderer than those of the chancel, with clustered shafts, hollow diagonals and moulded capitals. Some of the shafts in the angles of the windows have dogtooth ornament – the only example in the cathedral of this device, elsewhere so widely used at the time. The wall shafts are as in the aisles, the vault being treated as a series of separate cells, with quadripartite division, together with ridge-ribs in each direction. The soffits of all the arches are as richly moulded as in the chancel. The ribs cross in lively and delicate bosses. All in all, throughout the chancel, the impression is of concentrated energy, of richness without ostentation.

After this, the nave may seem something of a disappointment, so it is suitable that most people see it first. It has perhaps more of calculation and less

[17] The high altar originally stood [one bay] farther west.

[17a] As Dr. Fawcett has shown (*op. cit.*, p.28) the architecture of the chancel is closely related to that of Rievaulx Abbey (begun *c.*1225) and may derive very largely from northern English sources. The full cusping of the sub-arches of the triforium, however, is notably individual and advanced. It may in a minor degree have been anticipated in the retrochoir at Chichester (surely without influence on Glasgow); but other instances – Salisbury and the angel choir at Lincoln – are of the mid-century, and there the cusping is not in depth but essentially of tracery within conventional arch rings. Cusping is fully developed in the triforium at Beverley (whose chancel is contemporary with Glasgow's) but in a continuous arcade. Glasgow's continuous *clerestorey* arcade may possibly derive from the chancel at Whitby (begun *c.*1220), whose central member was likewise not vaulted in stone; but the only other example known to us of the division of the bay into three full-size arches between two much narrower occurs on the *exterior* of the nave clerestorey at Lincoln, where, however, the rhythm is varied: it was complete by 1233 and could have influenced Glasgow.

of inspiration than the chancel; but the calculation was very exact, and its greater simplicity makes an admirable complement to the richness farther east. There is far less of contrast between the two than with many churches built at different periods; the architect of the supposedly later nave evidently saw his work as integrally related with what was there already and used a self-denying hand: it is a pity that it is so rarely possible to see the two together now for the curtain which normally hangs in the chancel arch and the organ pipes on either side.

The nave is not much longer than the chancel, yet it has eight bays instead of five, **11**. The columns are smaller in section and their surfaces much simpler. Since they are closer together than those of the chancel, a perspective view such as one normally has gives an impression of numbers of verticals with no horizontal emphasis beyond the repetition of columns and arches: this impression is intensified by the treatment of the triforium and clerestory. The main arcade has clustered keel-shafts of a very simple kind, with moulded capitals (there is no leaf-carving anywhere in the nave), and moulded arches similar to, but plainer than, those of the chancel. Triforium and clerestory are treated as a single unit, being enclosed by shafts which run up the height of both storeys, a striking instance of the insistence on verticality.[18] It is strange that the main vaulting shafts are supported on corbels

17b

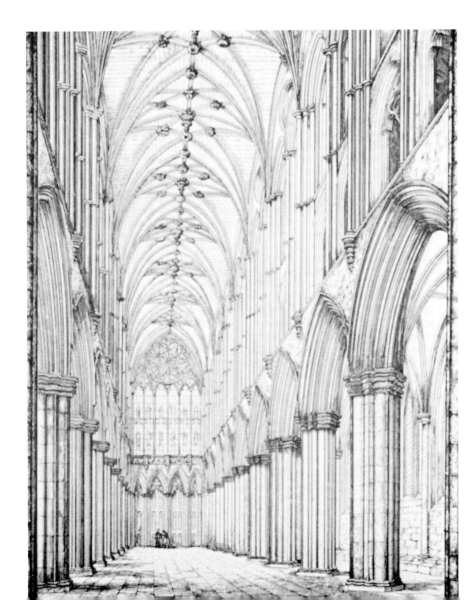

11. The nave looking west, showing the alterations proposed in 1835, with a large west window and the nave vaulted (Cleland).

[17b] In fact keel-shafts in the diagonals alternate with the characteristic broad-filleted shafts invented for the crypt (see below n.21c). The capitals have five distinct layers of moulding, boldly projecting like bracket fungus.
[18] This feature again seems to me to point to an early thirteenth-century date: cf. related designs at Jedburgh, Grimsby, Pershore and Selby.

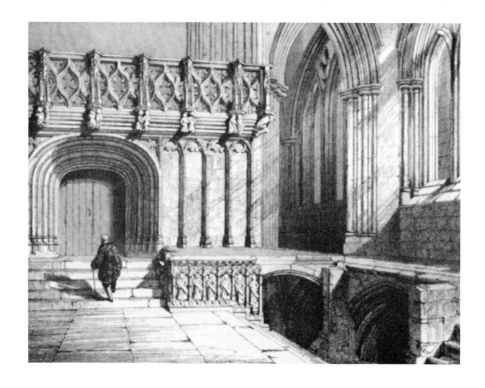

at the level of the triforium sill, rather than springing from the capitals of the main arcade as in the chancel: the chance of another vertical emphasis was missed. Each bay of the triforium and clerestory has two openings, in the clerestory quite plain with arches springing from the capitals of the two-storey shafts; the triforium is more ambitious but more coarsely executed: each opening has a trefoil over two cusped lancets. The somewhat similar but larger openings from the triforium into the transepts are finer: intersected tracery in which the openings between the intersections as well as the tops of the lower lights have trefoils in circles. All this, it has been suggested above, may be a fourteenth-century insertion into an earlier fabric. The nave aisles are similar to those of the chancel, with the same system of vaulting, though single keel-shaped wall-shafts: the bosses, not surprisingly, are more stereotyped and less interesting. The roof of the nave, long   18a plastered, has now reverted to its simple open timber form of exposed rafters and collars.

The only major addition to the interior of the cathedral after the early fourteenth century was the screen, **12**.[19] The date of this has been in dispute. MacGibbon and Ross confidently assigned it to the early fifteenth century (Bishop Cameron's time), but P. M. Chalmers saw no reason why it should not be as late as Blacader's aisle, which likewise has excellent figure-carving.[20] There is no documentary evidence (as there is for the altars which flank it), and it is almost impossible to judge by style alone in Scottish architecture of the fifteenth century, when aims were so confused and style so mixed. The floor of the chancel is about 3 feet higher than the nave; and the screen stands at the top of a flight of five steps. The opening into the chancel is really more substantial than elegant: it is almost square, with a very flat semi-elliptical arch. Seven bands of moulding run round without capital or break of any kind from base to base. On either side are four narrow bays of blank arcading, the top of each light being heavily cusped. Above all this is a

[18a] In the north aisle the longitudinal rib is missing from all but two bays: it appears simply to have fallen or been taken down as a result of outward settlement of the aisle wall. (There are rough rib-joints in the eastern ambulatory as well.)
[19] It is said that the screen may have been built to hold an organ: hence its great thickness. The date, however, is suspiciously early for such a purpose in Scotland.
[20] *Ecclesiastical Architecture of Scotland*, Vol.II, pp.198–9; Vol.III, pp.627–8.

13. (left) A detail showing the elaborate vaulting of the lady chapel (Billings).
14. (right) The eastern chapels of the crypt (Billings).

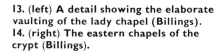

20a The shrine probably stood as a feretory behind the high altar in the easternmost bay of the chancel. The fine thirteenth-century pair of miniature arches now kept in the south-east chapel of the crypt has been plausibly seen as a fragment of this shrine.

richly moulded cornice supporting a large open-work parapet designed as a series of ogee lozenges, each cusped to contain a 'soufflet'. Alternate ones are crossed by uprights elaborately decorated with crocketed pinnacles standing above daring and lively pairs of figures. There is very little good figure-sculpture of the fifteenth century in England and almost none of any date in Scotland; so these are particularly precious. The rood, if there ever were one, above the screen, has of course vanished, and no record remains. (The east face of the screen now has a wooden arcade above which is an imitation of the parapet on the west face. The stone parapets above the stairs to the crypt are also modern and very ill-judged.) On either side of the steps up to the screen is a stone altar, certainly of Blacader's time: each has a frieze of standing figures, but these have been so defaced that it is very difficult to tell anything of their quality. The tracery on the altars is more definitely of a late – almost Tudor – type than that on the screen.

Steps down beside the altars lead to the crypt, the spiritual foundation of the whole building (for here is St Mungo's tomb), and the literal foundation of the east end, 15. It is rare for a Gothic church to be built on a steeply 20a sloping site; and the effect gained outside is in this case stupendous: it may even be compared (at a proper distance) to the building of the Parthenon on the *side* of the Acropolis, so that a massive plinth had to be constructed: its presence is magnificently enhanced. It was a remarkable stroke of genius – or perhaps we should say of good fortune – to have founded the shrine on this spot: at any rate it needed genius of a rare kind to make so much of the opportunity offered. The effect inside is utterly different, for the impact is not sudden and overwhelming: it strikes the visitor as having much the character of a true crypt, though (on a bright day) an unusually well-lit one. As such it is the finest thing of its kind in the world; but to appreciate the crypt one must explore it patiently, for the subtlety and purity of its design to tell as they should.

35

The spiritual function of the crypt is to house the grave in such a way that it could be properly visited and venerated by pilgrims. The shrine had to have a central position. At the same time the crypt had to fulfil the vital structural function of holding up the chancel, **15**. The principal columns must therefore correspond to those above. So the crypt is divided into a 'nave' and aisles. But this design was complicated by two factors acting together. In the first place the width of the lower nave (25 feet, identical of course with that of the central member of the chancel) is too large to mark off the shrine satisfactorily; in the second, the crypt is only about 17 feet high: to vault a width of 25 feet with any safety, the depth of the vault would itself

15. Cathedral: section through the east end (MacGibbon and Ross).

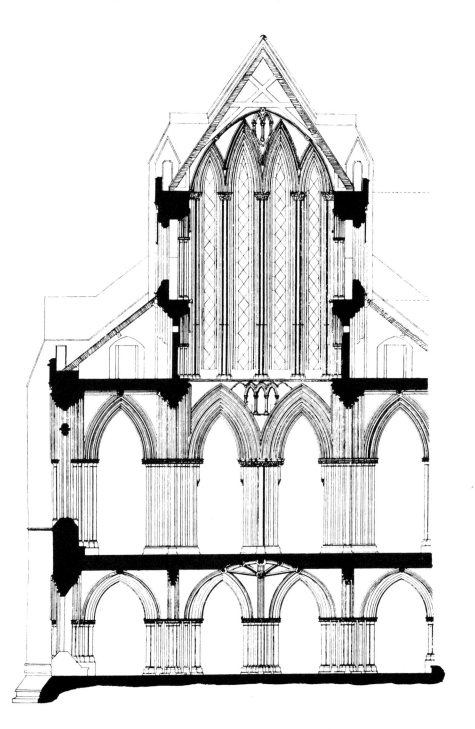

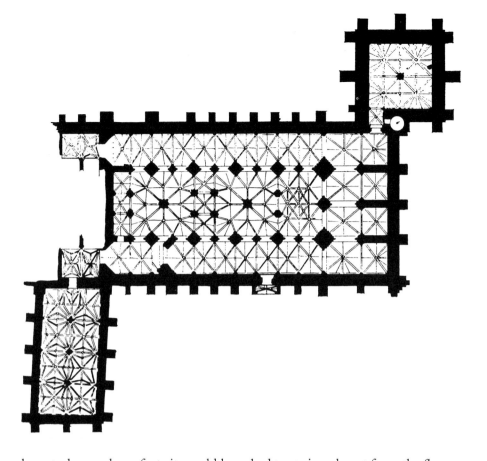

[21] T. L. Watson thought that it was originally intended to vault the lower nave in the same way as the aisles. MacGibbon and Ross at first accepted this view (*Ecclesiastical Architecture*, Vol.II, pp.172–3) but later rejected it when taken to the spot by Chalmers (*ibid*, Vol.III, Preface, p.v). They give no reason for the rejection; but a sufficient one is that it is not conceivable that a vault springing from the existing capitals could safely bridge the 25-foot space, when one remembers the weight of the stone floor above. The transverse arch would have been far too flat, the diagonals even more so.
[By examining rib sections Watson identified five distinct building programmes in the crypt vault.]
[21a] No: the high altar was three crypt bays further east.
[21b] Much more logic than at Gloucester, where the vault is essentially a pattern of ribs applied to a plain barrel; the Glasgow vaulting plan follows directly from the placing of the columns. Ingeniously the tomb is made to appear central in that the radically different treatment of the lady chapel vault marks off the two eastern bays as a separate element.

have to be nearly 17 feet; it would have had to spring almost from the floor. The lower nave had therefore to be laterally subdivided. Moreover a similar problem arose with the aisle vaults. An extra column was therefore introduced between each pair of principals, and the vaults are in simple quadripartite form, half the size of those above.[21]

In the nave the pattern is more complex. The shrine is a square. It is placed in the fifth bay from the west, directly under the high altar. It is marked by [21a] four columns at the corners: this divides the fifth bay, transversely, into three squares (or very nearly so, the bays being in plan rectangles whose sides are in a ratio of about three to one). Three bays to the east, two more columns are introduced transversely, and two again three bays to the west. The spaces between these and the shrine thus make two larger squares, whose sides are three bays long. At the centre of each of these stands a further column. The vaulting is (as MacGibbon and Ross put it) 'varied to suit this arrangement of pillars'. The vaulting is surely the most complicated in any church before the fourteenth century. Yet, granted the pattern of columns, it is entirely logical, with the same kind of geometrical logic as the vault of the chancel of Gloucester. The most involved section is the two [21b] eastern bays of the nave, treated as a unit transversely, to avoid the danger of the flat arch. The actual patterns are almost indescribable (but see the plan, **16**). All the columns, which vary greatly in section and area, are elaborated with a great variety of attached shafts and fillets; some capitals are moulded, some have excellent stiff-leaf work. And the bosses, some of which are unusually large, are of the same quality, **13**. Some have naturalistic sculpture of leaves with intertwining tendrils; others have circular designs which seem to be purely abstract. In the north aisle there are several heads, either in the centre of the boss looking down or at the side looking horizontally. At least two of these are portraits; all are very lively.

The aisles of the crypt are like tunnels, being of course uncommonly low for vaulted passages. Everywhere else the columns prevent any axial views; and indeed the crypt has no real axis: rather it has a centre at the tomb and a number of separate cells which open off it into one another. The whole design is one in which mystery and complexity (intensified by the deep shadows cast by the numerous columns, and the various shapes of different spaces) are substituted for clarity; yet it maintains a perfect order and co-herence. It is a wonderful and profound contrast to the chancel above, 14.

In the north-east corner of the crypt is the doorway to the chapter-house, 17 which must have had the most interesting carving in the whole cathedral; but the effect of the frequent flooding of the east end of the crypt has been to deface the stone very badly and to make the sculpture largely uninter-pretable. There are triple shafts and another single one, each with a kind of vigorous stiff-leaf decoration on the capitals which is on the verge of becoming naturalistic. Between the single and triple shafts is a continuous band of carving running round the arch from floor to floor without inter-ruption. Most of this is a nearly continuous leaf-scroll with a regularly repeated S-shaped motif. But at the bottom of the right-hand side are a monkey and a crocodile; and the left, as far up as the capitals of the shafts, is entirely figure sculpture. At the top is a Christ with hand held up in blessing, which looks distinctly Romanesque in feeling with rather stiff, stylized gestures and drapery. Underneath is a bishop, with mitre and cro-zier, the drapery more naturalistic and the face perhaps a portrait, possibly (like one of the bosses) of Bishop Bondington. Below this are two more figures now indecipherable. At the bottom is another monkey. All must have been very lively, and what can still be seen is of high quality.

The chapter-house itself was begun at the same time as the crypt, but apparently left unfinished until the fifteenth century. It is one of seven re-maining in Scotland (whole or in part) with a square plan and a central column; four of these have two storeys, but Glasgow is alone in having both storeys vaulted. The lower chamber, which is the chapter-house pro-per, is more severe in character than the crypt; but this is perhaps largely due to an extensive refacing early this century. The walls and wall-shafts are early, or at least begun early and continued to the same design: the main shafts are triple, with subsidiary single shafts at mid-bay. The central col-umn is square, with shafts at the corners and in the middle of each side; all these and the wall-shafts have plain moulded capitals, of a comparatively late date. The vault is divided into four quadripartite units, each with ridge-ribs in both directions and further subdividing ribs in the four cells nearest to the corners of the building. All this seems to be the work of Bishop Lauder[22] (d.1425), who is certainly responsible for the dean's seat in the east side. This is 'buttressed' with characteristically fifteenth-century crocketed pinnacles on each side, which do not very well agree with the flat (cusped) ellipse of the arch over the seat. The upper chamber, built by Bishop Cameron, c.1457, has a similar plan, though the vault is slightly simpler, and the central column is octagonal, again with eight shafts. The capitals on the wall-shafts have rather flat, as it were applied, leaf-carving which lies back against the principals. The north-east corner has a large contemporary fireplace, whose square opening has rounded corners, and two stone cupboards – all rather

21c Special and idiosyncratic features of the crypt include the extension of the convex surface of the principal shafts of the four shrine columns through their capitals into the concave soffits of the vault arches; and on others a broad fillet on the cardinal faces produced through the necking into the bell of the capital and thence leading to square projections of the abacus linked to the circular sections by reverse curves, in effect a horizontal ogee. Similar, though more 'elegant', capitals exist at Shrewsbury Abbey, dated by Pevsner to the late fourteenth century.

21d Mr. Patrick Morrisey has suggested that perhaps ordinary pilgrims did not approach the tomb closely but moved along one aisle to devotions in the eastern chapels, returning by the other aisle.

22 The chapter-house walls must have been substantially complete by the time the chancel was built, for it seems to have been the effective buttressing of these which prevented any serious settlement, during building, of the kind that happened at the south-east corner.

17. Chapter-house doorway (MacGibbon and Ross).

ugly. There is enough in the section of the vaulting-ribs, in the capitals and in other details to reveal the late date of this work; yet it is again conservative (and, perhaps in consequence, a bit lifeless), keeping well within the general lines laid down by the thirteenth century – something hardly conceivable at the time in England.

The Blacader aisle is later still, though the foundations of a chapel in this position may have been laid in the thirteenth century and later re-used. The design of the late fifteenth-century work is again conservative, but pleasingly fresh: it looks bright in its whitewash, though this clogs some of the carving; the painting of the bosses suits their rather brash, though attractive, pertness. The 'aisle' was apparently intended to support a continuation of the south transept, though it is considerably out of alignment, and out of square. It has the feel of an undercroft, though there is nothing above. It is four bays long, with a central row of columns, square in section and placed diagonally, with eight shafts. The vault is as in the chancel aisles, with added tiercerons to both longitudinal and transverse ridge-ribs. The columns have fairly modest stiff-leaf capitals, but the wall-shafts are more naturalistic and some have animals, perhaps subjects from a bestiary. These are lively and have been incorporated from an earlier building. The bosses are often livelier still, with a good many grotesques, singly or in groups; some more grotesques appear high up in the angles between wall and vault.[23]

Of the furnishings nothing is of interest apart from the over-enthusiastically repaired pulpit, an excellent early Renaissance design dating from the conversion of the cathedral to Protestant episcopalianism. It has classical panels containing characteristic Elizabethan strapwork. Nor are there more than three monuments worth mention. That to the Barons of Mynto in the south aisle is dated 1604: it has one of the rare Scotch brasses, rather crude and now badly defaced, showing a knight in armour kneeling to the rays of the sun, a curiously pagan idea for its date. This is set in a freely classical surround, with a big broken pediment over a semi-circular arch containing skull and crossbones. Archbishop Law (d.1632) has a large and very clumsy monument at the east end of the south chancel aisle, in which classical and Elizabethan motifs are freely jumbled: the recent painting adds to the confusion. More coherent is the one just outside the south door of the nave, to Thomas Hutchison (d.1641), fairly classical with the usual death's-head, this time under a scrolly pediment.

A few other early buildings now within the city boundaries deserve to be mentioned, though they do not belong to medieval Glasgow proper. Four small castles remain, all in the south-west corner of the city,[24] and one interesting late sixteenth-century house. The most important of these, historically and architecturally, is Crookston, standing on a ridge above the confluence of the Leven and White Cart rivers. It was built by Sir Alexander Stewart (the ancestor of the later Lennox family) in the late fourteenth century – a tower house standing within a dry ditch. The rectangular main block originally had square towers at all four corners: of these one is complete, very severe with only a light cornice to give relief from the almost uninterrupted masonry. The walls, over 7 feet thick (and containing staircases and small rooms), are of roughly dressed freestone; the remaining windows are exceedingly small, and the whole generally without architectural features.

22a

22a See above n.13b. The wall shafts of the vault are of an early section and contrast abruptly with the fifteenth-century work.
23 The extension on the north side of the cathedral, in line not with the transept but with the westernmost bay of the chancel, may have been the foundations of the hall of the vicars' choral: the doorway and low roof are modern.
24 A fifth, at Partick on the Kelvin, disappeared in the nineteenth century; a sixth, the Peel of Drumry on the north-west edge of the city, as recently as 1959, though by then only scanty remains were left.

The fifteenth-century Cathcart Castle had round towers at the angles and stood in a walled enclosure or barmkin, of which the southern end remains. The ground floor of the tower is rather crudely vaulted; above is the hall, of some architectural pretensions, but the whole building is now derelict. A third tower house, of the early sixteenth century, is now incorporated in the nineteenth-century castellated mansion of Castlemilk and has been considerably altered. The walls are now harled; the parapet is a renewal, perhaps according to the original design.

Haggs Castle, built by Sir John Maxwell of Pollock in 1585, reconstructed in the mid nineteenth century, is of a rather different type, dating from a time when the characteristic plainness of the small medieval tower houses was giving way to the exuberant detail of the Scottish Renaissance. The carved detail at Haggs – especially over the main entrance and on the dormers – is of unusual intricacy and of high quality: a very early example of the fashionable decoration that is prominent in better-known castles such as Caerlaverock, Huntly and Linlithgow.

Finally one small house of considerable charm though few ambitions: Provan Hall near the eastern boundary of the city was originally the manor of the same lords of Provan whose prebendary occupied Provand's Lordship. The Hall is a modest two-storeyed house with crow-stepped gables and a cylindrical cone-topped corner tower, probably built about the time of the Reformation. Walls, one with an elliptical arched gateway dated 1647 but perhaps earlier, join this house to an eighteenth-century one of the same size, built probably on the site of an earlier building.

Medieval Glasgow is in fact the Cathedral. It is, as has been said, a relatively small building. It is bullied by the ugly bulk of the Royal Infirmary, and the large open space to the south is bleak and windswept: its proper relation to the city has been ruthlessly disregarded, and the Cathedral itself grievously damaged at the west end. Yet it remains a building of silent and haunting beauty, all the more poignant and expressive in its isolated dignity.

25 It is still black with the grime of centuries – especially the last two. Yet cleaning would present unusual problems owing to the amount of internal patching often with Roman cement.
A new block is to be built across Cathedral Square to the south-west.

Chapter 2 — The Reformation and the Merchant City, 1560-1800

Until 1560 Glasgow was essentially an ecclesiastical town, dominated by a great medieval church with the largest and most magnificent cathedral chapter in Scotland. With the Reformation, and still more with the abolition of episcopacy, which was signalled at Glasgow by the assembly of 1638, the cathedral lost its pre-eminence, and the character of the town became primarily mercantile. The population grew fairly steadily throughout the seventeenth century (though there seems to have been a slight decline for a few years after 1660); but by 1700 it was still only about 12,000, so that, compared with Edinburgh, Glasgow, now the second largest city in Scotland, was still quite small.

By 1538 England was officially Protestant. The outcome of the Reformation in Scotland was in doubt for another twenty years; but Glasgow did not itself play a conspicuous part in debate, and the fabric of the city suffered remarkably little harm during the century of politico-religious struggles that followed the formal abolition of Catholicism. The town was, however, in considerable danger a few years earlier during the hostilities between the Earls of Lennox and Arran. Lennox, ambitious and unscrupulous, had – though, it seems, not with any special conviction – set himself up as the champion of the Catholic cause. Finding himself (as he thought) double-crossed, through the political miscalculations of Cardinal Beaton, Lennox aligned himself with England, married Henry VIII's niece (and so, through their son Darnley, became the ancestor of all future kings of both Scotland and England). At this time, 1544, Glasgow was held by Lennox's forces. They were attacked and beaten by Arran (now Governor of Scotland) at the Battle of the Butts, so called because it took place on the old Archery Ground, somewhere in the region of the present Paddy's Market. It was only with difficulty that Arran was dissuaded from burning the city. He became protector of the Archbishop but, already half-Protestant himself, finally abandoned Catholicism in 1559. The last Catholic archbishop (until the re-establishment of the see in 1878) left for France and carried the records of the diocese with him.

The final battle of the wars of the Reformation in Britain was also fought near Glasgow, at Langside, three miles south of the old city. By 1567 Mary Queen of Scots had abdicated in favour of her baby son, and the chief power in the land was the Regent, the Earl of Moray. In 1568 Mary escaped from her first imprisonment (which followed the murder of Darnley), mounted a sizable army and marched from Hamilton towards Glasgow. She was defeated, this time finally; the Regency remained, first under Moray and, after his murder, under the aging Lennox: a Protestant episcopacy was established in Glasgow. The power of the Protestant bishops, however, was only a faint shadow of that of their Catholic predecessors; and one immediate result was the rapid decay of the upper part of the town. The prebendary manses, which had been deserted when Archbishop Beaton left, were not reoccupied, and though the cathedral remained in use, the few other churches were neglected, the friars of course simply disappeared, and the hospitals were ruined.[1] In the early seventeenth century Archbishop Spottiswoode brought back some power as well as dignity to the bishopric; but in 1615 after only three years in Glasgow he was translated to St Andrews and became Chancellor of Scotland. He had only two successors in Glasgow before Archbishop Patrick Law was deposed by the Assembly in 1638. After the interregnum, the Archbishops returned with considerably greater power, but Glasgow remained loyal to the Covenant and was never again an episcopal city, though it was not until 1689 that the last archbishop left and episcopacy was finally abandoned.

By the middle of the seventeenth century, therefore, the centre of the city's life had definitely shifted to the Cross where the four main streets met. Attempts were made to revive the upper part of the town: one of these was a move of the salt market to Bell o' the Brae, the crossing of High Street and Drygate. But this was abandoned when the fullers and fishermen who used the market complained that it was too far from the river. In the early part of the century Glasgow's trade must still have been largely with the rest of Scotland; and it was not until 1688 that the building of a new harbour was started at Newark, twenty miles downstream from the city. Nevertheless, in 1655 a Cromwellian excise official reported an extensive trade with Ireland, France and Norway, and some ships going as far as the West Indies. Some factories had been set up, for cloth- and soap-making, sugar-refining, and even for candles – commemorated in the name of Candleriggs. Furthermore there was now a definite town council, and a guild of merchants, the Dean of Guild Court, modelled on 'the lovable form of judgement used in all the good towns of France and Flanders' – the Protestant ones, that is. The privileges of the Merchants' House and Trades House were regulated by charter in 1605. Not long afterwards the Council itself built its first Town House, the physical mark of the new government of the city, the new centre of power.

Of the merchants' town of the seventeenth century, however, hardly anything is now visible – no more than three towers, one insignificant house and the tortured remains of the façade of the College. But from drawings – and even from old photographs (for much of the destruction is quite recent) – it is possible to form an accurate idea of what the city looked like at this time. The plan remained substantially unaltered, the enlargements sporadic and unco-ordinated. Most of the population must have lived in the increasingly crowded closes built on the back-lands of the riggs behind the houses fronting the main streets. Many of these houses were rebuilt in a more orderly, and to some extent a grander, style than their predecessors. In the early part of the century the pattern of house design tended to follow the Edinburgh principle of tall, narrow façades, sometimes topped with gables, sometimes arcaded on the ground floor – the type of which Gladstone's Land in Lawnmarket, Edinburgh is perhaps the handsomest surviving example. The Glasgow houses were almost all smaller than the Edinburgh ones, never more than five storeys, and rarely more than four.

In the later seventeenth century, in the houses of the rich, the vertical accent characteristic of older buildings was abandoned, and a long low façade became the rule, though – in the public buildings – a tower behind the façade compensated the rather crouching horizontal effect with a vigorous point heavenwards. These houses had normally only two storeys, or two and an attic, but at least one was eleven bays long. This was the man-

[1] The church of the Black Friars, which stood immediately to the south of the old College, was later patched up as a parish church. It was destroyed by lightning in 1670 (see p.58 below).

18. A window in the Tolbooth Steeple.

19. The Tolbooth Steeple, c.1626.
The quadrant behind is by
A. G. Henderson (c.1922).

sion of the Campbells of Blythswood in Bridgegate, built (perhaps in two sections) sometime in the 1660s. Each bay was topped with a little gable, the six eastern ones being turned into rough approximations of a classical pediment, with a cornice and some kind of ornament at the apex. Silvercraigs Land, Saltmarket, was a more coherent and better proportioned design, owing something, it seems, to the façade of the College, with a little Renaissance decoration timidly applied and an elliptical archway into the court behind. It is probably a fragment of one of these houses which survives in a wretchedly mutilated state at No.28 Stockwell Street. Another important example of this class, long destroyed, stood on the south side of Trongate: mid eighteenth-century views show a ground floor arcade framed in pilasters and continuous entablature, a corbelled angle turret and a picturesque array of gables.

In comparison with the best English, and still more with the best Continental, examples, these houses were very modest, even meagre. The public buildings were more impressive. It was in the seventeenth century that Glasgow first had civic buildings of any importance; as the eclipsing of the city's ecclesiastical significance was marked by the disappearance of churches, monasteries and the palace, so its growing civic consciousness was exhibited in the ambitious – even pretentious – architecture of its public, but now secular, buildings. Fragments of several remain, though it is hard to appreciate them in their present state.

The most prominent of these works was the Town House or Tolbooth, built at the Cross, which was now the unrivalled centre of the city's affairs, **28.** It was not so large as the Heart of Midlothian in Edinburgh, but when built in about 1626 must have seemed an impressive assertion of the city's sense of its own importance. The Tolbooth was a square-fronted block, five storeys high, five bays wide, crenellated and with little turrets high up on the angles. The rather small, evenly spaced windows each had a minor pediment, but the

20. The old Hutcheson's Hospital, Trongate (begun 1641, demolished 1794).

general effect must have been severe. The chief architectural adornment, only added much later, though still in the style of the old building, was a large porch at first-floor level approached by two straight flights of stairs. The porch was an odd mixture of classical and Scottish elements, showing Glasgow's favourite elliptical arch, with coupled columns on each side supporting not an entablature but a corbelled and crenellated lintel. The style of the whole was that of a very up-to-date Court school, rather in the Danish manner. (Nearly contemporary examples of the same style survive in William Wallace's work at Linlithgow Palace, Edinburgh Castle and Heriot's Hospital, Edinburgh.) In 1814 porch and stairs were removed, during a rebuilding by David Hamilton, and the façade gothicized in the fashion of the time: it was all pulled down about 1921, but luckily the steeple was spared, and it now stands in rather affronted dignity above the most chaotic traffic junction in the city.[2] The steeple, **19**, is seven storeys high, with a tiny window at each level and no other relief except string courses until, above the clock, it bursts rather unexpectedly into an over-sailing parapet with square pyramid-topped turrets at the angles, the whole topped by a crown, four flying buttresses holding up another parapet and a tiny spire. The effect is crisp and nearly elegant – unlike those many efflorescences with which nineteenth-century town halls in Scotland were so often graced.

The Merchants' Hall in Bridgegate was an almost equally significant indicator of changing priorities. It was built in 1659 by Campbell of Blythswood, and the main façade was quite like that of his own house, though this time entirely symmetrical – of nine bays with a central entrance archway still only vaguely classical. The building was arranged round a courtyard, and contained a hospital and guildhall: all was demolished in 1817, except, again, the steeple, which stood behind the street block and which the merchants, with a flair for combining fame with profit, stipulated should remain as an

[2] Quite recently its demolition was proposed again: its historical and scenic value, and its architectural character, should surely put its preservation beyond question.

21. The trapezoidal doorway of the outer court of the Old College. The Lion and Unicorn stair was re-erected at Gilmorehill (Billings).

22. The second court of the Old College (probably by John Mylne, mid seventeenth-century).

historical relic. It is a relic now very difficult to see properly among the squalor of the run-down warehouses of the Fishmarket, and is in itself perhaps rather curious than beautiful. It rises in three stages, each topped by a pierced parapet, the first five storeys high, the others one, and each recessed slightly from the one below. The tower itself is very plain: the upper stages have, first, pairs of tall lancets, second a single broader window of generalized Gothic shape. Above is an octagonal spire with an onion at the top, all this making the upper part of the steeple look like a parody of that of the Cathedral. It has been attributed, more hopefully than credibly, to Sir William Bruce: the design of the top windows of the tower is like one that he used at his church at Lauder (Berwickshire), but used also by other builders: the evidence seems feeble, and the author of Kinross House or even of Hopetoun can hardly have been responsible for the crude attempts at classicizing the façade.[3]

Hutcheson's Hospital, **20**, formerly in the Trongate, was very similar in outward appearance to the Merchants' Hall, again with a tall steeple behind a nine-bay façade. Very possibly the same man designed and built both – which would rule out Bruce, who was only 11 when Hutcheson's was begun in 1641. It has vanished completely.[4]

So too, so far as the centre of the city is concerned, has the University, once probably the most distinguished collection of seventeenth-century architecture in Scotland. It was possibly the work of John Mylne, and consisted of two roughly square courts, arranged like those of a Cambridge college, with a tall steeple placed asymmetrically over the range which separated the two. One court was partly arcaded on the ground floor, with [4a]

[3] The attribution seems to go back no farther than Cleland. Unfortunately the relevant act books were lost at latest by the middle of the nineteenth century. Incidentally Bruce's drawings are bewilderingly difficult to read; and moreover only in the cases of a few large country houses did he supervise the building himself. Elsewhere a draft was given to the master mason, who interpreted it as well as he could. Even so, there is surely nothing in the Merchants' House story.
[The 'Bruce' drawings were in fact made by Alexander Edward. No Bruce originals are known.]
[4] It was replaced in 1805 by the building by David Hamilton which still exists (see p.81).
[4a] It is now known that the master masons for the College did not include Mylne: see further n.6.

classical detail which for the first time in Glasgow looks relaxed and confident, **22**. Above this the windows had more characteristically Scottish scrolly pediments; and there was an astonishing trapezoidal archway into the inner court, richly adorned and of a form without any very close parallel, **21**. The rest of the first court was rather plain, though with some decoration above the small windows. The second court had cylindrical staircase towers along two sides; the great tower was plain with a pierced parapet and had a small ogee cap of a kind still found on smaller public buildings of the seventeenth and early eighteenth centuries.[5] The façade to High Street was nearly symmetrical, two storeys with attic in the centre, three with attic at the ends, though the eave-line was continuous: (Five-bay extensions were added early in the eighteenth century.) It is the centre of this façade, **23**, which has been wrapped round a rectangle and re-erected as the Pearce Lodge at the foot of Gilmorehill, with one of the cylindrical towers added – a device which has resulted in an ungainly building but at least allows us to study the details.[6] Here once again the windows are topped with 'pediments' in the form of scrolly strapwork. The principal ones (slightly reduced in size and with a new glazing scheme) stand above a heavy corbelled balcony, originally covering the two bays on either side of the entrance. The proportions have been considerably altered and perhaps spoiled by a reduc-

23. The main entrance of the Old College (mid seventeenth-century). Re-erected at the Pearce Lodge on Gilmorehill in 1887 (Billings).

[5] See, for example, the town-house at Culross (Fife). A third court, made up of professors' houses, was added late in the eighteenth century.

[6] The architect responsible was A. G. Thomson (see p.93n). He campaigned for the façade to be preserved, and Pearce gave him the job; so much credit is due to him. The date is 1888.
[More has now been learned of the masons responsible for the seventeenth-century building: John Boyd had built part of the inner court by 1639; it was finished by John Clerk who also built the outer court (1654–60) (see *Munimenta Alma Universitatis Glasguensis* iii, 481ff.). Both were prominent Glasgow masons, Boyd having also had a hand in the tolbooth (*Glasgow Burgh Records 1537–1642*, pp.351ff.). The Lion & Unicorn stair was built by William Riddell in 1690 (MacGibbon & Ross, *Castellated & Domestic Architecture*, v, 563).]

24. No. 42 Miller Street (John Craig, 1775).

tion in the wall space above the principal windows. The centrepiece, with its stark half-hexagonal pediment or gable surmounted by three chimneys set diagonally, has been narrowed, so that the originally elliptical entrance arch has become semi-circular, and the decorations above are more crowded. The 'Gibbs surround' with its alternations of rock-face rustic and dressed stone is, however, original. (Similar surrounds to the ground-floor windows are not.) The chimneys have been reduced in height and their tops given extra emphasis. The reconstruction must therefore be looked at very cautiously: it is at least a reminder of the wanton destruction of a group of buildings which might have lent great heart to the architecturally depressed centre of the city.[7]

The seventeenth century was a thin time for churches throughout the country, and Glasgow is lucky to have one surviving fragment, the steeple of the Tron Church. The medieval collegiate church of St Mary and St Anne was reconstructed as one of the city kirks in 1592. A tower was added immediately afterwards and given a spire between 1630 and 1636. The church was burnt at the end of the eighteenth century and rebuilt in 1793 by James Adam, slightly to the south so that the steeple is now detached.[8] For some time the tron (the public weighbeam) was actually housed on the ground floor of the tower: it was removed in the mid nineteenth century, and arches were inserted (by John Carrick, 1855) to allow the pavement to run underneath. There is a curious mixture of styles, for the tower was built in the hesitant Tudor that one might expect during the uncertain period of the late sixteenth century, while the spire is a reversion to a more full-blown Gothic, being in fact quite closely modelled on the spire of the cathedral, though the details are coarser and the proportions clumsier: only the pierced parapet seems to be an original invention, made up of a row of elementary balusters.

Towards the end of the seventeenth century Captain John Slezer made several engravings of Glasgow for his book *Theatrum Scotiae*. The best known and most attractive of these shows the view from the Fir Park (the hill where the Necropolis now stands) 26: the great bulk of the cathedral dominates (as, alas, it cannot today), while in the middle distance is the town itself, with five towers of its own, each topped with an oversize weathercock, riding above the roofs of the houses. The whole is surrounded by trees and open hill-sides: the trees seem to reach right into the town and were no doubt partly responsible for the 'odoriferous smell' of flowers and fruit which John M'Ure reported in 1736.[9]

Rather more than a century after Slezer, Joseph Swan engraved a view taken from almost the same point, 25. The towers are still there, and so are the distant hills. But now, almost in the centre of the picture, are two tall factory chimneys (others can more dimly be seen in the distance). The trees have all gone, except from the hill of the Necropolis itself; and the city, which in 1690 was a compact but loose-knit little town in which individual buildings stood out, has become a much larger, solider and denser mass, obviously now extending outside the frame of the view. The eighteenth century was the period of Glasgow's first industrialization and of its first great expansion, during which the population multiplied six times: in 1801 it was 77,000, and Glasgow was the largest city in the country. Against all natural odds, including being thirty miles from the sea up a narrow and perpetually silting estuary, it became the first port of Scotland and was already an important manufacturing town. The most significant single booster to this

[8a]

[7] The Lion and Unicorn Stair from the Outer Court has also been rebuilt at Gilmorehill. It was reversed, and obviously heavily restored in the process. The doorway at its top is also original. A simpler, though similar, trapezoidal doorway (without columns) used to be at Gowrie House, Perth, others of a related kind at Aberdour and St. Andrews.

[8] George Hay (*Scottish Post-Reformation Churches*) attributed this church to *John* Adam, a distant relation of the famous brothers; but the date makes this impossible as this John died in 1790. He did, however, work in Glasgow (see below p.111n). Plans for the church are at the Soane Museum, and copies are among David Hamilton's drawings now at Glasgow University.

[8a] The engravings were actually made by Robert White, who was paid £256.10s. for the fifty-seven which made up the book; the original drawings were probably by Everhardus Kickius. (See Harris, *The Artist and the Country House*, 1979, p.90.)

[9] M'Ure was Glasgow's first historian – on the whole a biased and unreliable one; in this case, however, his report is backed by the evidence of less partial witnesses. M'Ure's material, including his mistakes, has been absorbed into a number of later histories. *Glasghu Facies*, of 1871, makes some attempt to sort it out.

activity was the Act of Union of 1707, which allowed Scottish ports to trade with the American colonies for the first time. Glasgow was in a natural position for Atlantic trade, and by the mid-century had something like a monopoly of the United Kingdom's tobacco trade – a business whose name is still marked in the name of Virginia Street, where a building once used as the tobacco exchange still stands.

Trade, however, for most of the eighteenth century still depended on the harbours much lower down the Clyde, at Newark (now called Port Glasgow) and Greenock. In Glasgow itself the river was hardly navigable even at high water. As early as 1556 the city had come to an agreement with Renfrew and Dumbarton burghs to remove the ford at Dumbarton, so that small boats might come up to Glasgow. But by 1770, just after the opening of the New Glasgow Bridge (forerunner of the present Jamaica Bridge), the depth of water at low tide 400 yards below was only 15 inches. A few years earlier, an Act of Parliament had been obtained for canalizing the river on the advice of Smeaton. Luckily this was not acted on. And in 1773 a new scheme of dredging and the building of frequent jetties for containing the drifting mud was begun under the direction of John Golbourne of Chester, who managed to increase the depth to 6 feet – still obviously inadequate for ocean-going ships. The work of narrowing continued, in order to deepen the channel

25. Glasgow from John Knox's Monument. (From Swan's 'Select Views of Glasgow', 1829).

26. Glasgow from the Fir Park. (From Slezer's 'Theatrum Scotiae', c.1690).

[10] See the letter from 'Senex' (Robert Reid) in the *Glasgow Herald* of 18 October, 1843: 'The different stripes of back garden ground, betwixt Candleriggs and Queen Street, gradually came to be formed into streets running northward from Trongate and Argyle Streets to Ingram Street. These were opened in the following manner: Virginia Street (1753), Miller Street (1773), Hutcheson Street (1790), Glassford Street (1793), and Brunswick Street (1790). Virginia Street was named by Mr Spiers in honour of the tobacco trade; his house has just been taken down by the Glasgow and Ship Bank Company. Miller Street got its name from Mr Miller of Westerton, through whose property it was carried. Hutcheson Street was so called because it occupied the garden of the hospital. Glassford Street received its appelation from Mr Horn, builder, who purchased Mr Glassford's house and back garden. About this time John Street, commencing at Ingram Street, was opened. It was so called from the circumstance of there being, at that time, a great number of gentlemen in office as magistrates and councillors, whose Christian names were John . . .'

further, and by 1821 ships drawing 13 feet 6 inches came to the city's own harbour, which by this time had grown extensive. The work of dredging goes on of course today. The Clyde is largely an artificial waterway.

An artificial waterway of a different kind followed a few years after Golbourne's work, when the canal from Grangemouth on the Firth of Forth reached Hamilton Hill, just north of the city. The junction with the Clyde was made in 1790. But by this time trade had taken a second place to manufactures. The revolt of the colonies ended the British monopoly of American tobacco; and other trading ventures had been unsuccessful. The first great cotton mills were well to the south of the city to take advantage of the Falls of Clyde (the greatest, though slightly later, group can still be seen at New Lanark); but the manufacturers were Glaswegians.

During the second half of the eighteenth century the ground plan of the centre of Glasgow took on much the form it has today: the medieval town was to some extent regularized, and the flat ground between Trongate and the modern Ingram Street (itself a rationalization of 'the common loan called School Wynd') was laid out with a series of streets running north-south, some of them being later extended north of Ingram Street. Though the layout is regular, this development does not seem to have been the result of any general plan. The opening of any given street depended on the decision of the owner of the land through which it was to pass, and the arrangement must for a long time have been haphazard.[10] By 1768, when the first Jamaica Bridge was opened, the city formally extended as far west as the line of Union Street–Jamaica Street. But most of the land was only sporadically built up and contained for the main part the comfortable town mansions and gardens of prosperous city merchants, while the bulk of the people still lived in the older part of the town and in its eastward extension along Gallowgate. The new streets, therefore, had not, to start with, the continuous façades of buildings that we see today. Late eighteenth-century drawings of Argyle Street show a mixture of large Palladian villas, cottages and gardens. Miller Street and its neighbours must have been almost entirely devoted to largish houses and gardens, one or two of which had to be removed for the cutting through of new streets.[11] One of these houses, perhaps a comparatively modest one, survives, now rather overwhelmed by its large commercial neighbours, at No.42 Miller Street, **24**. It was built in 1775 by John Craig and is a plain two-storeyed house of five bays, in an extremely simplified version of eighteenth-century Palladianism. The three centre bays project very slightly and are topped by a plain pediment, which is echoed in the quite proud doorcase, where it is supported on Corinthian pilasters. (The mansard roof and attic windows are modern and somewhat upset the balance of the design. Its appearance of being stuccoed is in fact due to thick paint: there is good ashlar underneath, as was amply proved when the building of Woolworths next door caused the house to subside.) Two other town mansions still exist but are difficult to see. The Dreghorn Mansion of 1752 is now buried in an indifferent Victorian warehouse at No.130 Clyde Street; the Cunninghame Mansion (1775) is the eastern half of the Royal Exchange, behind David Hamilton's portico and underneath his cupola. This house was obviously more ambitious than most; but its present appearance is due

[11] Glassford Street, continuing the line of Stockwell Street, goes through the site of the Shawfield Mansion which stood at the Trongate end; the old Hutcheson Hospital also went, being rebuilt at the north end of the street named after it.

27. Shawfield Mansion (Colen Campbell, 1712; demolished c.1795). (From 'Vitruvius Britannicus', Vol.I).

largely to Hamilton. Throughout the eighteenth century the most imposing of all was the Shawfield Mansion built in 1712 for Daniel Campbell by his namesake Colen (who was, it seems, no relation). The house, which Campbell illustrated in the second volume of *Vitruvius Britannicus*, is his earliest recorded executed design, **27**. Compared with Wanstead, Shawfield was modest indeed – a seven-bay house with pedimented and slightly projecting centrepiece, hipped roof and apparently a belevedere on top. Yet it has considerable historical interest: though retaining one or two Wrennish features, Shawfield was virtually a complete Palladian house on the scale of Palladio's villas. The type became popular in England in the 1730s and 1740s; but only one English example of the eighteenth-century Palladian revival is known to be earlier – William Benson's Wilbury Park of 1710. Since Campbell became (after Palladio himself, that is) the greatest single influence on Burlington, English Palladianism may almost be said to have begun in Glasgow.

By the beginning of the eighteenth century Trongate was the principal shopping street of the city. Defoe, visiting Glasgow in 1715, was much impressed: 'it is a large, stately, and well-built City, standing on a Plain, in a manner foursquare; and the Four principal Streets are the fairest for breadth, and the finest built that I have ever seen in one City together. The houses are all of stone, and generally uniform in height, as well as in front. The lower

28. Trongate c.1826, after the painting by John Knox in the Old Glasgow Museum: the Tolbooth and Tontine Hotel are in the centre, the Tron Church tower to the left. The building on the extreme left is part of John Weir's London Street scheme (see p.72).

29. The Tontine Hotel, originally the Town Hall (Allan Dreghorn, built 1737-60). This photograph taken about 1890 shows also the Tolbooth as rebuilt by David Hamilton, and beyond that a very early iron-framed warehouse, now destroyed.

[12] See *Glasghu Facies* (ed. J. F. S. Gordon, 1871), p.15.
[13] Perhaps de Caux was the real designer (see Summerson, *Architecture in Britain, 1530–1830*, p.83). The closest replica of this work now extant, apart from a passable copy of one house in Covent Garden itself, is the Brick Market in Newport, Rhode Island, begun by Peter Harrison in 1761 and modelled closely on the Somerset House design. Mr John Harris has recently pointed out that Tibaldi's Palazzo Magnani in Bologna is almost identical with the New Gallery, and that engravings of it were ready to hand for Webb to use. (See *Country Life*, Vol.cxlii, p.1249; 16 Nov. 1967).
[14] A motif of which Jones was fond – see the Banqueting House in Whitehall. [The building of the later section of the Tontine was in the hands of James Craig, but there seems every reason to suppose that Dreghorn, to whom payments are recorded in the Town Council minutes and who is known from St Andrew's to have been accomplished and skilful, was responsible for the Somerset House transcription, Craig simply doubling the original façade and having no choice but to continue the alternating pediments which, Palladianly correct over five bays, are something of a solecism over an even number. A fine section drawn by Alexander Hay in 1840 (see his *Modern Builder's Guide*, pl.10) shows mainly William Hamilton's work of adaptation.]

Stories, for the most part, stand on vast square Doric Columns, with Arches, which open into the Shops, adding to the strength, as well as beauty, of the building. In a word, 'tis one of the cleanliest, most beautiful, and best-built Cities in Great Britain.'[12] In a later edition of his *Tour*, it had become the 'beautifullest little city in Britain'. Defoe's description can be compared with a picture of the Cross by one John Knox, painted in *c*.1826 and now in the Old Glasgow Museum, **28**. The arcades (called, as in Covent Garden, 'piazzas') have almost all gone, but Trongate still has a most impressive dignity and width (perhaps slightly exaggerated in the picture). The buildings are still of a uniform height and 'front', though the tolbooth, now in Gothic dress, is properly allowed prominence. Next door to it is the Tontine Hotel, which was perhaps the most distinguished building of eighteenth-century Glasgow. It was built originally as the Town Hall, the five eastern bays in 1737–40 with James Cross as master-mason and (probably) David Cation as carver, the five Western in 1758–60 (Mungo Naismith, carver), at which time the whole design was perhaps spruced up. It is based on an historically influential formula of Inigo Jones, which first appeared in the piazzas of Covent Garden (begun in 1630 by Jones and Isaac de Caux), then in the New Gallery of Somerset House (1661–2, almost certainly designed by John Webb), which was demolished in 1776 to make way for the complete rebuilding by Sir William Chambers. Chambers himself produced a swagger up-to-date version of the formula in the Strand front of his palace, in which the pilasters are replaced by half-columns; but the Glasgow building was much closer to the design attributed to Jones.[13] It was a three-storey range, in which the two upper storeys were linked by a giant order of Ionic pilasters standing on a substantial plinth above a continuous arcade, both an echo of the Covent Garden design and a continuation of the piazzas reported by Defoe, **29**. The windows on the principal floor had alternating triangular and segmental pediments.[14] Above a dentel-moulded cornice was a balustrade (dating from after 1756), topped with urns. Since the building was ten bays long, no bay could be central: it could only be read as a continuous range – probably to be looked at in perspective – but the proportions were extremely happy. The Town Hall was bought by the Tontine Society in 1781 and the interior remodelled by William Hamilton: its principal feature was the coffee room, 74 feet long, $32\frac{1}{2}$ feet wide, $16\frac{1}{2}$ feet high, 'universally allowed to be the most elegant of its kind in Britain, perhaps in Europe'. The room was lit by a large glass dome supported on Doric columns 'with correspondent pilasters up the walls'.[15]

No civic building of anything like the grandeur of the Tontine Hotel survives from eighteenth-century Glasgow. Trongate itself, battered and shoddy as it now looks, still has a few minor Georgian buildings, Argyle Street rather more. The best is Spreull's Land (182 Trongate),† a four-storeyed tenement built about 1784: it has a fine oval cantilevered staircase, which used to 'hang' but now has cast-iron supports. The type, as doubtless of most of the rest of the street originally, is that of the plain tall blocks which are familiar in the eighteenth-century parts of the Royal Mile, though once again the Glasgow example is smaller.

By the end of the eighteenth century, when Glasgow had survived the slump that followed the American War of Independence and had gone over

[15] Chapman's *Picture of Glasgow*, 1820 (see *Glasghu Facies*, p.423). Allan Dreghorn (then at work on St Andrew's Church) measured Cross's work for the town council in September 1738. This makes it highly probable that Dreghorn himself was responsible for the Somerset House transcription. The town council minutes record payments to Dreghorn. A very fine section was drawn by Alexander Hay in 1840 (see his *Modern Builder's Guide*, pl. 10).
[15a] See Frank Worsdall, *The Tenement*, 1979, pp.72–3 and pl.24.

30. Candleriggs looking north to St David's Church. The best-preserved of the late eighteenth-century streets of the merchant city; the west side has lately been mutilated. (By James and William Carswell, c.1790.)

15a

31. Virginia Buildings, Virginia Street (c.1819).

to manufacturing cotton, most of the houses on the flat ground north of Trongate had been replaced by continuous façades of commercial buildings. Candleriggs is the street which preserves most nearly the character of the commercial heart of the city at this time, **30**, though a recent pointless 'face-lift' has partly spoiled the west side with unauthentic string courses and other little 'contemporary' features added. The buildings, dating from about 1790, are of five storeys, very severe, rather poker-faced, completely utilitarian, yet pleasingly proportioned despite the narrowness of the street: they have their analogues in Paris and Boston. More buildings of the same kind are in Cochrane Street and Ingram Street; and this was doubtless the rule in the whole area. Some builders were a little more adventurous: of their **15b** works the best surviving range is on the west side of Virginia Street, built late, in 1817. Here, opposite the end of Wilson Street is a five bay block designed as a unit, with tripartite windows in the centre, a doorcase with pairs of Ionic pilasters and a balustrade, **31-2**. Immediately to the south is another, plainer, but with beautifully delicate detail including two windows set into recessed blank arches. To the south again (Nos. 31–5) is the most valuable survivor of all, the so-called Tobacco (or sometimes Sugar) Exchange. It has a plain façade of seven bays which for a time was romanized and made quite grand by the addition of wooden pediments over all the windows. These have recently been taken down as dangerous, and the flat three-bay pediment is the only departure from maximum plainness. But – most precious – the galleried court (now called Crown Arcade) remains, a tall narrow rectangle, surrounded by timber galleries, **33**. The ground floor has been altered (though pleasantly) – presumably it had a Doric order – but the Ionic order above remains intact. A window at one end is said to be where the auctioneer sat. This is the only remaining example of the exchanges which at one time must have been among the most important public buildings of the city: it is of course tiny compared with later English examples, but a treasure to be carefully guarded. Though there have been so many changes, the general air of the commercial city of 1800 must have been in many ways what it is now – a straightforward workaday sort of place, little given to dressing itself up, but with a busy seemliness which, one supposes, reflected the activities of the people who caused it to be built. The rectangular layout was on a small enough scale not to become monotonous, particularly since all the views out were stopped, if not by buildings then by hills. A feature particularly notable in view of the piecemeal development of this period is the series of axial approaches to important buildings, which thus gain some formal dignity: examples are the Cunninghame Mansion, later Royal Exchange, on the axis of Ingram Street, St David's Church (Candleriggs), Trades House and Old Merchants' House (Garth Street), Bank of Scotland (Glassford Street) and Hutcheson's Hospital (Hutcheson Street).

Down to earth though most of this work is, the late eighteenth century also saw Glasgow's first attempt at formal civic design – more cautious than Edinburgh's, but an indication of the way the city would later turn. Glasgow's first square was laid out in 1768 – round the recently built church of St Andrew[16] immediately east of Saltmarket, thus setting a pattern which was to be popular in Glasgow for over a century, and which occurs also at the Royal Exchange in Liverpool. The houses were simple (almost all have gone now, and the square is very dingy indeed), with no attempt at any unifying principle other than repetition, the design, such as it was, rather

[15b] James Carswell (1767–1856) and his brother William (d.1852), who came to Glasgow from Kilmarnock in 1790, started building in Candleriggs. According to an article in the *Glasgow Herald* (25th Feb. 1856) 'almost the whole of Candleriggs owes its existence to them, including Commercial Court with its surrounding warehouses; this was the model upon which so many courts have been built by which business is conducted apart from the public street.' The Carswells also built part of Cochrane Street and Ingram Court.
[16] See p.58. [The houses in the square were not built until 1786–7; the architect was William Hamilton.]

32. Virginia Buildings: an early example of incised ornament, owing something to the influence of Soane.

cramped. In any case it was hardly on the east side of the town that one would look for experiments in urban formality. Much more important were the two squares at the west end of the city – St Enoch's laid down in 1782, George Square in 1787. St Enoch's Square was planned as the broad formal gesture which closed the south end of Buchanan Street, the big new promenade sweeping down to the river, which soon became Glasgow's fashionable shopping street. The square is now unrecognizable – even its plan confused by later buildings. It originally consisted of two sides of roughly similar houses with, on the south side, St Enoch's church, built in 1780 by J. Jaffrey (apparently on the site of an old chapel) and then again in 1827 by David Hamilton, who, however, kept Jaffrey's steeple. The church was just south of where James Miller's little underground station now stands and, though less absurdly insignificant than that building is, now that it is on its own, must have been on the small side when seen down the vista of Buchanan Street. George Square can still just be reconstructed, **34**, for the north side remains from the original design, much altered, with an extra storey on the North British Hotel and the rest badly knocked about; however the three-storey ranges with central pediments and pavilions marked by giant pilasters can still be picked out. This seems to have been the most ambitious – or at least the best built – side of the square, for John Leighton,

16a

33. Crown Arcade, once the Tobacco Exchange (1819): the balustrades have now been replaced by poor-quality boarding.

16a The eastern half of the north side has now been demolished.

34. George Square in the early nineteenth century. (From Swan's 'Views').

writing in 1838, reports that 'the houses on the other sides are an inferior order of buildings'. (In fact they were simple and dignified classical ranges, two and three storeys high, with a central pediment on the west side: rather like those on the north, though less imposingly adorned.) George Square has become, of course, the city's *Grande Place*: the garden, once fenced off and private to the occupiers of houses around the square, is now paved and public; and the very large buildings on three sides probably suit the huge scale and layout better than the 'inferior' ones. The excellent Scott monument still commands, despite the immense block of the College of Building on the hill to the north; indeed the contrast of the tall building above the horizontal square is exciting. But it is deplorable that the copious supply of 16b statuary has been given the addition of fussy flower-beds and the natty timber information bureau, which looks, and perhaps is, 'temporary': while it lasts it is certainly disruptive.

Socially Glasgow was also showing commendable progress at this time. Leighton gives the primary credit for this to the opening of the Coffee Room at the Tontine Hotel: 'Previous to the breaking out of the American war in 1775, the Virginia merchants, who were looked up to as the Glasgow aristocracy, had a privileged walk at the Cross, which they trod in long scarlet cloaks and bushy wigs, and such was the state of society that when any of the reputable tradesmen of the city had occasion to speak to these "Tobacco Lords", he required to walk on the other side of the street till he was fortunate enough to meet the eye of the patrician, for it would have been deemed presumptuous to have gone to meet him. Latterly, the rising generation of the middle classes, better educated than their fathers, engaged extensively in trade and commerce, and by honourable dealing and correct conduct, procured a name and place in society which had been hitherto reserved for those of higher birth. Since the opening of the public Coffee Room in 1781 the absurd distinction of assumed rank in a manufacturing town has disappeared.

16b It is hardly possible any longer to be excited by the College of Building: the plethora of tall blocks in and near the city centre has made such contrasts turn very sour.

17 *The Beauties of Clyde* (Glasgow [1838]),
pp.76–7.
18 A few small classical essays are slightly
earlier, notably William Adam's church at
Hamilton (1732), built on the plan of a
Celtic cross.
18a Wren had cautiously used three-dimensional
arches at St Clement Dane's and St James's,
Piccadilly, where, however, the principal
arch-rings are still vertical. Entablature blocks
or dosserets had first appeared in the
fifteenth century in Brunelleschi's two
Florentine churches of S. Lorenzo and
Sto. Spirito. (Our thanks to Mr. H. S.
Stevenson for pointing out inaccuracies of
formulation.)

35. St Andrew's Church from the south west. (Allan Dreghorn and Mungo Naismith, 1739-56)

Wealth is not now the criterion of respect, for persons in the inferior walks of life who conduct themselves with propriety, have a higher place assigned them in society than at any former period in the history of the city.' Nor was this improvement restricted to public occasions. 'The mode of giving entertainments is materially changed. Persons who formerly gave supper parties with ample potations, are now in the way of giving sumptuous dinners, entertaining with the choicest wines, and frequently finishing with cold punch, for which Glasgow is so celebrated . . . In drinking there is a mighty improvement. Formerly, guests were compelled to drink in quantity and quality as presented by their host; now every person drinks what he pleases, and how he pleases, after which he retires to the drawing room. Drunkenness and dissipation at dinner parties are now happily unknown. Profane swearing is considered highly reprehensible; so much so, that swearing in good society is scarcely ever heard.' As an afterthought, Leighton adds that 'the working classes are better lodged, clothed, and fed, than formerly'.[17]

The growing civic consciousness of the city was responsible for a number of individual buildings whose function was at least partly demonstrative and monumental. In this field, the design of churches, which had more or less stopped at the Reformation, was prominent (as, in another way, it had been in the Middle Ages). Apart from Blackfriars, an undistinguished replacement of the medieval church destroyed by lightning in 1670, St Andrew's (1739–56) was the first church built in Glasgow since the Reformation; and it is a building of an entirely new kind – the earliest large-scale classical church in Scotland,[18] slightly antedating those at Dumfries and Kilmarnock and finally finished at about the same time as Gibbs's St Nicholas, Aberdeen. It is not, however, to this, Gibbs's only Scottish church, that the architect, Allan Dreghorn, was primarily indebted, but rather to the considerably earlier St Martin's-in-the-Fields, London, on which the design of the Glasgow church leans heavily, **36**. Not only is the plan extremely similar – even to the point of including a liturgically useless chancel – but Dreghorn took over the giant Corinthian order, in which, on the inside, each column carries its own entablature, and the three-dimensional arches which lean inwards into the curve of the barrel vault. Both of these were inventions (or innovations) of Gibbs's, which he himself used again at All Saints', Derby.   18a

Again, Dreghorn repeats the Venetian window at the east end, the arrangement of plaster work on the vault is almost identical, and so is the hanging of the galleries between the columns. On the other hand Dreghorn's columns are fluted, while Gibbs's are plain; Dreghorn's chancel narrows abruptly from the nave, Gibbs's is angled inwards through half a bay: these changes, and the fact that his church is narrower, with a semi-circular, instead of an elliptical, vault, give Dreghorn's design a sense of greater movement, less spaciousness and perhaps less sumptuousness, rich though the rococo plaster-work is, particularly that surrounding the clock at the west end: this is the work of Thomas Clayton.

The exterior also owes much to Gibbs, **35**. Here again, the articulation is by means of a giant Corinthian order, pilasters along the sides giving way without interruption to the columns of a hexastyle portico at the west end (here the columns are not fluted). Unlike Gibbs's, Dreghorn's portico is the full width of his church, so that it gives the impression simply that the westernmost bay has been left open. The relation of portico to church is thus less complex than at St Martin's, where the portico (two bays deep – only one at St Andrew's) is an introduction to the church rather than a not completely explained part of it. The windows, in two storeys of course to take account of the galleries, follow St Martin's exactly – semi-circular headed above, depressed elliptical below, all with 'Gibbs-surrounds'. The steeple on the other hand is an attenuated version of another Gibbs design – proposed for St Mary-le-Strand, London, but later rejected. It consists of an octagonal drum standing on a slender square tower and surmounted by a tiny dome and a faintly Gothic finial. Dreghorn's steeple, though rather on the thin side, is very elegant: its chief fault – so common in churches of this type – is its externally arbitrary relation to the church roof; and here again the portico is partly to blame, for there is no division at all between its roof and that of the church. The steeple of St Martin's also emerges through the roof, and at the same place – over the intermediate bay between portico and nave; but the relation is clarified in Gibbs's design, because the narrowing of the portico articulates its roof from that of the church precisely at the point where the tower appears.[19]

Derivative and not wholly successful as it is, St Andrew's is an admirable building of a type rare in Scotland and deserves much more attention and much better treatment than the city generally gives to it.[20] Its interior is indeed of an unexampled richness, chiefly owing to the lustrous Spanish mahog-

36. St Andrew's Church (plasterwork by Thomas Clayton).

[19] St Andrew's, Edinburgh (by Andrew Frazer and William Sibbald, 1782–9) gets into the same trouble here as its Glasgow namesake; St Mary's (Thomas Brown, 1824) tries the heroic expedient of a plinth for the tower as wide as the portico, which thus appears seriously overweighted.
[20] The credit for the church should probably go as much to the builder, Mungo Naismith, as to Dreghorn. The craftsmanship throughout is of a high order.

37. The Assembly Rooms, Ingram Street (centre portion by R. and J. Adam 1792, wings by Henry Holland, 1807): demolished c.1890; the centre was later re-erected as the McLennan Arch.

any of its furnishings: the wood was imported by the tobacco lords. The pulpit is a specially fine piece, free-standing on a slender column in the centre of the church, its sides decorated with delicate rococo scroll-carving picked out in gilt.

Contemporary with this grandiloquent church is the much humbler St Andrew's-by-the-Green (1751), the first church built in Scotland for episcopalian worship (as a result of which its Presbyterian builder, Andrew Hunter, was excommunicated from his own church): it crouches almost unseen in its grime and is apparently now doomed by the inflexible inner ring road. It is a plain oblong, five bays by three, without steeple of any   20a kind. A pediment at each end is simply formed by the roof gable; on the longer sides is another pediment over the three central bays, which are articulated by 'pilasters' that are in fact no more than vertical bands of channel-jointed stone. The middle window of the north side is semi-circular-headed with a Gibbs surround; the others are all plain. The clumsy chancel is a fairly late addition. Inside, the loft fronts are original; the organ was built by Donaldson, of York, in 1795 and stood for some time in the cathedral before coming to St Andrew's in 1812. No architect seems to have been responsible for the church; probably Hunter made his own designs.   20b

Glasgow had few buildings with large-scale classical pretensions until the arrival of the younger Adams in 1792.[21] This event evidently coincided with an increased desire on the citizens' part for the elegancies of city life, which received their expression in the building of a new theatre, Assembly Rooms (the Tontine Hotel was already awkwardly far east), an infirmary, big extensions to the university, and, characteristically, several banks. (Glasgow had to depend on branches of Edinburgh banks until the middle of the century, but by this time had its own.) The Adams did not leave so firm a mark on Glasgow as on Edinburgh; and most of their work has now gone.

[20a] St Andrew's-by-the-Green is no longer threatened by the ring road (whose route has now changed), merely – like so many others – by neglect, closure, dereliction and vandalism.

[20b] The joint masons, as Mr. David McLees has shown, were William Paull and Andrew Hunter, with Thomas Thomson, wright. Only the west gallery was original.

[21] Their style had preceded them in the elegant work of James Craig, described as 'Architect to the Prince of Wales'; unfortunately none of his buildings, which included the Grammar School (1788) – later the Anderson Institution – and the old Surgeons' Hall in St Enoch's Square (1790), have been preserved.

38. Cathedral Square in about 1829 showing the Infirmary, Cathedral and Barony North Church (probably by John Robertson, 1793). (From Swan's 'Views'.)

Robert and James between them were responsible for the Infirmary and the Assembly Rooms, both long since demolished, though the centrepiece of the Assembly Rooms was rebuilt in 1894 and then again about 1922 as a surprisingly effective triumphal arch at one of the entrances to Glasgow Green. The large semi-circular carriage arch stands between pairs of Ionic columns, each pair with its own entablature and superstructure. Between the columns are small square-headed pedestrian openings. In its original position, the large arch was the central window of a façade, **37**, on which the detached pairs of columns were the chief architectural feature, though apparently much smaller than they now are and standing *on* an arcaded plinth up to the first-floor level: they were thus a giant order on the tall upper storey only. The Assembly Rooms were built in Ingram Street in 1796 (where the back of the post office now is), but already by 1807 were found to be too small, and wings were added in a modestly Adamesque manner by Henry Holland, who refused a fee for his work.[22]

The Infirmary, begun in 1792, took the place of the ruins of the Archbishop's Palace and stood till the present dreary monster was built early this century, **38**. Its principal façade must have been (except for the detail of the centrepiece) quite like the entrance front of Edinburgh University: a parallelogram with projecting wings and canted projecting aedicule centre, **39**. The familiar coupled columns standing on the basement plinth had a continuous entablature with a small pediment (thus with the window between forming an aedicule), set into a superstructure level with the main cornice. The wings had giant Venetian windows, two storeys high, with semi-circular windows in the basement.[23] The crowning dome was singularly graceful.

The house probably built by Robert Adam in Charlotte Street for David Dale, the philanthropic industrialist, has been demolished quite recently by the City Education Department. The additions to the University were

[22] Holland's authorship of these additions seems too well documented to question. Yet the ornamentation, particularly the curiously stilted blind tympana over the principal windows, is uncharacteristic.

[23] From 1850 the basement was a full ground floor, the earth having been dug away from the front during alterations by James Brown.

61

39. Royal Infirmary (R. and J. Adam, 1792): the photograph, taken shortly before it was demolished, shows the basement as converted to a full ground floor (by James Brown, 1850) Cf. fig.38.

swept away with the rest of the Old College, when the High Street site was abandoned; but two houses† designed by James Adam for the University still perilously exist in a miserably defaced state, on the corners of College Street, designed to flank a small vista from the main gate of the College, **40**. They were an early experiment in university staff housing, supplementing the old Professors' Quadrangle (an experiment repeated in frightful baronial gloom and inconvenience at Gilmorehill). Each house is of three and a half storeys, with slightly projecting wings, about a three-bay centre. (That on the south corner was altered in the nineteenth century.) The wings, of one bay each, have on the two principal floors a giant Corinthian order of the kind that includes the Prince of Wales's feathers, the order being carried round onto the side elevations. Columns stand between pilasters supporting a cornice continuous across the whole façade; between them is a recessed blank arch and inside this the windows. Only those on the first floor have pediments, and of these alternate (even) ones are left alone. The attic storey, above the main cornice, has square windows, which in the wings are flanked by circular plaques. Unfortunately the ground floors have been completely destroyed by modern shopfronts of a garishness remarkable even in Glasgow; but enough remains to show that the pair must have made a particularly stately and well-balanced group, their design if crowded certainly lively. The very pretty arcaded block on the north side of Wilson Street, **41**, is also perhaps a frail and mutilated survivor of the Adams' brief stay in the city. It has been given an unattractive and ill-proportioned mansard roof, the elliptical arcade has been filled in, and in one bay destroyed.[24] Nevertheless, with its quiet, crisp detail, now overlaid with thick paint, it makes an agreeable group with another, much spoilt building, also of *c.*1790†, and, between them, the solemn portico of the City and County Buildings.

James Adam's plain, but elegant bow-fronted parallelogram for the Tron Church (1793) is now a storehouse and virtually invisible. The only Adam

23a

[23a] No longer. The college houses were demolished as dangerous in the 1970s, despite worthy and appropriate attempts by the University of Strathclyde to save them, which were foiled by the City's being unable at the time to guarantee that the site would not be required for motorway works.
[24] Credit must go to the new owners for restoring this bay to the appearance of the others.

40. College Houses, High Street (James Adam 1793): the nearer one was altered in the nineteenth century.

41. No. 60 Wilson Street (probably by R. and J. Adam c.1790), with the portico of the City and County Buildings beyond. The ground floor originally had an open arcade, and the mansard roof is modern.

building surviving, and with some chance of continuing to survive, reasonably intact, is luckily one of the best – Robert Adam's Trades House in Glassford Street (designed in 1791–2, finished after his death in 1794). The rather cramped effect of this design is largely due to what J. M. Reid rightly calls the tall insignificance of its southern neighbours, though the single-bay side-pieces, which were a later addition, improve the general balance. The façade, 42, has been made unnecessarily bleak by the removal of the fanlights, alterations to the Venetian windows and the insertion of an architrave in the main doorway. The building is of two and a half storeys only: the principal storey is, however, unusually tall, with room for decorated panels over the windows in the central section. The wings again project slightly; but this time there is no giant order: only the centrepiece is an aedicule of coupled Ionic columns standing on the projecting rusticated entrance – seemingly almost a replica of the centrepiece of the Infirmary, though on a smaller scale. The principal floor has three venetian windows of a favourite Adam type in which the semi-circle is contained in a larger one of the same width as the rectangular opening below; these alternate with pedimented oblong windows under the decorated panels. The attic (over quite a light cornice) has small oblong windows punched into the wall; above is a balustraded parapet, interrupted over the centrepiece by a frieze of circular metopes, surmounted with the royal arms. Above again is the dome, topped by a tiny cylindrical cupola and standing on a cylindrical drum, with small pilastered and pedimented aedicules on the main axes. Like all the better Adam work, Trades House is a fairly complex balance of a variety of motifs on a strictly symmetrical basis: the symmetry is secured for the spectator by the building's standing on the axis of Garth Street. If the façade seems a little too crowded with incident, it is certainly vigorous, a good example of Robert Adam's abhorrence of flat, static surfaces. The interior was rebuilt by James Sellars in 1887.[25]

Two substantial and important country houses should also be mentioned to complete the picture of eighteenth-century buildings still or until recently to be seen in the city. Garscadden House was in fact begun shortly after 1664, the slightly projecting wings being added in the mid eighteenth century, the porch in 1778 and the elaborate Gothick gateway by Charles Ross in 1789. The house was a curious and engaging mixture of the naïve and the sophisticated, with old-fashioned hipped gables, yet an attempt at a pediment in the centre, and a purely classical porch high up and rather incongruous in the middle of the simple façade. Alas this entertaining house has now gone the way of so many others; the gateway was demolished only in 1965.

Pollok House, William Adam's only building in the immediate neighbourhood of Glasgow,[26] is a different thing altogether, a solid, rather solemn pile in a distinctly conservative idiom, 43. The main house is an oblong block, two and half storeys on a basement, seven bays wide, with quoins, hipped roof and broad eaves. The façade is articulated horizontally only by the greater width of the central bay, with a large Venetian doorcase[27] on the ground floor and swags on either side of those above. Vertically there is only a string course under the somewhat too small first-floor windows. The house, which was designed about 1737 and finished by his son John as late as 1752, hardly shows William Adam's power. It seems indeed a return to

[25] James Adam has also been credited with the old Barony North Church, which stood just south of the cathedral, a design in what, to judge by old prints, must have been a most unconvincing, indeed grotesque, mixture of Gothick and Baronial, a style that Robert adopted for Mauldslie Castle. However, the church was probably designed by Adam's nephew, John Robertson, who acted for him in certain Glasgow jobs. It was replaced by Burnet's Gothic church late in the 1880s. Drawings (1793) are again at the Soane Museum.

[26] He also built a library for the Old College, c.1740, never completed and now of course demolished.

[27] The now rather obscured entrance front has a pediment.

43. Pollok House (William Adam, designed c.1737). The garden front. Pavilions by R. R. Anderson 1896-1905. Anderson's original idea was to raise the wings to the full height of the house.

the manner of Bruce – paradoxical in view of the swaggering disregard that Adam showed for Bruce's work at Hopetoun when he built the new and wonderfully rich and grand east front there. But like his older contemporary M'Gill (cf. Blair Drummond of 1715), Adam liked uncompromisingly square blocks innocent of dormers or other accretions and distinctly Italian in general proportion. In its setting, provided by the admirable wings and terrace of Sir Rowand Anderson (1892, etc.) and the elegant eighteenth-century bridge over the White Cart, Pollok House is certainly a pleasant retreat from Glasgow noise. [The park of course now houses the great Burrell collection in a striking new building designed by Barry Gasson.[28]]

[28] [See below pp.274f.]

28

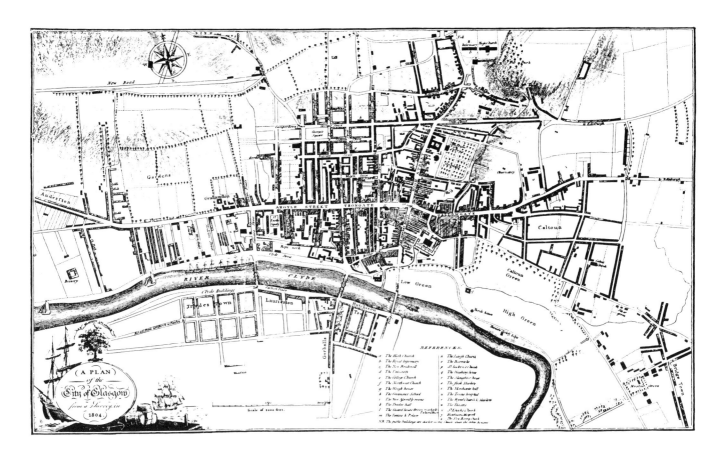

44. Glasgow in 1804 (From Denholm's 'History of Glasgow').

Chapter 3

1800-45: The First New Towns

In 1807 St George's Church was built on the west side of Buchanan Street, its steeple on the axis of George Street. Symbolically it is the central pivot of Glasgow. For it stands halfway along the street which has, despite its issuing in no bridge, become and remained the real north-south spine of the city, the street which divides the west end from the old town. It is also the street which marks the western expansion of Glasgow at the end of the eighteenth century, and this again despite the building of Jamaica Bridge farther west some thirty years earlier. St George's therefore stands not only at the physical heart of the city (and very properly makes traffic give way to it), but at the end of what may be called the natural – the relatively unco-ordinated – growth of the old town, and at the beginning of the series of planned and sophisticated developments which have given western and southern Glasgow the character that it still largely retains. Since it is itself a building of considerable interest, and since its architect, William Stark, almost immediately disappears from the Glasgow scene, St George's may be described here.

'The principal object' is, as noted in *Glasgow Delineated*,[1] the steeple, **45**. The body of the church is sober and restrained. The steeple, however, is an extremely vigorous design, clearly owing something to Wren (an unusual influence at this date), but showing the spirited invention seen fitfully in Stark's other buildings. The tower has three storeys, each with a semicircular-headed window, though the rectangular door has such a heavy cornice of its own that the semicircle above takes on an individual existence. (The treatment of the windows at the ends of the aisles is similar.) Above the tower proper come two small square stages and then an exceedingly neat cylindrical peristyle in the manner of St Mary-le-Bow, London, though the little dome and obelisk above this are like a tiny version of another Wren church – St Peter Cornhill. The most striking feature of the steeple is, however, the forceful vertical accent given by the clasping buttresses which run all the way up the tower and end in obelisks. This is an effect which recalls the spirit [1a] of the churches of Hawksmoor rather than of Wren, who only used buttresses of this kind on Gothic steeples and then never so emphatically. A curious contradiction in Stark's design is the cornice which runs rather too heavily across the façade at the eave level of the aisles and so weakens the upward thrust of the buttresses. But this may well be an alteration to the original design for which Stark was not responsible, for *Glasgow Delineated*[2] reports that he had intended the tower to project from the façade – in which case the cornice would not have had the weakening effect. The obelisks are also apparently a deviation: 'on the four upper Extremities, the Architect meant to place Statues of the four Evangelists, instead of which, slender and ill-proportioned Obelisks have been Substituted, which do not well accord with the beautiful little Peristyle which rises from the Centre'.[2] At least, however, the obelisks carry on the upward thrust of the buttresses and make some connexion with the design of the top, which the evangelists might not have shown. At all events, the east front of the church, if a little stiff, is an

45. St George's Church (William Stark, 1807). A photograph taken about 1870 before large buildings came to dwarf the church: cf. fig.224.

[1] 1826 (see *Glasghu Facies*, p.1085).
[1a] These octangular buttresses give even a hint of the Gothic: the effect of concavity on the topmost storey is decidedly Hawksmoorian. But the most likely source is the towers of churches that Stark will have seen during his visit to St. Petersburg in 1798.
[2] *Ibid*.

[3] His work outside Glasgow includes the Lower Signet Library in Edinburgh (where he died) and churches at Muirkirk and Saline. He is also to be remembered as W. H. Playfair's master and hence, perhaps, as the originator of neo-Greek in Scotland.
[4] Smirke's portico on the old Covent Garden Theatre was conceived earlier, and – owing to delays at Glasgow – built two years before Stark's; Smirke's building was burnt down in 1856. But John Sanders's Royal Military Academy at Sandhurst (Berks) was begun in the same year as the Justiciary Court and is on a very imposing scale. It still survives intact. Probably both designs come from a common French source.
[4a] Unfair and untrue. Craigie, whose brief was to work two courts into the place of the original one, made a surprisingly grand sequence through an Ionic colonnaded vestibule into a top-lit Ionic atrium flanked by twin-galleried courts whose bowed outer ends re-use the columns of Stark's courtroom. Probably at least the capitals in the vestibule and atrium also come from the early building which had already been partially remodelled by Clarke & Bell, incorporating in the atrium Buchan's plaster models for the sculpture at the south end of their City and County Buildings (see below, p.104). The original Justiciary Court was designed in limited competition with David Hamilton and Robert Reid (all the designs are now in the Strathclyde Regional Archives). The competition result was momentous in setting Scottish neo-classicism on its Ledoux-inspired way. Stark's colonnaded hemicycle closely followed Thomas Harrison's at Chester Castle (c.1795).
[5] Leighton, op. cit., p.97.
[6] Bentham championed this plan for prisons during Stark's lifetime; but Professor Pevsner tells me that it derives from the cross plan already found in Spanish hospitals of the early sixteenth century, and which itself derives from fifteenth-century Italian hospitals. Dr Helen Rosenau holds that the plan came rather via France.

original and arresting design, admirably placed in its street, though the dominance of the large office block immediately west of Queen Street Station is very unfortunate.

The interior of St George's is rather disappointing, very plain and showing nothing of the adventurousness of the outside. A gallery runs round three sides, supported on slender cast-iron columns with plain leaf capitals. The ceiling is flat with a large plaster rose in the middle, but the aisles have shallow transverse barrel vaults under the gallery. The best feature is the very pretty circular marble pulpit, standing on a pedestal and surrounded with a classical frieze containing a delicate shell motif over the panels. But it may not be original.

Stark died in 1813, and little is known of his life except that it was short. Nevertheless, he designed at least three other public buildings of considerable importance in Glasgow, though only a fragment of one remains.[3] This is the façade of the Justiciary Court, **46**, an ambitious neo-Greek design looking on to Glasgow Green. At the time of its design the Doric portico was probably the second largest in Britain.[4] The remainder of the front was recessed with very small projecting wings having giant coupled pilasters; but the present appearance is due to the almost complete rebuilding of 1910 by J. H. Craigie, who did, however, follow Stark's design roughly. The building is now, apart from the portico, of little interest.[4a]

Two other buildings of Stark's have completely gone. The Hunterian Museum (1804) went with the rest of the Old College, though it lingered on into this century. It too had a large Doric portico, this time with Tuscan columns, though contemporary descriptions refer to Stark ('distinguished for the purity of his taste') as choosing the 'Roman style'.[5] The sides, however, were evidently in the rather limp Palladian which Henry Holland had lately been popularizing. The small, centrally placed flat-topped dome looks as if it was insignificant in relation to the main block. Much more interesting and original, though perhaps less 'pure', was the lunatic asylum (1809), formerly in Bell's Park, **47**. This was possibly the earliest hospital in Britain to use the star plan which became popular later in the century.[6] It consisted of a large cylindrical drum, three and a half storeys high, from which projected four arms (originally of five bays, later lengthened to eight), the whole making a Celtic cross in plan. The arms were very plain, three-storeyed; the drum had giant pilasters and segmental headed windows; its attic storey rose above the flat roofs of the arms and thus could be seen all round. Above it rose a smaller octagonal drum, and above that was an octagonal, mainly glass, dome.[7] This was evidently considerably bigger than that on Soane's Consols Office of 1797 and antedates by about nine years the larger and more elaborate one on the Old Dividends Office. Stark was clearly an original architect of some talent: his early death was a misfortune for Glasgow, and the destruction of most of his important work lamentable.

By the end of the eighteenth century Glasgow was a large city; and thirty years later the population was three times as large again, just over 200,000. It was an architecturally fortunate time for a city to grow, and, like Edinburgh, Glasgow made the most of its opportunities. Craig's plan for Edinburgh's first new town was passed by the corporation in 1767, and building began quite soon afterwards. Glasgow was therefore a respectable distance behind in the formal planning of municipal growth, even if we take George Square into account. Moreover, in the direction of its most important expansion Glasgow had no loch to leap, and its new town was a less deliberate gesture than Edinburgh's. Nevertheless the work which had been done from the late eighteenth century onwards is of a consistently high standard, for which the city has not been given proper credit. When one remembers that

[7] Perhaps Stark was influenced by the dome of the Tontine coffee room. Sir John Summerson thinks that Adam's unexecuted design for Edinburgh University may also have played its part.

47. The Lunatic Asylum formerly in Bell's Park, but long demolished (William Stark, 1809). (Lithograph by D. M. Walker after a photograph taken about 1900)

48. (left) Carlton Place: the centrepiece (Laurieston House) after recent redecoration.
49. (right) Carlton Place (Peter Nicholson, 1802-4). From a photograph taken in about 1890. Note the sympathetic scale of the lamps.

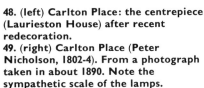

8 Each terrace has lost one of its end pavilions, so that, seen full face, it now looks lop-sided. Both are otherwise in excellent condition, having recently been face-lifted by the Civic Trust. The present salmon colour seems to me rather unwise.

the whole development was carried out in a completely opportunist fashion, with no coercion whatever and no overall plan, the coherence and dignity achieved are remarkable. Well-closed vistas were contrived, with added visual importance thus given to the principal public buildings. At the same time Glasgow invented a type of square for itself, normally on a smallish scale with a large building in the centre. St Andrew's was the first, followed by St Enoch's, Royal Exchange Place, St George's Place and the squares round the City and County Buildings (which was only achieved over thirty years) and the National Bank (which has now, regrettably, vanished).

Not that the growth was always as orderly. The pressure of a still very rapidly increasing population led to a huge expansion in all directions, including the south, where, crossing the Clyde, the city formally annexed the ancient suburb of Gorbals. As so often in British cities, the east end was left to get on as best it could: it was by this time very slummy, and there seem to have been almost no attempts at civic design east of the Cross. John Weir planned a handsome entry to London Street, which was opened with great pomp and destroyed only forty years later by the railway bridge, though fragments are still visible; the chief example that remains is part of Monteith Row, two terraces of plain three-storey houses, looking south on to Glasgow Green, that were built by Thomas Binnie in 1823 and 1830 – an agreeable, but very modest, achievement in comparison with what went on elsewhere.

The land south of the Clyde is, to begin with, quite flat, and consequently does not offer opportunities for dramatic urban scenery. But the boldness of the new work gives it an unexpected grandeur. Glasgow's first enterprise fronts the river itself – Carlton Place, a pair of identical palace-fronted terraces begun in 1802 by Peter Nicholson, 49.[8] The terraces are very long, forty bays each, arranged 5+12+6+12+5. The centrepiece has thus an even number of bays, and since it is pilastered, a central pilaster must come

50. Laurieston House: interior of the rotonda.

under the middle of the pediment, a rather uneasy arrangement (found elsewhere in the city), which comes from insisting on three-bay houses and incorporating two of these into the central unit: the architect has wisely kept his pilasters very quiet, **48**.[9] The rest of the terraces are quite severe, the pavilions projecting only very slightly: these have Ionic porches, with coupled columns, and there is a double porch for the centrepiece, again drawing attention to its duality. Because of their great length the terraces of Carlton Place can hardly be appreciated as a unit except from the north bank of the river or from the Suspension Bridge, from which they look very well – quiet and extremely dignified.[10]

The gap between the two terraces is the entrance to South Portland Street, which was evidently seen as the backbone of a civic development on a large scale (a work initiated by John Laurie, but never completed). South Portland Street is exactly on a line with Buchanan Street, a fact which, owing to the absence of a bridge at this point, is easier to appreciate on a map than on the site; but this can hardly be a coincidence. The continuation of South Portland Street is Abbotsford Place, which was originally Glasgow's Harley Street, **52**.† The doctors' sizable houses are still there, in long four-storey terraces with big Ionic and Corinthian porches but otherwise no articulation except an occasional very slight recession or projection.[11] No attempt is made to unify the design as in Carlton Place; the street, which must of course be seen in perspective, depends for its impressiveness on the admirable scale and the proportion of the height of the houses to the width of the roadway. Though somewhat monotonous, it is much the best reminder of the architectural dignity which this part of the city has largely lost. Like the other streets around it, Abbotsford Place was begun soon after Carlton Place was finished (in 1818), and itself finished in about 1830. Cumberland Street must come at the end of the period: it is smaller in scale (only three storeys) and shows the characteristic window detail of slightly later work north of the river. The now largely demolished Nicholson Street (c.1820) had a quality of its own, with scrolly pediments over the windows, which give an almost dainty effect to the fairly ponderous blocks of building.

The planned development working westwards up Blythswood Hill, though at first on a smaller scale than that south of the river, was more consistently carried through and has been much more influential on the later growth of the city. Blythswood Hill is quite steep, especially to the south where decidedly San Franciscan effects are found – a fact that has been very important in the townscape of this part of Glasgow,[12] for the hill gives a real shape to the rigidly geometrical layout, which would otherwise be monotonous and without direction. This distinction is now rather smudged in such streets as West George Street, where so many of the original houses have been replaced, usually by taller buildings, that the descent of the street cannot be read in the descending cornices of the houses. Bath Street has kept more than any other, though it was not built up until comparatively late in the whole scheme; and its slopes are gentle, so that dramatic effects are not to be looked for.

Leighton tells us that it was in 1800 that 'Mr Dugald Bannatyne, Dr Cleland and Mr William Jack purchased a portion of these lands and opened up Bath Street, which was the commencement of the splendid new town of Blythswood'.[13] What he does not tell us is that the history of the original

[9] Camden Crescent, Bath and Bedford Square, London have a similar arrangement of four bays and five attached columns. The centrepiece of Lansdown Crescent, also in Bath, has likewise four bays, but the architect, John Palmer, has left out the awkward central pilaster and linked his middle pairs of windows.

[10] Laurieston House (51–52 Carlton Place, built for Laurie himself) has a very fine interior, with rich and delicate plaster work, said to be Italian (though excellent local craftsmen were available). The most attractive feature is a rotonda with Corinthian columns and a good coffered ceiling, **50**. There is a general resemblance between Carlton Place and the smaller terraces on the north side of George Square, where, however, the centre is surprisingly played down. [Laurieston House has a porch segmental in plan and with fluted Doric columns: if these are original they antedate Stark's on the Justiciary House by several years and are among the earliest in the country.]

[11] It is possible that the bulky proportions of the Corinthian columns indicate David Hamilton's hand.

[12] See chapter 11, pp.231ff.

[13] Leighton, *op. cit.*, p.54.

development of this opulent area is one of bankruptcies, sequestrations, trusts, reversions and sudden flight. Nothing much seems to have been built by Bannatyne (who was, however, active in George Square), before William Harley opened the baths in 1804. Shortly afterwards Harley opened pleasure gardens near to a recently built mansion immediately west of the site of Blythswood Square. But by 1814 he was in difficulties, and in 1816 his affairs were put in the hands of trustees, who were themselves soon bankrupt. Some of Harley's feus were taken over by the Garden family who played a large part in the feuing of Blythswood. They first appear in 1816, when Alexander Garden started feuing in St Vincent Street (which had been begun in 1805). In 1820 Hamilton William Garden took over the family speculations here and extended them to cover a large part of the hill. His affairs were put in trust in 1826, but his trustees continued his schemes until well into the 1830s, when Garden himself fled to America. In 1827 Thomas Burns, who was building in West Regent Street, likewise failed. The development was, to start with, almost exclusively domestic; but by the 1840s the central part was already going commercial. Redevelopment started as early as the 1850s at the eastern end and has gone on steadily ever since.

It is unlikely that any of the buildings remaining on Blythswood Hill is earlier than about 1815; and development was so unco-ordinated that it is impossible to establish a chronological sequence of building. And unfortunately hardly any of the architects of this formidable quantity of work are known for certain, though some may confidently be guessed. But it can definitely be claimed that by the 1820s a distinctive Glasgow style had established itself. The handful of mid eighteenth-century houses left in the old part of the city are nearly all of a type of which Aberdeen has some better examples; the various Adam buildings might equally well be in Edinburgh. But Blythswood Hill is pure Glasgow. Except on the steeper slopes, the basic unit is a fairly short terrace, two or three storeys high, generally with centrepiece and end pavilions given considerable emphasis (sometimes by an extra storey, sometimes by projections beyond the main façade, sometimes by heavier cornices). Pediments are rarely used, though pilasters appear at times where houses were individually designed. There is a fair number of porches of various orders regularly punctuating the smoothish façades;[14] cornices are generally heavy and emphatic, those on the windows and window surrounds especially so – a characteristic local feature (perhaps with an inspiration from Rome). The facing is of course all ashlar, which the late eighteenth-century had made essential for any self-respecting Scottish city; mostly it is now a darkish silver-grey, but recent cleaning has revealed a lovely soft biscuity colour underneath. The contrast of the two is very attractive (though it is not improved by a number of very misdirected efforts at *painting* the stone, and it is a great pity that the cleaning has so far been so patchy[15]). Though the general character of these buildings is one of solid and upstanding dignity, the proportions have generally a quite expert precision, and the detailing – of porches, cornice, corbels, rustication – is frequently beautiful.

All the streets on Blythswood Hill have good buildings remaining from this period. Until recently St Vincent Street probably had most to offer: the most important remaining house is the hall of the Royal Faculty of Physicians and Surgeons, a one-time terrace mansion with some spectacular interiors mainly by J. J. Burnet. A beautiful little house on the north-west

[14] Three astonishingly clumsy ones in West Regent Street are presumably much later, probably of the 1860s.
[15] The north side of Blythswood Square was for some time of two colours asymmetrically divided – a most disturbing effect.

corner of Wellington Street has recently been demolished: it was of five bays, the three in the middle projecting slightly and emphasized by giant Ionic pilasters on the upper storeys over a rusticated ground floor: the porch, unusually, was pedimented and stood on coupled Corinthian columns. Its loss to the city is serious, and its successor appears to be designed with no feeling for the needs of the site. The range on the north side of St Vincent Street between Wellington Street and Hope Street may possibly contain the remnants of a complex terrace by David Hamilton. It would be surprising if the most powerful and (as we shall see) most influential Glasgow architect of his generation did nothing on this important site, and some of the details, particularly the console-type brackets supporting the window cornices, recall other work certainly his. West George Street has a fine row on the south side immediately east of Blythswood Square – not really designed as a unit, but linked by an ingenious parapet that steps downhill with the steep slope of the street.

Luckily Blythswood Square remains substantially unaltered (though Mackintosh put in a pert and charming little doorway at No.5). It was built in 1823 by H. W. Garden, who first called it Garden Square in honour of himself. The architect has now been identified as John Brash, **51**, whose hand is also seen in two plain but seemly churches – Tolcross (1806) and Macmillan

15a

**51. 196 West George Street (c.1830, probably by John Brash); a house of exquisite refinement, with some playful details; perhaps the finest individual house remaining on Blythswood Hill.
52. (overleaf) Abbotsford Place looking south (c.1820 and later).**

15a It now seems likely that Brash was working to an outline design drawn up by Gillespie Graham who produced a plan for the extension of Blythswood in 1820 and may have been consulted even earlier. By that date the layout of the square had already been settled.

Calton (1819). As a square Blythswood suffers from having two streets coming in at each corner, particularly unfortunate since the land falls away on all sides and a sense of enclosure is thereby largely lost; but it is unquestionably a most impressive piece of architectural design. The grand east side, **53**, now entirely occupied by the Royal Scottish Automobile Club, has kept its astragals (a rare thing in Glasgow[16]), though two of the doorways have presumably gone. One of its subtlest and most satisfying features, which is indeed used throughout the square, is the grouping of the windows in the central portion of the façade, each set of three per storey (i.e., each original house) being marked off from its neighbours by the slightly but perceptibly greater width of the masonry between adjacent windows – something that does much to give the building its very restful appearance.[17] The ranges on the four sides – which are very nearly identical – have the rather unexpected combination of pavilions and a principal section between, whose centre is in no way marked out.[18] The result is perhaps to link the sides of the square more effectively, since the only emphasis given to the individual ranges is at the ends, which are of course close to the identical end pavilions of their neighbours. Some of the recent refacing in Blythswood Square has unfortunately been lamentably ill done.

Bath Street is for the most part quite a lot later than the streets to the south. It is flatter and therefore offers fewer opportunities for scenic gestures. But as its range of early and mid nineteenth-century buildings is (at any rate west of Hope Street) very nearly complete, it gives the best impression of the original appearance of the area. The two best terraces are probably both the work of the elder John Baird and were built towards the middle of the century. One of these, the north side of Athol Place between Douglas and Blythswood Streets, follows closely the pattern of earlier terraces[19] – a straightforward sequence of three-bay houses with a larger one in the middle, the grouping of bays being 3+6+5+6+3. The pavilions and centrepiece project very slightly and have a raised and rather heavier cornice but no pediments: they also have the only porches in the terrace. The principal floor windows are rather tall, giving an air of slightly haughty elegance; the ground floor has banded rustication (with an appropriate appearance of strength) and has segmental-headed widows. These are also used on the terrace immediately west of this (Adelaide Place), **54**, which is in other respects more ambitious, though possibly slightly less successful.[20] It is one bay longer, the centrepiece having six bays projecting in two stages, 1+4+1. The middle four have one of Glasgow's rare central pediments; here and on the pavilions there is a giant order of Corinthian pilasters, and the cornice is unusually emphatic with dentel moulding beneath.[21] The even number of bays in the centrepiece means a pilaster under the middle of the pediment, as in Carlton Place. The weakness of the terrace is that its insistent symmetry demands a flat site (or at least a continuous basement plinth), and it has not got one. The land falls sufficiently for a break in all floor and cornice levels to be necessary between the centrepiece and the western half. The balance of an admirable design is therefore disrupted. The west end of Bath Street, beyond the terraces, is later still – probably about 1865; it contains several churches, including the excellent Elgin Place Congregational with a great hexastyle portico by John Burnet, Senior. Looking west the street makes a slight but definite and effective curve to the south before coming to a stop in front of W. B. Whitie's pompous 'Renaissance' Mitchell Library.[22]

[16] The rival motoring organization on the south side of the square has made a very nasty mess of the glazing of *its* windows.
[17] The same device was used centuries earlier by Vasari on the Uffizi in Florence, no more subtly than here, and to no very obvious internal purpose.
[18] Except on the east side by the unconvincing modern device of a two-bay porch centred on the division between the two middle houses. The porch is the work of James Miller. [The emphasis on the ends as against the middle had already appeared on terraces in Bristol begun as early as 1784 and 1790: the feature indicates a leaning towards neo-classicism. See p.154, n.3.]
[19] The terrace immediately opposite is similar, though the proportions are not quite so well worked out. Both were originally ventures of H. W. Garden, begun by his trustees in 1833.
[20] Like Athol Place, Adelaide Place was to have had a corresponding terrace opposite; but this was only partly built, and T. L. Watson's Adelaide Place Baptist Church eventually came to occupy the west part of the south site. [Adelaide Place is now known to be the work of Robert Black. The authorship of Athol Place is still unproven, but Baird's seems the best claim.]
[21] This has recently been fractured by the introduction of two ugly attic windows: every effort ought to be made to have these removed and the cornice repaired; for the effect on this fine building is serious.
[22] This effect will soon have to be spoken of in the past tense, for the Ring Road will cut away the end of Bath Street. [This prophecy has now alas been fulfilled.]

Blythswood when first built was a 'town' of rich individual houses (they are now nearly all offices). The layout continues without a break across the valley of Sauchiehall Street on to Garnethill. The map suggests complete continuity; yet in Garnethill one is in a different world. The hill is steeper (two streets are forced to end as stairs); the streets are narrower, the buildings taller, and moreover they contain flats, so that emphasis on individual doorways and the relative proportioning of different storeys were inappropriate. The streets have certainly a less princely air than their neighbours to the south. But they are lived in; and this fact – it cannot be missed by anyone walking over the hill – makes the contrast with the spacious and comfortable spread of Blythswood specially poignant. In between, Sauchiehall Street is an incident, a division rather than a link, not belonging to either. Curiously, this best-known of all Glasgow streets was not fully built up till the end of the century – and then in a very muddled way so that its numerous good buildings compete with, rather than support, one another.

The most considerable Glasgow architect of the early nineteenth century was David Hamilton (1768–1843), though he seems not to have taken any large part in the building of the new town. Like many of his time, he began as a classicist but tried his hand at other fashionable varieties: thus he built

53. Blythswood Square, east side (John Brash, c.1823). The central porch is a late addition by James Miller.

several Gothic churches (the tower and the nave of Bothwell show him at his best) and some Gothic houses. But, unlike most of his contemporaries, he took his personal idiom beyond the battle of the styles, and far enough to be an influence in his native town till the end of the century. Luckily, though Hamilton Palace, his largest completed work, has entirely disappeared, three of his most important buildings remain in the city.[23] The earliest of these is Hutcheson's Hospital, built in 1805 to replace the buildings destroyed to make room for a new street, **55**. Here, while most of the motifs have classical or Renaissance precedents, the composition is closer to the style – in so far as it exists as such – which has come to be called Mannerist. For wilful though Hamilton's details frequently are, they are more than simply *mannered*. Professor Wittkower has referred to the Mannerist architects' insistence on exposing the ambiguities inherent in some Renaissance buildings.[24] Hamilton, inheriting the post-Renaissance classical tradition, did something similar. Thus the principal articulating device of the façade of Hutcheson's is a giant Corinthian order; the façade is of five bays and almost as high as it is wide. The middle three bays are recessed, thus reducing any impression of central dominance; but the recession allows for attached columns in the centre, where the outer bays have pilasters that are only weakly emphasized. The stronger and weaker elements, then, appear together at each point. Moreover the outermost pilasters are not quite at the corners of the building – a small stretch of plain stone is left and the 'supporting' effect of the pilasters (which would normally make the visual claim of supporting the cornice and roof) is contradicted by what a purely classical architect would have treated simply as a screen *behind* columns.[25] The outer bays have niches (with statues of the founders removed from the previous hospital), the inner, recessed ones, tall windows which, instead of cornices have hood-moulds, decidedly unclassical but also decidedly un-Elizabethan in their design. Above the main entablature there is a balustraded superstructure which bulges forward over the outer bays in curious flattened ovals decorated with a tiny blank arcade. The side elevation is of course simpler, of two – very wide – bays only, articulated by coupled pilasters. The main windows are large and tripartite, with flattish triangular pediments supported on long, rather droopy consoles. Out of the centre of the building rises a tower, square in plan to begin with, then octagonal, the transference most neatly managed by coupled (Tuscan!) columns in the diagonals, each pair with its own entablature. Above this the octagon gives way to a circle with a small Ionic peristyle, topped not by a dome but by a fluted circular spire. It is as if, having shown his mastery of the difficult problem (not always solved by medieval architects) of the change from a square tower to an octagonal spire, Hamilton can afford to let that speak for itself while he explores another problem, only to remind us with his spire that that was what it was about all along.[26]

24a

Another spire of Hamilton's was unfortunately struck by lightning, and its stump has been cauterized with a miserable domelet: it used to belong to the aristocratic-looking Gorbals Parish Church (1806–10)† at the east end of Carlton Place. It was originally 174 feet high and evidently much more happily proportioned than it is now: again Hamilton made use of coupled columns in the diagonals for converting a square plan into an octagon, but the spire this time kept itself to the traditional octagon. The design, which offered one of the most interesting solutions devised of the problem of the

54. (left) Adelaide Place, Bath Street (by Robert Black, begun 1839). Note the curious disruption of the design by the slope of the site, and the ruthless spoliation of the cornice to the left of the centrepiece.
55. (above) Hutcheson's Hospital, Ingram Street (David Hamilton, 1802–05).

[23] Others of less note include the original block of Hutcheson's Boys School and the Dundas Vale School (formerly the Normal School, 1837). Hamilton submitted competition designs for the Houses of Parliament in 1835, for which he received a prize of £500.
[24] *Art and Architecture in Italy, 1600–1750* (Harmondsworth, 1959), p.161.
[24a] The columns are in fact free-standing.
[25] This particular device was, however, fairly common practice in the late eighteenth century; only in Hamilton's façade it gains a special emphasis from its conjunction with other mannerisms.
[26] The upper stages of the steeple have a curious resemblance to Nash's All Souls', Langham Place, London, which Hamilton's building antedates by seventeen years. Could Nash have seen Hamilton's fluted spike? (William Adam had long before proposed a fluted spire for Dundee Town House, but this was rejected on account of cost.)

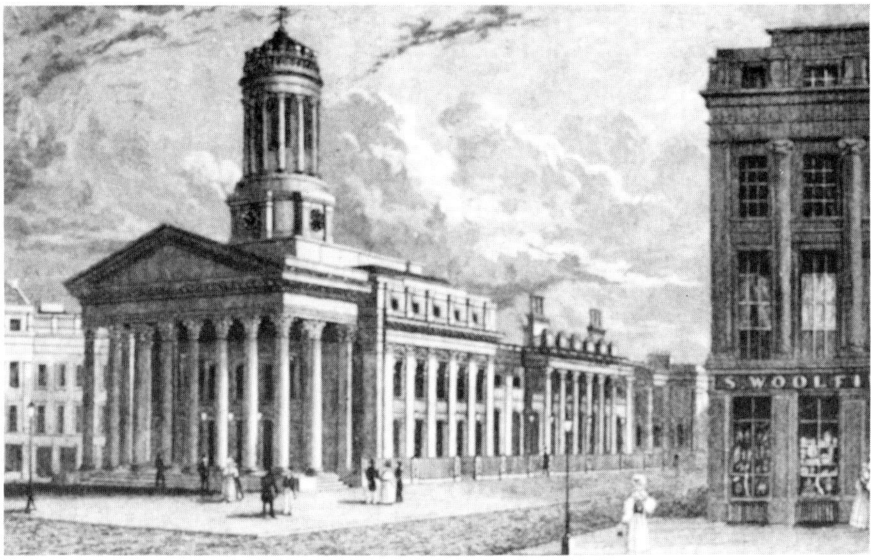

56. The Royal Exchange (now Stirling's Library). The Cunninghame Mansion of 1778 stands behind David Hamilton's portico (1827) and to the left of his colonnaded extension. (From Swan's 'Views') Later a platformed mansard roof was added to the front section, and David Thomson put a low attic on the rear.

relation of façade and steeple, was, however, never finished and the façade bears no relation to the church behind it. 26a

The Royal Exchange of 1827–9 has fared better, **56**. Like Hutcheson's Hospital it is designed to be seen first of all at the end of a long vista, closing the western end of Ingram Street. In this it is extremely effective: but on closer inspection the building appears more unsettling, a strange mixture of almost academic classicism and elements picked up from other contemporary architects with some that are surely Hamilton's alone. The huge Corinthian portico at the east end (octostyle and two bays deep) is a text-book essay in the correct neo-classic: the idea perhaps comes from the similarly planned portico of St Martin's-in-the-Fields. Behind it is the Cunninghame Mansion,[27] obviously much altered and with so many new details as to show that Hamilton must have quite encased the old house. A giant order of pilasters has a smaller order threaded through it on the ground floor, in the manner of Michelangelo's Conservatori Palace in Rome (though the inspiration may have come from Schinkel); the windows show Hamilton's characteristic scrolly brackets below the cornices. Above is a quite unexpected cupola, original enough, especially in its treatment of the top, but hardly making a very satisfactory union with the portico. Its drum is flattened on four 'sides' to suggest Hamilton's version of the drum of the Trades House; the very tall Corinthian peristyle above goes back to the plan of the true circle; above its cornice is a curious open crown with a flattish ogee dome. The mansion, of only five bays, was obviously too small, not only for the new purpose of the Exchange, but also as the body behind the great portico; and the western extension is as long as portico and mansion combined. Yet Hamilton chose not to continue the line of the portico's cornice (which is also that of the superstructure of the adapted mansion). On the contrary, he recessed his whole wall enough to allow a free-standing colonnade in front of the western half to be in line with the pilastered outer wall of the east end. But his colonnade is not a true continuation of the row of pilasters, though the two entablatures are in line. For not only is there a gap of two bays in between, but the colonnade has no superstructure, no attic storey, but instead a row of free-standing akroteria over the entablature. The model for the

[26a] Gorbals Church was demolished in 1974–5. Its original form is shown in Swan's *Views*.
[27] See p.231.

57. (left) 151-7 Queen Street (David Hamilton, c.1834). The decorated frieze is more ornate than is usual in Hamilton's work; but other details are highly characteristic.
58. (right) The Royal Bank of Scotland (Archibald Elliot, junior 1827): a building which well illustrates the seriousness of the neo-Greek in Scotland.

[28] Squares with a large building in the middle are a common Glasgow feature: cf. St Andrew's Square, St George's Place, the old St Enoch's Square. At times the central building is so large that the whole of the space is taken up, and one then merely sees it as a block, bounded by four streets: the City and County Buildings is the most obvious example.
[The development of the square was characteristic and interesting. The Royal Bank, which owned the Cunningham Mansion, built the new bank behind it, sold the mansion to the Exchange committee and feued the ground flanking it. It is clear that Elliot planned the layout, and he may well have provided elevations; but Robert Black was also involved, and the final responsibility for the executed façades is uncertain.]

whole device of this colonnade was almost certainly the Bartholomew Lane façade of Soane's Bank of England, which had been finished two or three years earlier. In Hamilton's building its want of true relation to the other parts of the building is only too clear: the north and south façades simply split in two; and the eastern half, lacking a proper continuation to the west, remains stumpy and ill-proportioned. (Moreover, the windows in the western part are different in scale, with much higher, semi-circular-headed ones on the ground floor denying the sill and lintel levels of the older ones.) Perhaps Hamilton was after all given an impossible task when he was obliged to incorporate the old house into a new design for a new purpose, while at the same time proportioning his portico to the vista along Ingram Street. At all events the resulting building seems deliberately to expose contradictions which a more tactful, if less independently-minded, architect might have done his best to conceal. The hall within is superbly self-confident in its bigness of scale and detail. It is divided into nave and aisles separated by massive Corinthian columns supporting an immense entablature. The aisle ceilings are flat, but the nave's is segmental in section; all are richly coffered in squares and circles.

The exchange (now Stirling's Library) stands in – indeed almost fills[28] – the small square between Queen Street and Buchanan Street called Royal Exchange Place; the whole group is the best piece of unified civic design in Glasgow. In detail most of it is Hamilton's work, but at the west end stands the Royal Bank of Scotland (1827) by Archibald Elliot the second, son of his better-known namesake, and to him the general design of the square is due. The bank is a very serious, even solemn, composition whose main feature is a big Ionic portico, flanked by a pair of splendid archways, with a massive entablature supported on coupled Ionic columns, which lead into the two arms of Royal Bank Place, small but formal pedestrian links with Buchanan Street, 58. The north and south sides of this square are two nearly identical ranges of houses and shops (one or two original shop-fronts remaining), with returns along Queen Street. These ranges are three-storeyed, with emphasis given to the pavilions at each end by a giant order of attached columns and an extra half-storey above the main cornice: here again is a small order threading through the main one on the first floor – evidence of the influence, at least, of Hamilton. The general spirit is still very Georgian, but there is some restless detail, particularly in the cornice and balustrade above, including (high up on capitals at the south-west corner of the square) perhaps the first appearance in Glasgow of the incised Egyptianesque detail that was later to become so fashionable in Thomson's time.[29] It is a moving experience to walk out of the noise and bustle of Buchanan Street, along one of the passages, through the arch and into the quiet of this stately, rather withdrawn square.

Perhaps the most remarkable of all Hamilton's designs is the Western Club in Buchanan Street (1841), **59**, in which he fairly throws a mass of almost violently conflicting motifs together, yet in the event produces a more interesting and much more unified design than that of the Royal Exchange. The main façade is basically of seven bays, the three middle (and larger) ones being very slightly recessed. But the outer pairs of bays are, on the two principal floors, linked into triplicated windows: only on the second floor do the separate bays assert themselves, so that a vertical tension is set up between the storeys. The ground floor is heavily accented with a massive porch on square Corinthian columns: the mullions of the triple windows rise into the corbels of lavish stone balconies, whose parapets are pierced

59. The Western Club, Buchanan Street (David Hamilton, 1841).

[29] A design which may be associated with these buildings is that of Nos. 151–157 Queen Street, built r. 1834 for Archibald McLellan, **57**. Here a giant order of pilasters links the two main storeys, with again a secondary pilastrade threaded through. Above an elaborately carved entablature is an attic whose centre has round-headed windows divided by deeply chanelled pilasters. The whole is very strongly Hamiltonian and is very likely his work. Compare the similar pilastrade on Henry Briant's nearly contemporary Royal Berkshire Hospital at Reading.

with elaborate scrollwork patterns. The intermediate bays at ground level have semi-circular headed windows, the whole linked by banded rustication. Glazing was originally as in the Queen Street block. On the first floor the mullions have the same capitals that we see on the porch: they are in fact substantial square columns. The three middle bays are now identical, square-headed windows under deep cornices that rest on fanciful scrolly brackets, the windows themselves having the tiny, but tellingly unclassical, feature of rounded corners. The second storey windows are all the same, in a rhythm of $2 + 1 + 1 + 1 + 2$, and here the detail is more distinctively Mannerist than ever; for each cornice is lifted over a blank recessed panel, and rests on bold jugged architraves which embrace the panel above and curve out at the bottom of the jambs: the effect is definitely to weaken our sense that the jambs support the cornice. Finally the attic storey has a restless rhythm of elaborate attenuated scroll corbels or consoles, single or in pairs, interspersed among small square windows and more recessed panels: the management of the angles here, though hardly delicate, is superbly sure, with coupled corbels marking the projections of the outer bays. The whole attic storey acts as an intricate entablature for the mighty cornice above, which thus becomes the chief unifying feature of the whole building. The Western Club to some extent foreshadows the less original and more Italianate experiments of

29a Could Hamilton have seen the windows set between paired brackets in the attic of Beningborough Hall, Yorkshire? The ultimate source is possibly the Palazzo Doria, illustrated as the first of the palazzi moderni in Rubens' *Palazzi di Genova*.

60. The Custom House, Clyde Street (John Taylor, 1840). The flanking bays are Edwardian.

29a

[30] Rochead was Hamilton's chief draughtsman at this time, and some details on the Western Club are his. A western extension was built by Honeyman in 1871 and has now been demolished. The Club itself has moved to Royal Exchange Square, and Hamilton's building now has an entirely new inside.

[30a] Repainting of the Western Club has drawn dramatic attention to the voids of the windows, the small ones in the attic now coming out especially strong and adding a further mannerist ambiguity: has the building three storeys or four? The interior of the Club has been gutted and the Honeyman extension removed.

[30b] After all it *is* the work of the Irish-born John Taylor, who was surveyor to H.M. Customs and designed the larger Custom House at Dundee in 1840. See Colvin, *Dictionary*, p.814.

[31] The same expertly tooled stonework can be seen on other classical public buildings of the time in various parts of the country, sometimes of commonplace or mechanical design: see for example the town hall of Stoke-on-Trent, begun by Henry Ward in 1834.

later architects like Rochead[30] and Sellars, who were hardly able to control their façades as Hamilton does here; and from it come most of the features that dominated Glasgow architecture for nearly half a century, including a window design which became the defining mark of the later Glasgow style. But the Western Club has much more than a seminal importance. In its different way it is at least as original as any of Barry's post-classical work – a more distinguished and original design, for example, than the Reform Club. It is Hamilton's final *chef-d'oeuvre*, an outstanding masterpiece of the early Victorian period in which the break with Georgianism is complete.

Just how far he had travelled may be judged by comparison with an almost exactly contemporary building not far away. This is the Custom House in Clyde Street, **60**, near the corner of Jamaica Bridge, which has been variously attributed to a certain John Taylor, who seems, however, not to have been a practising architect, to Dobson, of Newcastle, and most convincingly to George Ledwell Taylor. The restrained excellence of the design makes Dobson an attractive suggestion, but unfortunately the idea seems to be based on a confusion. Dobson apparently did an earlier Custom House in St Enoch Square, but this was quickly superseded, though it may possibly have influenced Taylor. The present building, which dates from as late as 1840, has a five-bay projecting centre which is recessed again on the upper storey to allow for a row of detached Greek Doric columns. Yet despite these incidents, the façade has none of the restless energy of Hamilton's work, and the details are all correctly classical, though instead of a pediment it has a free-standing coat of arms. The masonry is of the highest quality, and the detailing exceptionally refined,[31] a very fitting close to a stylistic phase which Glasgow in its rapid movement westwards was equally rapidly leaving behind.

Chapter 4 **The Move to the West**

Blythswood 'New Town' can hardly have been complete before further moves to the west were in hand, partly no doubt as a result of increasing commercial pressure in the centre. It is impossible to give a coherent chronological account of this work, since so many different schemes were in progress at the same time; nor was each carried out methodically: sometimes terraces stood isolated for ten years or so before others came to join them. As a generalization, however, it is safe to say that from the 1840s onwards the architecture becomes more eclectic, the planning of the streets more relaxed and more varied (though not always more satisfying). Along two streets –

and those perhaps the most important – the planning was of the simplest kind, consisting of no more than a succession of individually designed, though usually similar, terraces facing one another across gardens and a wide roadway. We are dealing throughout with residential development, which has remained almost uninterrupted in Glasgow's west end, though offices are steadily moving outwards.

For some time before 1850, terraces had been appearing along a western extension of Sauchyhall Road, 'which for its sylvan charms has long been the favourite promenade of the beauty and fashion of the city'. This stretch of Sauchiehall Street running west from Charing Cross with a series of pleasing terraces on either side for two thirds of a mile is still one of Glasgow's most attractive displays of urban domestic architecture: though hardly sylvan any longer, it still has plenty of trees, and the houses, though plain and sober for the most part, are also seemly. The earliest is Newton Place, by George Smith (begun in 1840), immensely long (87 bays in all) and very severe, in the main of two storeys, with three for the centre and pavilions. Newton Terrace (mid 1860s) and Sandyford Place, spec-built by Brown and Carrick, are later and clumsier. Somerset Place, now with a dull neo-Georgian block at its east end, is more of Baird's work (1840); Fitzroy Place (1847), never completed, is prentice work of John Burnet senior, still en-

62. Kirklee Terrace, Great Western Road (Charles Wilson, begun 1845). A grand Italianate palace design not perfectly adapted to the inevitable perspective view.

tirely in the earlier Glasgow domestic tradition. By far the strangest of these terraces is the farthest out, Royal Crescent (1839–49) by a certain Alexander Taylor about whom almost nothing is known, **61**. This is the only one of the Sauchiehall Street terraces in which classical precedent or inspiration has been almost completely abandoned. It is a shallow, three-storey crescent, with a slightly higher projecting centrepiece. The houses are designed in pairs, sometimes with big Ionic porches and flat windows, sometimes with plain doorcases and large bow windows. Where there are porches there are six bays on the lower floors but three on top, one (double) window per bay, the middle one divided between two houses. Where there are bow windows, there are only four bays on the lower floors, the outer ones wider than the inner, and again three on top. The rhythms are thus involved and indeed contradictory. All the top windows have small pediments; those shared between two houses have a slightly larger one flanked by little turrets. Most of the details seem individually to be derived from Hamilton (tripartite windows, pilaster strips, scrolly brackets and so forth), but the composition is something of a sport, without precedent in Glasgow and – probably fortunately – without followers either.[1]

Much farther out, well over two miles from the centre of the city, a completely separate group of terraces was begun along Great Western Road,

63. Part of the façade of Grosvenor Terrace (J. T. Rochead, 1855).

[1] Alexander Taylor also designed Clarendon Place† at the corner of Great Western and Maryhill Roads: it was originally to be a double feature in the manner of Edinburgh's Waterloo Place. [Only a fragment now remains.]

64. Woodside Terrace looking east to Woodside Crescent (George Smith, 1831-42).

65. (below) Lynedoch Crescent (George Smith, 1845).

66. (left) John Street Church
(J. T. Rochead, 1859).
67. (right) Claremont Terrace (John
Baird No.1). The projecting centrepiece was built as a mansion in 1842,
the remainder in 1847.

1a Mr. Frank Worsdall has now found
evidence that the design was by James Brown.
1b Now finely restored in synthetic materials,
following vigorous campaigning after its
partial destruction by fire in 1978.

the splendid new boulevard driving north-westwards straight out of the city
with no ghost of a bend for four miles, en route to Loch Lomond and the
Western Highlands. Great Western Road, which was laid down in the 1830s,
begins as a busy city street, bounded mainly by late Victorian tenements,
good-looking but of no outstanding interest. After Kelvin Bridge the road
goes on, but the buildings are more varied until we reach the Botanic Gardens, where the spacious, opulent atmosphere of western Glasgow is at its
most apparent. Here is a great succession of terraces, more lavish and more
independent than those in Sauchiehall Street. For some reason the earliest
to be built were well out to the west: Kew and Kirklee (formerly High
Windsor) Terraces, facing one another beyond the Botanic Gardens. Kew
Terrace (by J. T. Rochead, 1849) is an imitation of the Sauchiehall Street
ones though with much freer detail; Kirklee (begun 1845), **62**, is more ambitious – indeed somewhat pretentious – an early work of Charles Wilson,
the most important Glasgow architect of the generation following Hamilton's. Standing high above the road, though now rather obscured by trees,
the terrace has a self-assertive air, with heavy balconies and cornices and
very deep rustication on the ground floor: it also makes a feature of its roof –
something new in this type of terrace – and this and some of the details
suggest a direct influence from the palaces of the Roman Renaissance.

After this the terrace-building moved inwards with two interesting and
very different designs from J. T. Rochead in the 1850s. Buckingham is
really two terraces, of three and four storeys. They make use of the canted
bay windows which Baird had introduced slightly earlier: two of these
mark the centre of one terrace, and a row runs all along the front of the other.
Grosvenor Terrace (1855) is more appealing, in a style all its own in Glasgow, **63**. It is indeed something of a *tour de force*. It faces north-east, and to
make sure of as much light as possible, Rochead designed a continuous
three-storey range with an enormous number of identical semicircular-
headed windows on each floor and very little masonry showing, apart from
the columns which divide each pair of adjacent windows and the horizontal
bands between the storeys. The building looks almost as if a design for cast
iron has been adapted for stone, with as much glass and as little masonry

1a

1b

[2] Grosvenor Terrace is Rochead's most original design. He seems to have been too eclectic to make a genuinely individual architect, though one other building, the John Street Church (1859), with its direct-glazed colonnades, is remarkable in something of the same way as Grosvenor Terrace, **66**. His other work includes Queen Margaret College (the former Northpark House and now Broadcasting House) in a lavish and exuberant Renaissance style, several Gothic churches and some buildings in that worst of all revival styles which has come to be called 'baronial travesty' (see also p.276).

[3] See p.136.

[4] See p.244.

[4a] The lower end of Woodside Crescent has now vanished.

[5] 'Crescents' in Glasgow are of all possible shapes, from quite flat (Elmbank, but one side has been demolished and was in fact curved) to ranged round the four sides of a diamond (Lansdowne). They can be shallow (Clevedon), very shallow (Lancaster Terrace), or quite deep (Lynedoch), even semicircular (Belmont). Moreover they can be concave or convex (Crown Circus, Park Terrace).

[6] Inevitably Paxton has been credited with the design of Glasgow's principal green-house, the Kibble Palace, now in the Botanic Gardens, but originally built at Mr Kibble's house at Coulport, near Cove, Dunbartonshire. About 1871 'his offer to transfer the "palace" to Botanic Gardens, Glasgow, was accepted and the cost of removal and re-erection was estimated at £3000. It was formally opened in June 1873, as art palace, concert hall etc.' (information from Mr. Lochhead, *Architects' Journal*, 6th May, 1964, p.1030). Mr. Lochhead comments: 'I have found no evidence that Sir Joseph Paxton was its designer: Paxton made designs for a Winter Garden at Glasgow's Queen's Park in 1852, also in 1860, but these were not built. Kibble was an engineer by profession. Paxton was designing glasshouses in England from 1828 onwards – presumably Kibble was familiar with each of them. One might wonder if perchance he acquired one of the discarded designs made for that proposed Winter Garden at Queen's Park. Till evidence becomes available, I'm afraid we cannot ascribe "The Kibble" to Paxton.' Whoever did invent it, the Kibble is a delightful object, astonishingly light and delicate and quite worthy of the designer of the Crystal Palace. Its central feature is a flattish dome supported on cast-iron columns with a triple spiral running up them and elaborate wrought-iron brackets springing from the capitals like arches. James Cousland made a wire model.

[7] 'West' appears in a number of street names too: there are West Campbell, George, Graham, Nile, Princes and Regent Streets, though rarely an 'East' counterpart. I do not know the reason for this insistence on the west; possibly it is a distinguishing mark of the area's aristocratic character!

as could safely be allowed. The inspiration is clearly Venetian: in fact Grosvenor Terrace is surprisingly like a smaller version of the Procuratie Nuove, without the piazza but happy enough behind its trees.[2] All the Great Western Road terraces, each standing high above, or well back from, the road, are worth looking at. But one stands out, that by Alexander Thomson named after the road itself. And to this we must return later.[3]

The finest piece of architectural planning of the mid century – indeed perhaps the most striking piece of town design in Glasgow – has yet to be described. It cannot be appreciated as architecture alone, and an impression of it as townscape is given later.[4] Yet the architecture itself is very notable and contains the best work of Charles Wilson, an architect of great distinction, yet almost unknown today, at any rate outside Glasgow.

Woodlands Hill juts out in a rocky outcrop into Kelvingrove Park, but on the east the slope is much gentler, and it is here that building began in the early 1830s with Woodside Crescent. This takes off northwards from Sauchiehall Street just west of Charing Cross and then curves through a right angle to become Woodside Terrace, which runs level and straight along a contour looking south down the hill towards the northward-facing Woodside Place, **64**. All this is the work of George Smith, an Edinburgh architect whose designs are nevertheless entirely in the Glasgow tradition. The crescent is mainly two-storeyed, though the rising ground allows the central house to be higher than those to the south; the curve is held at either end by much taller houses, of three storeys with big parapets and plenty of emphasis given by balconies and window pediments. Even so, and despite the graceful curve of the crescent, the impression is rather severe. Woodside Terrace is really quite fierce, with its succession of identical, very large and very correct, Doric porches marking off identical three-bay houses, with its heavy window surrounds and a quite unadorned cornice. It would all be a little dour, were it not for the surroundings.

About 1842 John Baird built a mansion some way to the west of Woodside Terrace, and in 1847 added wings to make Claremont Terrace which is gentler, more relaxed than Smith's work and altogether one of the best of its kind in Glasgow, **67**. Here too the large porches (this time Ionic) are almost the only features that can be called at all decorative; Baird's real innovation in this terrace was to turn it into an extremely shallow crescent – a device which, with the help of very slight emphasis added to the end houses, gives an appearance of unified design which would certainly be less evident in a straight block which cannot be seen full-face.[5] (Unfortunately, there seems not to have been enough space for the design to be symmetrically balanced about the mansion, but this matters less since the terrace can only be looked at from an oblique angle.)

In 1854 Joseph Paxton (who had already designed Queen's Park in the south and the Botanic Gardens in the west) was commissioned with Wilson to lay out a new park to serve the growing west end.[6] (The park is still sometimes called West End Park, though its official name is Kelvingrove.[7]) At the same time Wilson was given the job of planning the rest of Woodlands Hill, which by this time, in addition to the work of Smith and Baird on the south side, had the beginnings of a still isolated development running up Lynedoch Street on the north-east. Here is Lynedoch Crescent (*c*.1845), **65**, a gentle feminine design making attractive use of the slope. All was designed as part of the original scheme in 1831 or thereabouts, and is also Smith's work.

8 The main architects of the mid nineteenth century in Glasgow formed so many partnerships with one another and moreover shared so few names that there has understandably been much confusion. There were at least seven Thomsons (only two of them related), five Hamiltons (father and son, and father and two sons, unconnected either with one another or with the Edinburgh architect), two Bairds (unrelated), five Wilsons (father, son and three others), as well as a Wylson and (from London) a Willson, and two quite distinct firms of Baird and Thomson (with no overlapping, though to add to the confusion Alexander Thomson worked at different times with both Bairds). Moreover both Bairds were John, two of the Wilsons were Charles, two of the Thomsons James; and to cap it all there is an Alexander George Thomson who is nothing to do with either Alexander or George Thomson. The genealogical tree on p.262 shows something of the intricacy of the relationships.

68. Park Circus: the north-east side (Charles Wilson, designed 1855, built 1857-8).

Wilson had been the Hamiltons' chief draughtsman in the 1830s, but left in 1837 to join his brother.[8] His real prominence, however, begins early in the 1850's, with the building of the new work at the Royal Bank in 1852 and the Royal Faculty of Procurators in 1854. By this time he had made an interesting and original personal style out of what Hamilton had done to the end of the Georgian tradition; and it is this that we see in three extremely different versions on the summit of Woodlands Hill. The centrepiece is Park Circus, which is now rather difficult to appreciate fully as the central garden has surely more and larger trees than the architect can have intended. The north-east side is the most impressive, **68**, for here the terrace is continuous along half of the flattened oval which is the plan of the whole circus (the remaining two terraces are almost quadrants). In fact this terrace consists not of a continuous curving crescent, but of a flat centre (itself with a centrepiece projecting in two stages) with curving wings, each rather less than a quadrant. This plan allows for a much more spacious and stately appearance than would be possible with a continuous curve of the same size: it recalls the Palladian principle of a mansion with curving wings. The vertical proportions are still basically those of a Georgian terrace, which may seem to bear out Professor Hitchcock's remark that the virtues of early Victorian terraces are still in effect those of late Georgian; yet Wilson is per-

haps the first architect of whom this is only superficially true. For most of the detail is quite new, and its cumulative effect is considerable, **69**. This is especially true of the ground floor, in bands alternately plain and vermiculated, with a change of pattern round each keystone (no cornice or even lintel, but a flat arch of upright stones), narrow slits of windows on either side of the doors (which again have keystone and no lintel), an ornamental string-course, and windows whose upper corners are shaved off in tiny quadrants – a feature perhaps consciously taken over from the Western Club. The sashes have each a single vertical glazing bar, and the upper sash is smaller than the lower. The decoration on the main cornice is extremely free, using oval medallions which had become a favourite motif of Wilson's.[9] Yet for all these very Victorian innovations, the appearance of the whole is exceptionally restful and dignified, if slightly austere.

The convex Park Terrace is totally different, and more whole-heartedly – or at least more obviously – Victorian, **70**. Here all classical precedents and pretensions have gone. The houses are now conceived much more as independent units: each has a large bay window (of two storeys) with a tripartite one above. The roof, which in Park Circus is quite visible from the ground, is now strongly emphasized, tall – almost mansard – with many dormers. Every third house is given rather more prominence with its separate,

69. High Victorian detail on Park Circus.

70. (left) The Park Area seen across
Kelvingrove Park from the
University tower. Park Terrace is in
the foreground, with Park Circus
behind: the steeples are (from left to
right) **Woodlands Parish Church
(Burnet, senior), Park Parish Church
(Rochead), the three towers of the
Free Church College (Wilson), St
Matthew Blythswood (Emmett), the
City Temple (Boucher and Cousland,
demolished), and St Matthew Bath
Street (Salmon, senior, demolished).
72. (overleaf) St Vincent Crescent
(Alexander Kirkland, 1850-5).**

[9] See also the friezes on the Royal Bank in
Buchanan Street and on the tenement at 543
Sauchiehall Street.
[10] David Thomson, Wilson's chief
draughtsman at the time, said later that the
idea of the French pavilions was to sweep
the hill up into a crown.

steeply hipped roof, like, say, the pavilions in the Place des Vosges in Paris.
In fact the general impression is distinctly French, but a French translated
into Glaswegian terms, the bay windows in particular taking over from
John Baird's experiments slightly earlier in Woodlands Terrace.[10] This is
not architecture to everyone's taste, but it is superbly self-confident and well
disciplined. It is hardly Wilson's fault if its style persuaded less talented
later men to cover the farther reaches of the city with the massive and
clumsy bay-windowed sandstone tenements which make so much of outer
Glasgow very gloomy. Wilson's example, however, may have encouraged
J. J. Burnet to exploit French idioms in the ambitious, not altogether lik-
able, Charing Cross Mansions.

But the best-known and most ambitious of all Wilson's buildings – his
crowning work on Woodlands Hill – is not domestic at all. The Free Church
College (now Trinity College) was begun in 1856, a year after Park Circus, **71**. To attempt to align it with any accepted 'style' would be impossible:
certainly it has elements taken over from the past: the original church entrance,
with a big pediment on four attached pairs of coupled columns, seems
definitely to owe something to Wren; and the main façade with its two storeys of round-headed windows between pilasters, rusticated below, smooth
ashlar above, carries echoes of Leo von Klenze's War Office at Munich and

73. The Queen's Rooms with related tenements in La Belle Place (Charles Wilson, 1857); the fenestration has now been altered.

more distantly of Queen's College Library, Oxford. The towers themselves have been called Lombardic, a resemblance which doesn't go much farther than their great height and a large corbelled cornice; the exceptionally tall attenuated lancets are quite new.[11] To combine such different things together into a thoroughly successful building which gives none of the impression of pastiche is the mark of an architect of high originality; and (though less clearly here than in his domestic work) Wilson developed a living tradition, carrying it several stages farther. Moreover, scenically the Free Church College marks a fresh departure: it is not a building designed to be seen from one, or even from one principal, position, as the insistent asymmetry and the use of a steeply sloping site indicate. On the contrary, for all its huge size and scale, it has affinities with the picturesque movement: it tells from a wide variety of positions both on and below its hill – as it were a moving element in the townscape.

The interior is less consistently good. The upper hall is certainly very impressive, with an imperial staircase rising through a colonnade into a pilastered room of great height with a well in the middle. The great hall below has a screen of columns at either end with the balconies of the upper hall carried on a half groin vault along the sides. This is processional architecture of considerable grandeur. The library is also interesting, though in a very different way and for different reasons – a longish room with a nave and aisles separated by Corinthian colonnades carrying an entablature, above which is a clerestorey. The segmental concrete vault is carried on iron beams with skylights between. But this is all the work of Colin Menzies, who rebuilt the college church as the library in 1908 after a fire.

Wilson's last building in the Park area is also one of his most remarkable – the great solid rectangle of the Queen's Rooms (1857, now a Christian Science church) at the bottom of the hill in La Belle Place, **73**. Its heavy, but well-tooled stonework and its many deep round-headed windows (in which an

11 These do occur earlier – in J.W.Wild's Christ Church, Streatham, of 1840. Wilson might possibly have seen this, though the effect in his much bigger towers is very different. There is a distinct resemblance between the top of the tallest tower (of which the design was not finalized until 1859) and that of Thomson's Caledonia Road Church (1856–7; see pp.128–31). An unexecuted design by Thomson in the Mitchell Library has the same feature and suggests, though there is no record of this, that the two architects may have been in close touch.

architrave separates the main opening from the upper semi-circle) give it a distinct flavour of the early Italian Renaissance, owing a good deal to Alberti. Yet the general shape is more like that of a classical temple, though there is no hint of a portico: the combination of the two themes gives the building a tremendous simple scale, though it is by no means specially large. (The adjoining houses, designed in the same year, cleverly accentuate this scale.) The details of the frieze and the devices over the windows, though classically inspired, are of the freely inventive character which gives piquancy to many of Wilson's best buildings. It is a pity that the Queen's Rooms is comparatively little known: having long deserved cleaning, it has lately been somewhat ill-advisedly painted, and the fenestration altered.

11a

Wilson is possibly (though doubtfully) a lesser man than Hamilton, certainly than Thomson; yet his impact on Glasgow was greater than those of either. And Hamilton did nothing better than the Free Church College, which is in its way a real masterpiece, one of the best mid nineteenth-century buildings in Britain.

By the 1850s building was going on at such a rate that only a few of the most interesting schemes can be mentioned. One of the most extraordinary is St Vincent Crescent (by Alexander Kirkland), a serpentine terrace facing the

11a A Wilson building of related character is the former Glasgow Academy in Elmbank Street (1846–7), later the High School and now the headquarters of Strathclyde Regional Council. Only the rich, freely Italianate frontage remains of Wilson's work, dominated by a powerful row of rusticated square piers carrying statues of Homer, Galileo, Watt and Cicero: technology among the older arts.

74. Queen's Crescent (John Bryce, 1840); part of the original delicate parapet can be seen in the middle; that on the right is a recent intrusion.

lower harbour almost continuously for nearly half a mile, **72**. Though not built till the early fifties, its style is that of a dozen years earlier. To the north of Woodlands Hill, another, less-imaginative layout seems to have proceeded in patches. Of these Queen's Crescent (by John Bryce, 1840 and a semicircle this time) and its surrounding streets are particularly charming, **74**: two-storey terraces and quadrants, with three-storey pavilions, all on a small and intimate scale. Other and later crescents and gardens are to the north again, on the other side of Great Western Road.

Farther west the layouts became extremely free, though Hillhead represents a partial return to the rectilinear pattern of Blythswood Hill. It is on yet another hill, small-scale and leafy, though now feeling the weight of the University. Though pleasant throughout, only two blocks need special mention: 27–53 Oakfield Avenue is by Thomson, carrying in the details of its upper storey the impeccable marks of his individual interpretations of the recurrent Glasgow theme of the two- and three-storey terrace. And near the north end of Hillhead Street is Granby Terrace (by William Clarke), an interesting development of the principle found first in Blythswood Square in which the windows of a long terrace are grouped in threes, marking off each separate flat and neatly articulating a façade that would otherwise be mono-tonous.[12] On the other side of Great Western Road from Hillhead is Bel-

76. Belmont Crescent (1869).

[12] See further chapter 9, p.186.

mont, with Northpark Terrace, also by Thomson,[13] and the handsome semicircular Belmont Crescent, bigger than Queen's Crescent but again of two storeys with three-storey pavilions and centrepiece, **76**.

A good deal farther west, south of the main Great Western Road terraces, is something quite different – the very mixed and very leafy suburbs of Partickhill and Dowanhill. The good things are more thinly spread here, though there is much to be seen. I shall mention only two. One is Crown Circus, a splendid and vigorous convex crescent, colonnaded on the ground floor (begun not later than 1858), **75**: the architect was James Thomson of Baird and Thomson (see p.262): his work is very finely conceived and looks like that of a more orthodoxly classical Wilson, though the design inevitably suffers from the impossibility of ever seeing the whole of a convex range with marked curvature at the same time. Nor does the shrubbery in front make it easy to get moving views; but it looks well from the south where the land falls away, and the crescent and its return along Crown Road can be seen together.[14] Wilson himself is supposed to have been responsible in part for Glasgow's version of Park Village, the garden suburb which arose on Partick Hill in the forties and fifties. There are villas of all sorts here, Grecian and Gothic and seaside and Thomsonesque (one indeed is claimed for Thomson though neither the details nor the proportions look quite right; and Hawarden Terrace, Partickhill Road, is probably by his partner, Turnbull). The whole has the very charming air of a semi-private enclave with houses spaced out among the trees.

South of the Clyde the impression is much less coherent. Between the river and the main railway lines it is all tenements – in the east giving way now to the new point-blocks and slabs of Matthew and Spence. To the south-west, Pollokshields is a 'town' of villas, only a few of which are worth looking at closely, chiefly in Albert and St Andrew's Drives,[15] though there are agreeable tenements farther east, particularly in Shields Road and Maxwell Drive. Strathbungo and the area round Queen's Park (as also the park itself) are consistently attractive. Moreover, Strathbungo has the most beautiful of all nineteenth-century terraces, Thomson's Moray Place. Indeed the outstanding things on the south side are nearly all Thomson's. Where Wilson was the dominant figure of the west end, Thomson worked primarily in the city and on the south side. But this work must have a chapter to itself, after an account has been given of many important changes in the centre which had been going on while the city spread to the west and south.

13 See p.140.
13a The two pavilions have now been demolished, following subsidence into old mine workings.
14 See also the nearby Princes Terrace and Princes Gardens, handsome and sturdy with big bays.
15 The older section of St Andrew's Drive, including Thomson's Green Gables and Boucher and Cousland's delightful Swiss Cottage was cleared in 1963–8.

Chapter 5

The Mid-Century in the City Centre

Though the west end grew so eagerly during the first half of the nineteenth century, it was not until about 1850 that a number of factors came together to make a substantial physical change in the old centre. By this time the economic basis of Glasgow's life had changed again. Trade continued to grow; but cotton was no longer of first importance, so that later, in the 1860s, when the supply from America was suddenly cut off by the Civil War, Glasgow suffered far less than Lancashire and simply allowed the manufacture of cotton goods to dry up. Iron had come to take its place, and the foundries were powered by local coal. The first ironworks in the city had in fact been started as early as 1786; but it was not until about 1830 that the foundries became really important. Blackband ironstone, in which iron ore is mixed with coal, occurred in large quantities in the lower Clyde valley; and soon after J. B. Neilson's invention of the hot blast smelter in 1828 transformed the manufacture of pig-iron, the whole of northern Lanarkshire and Ayrshire became predominantly an area of heavy industry.

Coal and iron not only brought more overcrowding in the centre; they brought also the railways. By 1840, even allowing for Glaswegian exaggeration, it seems likely that the area south-west of the Cross contained the worst slums in Britain. In that year the Chief Constable told the British Association that there was 'an accumulated mass of squalid wretchedness, which is probably unequalled in the British Dominions . . . [Here] is concentrated everything that is wretched, dissolute, loathsome and pestilential. These places are filled by a population of many thousands of miserable creatures. The houses are unfit even for styes, and every apartment is filled with a promiscuous crowd of men, women and children, all in the most revolting state of filth and squalor. In many of the houses there is scarcely any ventilation, and, from the extremely defective sewerage, filth of every kind constantly accumulates.'[1] The City Improvement Act, which gave the city power to tackle the slums directly, was not passed until 1866. But already there had been a good deal of evidently welcome destruction at the hands of the railway companies; and to this day the St Enoch's viaduct is the principal object between Trongate and the river. And, of course, the railways ended Glasgow's relative isolation from England and the rest of Scotland. But they did not end the intense feeling of locality that, despite its cosmopolitan population, is so marked a feature of the city even now. [1a]

The new tenements put up by the City Improvement Trust were obviously superior to what they replaced in almost every way. But as architecture they are, virtually without exception, negligible; and the architectural historian can have little to say about them. It is not with domestic work that we are now concerned. Though it took the rest of the century to eliminate the squalor into which the old city had degenerated, there was much wealth in Glasgow in the 1850s and 1860s; and to this we owe the great series of ambitious, even at times lavish, public and private buildings which together constitute the chief architectural interest today of the old heart of the merchant city. [1b]

[1] Quoted by J. M. Reid, *op. cit.*, pp.108–10.
[1a] No longer: station and railway were entirely removed in the 1970s; at the moment the site is a breezy waste.
[1b] This judgment is over-harsh: see further p.190.

In 1840 Glasgow had a population of more than a quarter of a million; and the machinery of its government had become correspondingly complicated and extensive: the Tolbooth was quite insufficient to house the army of local officials, sheriffs, clerks and the rest who were now necessary; and in 1842 the foundation stone was laid of a majestic new building called, rather drearily, the City and County Buildings, large enough eventually to occupy a whole block between Ingram Street and Wilson Street. The architects were Clarke and Bell, and the design was of course neo-classic – for, despite the Houses of Parliament, this was still the national style for the public building whose function included the impressive gesture of civic pride. In this case, however, 'classical' only in an extended sense of the term: the details have, most of them, classical precedents; the scale, the massing, the general method of composing the elements have not. There is indeed something almost absurd about the principal showpiece – a large Ionic portico at the south end high above the street on a substantial plinth, **77**. It would no doubt be an impressive stage-set for the pomp of a municipal blessing. Unfortunately there seems to be no way onto the plinth or into the portico: there are no stairs from the street, and in the wall behind only windows, no doors. (The doors at this end of the building are in fact ignominiously small, thrust in at the corners.) The portico is thus not a true portico at all, simply

77. The City and County Buildings, Wilson Street: portico at the south end (Clarke and Bell, 1842). The frieze is by Walter Buchan.

78. (left) 44-45 James Watt Street (c.1861). This grandest of all the dock warehouses of Glasgow makes an interesting contrast with the nearly contemporary Buck's Head (cf. fig. 123). 79. (right) The Old Merchants' House on the west side of the City and County Buildings.

² The north end was built much later, in 1871, but by the same firm. It represents a deviation from the original design and is of poorer quality; but this and the east façade were much altered during further additions and reconstructions in 1892.

a portentous gesture of civic solemnity: the adherence to classical forms is purely a matter of sentiment, and of a sentiment by this time rather out of date.

This said, the City and County Buildings must be admitted to be an impressive monument of its time. If one can ignore the irrelevance of its principal feature, the south façade has great dignity, with its temple-like frontispiece between projecting corner bays whose hefty superstructure gives an effect as of raised shoulders – perhaps the portico is even a little on the small side. The west façade is probably more interesting – twenty-nine bays long, the middle nine being solemnified by a massive row of attached Corinthian columns on the principal storeys, which projects slightly but has no pediment, **79**. (This part was originally the Merchants' House.) The effect, especially when seen from the axial approach along Garth Street, is quite germanically serious, though once again it is somewhat spoiled by the insignificance of the doorway, a single opening at street level with a hood over it, occupying only one bay. Once again, utility and civic grandeur have not been persuaded to come to terms. At least, however, a rule had been set; and from this time on Glasgow's public buildings are very conscious of the position they have to keep up.²

The merchants, industrialists and large shopkeepers who had indirectly been responsible for pushing Glasgow's civic architecture were quick to introduce elements of display into new buildings for their own use: the warehouses of central Glasgow provide perhaps its most fascinating and individual architectural form. But here a distinction must be drawn. Of warehouses in the conventional sense of the term – the vast dockside buildings so familiar in London and Liverpool and Hull – Glasgow has almost none, a remarkable fact considering its great importance as a port. The best group is in James Watt Street, with four large bonded warehouses, still very Georgian but built as late as the 1850s (one is dated 1854). Of these the most notable are Nos.65–73, of five storeys, pedimented with Doric pilasters, and above all, on the east side, Nos.44–54 (c.1861), of three and a half storeys with a huge Doric order expressed or implied along the whole front, the windows of the upper two storeys so deeply recessed that the impression in perspective is of a single huge storey on a high rusticated plinth, **78**. Unexpectedly this building has a pediment over the three bays at each end, but no central feature apart from a great round-headed archway: it is a design of great authority and grandeur. The only other building of this type which needs to be mentioned is the later Bell Street warehouse of 1889, a huge block, six storeys high, with small windows in pairs but otherwise completely unarticulated: it counts more for bulk and simplicity than for any refinement of detail, which passes unnoticed on the immense façade; yet as a feature in the townscape of a drab area it has immense virtues, only a few of which are now realized.

Again, Glasgow is disappointing in its industrial buildings. The docks have nothing apart from the unparalleled collection of cranes; nor is there anything to rival Dundee's jute mills.³ Of early industrial architecture the only thing of importance – and it is of great importance – is Houldsworth's Mill, Cheapside Street, almost unknown until recently, **81**.⁴ It was built between 1804 and 1806, probably to a design by Boulton and Watt (who cer-

2a

2b

80. (below) Diagram of the roof construction of Houldsworth's Mill. 81. (right) Houldsworth's Mill,† Cheapside Street (Boulton and Watt, 1804-6). Partially demolished.

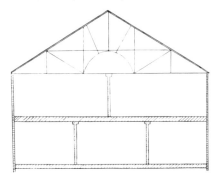

²ᵃ The great row of tea warehouses in York Street (only one now standing) built in 1843 for William Connal had a certain architectural presence, running indeed to a bracketed cornice. The architect was J. Stephen. See Hume, *Industrial Archaeology of Glasgow* (1974) pl.1.
²ᵇ But along North Speirs Wharf, in Port Dundas is a great tall parade built between 1851 and 1870 for the City Grain Mills and looking in its somewhat poker-faced way like a huge outpost of New Lanark. See Hume, *op. cit.*, pl.3.
³ Except perhaps Alexander's Mill in Duke Street (1842) [a plain but handsome five-storey façade by Wilson to a fire-proof mill built by Thomas Binnie. Between 1907 and 1909 Neil Duff converted it to the Great Eastern Hotel, adding a bit of architecture to the centre and an attic above the cornice.]
⁴ See the article by W. A. Skempton and H. R. Johnson, *Architectural Review*, March 1962, p.186.

82. (left) Randolph & Elder's Engine Works: the huge scale is repeated in the single-storey interior.†
83. (right) Randolph & Elder's Engine Works, Tradeston Street (William Spence, 1858).†

[5] Cf. Skempton and Johnson, *op. cit.*
The original fireproof scheme was in fact abandoned at the southern end, which was not built until the 1850s, to the same exterior design.
[John R. Hume has since shown that it is unlikely that Boulton and Watt had any hand in the design of the mill: see *Industrial Archaeology of Glasgow*, 1974, pp.26f. The mill was entirely demolished in 1969.]
[6] The station was only built after the Home Secretary wrote to the company in 1875, telling them that in the event of an accident due to insufficient accommodation, the attention of the Lord Advocate would be drawn to it.

tainly provided the engines) – one of the first half-dozen timberless mills in Britain and now the third oldest still standing. It is 224 feet long, seven storeys high, the framework throughout of cast iron, the tile floors supported throughout on brick arches; the outer walls are all of moulded brickwork, with pilasters between each pair of bays running the whole height of the building, topped by a brick cornice. The roof, 39 feet wide, is supported by a remarkable, seemingly almost perverse, iron truss, **80**.[5]

Equally interesting, and of an unusual type, is Randolph & Elder's Engine Factory† in Tradeston Street, designed by William Spence in 1858, completed in 1860, and now a seed warehouse, **83**. It is of colossal scale, a single-storey block over 50 feet high made of immense chunks of rough-hewn masonry deeply rusticated. The segmental arched doors are on the same huge scale; even the windows, with a slight batter and curious pentagonal lintels, are over 20 feet high. Inside there is the same massive simplicity, the roof and galleries supported on great iron stanchions with timber beams and struts, **82**.

A brief mention is also due here to the stations, and in particular to two whose future is in doubt. The more graceful is Queen Street, though the great segmental arch of its glass and iron vault can never have been fully visible from the outside. It has a clear span of 170 feet, the roof being carried on double arched trusses braced by diagonal struts. It was built in 1878–80 to a design by James Carswell, the district resident engineer of the North British Railway.[6] Behind the rather fussy façade of its hotel (by Thomas Willson of Hampstead) St Enoch's† has an equally fine roof, and here the external details, now partly obscured, that can just be seen from Howard Street, are specially vigorous, **89**. The engineers were Sir John Fowler and James F. Blair, 1875–9.

Glasgow's great contribution to commercial urban architecture begins in the 1850s with the remarkable collection of warehouses of a smaller type

7 Slightly earlier is James Wylson's recently demolished Canada Court, Queen Street (1848); the detail is of poor quality, but the elaborate design marked the beginning of a new adventurousness in commercial buildings in Glasgow. It is illustrated in Hitchcock, *Early Victorian Architecture in Britain*, fig.xii.9 and *The Builder*, vi (1848), pp.338–40. [Adventurous in another way is the appealing piece of Italian Renaissance at 109–115 Trongate, a speculation designed by Thomas Gildard to incorporate shops and a music hall. It has three superimposed arcades, the lowest using a form of Loire pilaster, the top managing to look like a dainty Umbrian loggia. The bones of the music hall survive inside.]

which have given so much of its character to the city centre. Almost the earliest of this group7 is also one of the very best – Arthur's, 81 Miller Street (1849–50), by James Salmon, grandfather of a more famous namesake, 84. Arthur's has almost continuous bands of windows on all three storeys, still – surprisingly – of Georgian proportions and with Georgian glazing. The centrepiece, however, has tripartite windows with segmental pediments filled with a shell-design. On either side of this is a range of six bays which has its own subsidiary centre, with more shell pediments over the two middle windows, except on the ground floor where the windows themselves suddenly go round-headed and form a curious little unit with three Corinthian pilasters and a separate small entablature. This is the only feature which does not look quite convincingly eighteenth-century. Like the rest it is full of refinement and charm, an unusually delicate treatment of a fairly large-scale project. What would the late eighteenth century itself have made of such a commission? Chambers, if we can imagine his taking it on, would have given it more bravado, Adam more applied ornament; it is safe to say that no one could have been guaranteed to design with a lighter touch than Salmon or a surer sense of the effect of his building as a piece of street architecture that must live with its neighbours as well as tell in its own right.

'rhythm' must be treated with caution when
we are dealing with an art form that does
not involve time as an essential ingredient
in its performance or even in its
appreciation. There is no close analogy
between the effects of architecture and of
music, from the discussion of which these
words may seem to be drawn. Nor is it a
matter of the movement of the eye along
the surfaces of the building, which is nearly
irrelevant in a symmetrical design like
Kirkland's which seems to ask to be seen
from a point opposite the centre of the
façade, or if not always from there (which
would in this case be nearly impossible in the
narrow street) at least not to be seen on the
move. The important point seems to be
that for a symmetrical building to make the
onlooker aware of the logic of its design,
the ratios between both the masses and the
details of its centre and its wings must be
carefully balanced to demonstrate that the
centre is the pivot of the design and not
just an arbitrary middle point. And for *any*
building the ratios of the sizes and details
on different storeys must be so calculated
that there is a visual reason why it stops
where it does and is not a storey or two
higher or lower: vertical symmetry is
nonsense in something that must stand on
the ground and be looked at only one way
up. When the masses and details take on
complicated and repeating patterns, then
we *may* be justified in talking of rhythm
and in suggesting that, for example, the
bays of a building may provide an analogy
with the bars of musical time.

Even a word like 'strength' (where, that
is, we use it to mean more than ability to
withstand a heavy knock) must be treated
with care: it implies an analogy with, say,
a potential for vigorous and concentrated
movement in a living creature (and the
appreciation of an elaborately undulating
façade may also be in part kinaesthetic).
But we know that no building has a potential
of this kind. The language of architectural
criticism, or that which we are obliged to
use to describe the effect of architecture on
us, is extremely primitive and inexact: the
dangers of this fact can be somewhat lessened
if we remember that we are – in talking of
balance, in using words like 'movement' –
primarily describing not the building itself
but our own reaction to it, or at least how,
in some sense, it stands in relation to us.

8a This building was gutted in 1979–80 and
has new interiors, but the façades have been
partly restored.

9 The Suspension Bridge is one of the only
two of Glasgow's present collection worth
notice. (It was finished only in 1871, with
George Martin as engineer.) The other is
James Walker's Victoria, which replaced the
old Stockwell Bridge in 1851, a noble
design, strong and graceful. The remainder
are a sorry lot, though the second Glasgow
(or Jamaica) Bridge must have been
delightful. It was designed by Robert and
William Mylne in 1767 and built 1768–1772
by John Adam of Glasgow (d.1790, a
relative of the Adam brothers). Hutchesontown

Almost next door to this delightful building is a masterpiece of a very different kind, Nos.37–51 Miller Street by Alexander Kirkland (1854), **85.**† This is an immensely strong and exuberant design, unconventional in plan, with a courtyard open to the street – the normal warehouse turned inside out to display as much as possible of the sumptuous vigour of its Venetian architecture. Everything about it gives an impression of concentrated energy, the effect of the chiaroscuro of the deep courtyard being repeated over and over again on the façades with their richly moulded windows recessed deeply between the columns and very heavy cornices on the lower storeys. No portion of wall is allowed to be inert or negative: there are columns between every pair of windows, coupled columns between every pair of bays; the combination of single and coupled columns, in different rhythms on the different storeys, fills the façade with a sense of restless movement enhanced by the contrasts of light and shade. This energy is conveyed in an upward as well as a horizontal direction through an arrangement of windows by which they get smaller but more numerous from floor to floor, each doubling the number below. Yet this richness is not allowed to get out of control. All the bays, except the centre one of all, are identical: that one is narrower, and the effect is a concentration of energy and attention into the centre, where of course the main doorway is. Moreover the management of the top storey, which must repeat the horizontal movement and at the same time arrest the vertical, is masterly. Each bay has four windows, compared with two on the middle floor and one large Venetian one on the ground. But on the top storey the windows are nothing like so deeply recessed, so that we have more the effect of a continuous band of windows than of the in-out movement so prominent below; and the band of windows carries a much lighter cornice; in the parapet above, with its recessed horizontal panels, the sense of movement has virtually disappeared – altogether a remarkable transition from the vigorous activity below to rest at the top.[8]

Also by Kirkland is the extremely interesting Eagle Buildings at the west end of Bothwell Street (1854–6), a two-storey range with a façade which looks as if made of iron and glass; but it is in fact of stone, though of a form (repeated round-headed windows with as little solid wall as possible) that seems more suited to iron and was in fact much used for it later. [8a]

Kirkland is an extremely perplexing figure. His recorded buildings are as varied in style as can be. The fine range, partly restored, at the east end of Bothwell Street (designed in 1849 in conjunction with John Bryce) is perhaps Florentine; 37–51 Miller Street is Venetian, as, in a different way, is Eagle Buildings. The tenements in St Vincent Crescent (1849) and Minerva Street (1853) are classical, the latter very much in the Edinburgh vein (cf. Atholl Place); the pylons of the Suspension Bridge (1851)[9] are pure Greek, **86.** Victorian architects were of course fond of this kind of free experimentation (less friendly critics might call it skylarking) among the styles; and these details would count for little, but that Kirkland's habits of collaboration were well known (G. H. Russell was, according to *The Building Chronicle*, involved in Eagle Buildings and Miller Street), and that the drawings of Miller Street were later in the office of John Hamilton, whose father James designed the Ulster Bank in Belfast in 1858 in a style that is very close to 'Kirkland's' Venetian. It is possible, therefore, that Kirkland may have been himself a shrewd business man manipulating various architects and without talent of his own as a designer, though he was a chartered engineer. Yet after

he emigrated to America, he became Commissioner of Public Buildings in Chicago. Perhaps his real talent lay in public relations.

All the warehouses discussed so far are of course in stone, and to them may be added one other impressive design – William Spence's at 21–31 Buchanan Street (now McDonalds) built about 1879, **87**. As so often before, it uses a giant order for horizontal articulation, absorbing two storeys of windows into the spaces between the pilasters. This, however, is a four-storey building, and the order is on the upper two. Between them and the now somewhat altered shop fronts on the ground floor is a row of pilasters without capitals which act as plinths for the main order. They have their own cornice giving a horizontal emphasis halfway up the building; but because this projects at each pilaster, a vertical connexion with those above is also asserted, and the design does not split horizontally into two. (Unfortunately the iron frames of the shop windows do not carry the apparent weight of the pilasters down to the ground, and the upper three storeys are therefore uneasily related to what is underneath.)

Historically even more interesting (though not necessarily finer architecture) is the collection of early iron-framed warehouses – a type that, in this country, Glasgow pioneered. The building still precariously surviving at the corner of High Street and Gallowgate represents two out of the four

87. (above) 21-31 Buchanan Street (**William Spence, c.1879**): the classically ordered warehouse style showed remarkable staying-power. With the taller domed corner section, H. K. Bromhead continued the same bay design into Argyle Street as late as 1902–3.
88. (right) **The Argyle Arcade looking towards Argyle Street** (John Baird No.1, 1827).

Bridge was rebuilt by Walker in 1829 to Rennie's designs but demolished in 1864 after scour had destroyed its foundations. [This dismissal of Glasgow's bridges was altogether too hasty and unconsidered. In particular it should be noted that Blyth & Westland, when widening Glasgow Bridge in 1894–9, virtually reproduced Telford's by re-using the original facings; only at the parapet was detail slightly amended. The cast-iron spans of Bell & Miller's Albert Bridge (1870–1) are also of interest; these engineers were responsible for later work on the suspension bridge. For the Kelvin Aqueduct see p. 269.]

89. St Enoch's Station: the vigorous ironwork of Sir John Fowler and James Blair, 1875-9.† The original span is 198 feet.

90. Royal Bank Buildings, Buchanan Street (Charles Wilson, 1850-1).

[10] The Buck's Head Building, by Alexander Thomson, with its very bold use of glass, was once thought to be of 1849. But this is now known to be the date only of the less daring part of the building, facing Dunlop Street. The rest is probably of 1863 (see p.145).
[No: even this was wrong: everything on the site was of 1863 or later. See below p.143 n.34a.]

[11] Arcades became popular in both Europe and America at this time. Baird's is small as they go, but is certainly one of the first, if not the first, in this country to be built entirely of iron. (Baird also designed the Wellington arcade, now demolished. The rather larger but similar Weybosset Arcade at Providence, Rhode Island, by Bucklin and Warren, was built in 1828.) To give a more complete indication of the range of Baird's work, two more things in the city centre should be mentioned. Greyfriars Church, Albion Street,† is an early work (1821): it has a solemn but very correct Doric portico. (Its Ionic sister in Wellington Street disappeared many years ago.) The attractive, withdrawn enclosure of Prince's Square (off Buchanan Street, 1854) has in detail something in common with Baird's domestic work farther west – plain, chiefly three-storeyed terraces round three sides of a small square, with a round-cornered lower building jutting out from the west side and occupying much of the floor area. Note the curious serpentine cornice at the angles where three storeys give place to four.

[12] Professor Hitchcock (*Architectural Review*, February 1951, p.114) points out that Gardner's has bays of wider span than contemporary American examples, perhaps because of Baird's use of framed girders consisting of flat bars of malleable wrought-iron with cast-iron distending frames, a recent patent of Robert McConnell.

storeys of a prototype in this field, apparently built in 1849–50. Then about 1850 came a much bolder design for Wylie & Lochhead, at 28 Argyle Street – the first to make really important use of cast iron. It was remarkably advanced for its time, having a tall narrow frontage with an immense window covering the entire upper storeys, the glass being divided only by two very slender iron mullions. Above was a fairly heavy attic with its own cornice, and at ground level a three-bay arcade whose shouldered lintels gave a somewhat Moorish appearance. (Much later, James Sellars's Queen Insurance Office (see p.153) was evidently much indebted to it.) After this the number of iron buildings multiplies rapidly.[10] 1853–9 seems to have been the peak period in Glasgow for cast iron and glass façades; though some of these have gone, several remain, including the purest and most beautiful of all. This is Gardner's, 36 Jamaica Street – the one that has become known simply as the Jamaica Street warehouse, **91**. It was built in 1855–6, and the designer was the remarkable John Baird, who had used an exposed iron frame as early as 1827 in the hammerbeam roof of the Argyle Arcade, **88**.[11] Gardner's is a most appealing building, friendly and graceful in appearance, straightforward and logical in its use of materials, which makes possible a sense of extraordinary lightness, which Baird has exploited to the full.[12] In principle the building is very simple – a four-storey iron frame, four bays by three, each bay divided into five lights (four on the side elevation) by simple iron mullions. All the iron members are moulded, the stanchions having a channel which runs all the way up and still further reduces the sense of solidity. And there is a delicate change of fenestration from floor to floor, the height of each storey being slightly less than that of the one below, **92**. On the first floor the lights have flattish segmental heads; on the second the heads are nearly semicircular; on the top floor they are semicircular, and the mullions have become tiny columns with capitals (the only use of a classical motif in the design except for the miniature balustrade at first-floor level). Each storey thus appears just a bit lighter than the one below, an effect increased by the little fretwork parapet under each window. By remarkable good fortune the original lettering has survived, and this too is beautifully in keeping – bold and tasteful, neatly occupying the horizontal beam between first and second floors. Gardner's is a lovely example of the functional use of a visually simple principle derived from a relatively sophisticated method of construction, carried out with a taste and restraint which make it appear nearly, but not quite, anonymous.[13]

Slightly earlier had come two equally unfussy iron buildings, which are not quite so dramatically simple as Gardner's. Kemp's, 37 Buchanan Street (now part of Wylie & Lochheads), was originally of three storeys only (it was later raised to five by Boucher & Cousland): it was essentially of the same type as one that has survived intact: this is Paisley's, almost certainly by Spence, 1854–5, **94**.[14] This has very emphatic horizontal divisions, which are moreover in stone, with quite a big cornice at each level. But the principal vertical members are not exposed: each floor thus shows simply a continuous band of windows separated only by very slender cylindrical iron shafts. Paisley's is therefore not quite so much for the purist; but it is an uncommonly restful and satisfying piece of street architecture.

In 1855 came the Lochhead section of Wylie & Lochheads, another bold combination of iron and stone, which has unfortunately long vanished. It

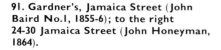

91. Gardner's, Jamaica Street (John Baird No.1, 1855-6); to the right 24-30 Jamaica Street (John Honeyman, 1864).

[13] It is a pity that Honeyman's otherwise very presentable Venetian warehouse next door should conflict at every floor level with Gardner's, more especially since the Honeyman building is the higher.
[14] Spence is known to have built a warehouse here, at this time; but Paisley's neighbour, the original part of the Colosseum, was rebuilt concurrently with Paisley's; so we cannot be sure.

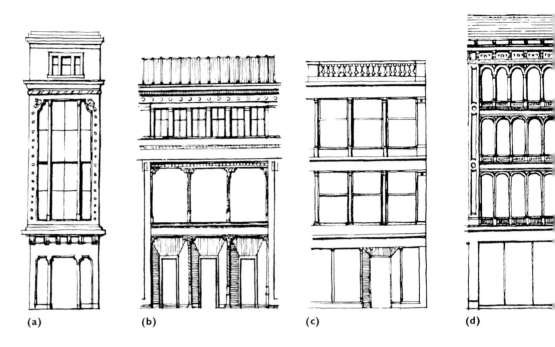

(a)　　　　　　(b)　　　　　　(c)　　　　　　(d)

92. Gardner's, Jamaica Street: the perfect relation of iron and glass. The lettering seems designed as part of the façade.

93. (above) The development of cast-iron façades in Glasgow:
(a) Masonry and cast-iron. Wylie and Lochhead's, 28 Argyle Street, 1850 (destroyed). Narrow frontage between tenements.
(b) Masonry and cast-iron. Design for Blair's, Howard Street-Dixon Street (Alexander Thomson, c.1851) (not built). One bay of façade.
(c) Cast-iron and composition between masonry gables. Kemp's (now Wylie and Lochhead's, 37 Buchanan Street: (1853-4, architect unknown). Three bays of façade; raised to five storeys by Boucher and Cousland later.
(d) Cast-iron. The Iron Building (Gardner's), 36 Jamaica Street (John Baird No.1, 1855-6; Ironfounder and patentee R. McConnel). One bay of façade.
(e) Masonry and cast-iron. Wylie and Lochhead's, Buchanan Street (William(?) Lochhead, 1855). Burnt 1883. One bay of façade of three bays; four-storey galleried salon of French type within.
(f) Masonry and cast-iron. 50-76 Union Street (William(?) Lochhead, 1855). One bay of façade.
(g) Cast-iron. North section of Colosseum, Jamaica Street. (H. Barclay and A. Watt, 1857). One bay of three, centre bay double width enclosed in wide arch. Ground and first floors conjectural.
(h) Cast-iron. 217-21 Argyle Street (James Thomson 1863; Ironfounder and patentee R. McConnel). One bay of three.
(i) Masonry and cast-iron. Gardner's, 120-36 Union Street (John Honeyman, 1872). One bay of façade (four to Union Street and five to Gordon Street).

94. (right) Paisley's, Jamaica Street (probably by William Spence, 1854-5).

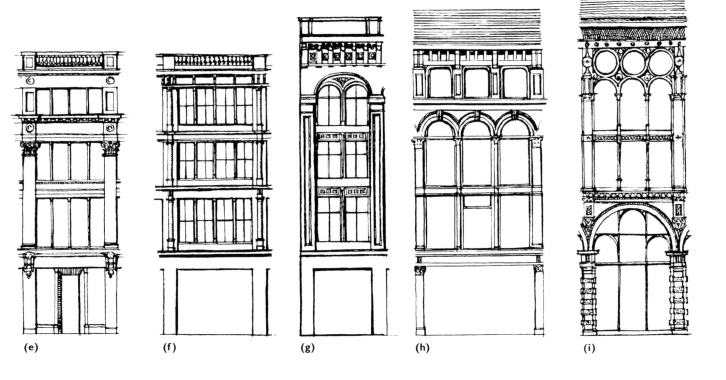

(e)   (f)   (g)   (h)   (i)

had a three-bay façade with giant pilasters linking the first and second storeys, standing on a chunky stone ground floor, and a much lower attic storey with balustrade. Each bay was divided into four by slim iron mullions, so that, as at Gardner's, the principle of the façade was of a bold, rectangular grid-pattern, with a smaller one threaded through it.[15] Another, not quite so striking, example of the same type remains at 54–76 Union Street, which has a wide-span exposed iron frame, with simple mullions between the windows and a substantial strip of superimposed masonry orders on the main stanchions. This was likewise built in 1855, by William (?) Lochhead, and was soon followed by the now much mutilated iron section of the Colosseum Building in Jamaica Street, by Barclay and Watt (1857) **93**.

Thus much for the warehouses. The other commercial buildings which have given a special character to the city centre are the banks, of which Glasgow has a number of handsome examples from the early nineteenth century onwards, though some, including Robert Black's City of Glasgow Bank in Virginia Street (1838) have long since disappeared, and one by Hamilton in Queen Street went in the last few years. Wilson is represented by a characteristic building – the Buchanan Street front which he added to Elliot's Royal Bank of Scotland, **90**. This sturdy oblong fills in the end of Gordon Street, as the Exchange does for Ingram Street, though it is now dwarfed

95. The Commercial Bank, Gordon Street (David Rhind, 1857). Note the exquisite refinement of the detail.
96. (opposite) 81-91 St Vincent Street (perhaps by David Rhind, c.1860): a dignified office variant of themes from the Commercial Bank. To the left, offices by J. J. Stevenson (c.1890).
Leon's art-nouveau shop-front (1928, since destroyed) was the first independent work of Jack Coia.

[15] This building was destroyed by fire in 1883 and rebuilt by James Sellars, who took advantage of the lessons learnt from the great Chicago fire to case the frame in terra-cotta, which protects the iron from the effects of intense heat.

by the buildings which frame the view. Its rows of evenly spaced windows extend almost to the edge of the building, giving it an appearance of greater width than the site would otherwise seem to allow.[16] And though the detail may seem largely to derive from the Renaissance, the proportion of window to wall is much higher than in any possible prototype and gives it a distinctly Glasgow air. The fanciful scrolls of the plaster frieze below the main cornice are another local device; the oddest single feature is the appearance of small scrolly piles which intervene between the windows and their cornices, which are thus lifted higher than one would expect to give the windows a slightly haughty expression. The interior has lately been entirely rebuilt.

The head office of the Commercial Bank of Scotland in Gordon Street (David Rhind, 1857) is more ambitious – a three- and four-storey block with definite pretensions, **95**. Professor Hitchcock says that Rhind 'followed intentionally the Farnese Palace',[17] but the building is nothing like as pure as this would suggest: indeed the connexion with the Farnese seems remote, except in the three first-floor aedicules which may well come from the grand entrance inserted by Michelangelo into Sangallo's façade. If one is looking for precedents, Raphael's Vidoni-Caffarelli is generally rather closer, though the central attic storey with its row of small attached columns seems to follow a Tuscan rather than a Roman original. But in fact Rhind articulates

[16] The Farnese Palace seems to me more likely to have had an influence on Wilson in his use of this feature than on Rhind in the building discussed below.
[17] *Early Victorian Architecture in Britain*, p.366.

97. Royal Faculty of Procurators, St George's Place (Charles Wilson, 1854).

98. The National Bank (John Gibson, 1847-9), later re-erected in Queen's Park as Langside Hall.

his design in a way more characteristic of the Baroque than of the Renaissance: here is no long façade with a regularly repeated pattern of windows and columns, but a five-bay centre and lower three-bay wings, each with an identical subsidiary centrepiece, so that there are three foci of visual attention. The principal cornices are indeed continuous, but apart from the extra storey, the centre is marked off emphatically by double bands of rusticated stonework running the entire height of the building; rustic also are the columns and arches of the ground floor. This palazzo is extremely self-confident, yet it has impeccable manners – though once again one has to deplore the effect of its assertive neighbour (an addition to the bank by Sydney Mitchell, 1887), which – half-heartedly and not consistently picking up motifs from Rhind's work and adding a tower and dome at one end – completely upsets the balance.

Though Rhind was an Edinburgh man, his pleasure in Italian forms set something of a fashion in Glasgow. But Rhind had in fact been preceded in this by Wilson, whose admirable hall for the Royal Faculty of Procurators was built in 1854, **97**.[18] This too has links with Roman palazzi, though rather more with the Venetian seicento, and though it is a relatively small building (only two storeys) it gains prominence from a slightly raised site, which allows it to have three exposed façades. The two storeys are treated very differently. The ground floor is quite plain, with round-headed windows set in heavily rusticated masonry; the rustication is droved only at the angles and round the windows, which have keystones in the form of sculptured heads of law lords. The whole ground floor acts as a substantial podium for an order of coupled Corinthian columns between which are more round-headed windows, this time with cartouches for keystones. The frieze above these is very free, with elaborate sculptured swags. The end elevation is less successful: here a feature is made of a Venetian window between columns which are separated by niches from more coupled columns. There seems a

[18] The Faculty had originally commissioned a design from Emmett, which was naturally in Gothic. They took fright at his estimate of £7000 and decided to ask for local plans in the 'Roman or Palladian' style. Wilson's design was preferred to one by Clarke and Bell: in the end it cost a lot more than Emmett's estimate (see *Glasgow Herald*, 18 November 1950).

[19] Smirke's building was completely refaced by Blomfield in 1921 and finally ruined in the second world war (see Hitchcock, *op. cit.,* pl.VI.7).

[20] One more Italian building should be mentioned here, though it is no longer in the centre – John Gibson's National Bank (1847) formerly in Queen Street and moved in a moment of wisdom in 1902 to Queen's Park, where it is now Langside Public Hall. The task of re-erection was most skilfully done, and we must be grateful that a modest and gracious little building was saved when its central site was given up to a strident warehouse by David Barclay. But it undoubtedly misses the square of chambers which used to surround it and does now look rather lost, **98**. Gibson was a London architect, and his Italianate is perhaps more academic than a Glasgow architect would have made it. (Cf. his contemporary Imperial Assurance Office in London.) He uses the 'Scamozzi order', and apart from the Royal Arms, the building seems to have strayed rather from Vicenza than from central Glasgow. It is a less self-consciously tough building than Wilson's, and may for this reason be found more attractive. It seems to have had some local influence: see for example the work of Boucher and Cousland, notably the fine villa at 998 Great Western Road (1877).
[There is another (simple) Italian façade to the former Fishmarket (Clarke & Bell 1871–3), but the main frontage, to Clyde Street, is in a jolly Franco-Italian baroque – a much-needed architectural refresher in Glasgow's rather seedy riverfront.]

little too much incident here (it stops abruptly halfway along the façade); but the most uneasy detail is the treatment of the corners, where the wall behind the columns is carried a few inches beyond them on each façade (recalling a mannerism of Hamilton's on Hutcheson's Hospital). The entablature, however, is not: hence at the levels of the frieze, cornice and parapet there is not one right angle at the corner, but three. It is difficult to see how Wilson could have turned his corner in a more convincing way once he had settled on his coupled columns; but the effect is to crowd and weaken the design at these crucial points. This feature also occurs on Sansovino's Palazzo Corner Ca' Grande at Venice, and on its descendant, Longhena's Palazzo Pesaro. In neither of these do I feel the corners altogether happily managed. (Sanmichele's Palazzo Grimani which, though more austere, likewise makes use of coupled columns, is bolder in its handling of angles, with square columns at the extreme corners and a plain rectangular cornice.) Both Sansovino's and Longhena's buildings likewise have the keystone heads and what David Thomson called the sur-bases on top of the pedestals of the columns. Quite as close in spirit and detail is Sydney Smirke's competition design for the Old Carlton Club in Pall Mall, London (1847), which, however, was not completed until 1854, the year of the Procurators. Parapet, frieze, columns and windows (though not the corners) are in fact so similar in the two designs that it is reasonable to look on Wilson's as a simpler, smaller and rather less happily proportioned version of Smirke's. It seems hardly conceivable that the two can be entirely independent; yet Wilson is the last architect to be accused of plagiarism.[19] It is likely that both designs were independently inspired by Sansovino, a frequent source at this time.

Inside there is an almost painfully high and narrow staircase hall with three arches in the Genoese manner. But the library which occupies the whole length of the building on the upper floor is very different – an astonishing display of rich colours and varied surfaces. The plan is of a five-bay nave with aisles, separated by an arcade of square Corinthian columns in green marble with gold capitals. Along the aisle walls are similar green wall-shafts, and above these the aisle vaults are quadripartite with gold chains on the broad flat bands which take the place of ribs; more gold decoration is in the spandrels of the arches. The ceiling of the 'nave' is flat, with elaborate plaster strapwork. The woodwork is everywhere richly polished mahogany; and the whole effect is of a lavish exuberance of decoration which reduces architectural qualities almost to a minimum. Though Italianate designs continued to find favour with later architects (reaching a fevered climax in the City Chambers), such a building as the Royal Faculty of Procurators was hardly imitable even in the opulence of mid-century Glasgow. By the time it was built Thomson had had his own firm for five years, and the earlier part of the Buck's Head was already four years old.[20]

Chapter 6

The Individual Contribution of Alexander Thomson

99. Old Stirling's Library, Miller Street (James Smith, 1863–4)

Thomson has been 'Greek Thomson' for too long. The phrase sets up expectations which are at best misleading, and may seriously distort a proper appreciation of his architecture. For it contains just enough truth to be easily taken by the unwary for the whole truth; and Thomson's profound and daring originality is obscured. The unwary in this context can include even so astute and well-documented an historian as Professor Hitchcock, who, for all his evident delight in Thomson's churches and terraces, insists that they can all be understood as late examples of 'romantic classicism'.[1] Now it is true that Thomson used Greek porticos on two of his churches, one of which even has the general shape of a temple; true also that he used classical details on the porches of Great Western Terrace and the Ionic columns of Westbourne, that the shape of Moray Place may have its distant original in a Greek stoa. But not only can we find equal numbers of details drawn, say, from Egyptian sources; not only are many of his designs not classical in form or detail: they are without important precedent of any kind. This is less obviously true of his domestic than of his commercial work, which has in consequence not always been found so attractive. But it seems to me unwise anywhere to regard Thomson as basically neo-classical: he was capable of using an exceptionally wide vocabulary of motifs and subordinating them to his own greater architectural purpose.

What this purpose was may be suggested by a question which he put in his presidential address to the Glasgow Institute of Architects: 'How is it that there is no modern style of architecture?' The period of Thomson's maturity was one which – more or less the country over – was completely astylar. Certainly in Glasgow architects played their variations over an extraordinary range and often confusion of stylistic devices, sometimes lacking any coordinating principle in their work. No man can change art alone, but if Thomson did not by himself create a 'modern style' he certainly created an extremely individual personal one, so that his hand can always be recognized even among his amazing variety. Yet this style is not personal in the sense of being the expression of an assertive *personality*. We cannot guess much about the man from his work. On the contrary the best of it all has a curiously detached air, an air of impersonality, telling its own tale and pointing to the artist behind only implicitly if at all.

Thomson was highly regarded by his contemporaries in Glasgow, and often imitated before and after his death. Yet few other architects appear to have been aware of him as an *influence*, changing and extending the possibilities of expression for other practitioners as every truly original artist must. Today his architecture seems astonishingly ahead of its time, not only in the freedom and daring of his use of new kinds of expressive detail and (though less markedly) new ways of handling materials, but above all in the recognition, which is clear from work as early as 1850, that architecture could not grow merely by *playing variations on* traditional themes in the manner of the fashionable revivals of the period. Thomson was greatly more than a revivalist like, say, Smirke. He can now be seen as one of the

[1] See *Architecture: 19th and 20th Centuries*, pp.61–2.

100. (right) 25 Mansionhouse Road:
detail of elevational drawing.

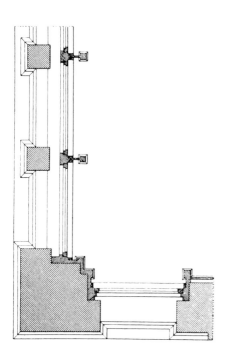

101. (above) 25 Mansionhouse Road,
Langside(1856): detailed plan of bay,
showing glazing behind
free-standing stone columns.

[2] And I think that Graham Law (*Architectural Review*, May 1954, p.314) is certainly right that Thomson was not interested in the use of new materials and techniques as the foundation of a new aesthetic. Architecture was for him an expressive medium, and its methods and materials were means to this end. At the same time it is not contradictory to claim that his stylistic inventiveness, which itself made free use of these, also made it easier and more natural for later architects to derive an aesthetic directly from them. [We shouldn't now want to lay stress on Thomson's 'proto-modernism' – an attitude which seems to us to smack of whiggery, and is in any case torpedoed by recent discoveries about the chronology of the warehouses: see below p.143 n.34a.]

great forerunners of the Modern Movement, and in this country the earliest of them all, unless one should here mention Soane. But, as with so many truly creative artists, one is with Thomson at least as aware of the tradition from which his work organically grew as of the originality of his own genius.[2]

One important influence on Thomson's work should be acknowledged, indeed emphasized, at the start – that of Karl Friedrich von Schinkel. Not only does Schinkel seem to have been almost the first to have used the horizontally linked bands of windows of which Thomson was so fond (see

the Berlin Schauspielhaus, 1819), but he combined this with classical elements on the largest scale: the Schauspielhaus has a giant Ionic portico. (Some of his most important buildings were, however, purely classical in detail if not always in spirit – something never found in Thomson.) Such buildings, therefore, as Walmer Crescent or the printing works in Stanhope Street, which are unprecedented in Britain, must be held to owe some detailed inspiration to Schinkel; and the combination, in the churches, of classical portico and horizontal bands of windows punched deeply into the wall suggest quite close study. Furthermore, the much freer *Rundbogenstil* (round-arch style) which Schinkel developed for his villas can also be seen in early villas by Thomson: for example, No.301 Albert Drive of 1857.[3]

It may be remarked that in the mid nineteenth century the use of Schinkel as a model is itself the sign of an independent spirit. But Thomson did have a precursor in this. Barry's Royal Institution (now the Art Gallery) in Manchester used very markedly Schinkelesque forms as early as 1824, though thereafter Barry retreated to his more easily acceptable Italianate. The Royal Institution is indeed in many ways like a small, rather timider version of the Schauspielhaus: in particular the portico, with a high attic storey of horizontally banded windows above, seems almost a deliberate pastiche; the wings of Barry's building, however, are closer, say, to Holland's Carlton House.[4] By contrast Thomson's use of his great predecessor is always more full-blooded, adapted moreover to compositions whose principle of invention is wholly Thomson's own.

Thomson was a very prolific architect.[5] Yet, tenements apart, hardly ever does he repeat himself, except through the fresh use of detail adapted from one building to another. Very likely he was largely responsible for some designs while chief draughtsman to John Baird 'No.1'. But no major building can definitely be authenticated as his before the Dunlop Street section of the Buck's Head, of 1849–50, that is, after he had set up his own firm. And if

3 Ludwig Persius and von Arnim were probably also early influences. Thomson's study of the work of all these architects was through books of illustrations: he never went out of Britain and only rarely out of Scotland.

4 The old Stirling's Library (48–56 Miller Street), by James Smith, 1863–4, is the most distinguished of the few buildings in Glasgow to owe something directly to Barry: note the use of both Renaissance and Mannerist windows, 99. There is nothing of Thomson in Smith's admirable building. J. T. Rochead's Bank of Scotland in St Vincent Place (1869) should also be mentioned (see further p.157). This is in the bold Italianate of Barry's club architecture and really quite as good as Barry's own work in this style, though of course very late in the day.

5 For much interesting biographical and other information, see the article by Graham Law cited in n.2, above. [We now also have the idiosyncratic and richly illustrated book-length study by Ronald McFadzean (1979).]

any previous work has survived, it seems clear that he had not developed his personal style much earlier than this – or at least had not been able to make use of it. All the work by which he is now known belongs to the last twenty-five years of his life, most of it to the period between about 1856 and 1870. He produced buildings of all the kinds needed in the Glasgow of his time – churches, houses, terraces, tenements, warehouses, offices. A rough chronology can be made out;[6] but Thomson's career shows less a *development* than a continuous inventiveness and experiment.

Nevertheless, a few generalizations can be made. Thomson's use of classical features is more marked early than late. Both his remaining churches[7] (1856 and 1859) have correct classical porticos, in both cases raised high above the street on an immense plinth. Where unaltered classical motifs are use in his later work, it is on a (proportionately) smaller scale and far less insistently, for example, the Ionic porches on Great Western Terrace, the columns in Hyndland Road. On the other hand, his earliest dated commercial work is as free in its use of detail as his latest. Equally, in his earliest terrace designs we find those either without classical precedent at all (Walmer Crescent) or with features so modified and adapted to his personal idiom that the possible classical origins do not seriously count (Oakfield Avenue). In these, however, what does remain, even in such personal, such idiosyncratic creations as Northpark and Westbourne Terraces is the basic relation of floor and window heights which had been worked out in the eighteenth century or earlier. In Thomson's three-storey terraces there is plenty of variation even here: in Westbourne Terrace, for example, the top storey windows are hardly more than half as high as those below, while in Northpark Terrace the proportion is about 3:4. But prominence is still given to the first floor, and its windows remain the largest. (In the two-storey terraces, of course, a quite new relation has to be worked out.) This seems to me a matter of adherence less to the principles of the classical revival than to

[6] See p.280; McFadzean, *op. cit.*, pp.295ff.
[7] A third in Ballater Street (1859) partly survives, shorn of one end and converted into a factory.† It was built in Thomson's villa style, with low-pitched roof, and is quite small. [Now destroyed.]

certain stubborn facts about the human sense of proportion. In a building with predominantly vertical emphasis to the main features (especially the windows), a top storey as large as those below makes the whole look top-heavy: hence the need (as in Northpark Terrace) where the top windows are relatively large, to reduce the stonework of this storey to a minimum.

At the same time as Thomson freed himself from the rules of orthodox academic classicism, he experimented widely, in his individual way, with new techniques. The unexecuted Howard Street warehouse design of *c*.1851 is one of the earliest in Britain to use an exposed iron frame, and none earlier had been on this scale. At the Buck's Head, somewhat later, the continuous glass is set into iron mullions at the back of the exposed stanchions,[8] and in the top storey behind stone columns. This device had in fact been carried a stage further in the double villas at 25 Mansionhouse Road, Langside (1856). Here, in the projecting bays, the window frames lie behind and separated from the mullions, which are thus essentially a row of free-standing columns, with the windows entirely clear of the stonework, **101**. This, as Elizabeth Beazley has remarked,[9] is like a curtain-wall turned inside out. The logical conclusion was reached in the following two years in Thomson's finest and most elaborate house, Holmwood, where the glass stands quite free of the peristyle – a feature which took on greater significance in the

104. Queen's Park Church: portico (drawn by W. J. Anderson).

[8] These stanchions are lightly clad in wood. [Partly at least in masonry: see further p.146 n.37a; also McFadzean, *op. cit.*, p.145.]
[9] *Architects' Journal*, 6 May 1964, p.1016.

105. (left) **Caledonia Road Church (1856).**
106. (right) **Caledonia Road Church: interior (destroyed by fire 1965).**

[10] Curiously the design was not published until 1872 in the *Building News* of May 31, and then not exactly as built: perhaps after seeing the Egyptian Halls the publishers asked if he had done any more like it. The date of building shows how early Thomson's treatment of the relation of pilaster and void had reached a very advanced stage.

[10a] From Thomson's Haldane lectures it is plain that his unease derived from the fact that, the Erekhtheion apart, no surviving Greek building has architraved windows.

warehouses and offices of the 1860s, most notably in a fine building in Bath Street (dating from 1860,[10] now alas demolished), whose top storey consisted of continuous glazing along the length of the building behind a colonnade, and in the top storey of the Egyptian Halls in Union Street (1873). It is said that Thomson disliked 'openings': by these methods he was able to indulge this dislike, while at the same time articulating a façade into units and preventing the dangers of monotony so rarely avoided by twentieth-century glass buildings. [10a]

Thomson's best-known works are his two remaining (or partially remaining) churches, both built in the 1850s. A third, Queen's Park Church of 1869, was the only serious wartime casualty that Glasgow suffered, and one of the unhappiest architectural losses in Britain, **102.** It was unlike either of the two that we still have in largely abandoning the reproduction of classical motifs. It had a strange high dome, developed from St Vincent Street, rather 'Indian' in character; and the front elevation was unlike anything else that he ever built. Below the octagonal plinth on which the dome stood, the main body of the church ended in a pedimented wall, into which a grotesque, squat, free-standing colonnade was inserted near the top. Below and in front of this was what could be called a kind of 'Egyptian' portico; but it consisted rather of a colonnade set within a huge pylon, whose slightly battered uprights were decorated in the Egyptian manner, **104.** The colonnade did not reach the top of the pylon uninterrupted: a massive, elaborately incised lintel ran across about three-quarters of the way up, above which the columns sprouted baluster-like capitals which 'supported' the main lintel of the pylon. The lower lintel was in fact the entablature of a big square colonnade which ran across the whole front of the church and was threaded through the big pylon. (More small pylons stood high up at the ends of the 'aisles'.) The whole was a characteristically individual variation on Nubian temple designs which

Thomson could have seen illustrated in Denon's *Voyage dans la basse et la haute Egypte*;[11] the archaic Treasuries of Massalia and Syphnos at Delphi are also possible sources, though their reconstruction is later than Thomson. The interior of Queen's Park Church was evidently sumptuously coloured in a vein still to be seen on a smaller scale in at least two villas, **103**.

Of the two remaining large churches, St Vincent Street has much the more impressive site, and externally the composition of the whole is perhaps finer. Caledonia Road's (1856–7) real triumph is its magnificent tower, a great square pile of masonry rising unadorned except for very severe triple bell-openings near the top and a smaller square clock-storey with cornice above, **105**. This absolutely uncompromising design is in its way more strikingly original than the strange accumulation of motifs that go to make up the steeple of St Vincent Street.[12] What is, however, really odd about Caledonia Road is the appearance of the temple motif in distinctly unorthodox surroundings. Professor Hitchcock observes that the tower 'reduces the temple front to a subordinate element in a sort of Italian villa composition'.[13] It does not, however, reduce it enough to prevent the portico from being an oddly disturbing element. It seems to have come from another world into the harshly rectangular context provided by the tower and the body of the church with its deep-set Schinkelesque windows, an impression in-

107. (above) **St Vincent Street Church from the south: a photograph taken in about 1890.**
108 (right) **St Vincent Street Church (1859) from the north west with its now demolished linked tenement.**

[11] The Egyptian revival is discussed in an article by N. Pevsner and S. Lang in the *Architectural Review*, May 1956, p.242 ff. P. F. Robinson's Egyptian Hall in Piccadilly disappeared long ago; but survivals include Foulston's Library at Devonport, a house at Penzance, a factory at Leeds and a Masonic Lodge at Boston.
[12] There is an amazing small-scale forerunner of this tower at St Mary's, East Cowes, Isle of Wight, built by Nash in 1831. This too is square and unadorned except for the bell-opening near the top, which has two squat columns rammed into it. Can Thomson possibly have seen it? It is illustrated in David Lloyd and N. Pevsner, *The Buildings of England: Hampshire and the Isle of Wight*, (Harmondsworth, 1967), pl. 69.
[13] *Architecture: 19th and 20th Centuries*, pp.61–2.

109. (left) 25 Mansionhouse Road, Langside (1856), a house which seems to look forward half a century to the early work of Frank Lloyd Wright.

creased by what at first sight seems a lack of co-ordination of dimensions. The portico is three bays deep (most of the side elevation is solid) and then suddenly the temple stops and is replaced by the main upper storey of the church, which is much wider but also lower than the portico – its parapet comes to about the height of the temple frieze – and its roof, always lower than that of the portico, was invisible from street-level. The combination of somewhat discordant and certainly uneasily linked elements nearly manages to give the impression that Thomson felt under some obligation to introduce a classical motif into a design which it did not fit and took his revenge by demonstrating its inappropriateness in the most emphatic manner possible.[14]

I am not of course suggesting that this is in fact what happened. Thomson was a great admirer of the classicizing work of some of his predecessors and contemporaries,[15] and at St Vincent Street showed his own complete mastery of the temple, there carried through much more wholeheartedly. Nor should I like to leave Caledonia Road without recording my feeling that, in the face of its overwhelming majesty and sureness of proportion, the objections I have raised seem to me crabbed and pedantic: a compelling overall logic pulls all together. What strength comes from the placing of the doorways and the alternating broad and narrow bands of stone! What a perfect sense of balance one has, as one looks at the church from its main viewpoint, the south-east! How sure is Thomson's eye in relating the height of his asymmetrically placed tower to the horizontal lines of the street front to the right! How convincingly the mass of the 'temple' helps in the linking of the vertical and horizontal accents which, without it, would be far too starkly juxtaposed! And how much Thomson has made of so unpromising a site! It is one of Glasgow's greatest buildings – indeed one of the greatest nineteenth-century buildings anywhere; yet, in a way only too characteristic of Glasgow, the church, after years of ill-treatment amounting to dereliction, has in 1965 been, almost casually, gutted by fire and the superbly detailed roof and interior destroyed, **106**. For some time ominous rumours were about that the ruins (including the undamaged tower) were to be demolished, and the site used for a roundabout. But the Corporation has lately voted £37,000 for immediate repairs to the tower, portico and outside walls. Partial survival therefore seems assured; but we need the whole church: in almost any other country than our own, so great a work of art would call out enthusiastic and complete restoration as a matter of course.[15a]

The site of St Vincent Street (1859), which Thomson handled with spectacular drama, is the first ingredient of his success there, **108**. Since the land falls steeply both to the west and more particularly to the south, a large substructure had to be built up. This was turned into a gigantic plinth which juts out from the side of the hill in imitation, surely, of the substructure of the Parthenon, or at least the temple of Nike Apteros. This 'plinth' contains in fact the ground floor of the church (as well as basements, entered from street-level lower down the hill to the south); but it appears as an unusually large foundation for the temple which stands above. This temple has columns only at its ends; for along the sides, below a row of square clerestorey windows, are 'aisles' with nearly continuous glazing divided only by pairs of coupled square columns, **107**. (The aisle walls in fact continue upwards the outer walls of the sides of the plinth and contain the galleries: apart from slender supporting columns there is no internal division at the floor level of the church.)

[14] There may be a parallel to this strange composition in the Erekhtheion at Athens, whose curious lateral portico produced a similar clash of scales and roof-lines. Here, however, the dominating Ionic order provided a linking motif throughout the whole temple.

[15] He thought Edinburgh High School and St George's Hall, Liverpool unquestionably the two best modern buildings in Britain. The first is an example of 'interpenetrating masses', as Thomson pointed out – he was later to use the principle himself; the architect of the second, H. L. Elmes, was also strongly influenced by Schinkel. Unlike Thomson he went to Berlin to study his work directly while working on the Liverpool designs.

[15a] Deplorably demolition, or at least drastic reduction, has once again been under consideration, and there has been further vandalism of the ruins. A recent suggestion has been its rebuilding as a focus to the top of Buchanan Street.

(a)   (b)   (c)

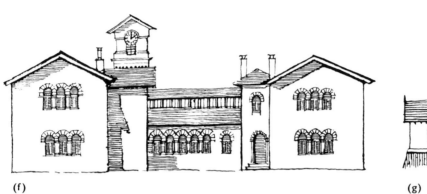

(f)

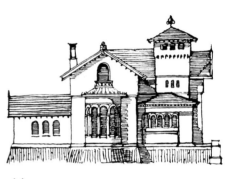

(g)

110. The development of Thomson's villa style:
(a) Green Gables, Pollokshields (c.1851), demolished.
(b) Balfron Manse, (c.1860).
(c) 25 Mansionhouse Road, Langside (1856–7).
(d) Busby House (c.1860).†
(e) 202 Nithsdale Road, Strathbungo (c.1870).
(f) Pollok School (1856) (right-hand wing probably raised later).
(g) Craig Ailey (1850).
(h) Greenbank, Bothwell (probably 1850s).
(i) Tor House, High Craigmore (c.1868).
(j) Arran View, Airdrie (1868).

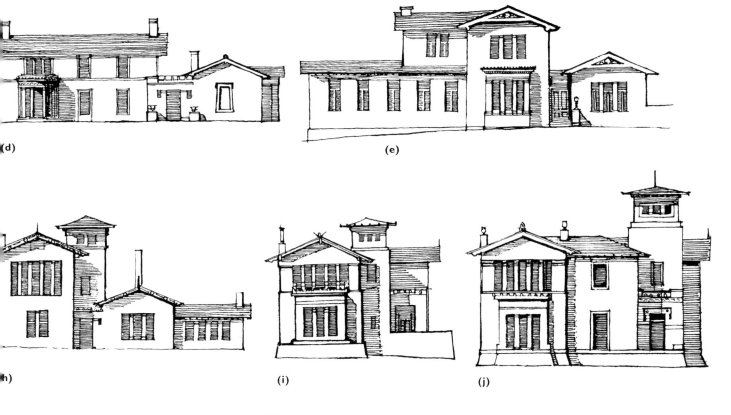

(d)

(e)

(h)

(i)

(j)

Near each end of the outer aisle walls is added one of Thomson's strangest and most arresting devices, a tall, nearly rectangular pylon imposed on the outside of the coupled colonnade and rising well clear of the cornice; the slight batter of the uprights of these pylons gives a distinctly Egyptian effect. Their effect on the design of the church as a whole is to provide a most satisfactory stop to the ends of the aisles which might otherwise appear a little arbitrary, and also to give a needed vertical accent to the very horizontal character of this part of the design.[16]

The appearance of great strength in the substructure is reinforced by the treatment of the lower windows. A band of stonework five courses deep is recessed all round the church: into this is set a continuous projecting band of stone in the form of a square zig-zag, rather like a very elementary key-pattern. The square spaces between the uprights of this pattern are filled alternately with windows and blank panels: the uprights act as window jambs, the horizontals as lintels to the windows (which have no projecting sills) and sills to the panels (which have no projecting lintels). Since the windows are set very deep, there is heavy cast shadow between the uprights: the effect is unusually massive.

Above all is the nearly indescribable steeple. This begins as a plain tower, square in section, near the top of which is, on each side, a large T-shaped opening, in the horizontal part of which are inset two Egyptianesque caryatids in the form of sideways-facing busts which support the lintel. Above this the tower has four small, slightly bulging corner turrets which end in pinnacles. Between the pinnacles is a cylindrical drum flattened on four sides with a recurrence of the pylon motif used at the ends of the aisles enclosing a completely black opening. The drum is topped with a cylindrical peristyle which has columns in the shape of fat corn-shocks or shaving brushes. Finally the dome is like a long-drawn-out policeman's helmet with a kind of sugar castor at the top, for which the inspiration appears to be Hindu.[17]

[16] Graham Law writes that 'it is as if a Gothic church had been Grecianized by building the clerestory and nave roof as a Greek temple, with porticos on the gable ends and the rest of the church as a base, with the triforium expressed as a subordinate mass along the side'. But the basic shape is also that of Vitruvius's Egyptian Hall, which had been used by Burlington for the York Assembly rooms early in the eighteenth century. [Conceivably the pylon motif might have been suggested by the choragic monument of Thrasyllus, which Thomson could have found illustrated in the second volume of Stuart and Revett's *Antiquities of Athens*.

Though the St Vincent Street church looks outwardly very different from Caledonia Road, the fascinating (but unsuccessful) competition design of 1858 for St Mary's Free Church, Edinburgh, of which the original perspective is now in the Glasgow School of Art (see McFadzean pl.81, where the design is incorrectly identified as for St George's), shows how the later church grew out of the earlier. A comparative study of the towers and of the absorption of the portico into the upper storey is especially instructive.]

[17] The steeple of St George's Tron Church and the dome of the asylum are also possible inspirations.

111. Holmwood, Netherlee Road, Cathcart (1856).

It is all – intentionally of course – very odd, Thomson's most extravagant and capricious display of the heterogeneous motifs which continued to fascinate him all his life.[18]

The interiors of both churches are in marked contrast to the huge solidity of the exteriors. For roofs and galleries are supported on slender cast-iron columns, the galleries being incorporated into what Professor Hitchcock rightly calls interior architecture (no mere galleried hall). Caledonia Road only had a gallery at one end, on two slim columns with foliated capitals; but in St Vincent Street (whose inside may not be all Thomson's work) the gallery goes round three sides, as it did at Queen's Park; and at the south end a great set piece is made, with a huge preaching desk, behind which the organ is incorporated into a symmetrical design with pediments at each end, Egyptian doorways and much use of Egyptian detail in akroteria and incised carving. In front the seats are banked in a curve as in a theatre: the prototype was probably the hall of Thomas Hamilton's Edinburgh High School.[19]

Thomson's houses and villas, of which he probably built a large number, are at present very poorly documented. The earliest of all seem to have been 'cottages ornés' in a free, picturesque Gothic, many of which remain near Kilcreggan. In Glasgow (perhaps influenced by his partner and brother-in-law, John Baird 'No.2') he early favoured the *Rundbogenstil* also used by Schinkel for villas, with small, round-headed windows with deep reveals, arches and flattish roofs and gables. Possibly a number of houses in Pollokshields are by Thomson:[20] 'The Knowe' (301 Albert Drive) certainly is. It seems to have been built about 1853. The composition of Romanesque windows, deep-eaved, wide gables, a squat tower and a nearly free-standing porch of columns and arches, is loose and picturesque. Yet a few years later this formula, identical in principle save that there is now no porch, was used for the most complex but highly organized of all Thomson's villas, Holm-

[18] Many of these details had been anticipated by the early nineteenth-century New England architect Minard Lafever, some of whose churches appear strikingly Thomsonesque. It seems unlikely, however, that there could have been any direct influence. William Strickland's Presbyterian Church at Nashville, Tennessee has an Egyptian frontispiece which may be contrasted with that of Thomson's nearly contemporary Queen's Park.

[19] A special note should be made of the admirable tenements which in each case have been incorporated into the design of the adjoining church: 37–39 Cathcart Road is the most striking.
[All have now been destroyed.]

[19a] But now see McFadzean, *op. cit. passim.* A number of Thomson's villas are included in the admirably illustrated *Village and Cottage Architecture* published by Blackie in 1868 etc.

[20] Claims are made in Partickhill also: there is a villa in the *Rundbogenstil* at No.74 Partickhill Road; but the detail is wrong. This style is also used in Thomson's recently demolished Pollok School annexe, 2097 Pollokshaws Road (1856).

[20a] Dr. McFadzean has found that Thomson made extensive additions in 1855–6. *Op. cit.* pp.33ff.

192

202

wood, in Netherlee Road, Cathcart (1856–8, now the Convent of Our Lady of the Missions), **111**. Here again is a façade of two gables, the right-hand one lower than the other, joined by a yet lower flat 'hyphen', above which is the tower, now a circular drum, glazed all round between square columns and standing on a square block of masonry. The design is further extended by including a stable block, to which the house is joined by a long wall. Like The Knowe, Holmwood is an example of Thomson's habit of building up a complex design by means of small units interpenetrating each other. The great difference, however, between the two houses is that whereas in the earlier the small windows are simply punctuations in solid walls, at Holmwood the glazed colonnades articulate and relate the whole façade. The horizontal emphasis given by low roofs, flat gables and long walls produces an effect similar to that of houses built early this century by Frank Lloyd Wright. But the window design and its elaborate use as the co-ordinating element of the whole house are Thomson's own. Nearly all Thomson's asymmetrical villas build up from right to left – whether their style is Greek, Romanesque or Gothic (and the same is true in a modified way of Caledonia Road), **110**. Another exceptionally interesting example is roughly contemporary with Holmwood – the double villa at 25 Mansionhouse Road, Langside (1856), **109**. This has only one gable on each façade, projecting from it

112. 200 Nithsdale Road, Pollokshields (1871).

113. Ironwork railings on Great Western Terrace.
114. (opposite) Great Western Terrace (1869).

21 See p.124. [The semi-circular bow window to the parlour at Holmwood is in fact contemporary.] Professor Pevsner thinks that Thomson must have had access to a copy of Ledoux's *Architecture*, from which the flat gables with colonnaded windows would have come.

21a 'Light-hearted' is not after all the word for Ellisland (200 Nithsdale Road): though the other adjectives may stand, there is always a solemnity about even the most freely inventive of Thomson's designs.

22 Big Ionic columns appear also in the hallway of each house as an inner screen.

23 For this question see Summerson, *Architecture in Britain 1530–1830*, p.231. Two-storey terraces always have been specially difficult to handle, particularly where (as so often) they are very long. In Baltimore are terraces, approximately contemporary with late Thomson, continuous for nearly half a mile with no interruption except small flights of steps to the doorways.

and with a square bay on the ground floor projecting still further. The rear elevation is an exact replica of the front, the two houses being most ingeniously fitted together with reversed plans. The villa contains Thomson's first experiment of a load-bearing colonnade from which the glazing is entirely separate.[21] If anything, the articulation of the façade by the fenestration is even more marked here than at Holmwood; in both, Thomson's terrace style is already clearly formulated on a small scale: one can see the gables turning into the pavilions of Moray Place (which may perhaps have been designed as early as 1857). A further point of interest about Mansionhouse Road is the porch, a huge chunk of masonry set into the re-entrant angle made by the projecting section of the façade, moulded in a way that looks forward to Mackintosh.

The interior of Holmwood is exceptionally fine, a rich display of free 'Greek' ornament and bold colours, with blue and gold predominant, and brimming over with original ideas such as top-lighting of the sideboard in the dining-room (now ingeniously adapted for the altar). An equally fine but no longer complete interior was at one of Thomson's rare symmetrical villas, No.200 Nithsdale Road, **112**. This entrancing *jeu d'esprit* seems not to fit into any category whatsoever, though its weird fantasy may be seen as a prevision of the inclination among some architects of *c*.1900 to make stone as much like vegetation as possible: the columns at the entrance suggest above all bulging tree trunks. (Even so the outline remains hard: the stone does not appear to deliquesce, as with Gaudi.) The house needs a setting a little more exotic than the Glasgow climate can allow it, though its owners have done their best. The whole design is irrepressibly gay, happy and light-hearted without being frivolous.

The terraces are at least as varied as the houses. Each is a completely individual answer to an individual problem: Thomson never automatically applied solutions that he had found elsewhere, for the new situation demanded a new approach from the start. Of the most famous of them all perhaps the least need be said. Great Western Terrace (1869) is normally taken as a typical example of Thomson's Greekness, **114**. Yet the true Greek appears only in the porches which regularly punctuate the smooth ashlar façade, a façade in which the proportion of window to wall is markedly less than was Thomson's habit.[22] As the terrace is basically two-storeyed over a low basement (largely concealed by the area railings), the 'classical' proportions of the three-storey terraces do not hold.[23] Only the pavilions are three-storeyed, and they stand not at the ends but six bays in from each end. There can be no doubt that this gives a much better balance to the very long terrace (which, again, must be seen in perspective) than the normal Glasgow solution of pavilions at the end and perhaps a higher centrepiece: since the lower section appears to continue *through* the slightly projecting higher ones, there is less tendency for the eye to feel the central section as sagging – the terrace is braced by the pavilions. Windows throughout are as plain as they could be – no cornices, no projecting jambs or lintel: only the wide corbelled eaves and the delicate iron railings, **113**, relieve the severity of this magisterial, almost haughty building. But its superb sense of scale and proportion raises it above all the other terraces in the road.

By comparison Moray Place (built in 1859 but probably designed earlier) is quite tiny, with only two storeys throughout, **115**. Yet it is even more elo-

quent; and it is in relation to such a design that it becomes most misleading to talk, with Professor Hitchcock, of Thomson's remaining in his domestic work 'closer to the conventional norms of the Greek revival than in his churches'.[24] Professor Hitchcock goes on to call Moray Place 'the finest of all Greek terraces'. Yet in what sense is it Greek? True it has pediments, and these stand above an entablature which rests on four giant pilasters, so that the whole might be taken as a residuary portico.[25] But this is not in any real sense a portico: it stands not in the centre but on a pavilion, its axis at right angles to the main block. The unbroken row of square stone mullions on the upper may, if one so desires, be described as a colonnade (and thus echoes a similar usage in Schinkel). But they are not Greek columns, and they do not become Greek by calling them *antae*: they are oblong blocks of stone with only the ghost of a capital incised with a tiny key-pattern. The essentially un-Greek squareness is what tells most emphatically about this 'colonnade' – that and the way in which it stands out not from a wall containing windows, but from apparently continuous glass: this is no longer a row of engaged columns, for there is nothing for them to be engaged to. (Note the way in which the row is made continuous, and as unvarying as possible, by recessed stone panels where divisions between houses make windows impossible.) On the ground floor there is even less of

115. Moray Place, built in 1859 but designed perhaps two years earlier.

24 *Op. cit.*, p.72.
25 Note the resemblance between these end houses and the Dunlop Street warehouse (see below, p.143).

138

the Greek: merely a series of deep oblong holes in the wall for the doors and windows. These do, to be sure, have pilasters, of the same rudimentary kind as the columns above; but the pilasters stand not against the wall but at right angles to it – in the reveals of the doorways and windows. If there was any kind of classical model for Moray Place, it was presumably a stoa – the long open colonnaded hall, for casual or processional use, of which one example has recently been reconstructed in the Athenian agora.[26] But the important point is that the precedent, whatever it was, has been left far behind, or rather so completely absorbed that classical features like colonnades and pediments are only the starting points for the intensely original inventiveness of this unpredictable architect. What counts for the onlooker today is the severe withdrawn serenity of Thomson's building, its simplicity and absence of fuss, the uncanny accuracy of Thomson's eye in judging the proportions of his long façade, the exquisite, near mechanical precision of the incised details on the cornice and panels, **116**.

Moray Place cannot be said to lean heavily on the Greek; the slightly earlier Walmer Crescent (begun in 1857) scarcely appears classical at all, **117**. Here again, the tremendous and nearly unbroken sequence of large square mullions on the top storey may be seen as making up a sort of residual colonnade; but here again, as in Moray Place, there are twice as many windows on

116. The exquisite incised detail of Moray Place: note the direct glazing to the colonnade. The contorted object in the foreground used to be a tree.

[26] The two wings of this have hexastyle porticos, but they are wings, not mere pavilions: they enclose a recessed range whose columns are more widely spaced than those in the wings – not more narrowly as at Moray Place. For a local (though primitive) version of the stoa, see Playfair's Royal Institution at Edinburgh, now the R.S.A. Galleries.

117. Walmer Crescent (1857).

this floor – and hence twice as many 'columns' – as on the ones below: there is no simple, 'classical' vertical articulation from floor to floor. As for the huge two-storey projections which punctuate the façade and link pairs of houses, there seems no possible precedent for these. What on the other hand it may be possible to say is that the square mullions, the rectangular severity (even the apparent curve is in fact made up of subtly angled straight frontages), the sense in the whole design of an overriding mathematical logic, and perhaps, too, the mechanically accurate stone carving, represent a rationalization in terms of an oncoming machine aesthetic of motifs devised and developed in a more humane age. Walmer Crescent is one of Thomson's grandest and most imposing designs,[27] but it is also his most austere and uncompromising, the freest from humanizing detail. Only the idiosyncratic hood-moulds over the first-floor windows (similar to the 'key' motif at St Vincent Street) suggest the humanity of a designer. The rest is authoritative, detached, remote. The fantastic caprice of 200 Nithsdale Road may have been a necessary release from the rigours of Walmer Crescent, or even of Moray Place.[28]

Northpark Terrace, Hamilton Drive (1866) is roughly contemporary with Great Western, **119**; documentary evidence for Thomson's authorship is lacking. We can, however, be perfectly confident, for who else would have been capable of such accuracy and restraint, and above all of such a powerful composition out of so few and such simple elements?[29] This terrace again has a continuous square 'colonnade' on the top storey, with alternating windows and blank panels, though neither is at all so deeply recessed as in Moray Place or Walmer Crescent. In perspective, however, it is the row of columns or mullions which counts – an important point in almost all Thomson's terrace designs, which are not made for the frontal view that is in any case almost never physically possible: this is often the secret of their balance – of why, for example, he avoids the high centrepiece which cannot tell *as a centrepiece* in oblique views.[30] At Northpark Terrace, only in very sharp perspective is the whole visible at once. The first-floor windows make use of the square zig-zag device from the podium of St Vincent Street Church,[31] but here in very flat relief; and the lower horizontals are two thirds of the way up the windows across the intervening stonework, the upper ones continuing to act as lintels. The motif is here treated much more lightly than in the church, with applied dots and an akroterion over each window. The general effect of the terrace is Schinkelesque, though no single detail seems to derive from him. The design is one of Thomson's quietest, with absolutely nothing theatrical about it. Yet it shows his mastery of the relation of detail to mass, of the essential scale of detail in a long continuous façade, as impressively as any.

The last true terrace I shall discuss was once Westbourne Terrace but now has no name of its own – it is merely Nos. 21–39 Hyndland Road (1871), **120**.[32] Here the two upper storeys are recessed; or (another way to put it) the ground floor has a series of square bay windows and porches under a continuous entablature. The porches have Ionic columns close up to the jambs. Above, on the first floor, pairs of tall flat windows alternate with canted bays resting on the cornice of the projecting ground floor (possibly the only time that Thomson used the familiar Glasgow motif of the canted bay). The top storey again has more windows than the storey below – this time in a proportion of five to three – but they are not linked to one another except by a

[26a] Or rather, the ends and the stretches with projections are straight, the intermediate sections being curved on the radius of the overall crescent.
[27] Mr Law (*art. cit.*, p.313) finds it 'rather bald and clumsy'.
[28] Another terrace (84–112 Nithsdale Road) reduces austerity to the point of bleakness, which is confused but hardly lessened by the curious mixture of dark and pale stones on the façade. It was begun about 1873.
[29] Thomson did in fact produce plans for developing this area, though they came to nothing. So the owner of Northpark House must have been a client.
[30] Wilson's Kirklee Terrace miscalculates here, though perhaps when first built it may have been visible from a viewpoint directly in front.
[31] See p.133 and Walmer Crescent, above.
[32] One more should be briefly mentioned: 41–53 Oakfield Avenue (*c.*1865), two-storeyed, with pedimented three-storey pavilions. The glazed colonnades at the ends are familiar from Walmer Crescent and Moray Place, but the main façade is more conventional, except for certain idiosyncratic details.

string-course at sill level. The haphazard dormers are of course later (and unfortunate) additions. This terrace is a more relaxed design than most of the others, less stern, and therefore perhaps a little easier to live with, though the ground floor is eminently characteristic of its author.

These two last terraces have no end pavilions to stop the design (Westbourne has rudimentary pavilions in that at the ends its upper storeys are brought forward to the line of the ground floor of the whole). But there is no doubt that the proportion of length to height has been carefully calculated – again for the perspective view. The same can be said of the most distinguished of Thomson's tenement blocks† – the so-called Queen's Park Terrace, Eglinton Street (1857), **118**. This is, following the normal tenement pattern,[33] four storeys high. Moreover the fact that this is a block of flats, not a row of houses, means that the familiar proportion of windows to one another cannot be maintained: it is no use having those on the top storey the size of the attics in Hyndland Road. The windows do in fact slightly decrease in height from first floor to third (the ground floor is entirely occupied by shops); and the change in height is given false emphasis by the changing treatment of the window surrounds – on the first floor aedicules with slender columns and substantial cornices; on the second lighter, with drip-moulds and akroteria, once again making use of the square zig-zag now reduced to a

[33] See chapter 9. Thomson reached his mature tenement formula in 1856 in the Caledonia Road group.

118. Queen's Park Terrace, Eglinton Street (begun 1857).†

119. Northpark Terrace, Hamilton Drive (1866).

barely noticeable string-course. On the top floor the windows have no surrounds of their own though they are linked by a string course at sill level; but near the top of the panels between them the stonework is recessed, leaving small incipient columns adjacent to the windows which carry a very slightly projecting band of plain masonry. A light shadow is thus cast along the length of the building, so that the band of stone acts as a primitive crowning entablature to the whole block. There is no horizontal variation along the whole considerable length, apart from a slight widening of the very end bays and chamfered corners. As the perspective view is the only one obtainable, one does not read the vertical bays as individual units: though the verticals are strongly emphasized (the windows are unusually tall and narrow), the horizontals, by force of the perspective, are what really tell; and the block is saved from monotony by the handsome proportion of height to length (a ratio in fact rather greater in Queen's Park Terrace than in Westbourne, despite its much greater length). Lamentably this excellent block has now been declared beyond repair. How many fine things we seem likely to lose through lack of care or foresight!

Thomson very probably built a number of other tenements on the south side: one at Gorbals Cross† deserves particular mention for its use of a difficult corner site, and for the vertical articulation of the windows by means of continuous masonry strips. This last seems to be a device used to prevent the top-storey windows from appearing awkwardly large (they are about the same size as those below), by asking the eye to read the first- and second-floor windows together as single units.[34] Unfortunately this effect is now completely ruined by the crude painting which at present splits the building horizontally in two above the first-floor windows. It must in any case have been a difficult point to grasp visually, since owing to the shape of the Cross, this is one of the few Thomson buildings which one can, and normally does, see in full face, so that the dark voids of individual windows appear as the

[33a] In fact the treatment of the second floor is identical with that of the first floor of Northpark Terrace.

[33b] Alas, after much debate and despite an admirable scheme for rehabilitation by the Pollokshaws Housing Association, Queen's Park Terrace was demolished in 1980–1 when the façade had been so ruined by water penetration that it would have required almost complete replacement.

[34] Compare the warehouses in James Watt Street described on p.105.
See McFadzean, pl.157.

33a

33b

120. Westbourne Terrace, Hyndland Road (1871).

³⁴ᵃ The date of this range (which was demolished in 1974) has been much in dispute; but now, thanks to the researches of Mr. R. S. G. Nicol (who has recently completed a structural survey of the Buck's Head building and generously shared his discoveries with us), it is possible to be fairly confident that its construction in fact post-dates the Buck's Head itself, to which it seems to have been added, probably in 1864, after the whole site had come into single ownership. (A small building *had* been put up in 1849, on the site of No. 1 Dunlop Street; but it was an annexe to the old hotel building and was pulled down with the rest in 1863.) The large number of flues in the building which survived until 1974 must be explained by its having been designed originally as a combined warehouse and tenement. The conservative treatment of the façade, which contrasts strikingly with that of the corner block and prompted the attribution of an early date, may imply the re-use or adaptation of an earlier design (in detail it is close to Moray Place and in overall design to the Washington Hotel of 1857–8: see fig. 128(d)); but it is plain that, though we may arrange Thomson's warehouse designs in a sequence to 'demonstrate' increasing unconventionality and experiment, this would not in fact correspond with the chronology.

³⁵ See p.150.

³⁶ Direct glazing of this kind had been used by Isaiah Rogers in Boston (Massachusetts) in 1843; but the only previous instance in Scotland was on Archibald Simpson's only slightly earlier New Market in Aberdeen.

obvious visual units. The execution of the design is faulty and may be the work of a builder carelessly following a Thomson sketch.

It was said before that Thomson was essentially an architect of the south side of Glasgow. The one field in which this cannot be true is his commercial work. Thomson's series of warehouse and office buildings is the greatest contribution made by a single architect to the centre of the city, with the possible exception of J. J. Burnet. The dating of some of these buildings is still in doubt. The chronological account attempted here must therefore be regarded as tentative, though stylistically the order proposed seems at the moment the only possible one.

The earliest authenticated Thomson building dates from the very start of his commercial practice. This is the rear (Dunlop Street) portion of the Buck's Head Building,† so called from the inn whose site it occupies, **121**. The date is 1849, the design not yet very adventurous, and the influence of Hamilton marked, particularly in the relation of the pilastrades on the first and second floors, which can be compared with 151–155 Queen Street.³⁵ These two floors are treated as a single unit, in that a giant order encloses them both (as also at Gorbals Cross). But there is now direct glazing to the pilasters on the second floor, where Hamilton had always inserted a subsidiary pilastrade or at least independent jambs.³⁶ The top storey stands on a big cornice and consists simply of oblong glazed holes alternating with plain ashlar with some idiosyncratic detail at the top. Above another cornice stands a row of akroteria, which perhaps derives from the Royal Exchange and would give an appearance of castellation, were it not for the dormers which have later (it is said) been inserted between them.

There is then no securely datable design for a decade, except for the unadventurous one in Howard Street (recently demolished) – until the Grosvenor Building, 68–80 Gordon Street, **125**, designed in 1859, built in

34a

121. (left) 7-11 Dunlop Street (1864),†
note the subsidiary pilastrade on the
first floor and direct glazing on all the
upper floors.
122. (right) Bath Street in about 1908.
The building in the foreground is the
Mechanics' Institute (James Salmon,
senior, 1861) with Thomson's Bath
Street warehouse (1860) beyond.

1860 as a speculative venture, which was owned and let by Alexander and
George Thomson and was a liability to them all their lives.[37] Here the vertical articulation of first and second floors is less marked, for though the giant
order of pilasters remains, the subsidiary pilastrade on the first floor has
been pulled out to form a series of small aedicules, whose entablatures both
jut out enough to establish an extra horizontal line and actually cut into the
width of the pilasters. One is therefore more likely to read this part of the
façade as a row of single-storey pilasters which grow out of the window
divisions below them. The second-floor cornice is especially heavy, and above
it now is a primitive eaves gallery supported on elaborate and heavy consoles
with direct glazing immediately behind. The general effect of this building
is less coherent than that of the previous one, perhaps because there is too
much incident on the façade, whose main and subsidiary structural elements
are not clearly distinguished. And of course the grotesque Greco-Baroque
top-hamper added by J. H. Craigie in 1907 adds to the general confusion.

An exceptionally interesting development of the Grosvenor design appeared about 1860 at No.42 Bath Street: it has unfortunately long been
demolished, its place being taken by an extension of the doubly wretched
Corporation Transport Offices. It was once again four storeys high, with
the window system of Queen's Park Terrace at first and second floors with
the familiar square zig-zag over the second-floor windows, the akroteria
being here one over each horizontal. From behind them at third floor grew
the columns of the Grosvenor Building, but here the glazing is pushed back
to form a continuous window-band free of the columns – a commercial ap-
plication of the glazing system of Holmwood. Above this again was a sloping skylight running the full length to light the attic. This warehouse was
probably the most adventurous of Thomson's commercial designs, **122**.   37a

In 1863 comes the Argyle Street section of the Buck's Head; and this represents a quite new development, **124**. For it is an iron-frame building, and the

[37] The money paid for the site by the
Thomsons financed St Vincent Street
Church, whose congregation had previously
met in Gordon Street. The building was
burnt in 1864 and immediately rebuilt
to the same design.
[37a] A measured elevation is given in
McFadzean, pl.98.

37b The structural implications of this account need to be modified. Dr. McFadzean asserts that 'the walls are constructed of masonry strengthened with cast-iron beams and columns which are concealed within their thickness. The external columns are purely decorative and only support the iron balcony which is also ornamental' (*op. cit.*, p.145). Mr. Nicol's survey (see note 34a above) has shown this to be incorrect. In brief the ground floor had a row of very large circular cast-iron columns (some of which remain): from their tops flanges parallel with the front carry the ground-floor lintels and very large flanges at right angles carry the first-floor pilastrade which is of stone, probably without reinforcement. The second-floor pilastrade is of wood into which cruciform iron stanchions are bedded. The exposed outer iron columns are spigoted at their bases into the ground-floor columns

123. The free-standing iron stanchions of the Buck's Head in front of a wood-encased iron frame above masonry columns.

main part of the façade consists of an exposed free-standing cast-iron frame (cased in wood), with additional slender iron shafts which run up to a wrought-iron balcony, **123**. Glazing is now direct to the iron frame; and so on two storeys we have a façade as nearly glass-fronted as possible, at least before the curtain-walling of the twentieth century was devised. The ironwork and glazing have slight affinities with Peter Ellis's famous and nearly contemporary Oriel Chambers in Liverpool, though the Glasgow building has a less-marked vertical emphasis and its detail is less fastidious. It is interesting that the problem of the corner, which is the least satisfactory feature of Ellis's design, has simply been shelved by Thomson: there is no true corner, just a quadrant occupying three bays of the façade. It is a pity that the building is not symmetrical about this quadrant, for what seems evidently designed as a central feature when seen from the diagonally opposite corner of the cross-roads is in fact off centre, though the present owners, having completed the ruination of the ground floor, have done their best by painting part of the Dunlop Street range to link it with its neighbour. The treatment of the attic storey, carried on the double iron stanchions below, is not very successful. Here there is a development of the eaves gallery theme from the Grosvenor; but the iron stanchions are now encased in thick, though tapering square masonry columns, which look much

124. (left) The Buck's Head, Argyle Street (1863).
125. (right) Grosvenor Building, Gordon Street (designed 1859), a photograph taken about 1895 before the huge top storey was added.
The tall block on the left is James Thomson's Standard Life Building as originally built in 1890.

just below sill level. They have no part in supporting the second-floor load; but the massive stone attic is carried jointly by the cruciform stanchions and the exposed ones: it is still not clear whether the two sets are jointed at the top. A horizontal iron ring holds the corner stiff with frames between the stanchions and subsidiary ones slotted into the angles of the cruciform columns. The use of lattice girders made according to McConnel's patent made possible a remarkably daring structure: the girders are bedded into the pilastrade at second-floor and attic levels. The glazing is of course not direct to the iron frame but to its immediate cladding. The motif of the free-standing iron columns probably derives from Thomas Hamilton's 93 George Street, Edinburgh.
37e In fact wedges of stone project backwards from the columns to provide hidden mullions for the glazing.

too heavy for the slender uprights below: it is almost as if Thomson has forgotten that this is an iron-frame building, and not one with load-bearing masonry columns, or as if he wanted to show off the strength of the frame by pretending that it carries a solid stone top (as indeed it possibly does). There seems at any rate some confusion of aim.

An interesting forerunner of the Buck's Head is an unexecuted design for a warehouse in Howard Street, dating from before 1853. This too would have been an iron building, three storeys high, the two lower storeys operating on a very wide frame with subsidiary iron mullions, the top having another almost continuously glazed colonnade, 126. There was to have been a nearly cylindrical cornerpiece with a flat conical cap; but the client appears to have been afraid of structurally so adventurous a design, and the executed building is fairly orthodox Greek.

The 'Grecian Building', 336–56 Sauchiehall Street, follows next, a partial return to the principle of the Grosvenor façade, 127. The scale is modest – only three storeys – and the two upper storeys represent a telescoping of the upper three of the Grosvenor with the Bath Street treatment of the eaves gallery. Here the first-floor pilasters turn into columns, or the top-floor columns grow out of the wall-spaces between the windows. As at Bath Street the columns are completely free-standing, the glazing of the top floor set well back, and the gallery thus forced outside the cladding. Despite the building's name, the columns are Egyptian. The end bays and side elevations are treated differently – no gallery, and two first-floor windows gathered together to make a single large feature; for unlike Thomson's other warehouses the Grecian Building is not part of a continuous street elevation and must therefore have a convincing corner. As with all the others, however, the original ground floor has been destroyed; and in this case the shop-fronts are among the nastiest in the city.

37c

**126. Unexecuted design for a
warehouse in Howard Street (c.1851).**

**126. Unexecuted design for a
warehouse in Howard Street (c.1851).**

[38] Three other buildings should be
mentioned here for the sake of completeness.
Cowcaddens Cross (1872)† is a three-storey
convex crescent whose stone and glass front
conceals a cast-iron frame; the former
Blackie printing works in Stanhope Street†
(1871) uses Schinkelesque details in a
manner more characteristic of Thomson's
domestic than of his commercial work;
No.99 West Nile Street is similar and
similarly modest but has continuous glazing
on the top floor. It was long thought to be
Thomson's own, but seems now to be an
early imitation by John Gordon (1858).
[No: it is quite definitely by Thomson, as
Dr. McFadzean has shown.]

[39] See p.115.

[39a] This capital-cum-console (another form
of which appears on the second floor of the
Buck's Head) is probably again derived from
Thomas Hamilton, whose National Gallery
design Thomson would certainly have known.
Despite his never having built there, Thomson
would be familiar with Edinburgh architects
through the Architectural Institute of
Scotland, the importance of which as a
meeting-place for the principal architects in
Edinburgh, Glasgow and Aberdeen has
hitherto not been sufficiently appreciated.

[40] The pilasters on first and second floors
are in principle similar; for the triple ones
can be looked on as pairs with a third slotted
into the space between them.

The last warehouse of real note is the Egyptian Halls, 84–100 Union Street (1871–3),**129**: its contrast with its predecessors is most remarkable.[38] The advance toward a complete co-ordination of the whole façade, both horizontally and vertically, is so marked in Bath Street that it is astonishing to find it abandoned for a seeming reversion to an earlier type where the horizontal divisions are extremely strong and vertical links quite absent. Yet here too there is daring experimentation. Though only on the top floor is the colonnade, as in Bath Street and Grecian Buildings, free-standing, the lower floors are no longer masonry walls pierced with window openings but colonnades apparently engaged to a continuous glass wall. Hence, though naturally the columns are vertically, as well as horizontally, aligned, each colonnade has its own entablature, with uninterrupted cornices, so that the columns in no way grow out of those below. The principle of the façade has indeed something in common with that of Paisley's Warehouse;[39] but where that design is identical on each of the three upper floors except for very slight changes in height, Thomson has endeavoured in Egyptian Halls to make his three main horizontal divisions as different as possible. Above the usual horrible shop-fronts (contrast their original appearance in fig.**129**) the first floor has a row of triplicated pilasters in Michelangelo's Farnese manner, though here, instead of being set against a wall, they appear to be units in a free-standing colonnade, so deeply set are the windows which occupy all the space between. (In fact there is nothing that could properly be called a masonry wall in the whole façade: rather what we have is a series of superimposed, load-bearing colonnades.) The middle one of each of these trios of pilasters has a kind of fanciful curlicue capital which spreads to cover all three, and indeed almost meets its next-door neighbours, so as to form a kind of arch over the windows.[39a] Above these is an architrave with incised fretwork ornament and a cornice (with tiny rudimentary akroteria) which is the sill for the next colonnade: coupled square pilasters this time,[40] with a more conventional entablature again providing the sill for the one above, which is strangest and (in appearance) heaviest and most massive of all – very squat and fat round columns with exaggerated entasis, standing well clear of the glass wall, so that the eaves gallery is a walkway behind the supporting colonnade but

127. Grecian Building, Sauchiehall
Street (1865).

127. Grecian Building, Sauchiehall
Street (1865).

outside the cladding of the building – all this is similar to, but bolder than,
the equivalent in the Grecian. The gigantic entablature, itself as deep as the
height of the squat columns that support it, is made to appear yet bigger by
the deep shadow cast on the glass wall: it has a preliminary cornice with a
row of small akroteria, then tiny incipient columns of its own, and finally a
great overhanging cornice, itself topped with yet more akroteria. Above
again, though invisible from the street, is another of Thomson's continuous sloping skylights.

Egyptian Halls is one of Thomson's most fantastic inventions and represents an aspect of his creative imagination very far removed from the
rigid logic of Walmer Crescent or Great Western Terrace, or indeed from the
Bath Street warehouse. But the same devotion to detail of a machine-like
precision is in them all. Egyptian Halls may go Egyptian on its top storey.
But behind those unpredictable columns are the machine-made metal frames
of the windows. Thomson appears to have been an architect whose skill and
inventiveness looked forward to the method of mechanical mass-production
of our own day. And there are buildings of his which seem to go a long way
towards demonstrating the ultimate in the elimination of human differences.
At the same time we have not only the abandon of Nithsdale Road, or the
St Vincent Street steeple, but the refusal to give up human, even quirky
details on his most serious buildings. These do not always come off. The
peculiar triumph of Egyptian Halls is to combine a sense of personal style
unexcelled by any other Scottish architect with the detachment from mere
idiosyncrasy which not only gives the building a compelling visual logic of its
own but makes it so convincing a part of the street and city in which it
stands.

There remains one more office block, said to be Thomson's, though not
completed until two years after his death. This is 87–95 Bath Street,† which
certainly looks Thomsonesque, but represents a complete abandonment of
all his commercial experiments, and returns to the simple load-bearing masonry wall pierced with 'openings'.[41] Presumably this is a case of an obdurate
client. The development from 1849 to 1875 may be summarized as follows, 128.

[41] It is worth noting that this building
has a masonry ground floor. One suspects
that Thomson disliked the weight of plain
walls bearing down on ground-floor voids,
and that with a solid ground floor he felt
it less necessary to avoid them.
[It is now known for certain that the design
was Thomson's: it was already half-built by
the time of his death in 1875.]

128. The development of Thomson's warehouse style: these are not drawn to scale, but to a uniform second-floor cornice line to show mutations of design more clearly: (g) is in fact larger than the others.

(a) David Hamilton (?), 151–7 Queen Street. Giant pilastrade with subsidiary first-floor pilastrade. Orthodox fenestration at second.

(b) c. 1849(?) Warehouse, north-east corner, Glasgow Cross (destroyed). Superimposed pilastrades on first and second floors. Original ground floor not known.

(c) Alexander Thomson 1864. Dunlop Street Building. Giant pilastrade with subsidiary pilastrade, area between pilasters at second floor fully glazed. Top-floor design frequently adopted for tenements.

(d) Alexander Thomson, 1858 or later, Washington Hotel, Sauchiehall Street (destroyed). Giant pilastrade with subsidiary pilastrade at first floor, dwarf pilastrade at third.

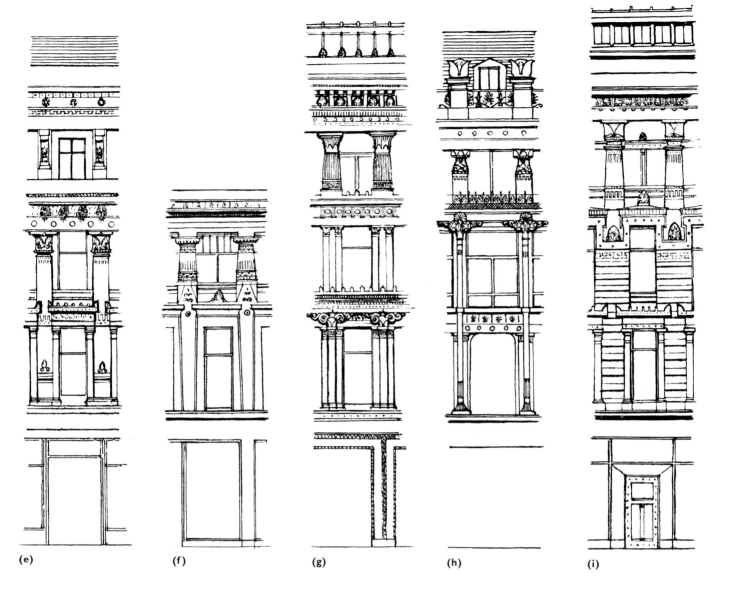

(e)   (f)   (g)   (h)   (i)

(e) Alexander Thomson, 1859. Grosvenor Building. Giant pilastrade with aedicules at first floor, consoles at third.

(f) Alexander Thomson, 1865. Grecian Building, Sauchiehall Street. Egyptianizing architraval openings replace aedicules; 'piers' between become dwarf columns at second floor.

(g) Alexander Thomson, 1871–3. Egyptian Halls, 84–100 Union Street. Highly developed synthesis of all previous designs. Dwarf colonnade at third floor; complex pilastrade scheme at first and second; superimposed coupled anta pilastrades with additional bracketed pilastrade slotted into the interstices at first floor. Note that end pilasters (not shown) run through from first to second floor without entablature, and resemblance of bracket capitals to cast-iron ones in (h).

(h) Alexander Thomson, c.1863. Buck's Head Building, 63 Argyle Street. Continuation of the 1864 Dunlop Street Building. Double stanchion iron frame, innermost stanchions wood-clad, outermost treated as giant order; masonry third floor. Tapered capitals occur also in end bays of (f) (not shown). Original ground floor not known.

(i) Alexander Thomson, 1860. Cairney Building, 42 Bath Street (destroyed). As executed; differs slightly from elevation published in 1872. Enriched version of tenement designs at first and second floors. Third-floor piers free of glazing for the first time in commercial designs. Note similarity of aedicules and piers to those of (e).

129. Egyptian Halls, Union Street
(1871–3): a late nineteenth-century
photograph showing the original shop
fronts, all of which have now vanished;
the present ones are disgraceful.

1859:
Grosvenor Building, Gordon Street. Subsidiary pilastrade has been pulled out as a row of aedicules. There is now an eaves gallery supported on consoles.
1860:
Bath Street (demolished). Tenement and warehouse themes combined with square columns and free glazing behind, but no walkway.
1863:
Buck's Head, Argyle Street. Eaves gallery now has tapered square columns. First and second floors have exposed iron frame (lightly encased in wood) with direct glazing, and additional free-standing iron stanchions.
1864:
Dunlop Street. Hamilton-type relation of pilastrades on first and second floors, except for direct glazing at the second.
1865:
Grecian Building, Sauchiehall Street. Eaves gallery with circular columns.
1871–3:
Egyptian Halls, Union Street. Pilastrade theme developed further with subsidiary pilastrade pulled out in front of giant one. Top storey as at Grecian Building with completely free glazing behind detached colonnade.
1875:
87 Bath Street. All themes given up, presumably at insistence of client. Building without marked individuality, except for details of door, etc. Proportions of wall to windows reminiscent of Great Western Terrace.

An observation by Campbell Douglas (obviously of Thomson) is worth recording in conclusion: 'In my experience I have only known one man who confined himself to one style, and if his proposed employers insisted on building in a different style, why, then, he let them go elsewhere. That architect was a great man, who probably made less money that some others did, but he left behind him monuments more worthy of his genius.'

Chapter 7   **The Later Classicists**

Thomson had a number of imitators, but, it hardly needs saying, no real successor. For the moment, the more superficial elements of his style, which mean nothing by themselves but can easily be copied, were very fashionable. All pediments now had to have akroteria; incised ornament or 'chip carving' (usually Egyptian) was everywhere. Yet Thomson was, to start with, a more potent and more serious influence than this imitation would suggest. And through him the still beneficial influence of Schinkel continued to be felt. Indeed Schinkelism was taken to its most extreme in Glasgow two or three years after Thomson's death by the most able of his immediate followers, James Sellars. Kelvinside Academy (1877) is, it must be confessed, rather a frigid building, **130**: in this, however, it is well within the Scottish school tradition. The main building is two-storeyed, quite long, rather coarse, with slightly projecting pavilions; the windows, mere oblong holes with a ghost of a Thomson pilastrade showing, are frowningly severe. But in the middle of the composition is a very odd device: a somewhat higher lateral block, with blind Ionic portico and pediment, sits like a saddle across the main range, the columns resting on a single-storey podium which contains the main entrance.[1] This really has nothing to do with the design of the long block, which appears to go straight through the lateral one; yet the effect, though surprising, is not incongruous, for the façade is altogether very well balanced, the height of the centrepiece being nicely calculated in relation to the total length. The formula of Kelvinside is similar to that of Thomas Hamilton's Royal High School at Edinburgh, which had given Thomson his theme of interpenetrating temple shapes (see his unsuccessful entry in the South Kensington competition, illustrated in Law's article). But Sellars has combined Hamilton and Thomson, and his design, lacking the colonnades which explain the placing of the central temple, lacks also the complete coherence of Hamilton's.

Sellars was an eclectic architect, open to any style that suggested itself or was suggested to him; but he seems temperamentally to have been a classicist, though this has been obscured by the unlucky fate of several of his most important buildings. The Queen Insurance Building in St George's Place (c.1877), **131**, containing his most extreme use of Schinkelesque forms, survived for only twenty years; it was most remarkable for its giant order of iron columns on the first and second floors, with direct glazing over two storeys, on a theme suggested, no doubt, by the Wylie & Lochhead building of c.1850 (see above, p.114). The City of Glasgow Bank (1878) lasted somewhat longer. It was an admirable design, Renaissance rather than Greek, whose principal feature was a row of giant Corinthian columns on the two main storeys, behind which the seven central bays were deeply recessed: lavish and dignified without being ostentatious, **132**.[2] Recently we very nearly lost completely another Sellars work – and that perhaps his *chef d'œuvre,* the St Andrew's Halls (1873). The interior, with its rich panelling, has gone, destroyed in the disastrous fire of 1962: Glasgow seems particularly prone to loss through fire. The shell, however, remains; and the sensible and proper deci-

1a

[1] The pediment is repeated not only on a small block which crouches at one side, but also on the substantial gateways from the street, which look rather silly standing not in a wall, but an iron railing.

[1a] George Angus's Dundee High School of 1832–4, likewise a derivative of Hamilton's design, likewise lacks the colonnades; but the temple portico is a genuine entrance as Sellars' is not. Cf. the City and County Buildings, p.105 above, and fig.77.

[2] Visitors to Stamford can get a hint of the appearance of this building in the Stamford Hotel, designed by J. L. Bond in 1810; the principle of the façade is identical, though the earlier building is less exuberant. It seems unlikely to have been Sellars's model. Owing to the crash, the bank was never completed. It was to have had a top in the manner of the Glasgow Herald Building.

sion has now been made to house within it the extension that the Mitchell Library has needed for years. The showpiece is the west front, **133**. Here, as in the Bank, a row of giant columns (the shaven Ionic capitals are to be restored) is the dominant feature – longer, higher and prouder than on the Bank. The row in fact runs the length of the façade and recalls the immense columnar front of Schinkel's Altes Museum in Berlin, though now raised above the ground floor. Sellars divides his row into three, the groups of five, nine and five bays being divided by massive square stone piers. The wall in the nine bays of the centre is more deeply recessed than in the pavilions, and its columns therefore stand out from the façade more sharply. Above the colonnade, however, the centre is not emphasized at all, having merely a recessed plain parapet (which was, however, originally intended for a rich sculptured frieze), while the pavilions have a superstructure of a heavy entablature supported on unexpectedly graceful caryatids. One effect of this change of accent seems (remembering once again the importance of the perspective view) to be to throw more emphasis on to the central colonnade;[3] altogether a composition of force, dignity and coherence – perhaps the most extreme example in Glasgow of the use of classical features on a grand scale to a distinctly anti-classic end; for this façade has none of the restfulness of the true classical: it is tense rather than poised.

[2a] Unfortunately it has been found possible to retain only the west façade and three bays of the return elevations; what remains, however, has been handsomely cleaned and restored.

[3] Sellars here is in line with the characteristic neo-classic reluctance to emphasize the centre. Cf. the tendency to bring forward the wings in such a work as Smirke's British Museum or Cockerell's New Ashmolean at Oxford. Thomson on the other hand does make a special point of the centre of his symmetrical temple design for South Kensington.

130. Kelvinside Academy (James Sellars, 1877).

131. (left) The Queen Insurance Building, formerly in St George's Place (James Sellars, c.1877). The (surviving) building on the right is by James Boucher, 1875.
132. (right) The City of Glasgow Bank, Glassford Street (James Sellars, 1878): the top storey was never built, and the building was demolished in 1959.

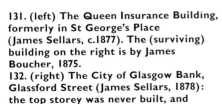

[4] For 24 George Square, see below, p.157.
[4a] Some of the details are nevertheless extremely elegant. The last remains of Sellars' interior went in 1980–1 when the building was redeveloped behind the façade.
[5] Several other churches are Gothic (see chapter 8, pp.174–5).
[6] See p.171.
[7] See p.64n.
[Kelvingrove is now disused and its future very uncertain. Barony North is now Glasgow Evangelical Church.]

Apart from St Andrew's Halls, none of the buildings remaining near the city centre represents Sellars at his best.[4] The restless Renaissance details of the Anderson College of Medicine, 56 Dumbarton Road, which suggests a new departure, are, nevertheless, clumsily and confusingly handled, though this may be the fault of John Keppie, who finished the building in 1889 after Sellars's death. And the New Club (144–6 West George Street, 1878) is frankly perplexing – large, restless and undisciplined, the details (mainly in a post-Thomson vein, though some Frenchified ones, notably the doorcase, may have been suggested by William Leiper's burgh hall at Partick) very mixed and the scales confused: its seemingly pointless asymmetry comes from the recurrent refusal to allow any central emphasis. Much more attractive is Sellars's one classical, or classically inspired, church.[5] This is Finnieston (now Kelvingrove) Parish Church, at the corner of Derby and Bentinck Streets, (1878), 134. It is quite small, its portico only tetrastyle, with a plain entablature and pediment and a single small doorway. Again, Sellars's favourite device of columns *in antis* appears on the sides – this time they are square and coupled, and the windows are deep-set between them. Behind the portico is a squat square tower with an octagonal cupola above: it is all very neat and unassuming.

As a church architect Sellars is probably not the equal of John Honeyman, another eclectic architect whose Lansdowne is one of the best Gothic Revival churches in Glasgow.[6] Barony North Church, 135, which was built in 1878 a little east of the site of the Adam-Robertson building,[7] is a very different matter: a lively, inventive design with Mannerist elements, in particular the row of engaged Corinthian columns with individual entablatures along the sides. These have small figures standing on podia above each separate cornice – an unusual feature in Glasgow, which on the whole does not go in for figure-sculpture until the end of the century, and then in a different manner on the large office blocks. Low, square towers are at each

corner of Barony North, except the north-west where is a bigger tower with a somewhat Hawksmoorish upper storey and a nice octagonal cupola and dome. The detail here is very careful and stylish, and all seems to come from the early eighteenth century with urns and swags of flowers;[8] the tower is the most attractive of its kind in Glasgow. It stands against an unexpected and liturgically dubious apse (which in fact turns out to contain the gallery stair). The design as a whole is not completely lucid, but it is full of charm.

So is Westbourne, very slightly later (1880) and the most lovable of all Honeyman's churches, standing in a delightful leafy enclave behind Great Western Terrace, **139**. It has a tiny pedimented façade on the principle of St Paul's – a shallow portico with two superimposed orders of coupled columns, Ionic below, Corinthian above. The aisles have coupled Ionic pilasters and lean-to roofs which make half-pediments echoing the slope of the main one. Standing well back where the body of the church widens are small square towers with semicircular-headed bell-openings and square onion-domes of a familiar Scottish type. The design is continued at one side into a single-storey hall with three blank arches set between pilasters. The quietness and modesty of the whole design should not lead one to ignore the exceptional refinement of the detail (note the use of banded stonework to tie in the design horizontally) and Honeyman's masterly and delicate sense of proportions. Of all the later churches there is none which shows a surer hand in the management and functioning of classical motifs or a better understanding of the place of classical detail.

For its size Honeyman's principal commercial building is also surprisingly delicate. This is the Ca d'Oro in Gordon Street, built in 1872 as a furniture warehouse, **138**. Its present name records the re-use of a favourite Venetian device which appears on its famous namesake: window tracery whose top is a figure of eight with its lower end open. In Honeyman's building this tracery is continuous along both the principal façades, and it is all in iron and

[8] Compare the chapel of Trinity College, Oxford (by Henry Aldrich, c.1710) for a very similar tower.
[The cupola and dome seem to come from Archer's St Philip's, Birmingham, with its more baroque features straightened out.]

134. (left) Finnieston (now Kelvingrove)
Parish Church (James Sellars, 1878).
135. (right) Barony North Church,
Cathedral Square (John Honeyman,
1878).

8a This entablature design perhaps owes
something to the attic of David Hamilton's
Western Club: see p.84, fig.59.

glass. The two upper storeys are thus covered in the lightest and sunniest
manner; below these is a giant arcade, two storeys high, each bay as wide as
three above – in stone. If only the miserable shop fronts would allow one to
appreciate it, this arcade would give a satisfying solidity of support to a
very substantial building – even including the unhappy mansard attic added
in 1925–6 by J. G. Gillespie.

John Burnet, senior must be included here for want of any more obvious
place. He worked in a variety of idioms surprising even in nineteenth-century
Glasgow; but of his large and uneven output there is reason to mention only
a few items. One of the most curious of these shows Burnet in an unusually
self-denying mood, taking part in the odd composite design of the west side
of George Square, **137**. This was begun by Rochead, who set the style for the
whole range in 1869 with the south portion at the corner of St Vincent
Place, built for the Bank of Scotland. This is in a quite vigorous Barryesque
Italian mode, with a very high ground floor covered in alternating bands
of vermiculation and ashlar, and big segmental pediments over the first-floor
windows. The design of the main frieze and cornice is very restless. Sellars   **8a**
followed in 1874 with the central section, also for the Bank of Scotland. His
design follows Rochead's fairly closely, though the first-floor windows now
have aedicules, and the restless ground floor has the added complication of a
mezzanine storey inserted above the lower windows. A top storey is added
over the main cornice with wide eaves and a hipped roof. Finally at the
north end, and turning the corner into West George Street, Burnet added
the Merchants' House, a wing whose front elevation almost exactly echoes
Rochead's (the side is much freer), so that in the mid 1870s the whole range
formed a single palace design with a higher central section – a larger example of the principle used by Rhind for the Commercial Bank in Gordon
Street. But the symmetry of the George Square range was to some extent
denied by the tall tower added by Burnet to the corner of his part; and in

136. (left) Lanarkshire House, Ingram Street (John Burnet, senior, 1876).
137. (right) The corner of George Square and St Vincent Place: in the foreground the Bank of Scotland (J. T. Rochead, 1869) with, beyond, continuations of the same design by James Sellars, (1874) and John Burnet, senior (1874). On the left James Miller's faience Anchor Building; on the right Queen Street Station.

this respect the outline may recall (at some distance) the town hall at Siena. Since 1907, however, it has all looked very lopsided, for then Burnet's more famous son was given the thankless job of adding another two and a half storeys to his father's portion (a task which he carried out with an uncomfortable columnar treatment), so that now the building goes up in steps from left to right.

Another Italianate design of the same period is that of the former Lanarkshire House, now the courthouse, 191 Ingram Street, 136. This was originally a mansion which was rebuilt in 1841 as a bank by David Hamilton, who gave it a tall portico, the columns from which are now on the front of the Citizens' Theatre. Burnet's façade, which replaced Hamilton's, was built in

138. The Ca d'Oro, Gordon Street (John Honeyman, 1872). The unhappy attic was added by J. G. Gillespie later. The equally discordant shop fascias are alas later still. Now being restored.

1876–9. The two principal floors have a pilastrade and a colonnade. The pilasters and columns are not coupled, but nor are they evenly spaced. Narrow and slightly wider spaces alternate – a characteristic Mannerist device. On the first floor the narrow gaps are filled almost flush to the front surface of the pilasters with banded stonework, the wide ones with direct glazing. On the top floor the windows are deep-set within arches, while the narrow gaps have niches with elaborately sculptured figures by John Mossman. It is a design which very successfully combines dignity and liveliness, and probably owes as much to C. R. Cockerell as to Venice.   8b

Quite different, though also doubtless Italian in inspiration, is the Clydesdale Bank in St Vincent Street (1870–3), **140**. This is Glasgow's most lavish display of ornamental Baroque stonework. The whole façade is devoted to exuberant and lively incident, the energy not concentrated in a few verticals and horizontals but spread opulently over the whole building. Yet it is surprisingly well organized, though unfortunately the three easternmost bays were never built (the *Citizen* newspaper having beaten the bank to the ownership of this end of the site), and the symmetrical design has thus been upset. The controlled treatment of the windows (especially on the top floor) is an important restraining factor, for there is no inert wall anywhere. Columns and pilasters are all coupled or tripled, or a column stands forward between two pilasters. The two broken segmental pediments on the centrepiece are filled with flower carving, and the principal one is flanked by figures, the upper one by spiked urns. The centrepiece projects, but its top storey does not; the one existing pavilion has a squat tower, and its façade is marked off by pairs of detached columns with their own entablatures. All corners are strengthened by additional columns or pilasters. Everywhere is a multitude of different planes; everywhere suggests activity as if there is plenty of energy to spare. The building has an expansiveness unusual in Scottish architecture.[9] Yet its appearance of self-confidence may be to some extent illusory. The energetic accumulation of detail lacks something of the sense of logic and purpose evident in the best work of the true Baroque period; nor has it quite the coherence of, say, Kirkland's splendid Italianate warehouse in Miller Street. At any rate it is

8b The disposition of the sculptured figures and the sharpness of the detail suggest that the younger Burnet, at this stage at the Ecole des Beaux Arts, may have touched up his father's design.

9 Perhaps this is a momentary re-emergence of the spirit that 300 years before blossomed so unexpectedly in the fantasy of Roslyn Chapel. *The Baillie* disappoved of this new departure in Burnet's work: "He is here more of a decorator than an architect. He has left the large lines of the magnificent entablature of the Madeira Court warehouse [1856, destroyed] for petty prettiness of broken pediments, three-quarter columns and mansard roofs." The mansard, if indeed intended, was omitted in execution. [We now know that the original design consisted only of the five right-hand bays (making a smaller symmetrical façade); the enlargement was an afterthought.]

**140. Clydesdale Bank, St Vincent Place
(John Burnet, senior, 1870).
A symmetrical design with added
bays on left. (Photograph taken
before the building of the Citizen
Office in 1889.)**

difficult not to feel that the choice and placing of the ornament on the Clydesdale Bank is somewhat arbitrary: the decision to use this rather than that does not always seem to spring from a coherent principle: the building is perhaps better described as theatrical than dramatic. Yet such a work, taken in a fairly relaxed spirit, can give much pleasure.[10]

While the extravagance of the Clydesdale Bank obviously comes from an unexpected accumulation of details used more sparingly by the architects of the Italian Baroque, Italian influence of another kind was responsible for the nearly contemporary design of the Stock Exchange only a few yards away – Glasgow's only example of municipal Gothic.[11] And as if to emphasize the firm's versatility, its mastery of any and every style, again of almost the same date is Cleveden Crescent (c.1876, well out to the west, behind and above Great Western Road), **141**. This is in no sense a revivalist piece; but nor is it a carefully balanced symmetrical design like most of the good Glasgow crescents; rather a row of identical individual houses arranged on a curve and up and down a slight slope, over which it almost disappears at one end. Each house has a single asymmetrically placed canted bay window in a modified Thomsonesque form and five plain oblong windows on the upper floor. The houses, though only of two storeys, are on the wealthy scale of Great Western Terrace (with more than fifteen rooms each); despite the lack of continuous design from house to house, the crescent has a severe and upright dignity: it is all solidly, unostentatiously sumptuous.[12]

A much earlier work of Burnet's may be used to introduce the important group of late classical churches which demonstrate strikingly the surprising tenacity of the ecclesiastical attachment to antique forms in Glasgow. Elgin Place Church, Bath Street (1856), **144**, has generally been found one of Burnet's most enduringly attractive designs, though it looks, alas, as if the building itself will not be allowed to endure much longer. Like Thomson's churches

[10] Nos.65–75 St Vincent Street, by J. J. Stevenson (c.1890) is surely a child of the Clydesdale Bank design, more restrained, perhaps indeed a bit timid. But the upper storeys, with their segmental pediments, are attractively carefree.

[11] See p.178.

[12] [Mr. Colin Holroyd points out that Cleveden Crescent *is* a symmetrical design: the bays are reversed from left-hand to right-hand half of the crescent and the middle two houses have two bay-windows each. Mr. Holroyd comments that the end houses seal it off nicely; the rise and fall of the land allows the central pair a slight prominence.] The precise authorship of Cleveden Crescent is still in doubt. For while the design has generally been assumed to be the work of Burnet senior, it was apparently noticed when the drawings were last seen thirty years ago that they had metric measurements – which could hardly be accounted for save by their being the work of J. J. Burnet then at the age of 18 getting himself into trim for the École des Beaux-Arts. But the restrained excellence of Cleveden Crescent would be a remarkable achievement even for a Burnet at that age (when one would expect more boyish delight in display of power); and Mr Lochhead suggests that the frequently used one-tenth scale may have been misread.

141. Clevedon Crescent (John Burnet, senior, 1876).

of the 1850s, it uses the temple principle; unlike them it uses almost nothing else. It has no steeple of any kind, and the plain oblong plan is broken only by a lower addition near the west end. For the rest everything follows logically from the great hexastyle Ionic portico at the east end, whose breadth defines the width of the church and whose pediment its roofline: the side walls are blank, except for a row of simply treated oblong windows. The church is in fact an example of the simple form of temple design without the peripheral colonnade but with a big prostyle porch. The south-east view of the Erekhtheion at Athens must have been something like that of Elgin Place, whose small western addition would then act in place of the caryatid porch on the Greek temple. Perhaps indeed the Erekhtheion was the model for Elgin Place, though the columns of the portico of the Scottish building are more widely spaced and not quite so slender, and there is of course nothing to compare with the great north porch of the temple.[13] At all events Elgin Place is the purest example of the neo-classic in Glasgow: the purity of the style is doubtless what makes it so satisfying; the grand interior carries on the splendid simple scale, its austerity refined by the superbly sure but delicate detailing, **143**.

13a

Three churches all using the temple front in one way or another form a late group which, while it is the swansong of Glasgow classicism, shows a lingering spirit of inventiveness even in the re-use of ancient forms. The earliest and most correct is T. L. Watson's Wellington Church in University Avenue (1883), a latter-day Madeleine staring in obvious and prim reproof at the baronial extravagance across the road, **142**. Not of course that Glasgow went in here for the expense and show of a peripteral temple as Paris did: Not that Glasgow ever did this: the purpose of Glaswegian classicism was not to demonstrate the opulence of empire. Nevertheless Wellington is Roman and quite lavish; its huge Corinthian portico may even seem something of a folly. And if it has no peripteral colonnade, it has enormous col-

[13] This north porch may perhaps be seen as an example of the interpenetrating blocks which at the period of Elgin Place and later were a favourite feature of Thomson's work (cf. above, pp.127 and 135). [And compare perhaps H. W. Inwood's St Pancras New Church, London, of 1819–22.] [13a] Elgin Place has now been reprieved with the help of a handsome grant from the Historic Buildings Council. It has been converted into a disco-restaurant.

142. (left) **Wellington Church,
University Avenue**
(T. L. Watson, 1883).
143. (right) **Elgin Place Church**
(John Burnet, senior, 1856), interior.

142. (left) **Wellington Church,
University Avenue**
(T. L. Watson, 1883).
143. (right) **Elgin Place Church**
(John Burnet, senior, 1856), interior.

umns in antis along three quarters of each side wall (an idea perhaps deriving from Sellars's Finnieston Church); one can hardly see these now for the trees, and in any case it is not really possible to believe that they could ever satisfactorily be read as part of the same temple to which the portico belongs, for the hefty ashlar corners of the church will always have been too big an interruption.[14] The interior goes Renaissance on quite a grand scale.

St George's-in-the-Fields, by the brothers Hugh and David Barclay (1886) is rather less solemn, **145**. Like all the rest it has a hexastyle portico, and as at Elgin Place, this is Ionic with sumptuous figure sculpture (by Birnie Rhind) in the pediment; on the other hand, as at Wellington, the body of the church is wider than the portico. The side pilasters are of the simplest, without even capitals. The most interesting departure from classical precedent is in the greater height of the roof than the pediment: from the east, the shape of the pediment appears repeated above and behind by the end of the nave roof, and it is this second 'pediment' which has not only Thomsonesque decorations but the akroteria which one might have expected to find rather on the pediment itself.

13b

The Barclays, or more accurately the more talented and more adventurous Hugh Barclay, are, however, best represented in their schools, of which Glasgow Academy is the most famous and Govanhill and Rutland Crescent perhaps the best. Govanhill (1887), which stands among uninteresting neighbours in Annette Street, is a return to the Renaissance palazzo form, but with a markedly individual treatment of the principal façade, **146**. Thus each end bay on the main floor has not a window but a blank niche; and the whole of the quite low attic storey has for windows square holes punched into the wall and divided into two lights by tiny free-standing Ionic columns. Altogether a handsome, as well as substantial, block. Rutland Crescent (1883)† is more severe, with gaunt, tall windows set in bands of rustication, in a style which may be called squared-off classical, though the windows are more

13b This is yet another church which is now closed and its future in doubt. Its interior, though less spectacular than that of Wellington, has retained its rich stencilled decoration.
14 The arrangement of square blocks flanking the approach stairs below the portico is taken from Wilkins's University College, London.

144. Elgin Place Congregational Church
(John Burnet, senior, 1856).
145. (opposite). St George's in the
Fields (Hugh Barclay, 1886). The last
of the pure Greek churches.
The sculpture is by Birnie Rhind.

strictly utilitarian than this would suggest. It is at any rate a reduction of the classical to its barest outlines, little more than a nod of acknowledgement in the direction of its remote origins. The building is pedimented, long and low and on a very flat curve: it stands next to a graceful curve of houses with Ionic porches and continues their line in a neighbourly fashion. Sellars incidentally was a pupil of the Barclays and greatly influenced his masters. [15]

The last classical church of Glasgow was built as late as 1895–6. This is Langside Hill Church, south of Queen's Park, by Alexander Skirving, the general shape of which clearly comes from St Vincent Street. It is the only one of this late group whose portico is not a true porch but stands high above the street on a great podium of banded stone. The real entrance is under the central three bays of the portico: with its square columns, mere hints of capitals, frieze of small blank circles and rows of akroteria above the cornice, it is frankly imitation Thomson. (Skirving had been Thomson's draughtsman.) The pediment, however, is something new, for it is partly filled not with figure sculpture but with an abstract pattern of projecting squares and rectangles, which give a curiously unfinished effect. Were these bits in fact waiting to be carved later? Again unlike the other later classical churches, Langside Hill has lower side aisles – this too, presumably, a derivation from Thomson. Here they look too much like plain additions to the temple, rather than integral parts of it. At the end, and level with the end wall of the church, they stop not square but in cylindrical drums, in plan about three quarters of a circle, tucked into the re-entrant angle between 'aisle' and 'nave' – a desperate gesture to pull unrelated elements together, for the drums sit very uneasily against the temple front. The side elevations lose any classical pretensions and go Renaissance, with a row of semicircular-headed windows and little pediments near each end. The windows probably derive from Wilson's Queen's Rooms, but are coarse and undistinguished in execution. [16]

15 [For Hugh Barclay see further p.262.]
16 [Were these perhaps suggested by the drum feature worked in by Thomson to one corner of his unexecuted design for St Mary's Free Church, Edinburgh, which is overall a little closer than St Vincent Street to Langside Hill? See p.133 n.6 above and McFadzean, *op. cit.*, pl.81. It is certain that the square blocks in the pediment were for unexecuted sculpture.]

146. (left) Govanhill Public School,
Annette Street, Govanhill
(H. & D. Barclay 1887).
147. (right) Ewing Place Church
(Hugh Barclay 1858): a design of
much strength and originality, alas
demolished a century later.

17 [The massive classicism of the inter-war
years has found recent admirers.]

Though he makes clever use of a difficult, sloping site, it is hard to feel that the architect's heart was really in this somewhat patched-up job. But then how could it be? In the year in which Langside Hill was completed, Mackintosh designed the north wing of the Art School. And if he remained, in his own time, a lone and largely unappreciated genius, the way ahead lay with the kind of experimenting then being done by J. J. Burnet, who had abandoned even his modified Beaux Arts classicism some years before. Classicism had in fact by now turned into little more than a roomy dead end – as was to be shown on a depressing scale by James Miller in the 1920s and 1930s. Alas that none of Thomson's direct successors really knew how to 17 benefit from his example or to understand what he had done to the remnants of the classical tradition. Like all great artists who have inherited a tradition formed in a different context of civilization, Thomson not only absorbed it into himself but adapted it and reformed it into something which could once again be a living and expressive medium. Proportions which have in some sense an eternal validity because they depend intimately on the substantially unchanging shape of the human body can nevertheless find expression in different outward manifestations. When Thomson turned a classical colonnade into a nearly continuous window band divided by stone mullions, he was indeed changing the possibilities of expression for a new generation. But by then the artistic consciousness of the time had become too fragmented to respond.

148. The main front of the University
(begun in 1866 by George Gilbert Scott);
the spire by J. Oldrid Scott (1887).

Chapter 8 Victorian Gothic

For a city which grew so hugely in the nineteenth century, Glasgow has remarkably few buildings of the Gothic Revival, and fewer still of special note. Those that it has suggest that Gothic in its various revivalist forms is somewhat alien to the homogeneous local style which the Victorian architects of the city created. The Gothic inclination which in the south became so prominent in the middle of the century was initially prompted largely by archaeological, literary or liturgical motives. It could hardly be called an essentially architectural movement. But neither Ruskin nor Pugin had much influence in Scotland. When Glasgow churches do go Gothic, they do so with an air of being fairly up to date and in the fashion, though often cocking a snook at the more correct practitioners of the style. It is worth noting that, of the major church architects in nineteenth-century Glasgow, only William Leiper was a consistent Gothicist; most of the other Gothic churches are the work either of men, like Honeyman, equally at home, or of those, like Sellars, rather more so, in totally contrasting styles.

English Victorian Gothic was at the start not only essentially literary in inspiration; it was also a phenomenon generated largely from London, and its chief exponents are either London-bred or London-trained. Few of these did much in Scotland; and in Glasgow the only big English name to be represented by work that could be called major is Scott's. Yet neither of Scott's two large buildings in Glasgow shows him at his best. St Mary's Episcopal Cathedral in Great Western Road (1870, with a good spire by J. Oldrid Scott, 1893) is indeed a frigid affair, uninteresting and coarse in detail, unhappy in its mixture of random stone and ashlar, and poorly sited. It is similar in outline to Scott's much earlier and more famous church of St Giles, Camberwell, though the details come from the early rather than the late thirteenth century, and the tower, instead of being over the crossing, stands in the angle between chancel and transept (a feature appearing also in the contemporary St Mary Abbots, Kensington). At least, however, it looks like a Victorian church instead of like one of Scott's own heavy restorations. The wrongness of scale and material is doubtless the result of a design made from a distant office without thought for the site.

The University, begun a little earlier than the Cathedral, is much more interesting: an ambitious and flamboyant design something in the manner of the municipal buildings then going up in English industrial cities, but – unlike St Mary's – slightly closer to the Scottish than to the English Middle Ages, **148**. Thomson contemptuously dismissed the whole affair as sixteenth-century Scottish architecture clothed in fourteenth-century French details; and indeed Scottish or Franco-Scottish (sometimes baronial) features abound: corner towers with saddleback roofs, round turrets with conical caps, crow-stepped gables, and a huge top-heavy central tower of the type which had few medieval precedents, but seems somehow to have become established in the nineteenth century as distinctively Scottish. The inspiration for the principal façade may indeed be thought rather Flemish than Scottish: the Cloth Hall at Ypres suggests itself as the source for the long horizontal

**149. St Matthew Blythswood
(J. T. Emmett, 1849–52).
150. (opposite) The undercroft of
the Bute Hall of the University
(J. Oldrid Scott, 1878–84).**

1 [The elegance of Emmett's steeple is after
all not surprising and not much to his credit,
for it is an almost exact copy of that of
Pugin's St Giles', Cheadle, finished in 1846.
Emmett seems not to have had much idea of
what he was doing in bringing Pugin's
Catholicism to the Independents of Glasgow.
In the repair of the church the lucarnes and
much else were stripped away to save the
expense of restoration.]

1a Salmon was himself the author of the
much to be lamented St Matthew, Bath
Street (1849),**151** demolished not very long
ago. It was in a delicate and graceful early
Perpendicular style. Wilson produced some
ascetic Early English churches, all of which
have gone.

2 *The Beauties of Clyde*, p.99.

3 'Gothic' is hardly the word for Rickman's
building, which was dictated more by the
current taste for the picturesque than by
any strong grasp of Gothic principles. It is
greatly inferior to his iron churches at
Liverpool. Professor Pevsner draws
attention to its exceptionally early use of
geometrical tracery. The tall proportions
result from Dr. Cleland's insertion of a crypt.

range with big central tower. (The openwork spire of 1887 is an attractive feature – a great improvement by Oldrid Scott on an earlier version of the design which had a heavier spire with gablets and clocks on four sides and extra pinnacles on four corners.) As a whole, however, the University cannot be called a success: though it looks well enough on its height above the Kelvin, especially when seen from a distance, the calculated symmetry of the very long principal front is ill-served by the diminutive scale of just those features which rather weakly insist on the symmetry; and in this it may be contrasted with Ypres: the tower is too high for the long, low ranges on either side, or alternatively these are too long for the tower; there is an uneasy tension between the two. Internally, too, the quadrangles with their numerous gables and their small fiddly windows are pretty gloomy; nor does the baronial style go very happily with the more orthodox Gothic of the central range that divides the two quadrangles, which is again the work of Oldrid Scott (1878–84), **150**. Only this central range is likely to give much pleasure now (though the elder Scott's treatment of the fall of the land to the north and east is skilful). There is indeed enjoyment to be found in the fat, substantial columns of the undercroft, and more particularly in the slender and graceful cast-iron columns and vault of the Bute Hall above. The Bute Hall has been cheered up a lot by its repainting, though it is perhaps doubtful whether the architect himself would altogether have approved of the colours. (It should be remembered in partial exoneration of Gilbert Scott that he was stuck with a layout devised by Baird in the 1840s for a much smaller building.)

Of buildings by other English architects, J. T. Emmett's St Matthew Blythswood (1849), built for an Independent congregation, is certainly the best, with its excellently detailed graceful spire rising to 220 feet among the sober tenements of the west end of Bath Street – a beautiful and much-needed punctuation and landmark which has not been allowed to disappear, **149**. The interior is equally good, in a carefully detailed idiom of the English fourteenth century – a surprising choice for an Independent church; and it can hardly be claimed that the Camdenian principles out of which the design grew fit the Congregational worship for which the church was intended. The glass is unfortunately very poor.[1] There is one church built by James Salmon the elder from a sketch by Pugin† – the Catholic Apostolic Church in McAslin Street, well detailed though not exciting; and one, the Ramshorn Church in Ingram Street, by Thomas Rickman (1824). This was evidently much admired in its early years, Leighton reporting that 'its general effect . . . is very fine, its details peculiarly classic [!], and its proportions perfectly just and symmetrical'.[2] In truth, however, the church is a staid affair suggesting the currently fashionable institutional Tudor that Rickman used on an enormous scale in Cambridge (though the details and tower come from *c*.1300), and only worth mentioning here for its early date, **221**. 1a

But Glasgow had in fact two more or less indigenous Gothic churches of this time or slightly earlier.[3] David Hamilton's St John's Church in Bell Street (1819) was not one of his more successful efforts, a rather pinched design in a kind of free Tudoresque Gothic of no special character. It has now been demolished. Much nicer is Gillespie Graham's Catholic Chapel (now the Cathedral), whose quite humble but bristly front looks out between warehouses on to Clyde Street. From the outside, though the detailing is pretty (with 'graceful turrets' and a 'splendid tabernacle'), it suffers from

4 See *Glasghu Facies*, p.1107. By this date New College Chapel had been given a plaster vault by James Wyatt: presumably Wade referred to this, not to the original. [After various plans for replacement or enlargement the cathedral is now to be restored. It was built in 1815–17.]

4a Park Church has now been demolished except for the tower which was suffered to remain as a mark of its value in the townscape. Cross gables were perhaps less rare in the English Middle Ages than we supposed. They survive on the apse at Bluntisham (Hunts), and Street, restoring St Mary's, Brewood (Staffs), claimed to have evidence of medieval predecessors for those he supplied; of course Victorian restorers did sometimes find the evidence they wanted. See **237**.

151 (left) St Matthew, Bath Street (James Salmon, senior, 1849). Now demolished.
152. (right) Lansdowne U.P. Church, Great Western Road (J. Honeyman, 1862).

having no marked vertical accent. But the interior is something of a surprise, loftier and more graceful than one might have expected. Wade's *Tour of Modern and Peep into Ancient Glasgow*, published in 1817, describes the 'groinings' (he means the ribs of the vault) as being 'like those of New College Chapel, Oxford, but more multiplied and more beautiful'.4 However that may be, Wade is no doubt right that 'both fine taste and correct taste seem, on the whole to have presided over the Designing and Decoration of this Fabric'. A care for expense also presided: the vault is entirely of wood, painted to resemble stone.

Of later Gothic churches only a few are worth individual mention. Rochead's Park Church (1858)† is perhaps the earliest from the period corresponding to what is known as High Victorian in England. It has a spikey tower and an air as if of surprise at finding itself among so much classical company. Above the clerestorey is a row of gablets marking the transverse sections of the nave roof – a feature which appears fairly often on medieval Continental churches but, I believe, only twice in Britain, on the nave of Elgin Cathedral, now alas destroyed, and at St Giles, Edinburgh (where the gablets marked individual chapels): it was later used in Glasgow by William Leiper on Dowanhill Church and elsewhere. Honeyman's Lansdowne United Presbyterian Church in Great Western Road (1862) seems to be the

4a

first full-blooded piece of indigenous Gothic, in a fairly free version of the 'first-pointed' (i.e. Early English) style, with slender lancets (a triple lancet at the west end) and an exceptionally slim and elegant, even dainty, steeple, **152**. Its plan has a special, perhaps unique, interest in that the aisles are vestibules separated from the nave by a panelled partition, in which are set individual doors to each pew – a beautifully quiet piece of snobbishness in the allegedly egalitarian U.P. Church, but a gesture which at least shows awareness of the anomalies which are bound to crop up when a cellular medieval plan is adapted for a form of worship based on preaching, a problem which Emmett glossed over rather than grappled with. Externally Lansdowne is perhaps the most attractive Victorian Gothic church in the city.

In 1866 Leiper set himself up as a rival to Honeyman with Dowanhill Church. Its spire is 195 feet high (25 feet less than Lansdowne), and the steeple with broach spire again Early English but rather more correctly proportioned – looking indeed, apart from its darker stone, as if it had come out of Northamptonshire or Rutland. The body of the church is rather freer and more in the second-pointed manner, with cast iron columns inside, whose slenderness allows for some flexibility in use.[5] Leiper's later church, Camphill-Queen's Park (Balvicar Drive, 1878), is a stronger design, more confident and cleaner, **154**. The steeple, finished in 1883, is particularly good

153. Renfield Street Church (James Brown, 1849): the church was demolished in 1963 and this lovely interior is one of the saddest of recent losses.

[5] The main roof is, however, a single-span hammerbeam inspired by Godwin's at Northampton Town Hall. An exceptionally graceful iron and timber interior used to exist at James Brown's recently demolished Renfield Street Church (1849), hidden behind an unpromising front, **153**.

and more obviously shows the influence of Normandy Gothic that is to be expected in a pupil of J. L. Pearson. The tall coupled lancets of the tower and the use of small pinnacles to mask the transition from square tower to octagonal spire are close to Norman work of the early thirteenth century, particularly in and around Caen.

Sellars, not surprisingly, is freer and more eclectic than Leiper in his use of Gothic. His churches have a somewhat forbidding air, but are always liable to burst out into some detail without precedent or authority. For example, Queen's Park High Church (40 Queen's Drive, 1872), where, it should be said, Sellars's contribution is uncertain, is fairly conservative except for the spire, which is crammed with ancillary spirelets in a loosely French manner, but with some additional small arches which look Moorish, **156**. This rogue design, undeniably clumsy but undeniably original, may in fact be due to the influence or even to the direct participation of J. J. Stevenson (architect of the better-known Kelvinside Parish Church), who had recently left Campbell Douglas's firm for London.[6] Belmont and Hillhead Parish Church (Saltoun Street, 1875–6) was the result of a limited competition which, rather surprisingly, Sellars won over the heads of Leiper and Honeyman, **155**. Its design, which is a variation on the Sainte Chapelle theme, was in fact claimed by W. H. McNab to be largely Leiper's. The interior is groin-vaulted in

[6] See p.280. Kelvinside Church (of 1862) has one of Glasgow's best steeples: it is much in the manner that Street was at this time introducing in London.

154. (left) Camphill Church of Scotland, Queen's Park (William Leiper, 1878).
155. (right) Belmont and Hillhead (now Kelvinside-Hillhead) Church, Saltoun Street (1875), James Sellars's version of the Sainte Chapelle, perhaps based on a design by William Leiper.

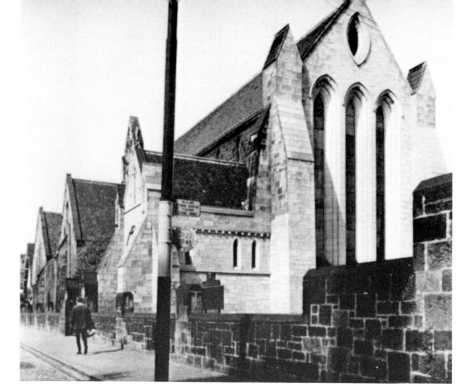

156. (left) Queen's Park High Church
(Campbell Douglas and
J. J. Stevenson, 1872).
157. (right) Shawlands Old Parish
Church (J. A. Campbell, 1888), a
smaller exercise in the Dunblane
manner.

6a Two Pearsonesque churches somewhat
similar to Belhaven may be briefly mentioned.
Both are by W. F. McGibbon: Pollokshields
East (Leslie Street, 1882–3)† and the rather
fussier Sherbrook St Gilbert's (Nithsdale
Road, 1895–9). Presbyterian worship having
no use for a more complex plan, each church
has the appearance of being the left-over
western limb of something much larger –
reminiscent of Paisley Abbey before its
crossing and chancel were reconstructed.
7 An enormous copy of Belmont Church,
with inferior detail, used to exist at
Kelvingrove U.P. Church: it was designed
by Robert Baldie in 1879 and burnt down
in 1925.

wood; the exterior has the fashionable French gablets with late thirteenth-century fenestration, and two thumping octagonal turrets heftily buttressing the entrance front. The church is seen at its best from the east, where the land falls away and the church thus gains an added height; from here the attractive many-sided polygonal apse is dominant, and the *flèche* does not seem disproportionately small.[7] The main front of Sellars's Belhaven Church (now St Luke's Greek Orthodox, 29 Dundonald Road, 1877) is much happier than that of Belmont, **158**: the flanking buttresses are now convincingly related to the body of the church, and the tall lancets give to an already lofty building a fine upstanding air, so that the absence of a tower is not seriously felt as a lack. The detail is all very refined and precise, without being mechanical.

Honeyman's Barony Free Church (49 Castle Street, 1866–7),† one of the remarkable group of four churches facing Cathedral Square, is outwardly more Scottish than any of those previously mentioned, at least so far as its saddle-back tower is concerned; the church itself has nearly crumbled away. Nearby is a much more powerful building, unquestionably the most important Victorian Gothic church in Glasgow, perhaps even in Scotland. This is Burnet and Campbell's Barony Church of 1886–90, won in a competition assessed by J. L. Pearson. The outside of this large T-shaped building is strong but severe, **159**. It has a 'west' front (actually south-facing) closely modelled on that of Dunblane Cathedral, with tall lancets between clasping buttresses and the famous vesical window in the apex of the gable. The French *flèche* over the crossing is rather inadequate as the only vertical accent above the roof; the immense transeptal porch is very powerful – a deep black hole into the side of the church – and the whole church builds up impressively from the north-east. The interior is one of the few appearances in Scotland of the plan of Gerona Cathedral, in which the aisleless nave is as wide as the tripartite chancel, **160**. Actually the Glasgow design is a

6a

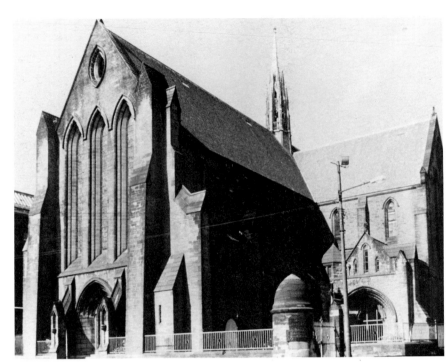

158. (above left) Belhaven (now St Luke's Greek Orthodox) Church, Dundonald Road (James Sellars, 1877).
159. (above right). Barony Church, Castle Street (J. J. Burnet, and J. A. Campbell, 1886).
160. (right) Barony Church: interior looking towards the chancel. The reredos was added in 1900.

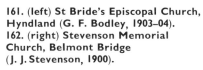

161. (left) St Bride's Episcopal Church, Hyndland (G. F. Bodley, 1903–04).
162. (right) Stevenson Memorial Church, Belmont Bridge (J. J. Stevenson, 1900).

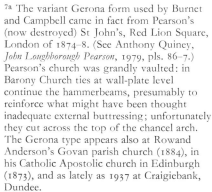

7a The variant Gerona form used by Burnet and Campbell came in fact from Pearson's (now destroyed) St John's, Red Lion Square, London of 1874–8. (See Anthony Quiney, *John Loughborough Pearson*, 1979, pls. 86–7.) Pearson's church was grandly vaulted: in Barony Church ties at wall-plate level continue the hammerbeams, presumably to reinforce what might have been thought inadequate external buttressing; unfortunately they cut across the top of the chancel arch. The Gerona type appears also at Rowand Anderson's Govan parish church (1884), in his Catholic Apostolic church in Edinburgh (1873), and as lately as 1937 at Craigiebank, Dundee.

8 For whom and Burnet, see further, chapter 10. A draughtsman called A. R. Scott is understood to have assisted on both churches. A late Gothic work by Burnet's Glasgow firm, with which J. Taylor Thomson assisted, is the chapel in the west quadrangle of the University (1923). It is stylistically rather tame, though impressive in scale, in a squared-off version of first-pointed, without any of the brash inventiveness of the Scotts. [The design is mainly by James Napier, working in close collaboration with Burnet himself.]

variant on this, for the nave has aisles, but the chancel has wider ones, so that the central space of the chancel is still narrower than that of the nave, and one is still faced, as at Gerona, with the west-facing wall in which the chancel arch is flanked by the much lower and narrower openings into the chancel aisles, here quite slit-like with sharply pointed arches. It is not clear what superiority over a plain unaisled hall this plan has for Presbyterian worship, though the aisles are in fact all so narrow that they are mere passageways surrounding a virtually single-celled hall – a rare example in Scotland of nineteenth-century Gothic moving away from essential imitation of medieval prototypes. In any case the Gerona plan was, like Dunblane, known to be a favourite of Pearson's, and it has certainly resulted in an extremely noble design. All the internal arches are richly moulded in the Early English style, for which presumably the cathedral across the road served as the model. But the fat round columns of the nave rather surprisingly have no capitals, and the arch mouldings grow out of them in a not altogether satisfactory way. The cost of the church was less carefully calculated than the assessor's inclinations and was long unkindly remembered, particularly by some of the unsuccessful competitors.

It seems impossible now to say which partner was chiefly responsible for the design. The credit has usually been given to J. J. Burnet; but the contemporary Shawlands Old Church, **157**, which is undoubtedly Campbell's, is very close in style of detail, and also has a Dunblane end; it is unlikely that Campbell would have simply copied. The Shawlands church is an attractive minor work of a major architect, then still quite young.[8] But Burnet was only two years older.

Secular Gothic buildings are extremely rare. Apart from the University, only two need to be mentioned here. Honeyman's Henderson Street School (1874) is in fact not really Gothic – an oblong with coupled windows under flattish segmental heads on the ground floor, and pairs of pointed ones above,

7a

the upper storey also adorned in the middle of one side with an oriel surmounted by a little Gothic belfry: mildish. Much more striking and lively is the Stock Exchange (1875–7) at the corner of Buchanan Street and St George's Place, **163**. The main building, amassed by the elder Burnet, is distinctly Italianate, a gorgeous display of North Italian Gothic, with an arcade of large square-sectioned arches on cylindrical columns on the ground floor, topped by hood-moulds with oval sculptured plaques in the spandrels, and above, small similar arches in threes, making an almost continuous arcade on a smaller scale: the glazing on this floor is set well back from the arcade. The attic storey, over an elaborately corbelled parapet, tries too hard and becomes confusing in its accumulation of detail.[9] The western addition by the younger Burnet, less clearly national in style, makes an unfortunate change in floor levels to accommodate three storeys within the height of the main building's two. His work is rather less hefty than his father's.

Of later Gothic churches two by London architects are worth notice. J. J. Stevenson designed the Stevenson Memorial Church, Belmont Bridge, on a return visit to Glasgow in 1898. The exterior is finely conceived, especially the massing of the church when seen from the south-west (from the north-west the body of the church looks stunted); but the detail is surprisingly inconsistent in style – smooth English fourteenth-century on the

163. The Stock Exchange (John Burnet, senior, 1875) with J. J. Burnet's extension of 1894 beyond.

[9] Burnet's design is in fact essentially a cut-down version of part of Burges's unsuccessful competition entry for the London Law Courts (1866): see R. P. Pullan, *The Architectural Designs of William Burges*.
[The Burges designs are also illustrated in Summerson, *Victorian Architecture*, 1970, pl.71, and in J. Mordaunt Crook, *William Burges* (1981), pls. 60 & 61.]

south side with very tall clerestorey windows which make it look like a monastic refectory; little gables and round windows on the north; crow steps at the west end with an immense square tower tucked into the north-west corner and topped by a crown steeple, made up of four flying buttresses meeting under a central pinnacle – a rather more graceful top than that of the Tolbooth tower. The dark red sandstone is perhaps not a very suitable material for this kind of design, though it was used for fourteenth-century churches in Galloway and the east. The interior produces further surprises and oddities, **162**: the two arcades of the nave are quite different without even the same number of bays. The north has three wide arches rather like those in a fifteenth-century Gloucestershire wool church, but, halfway up, the columns carry the front of a gallery stretching back across the exceptionally wide aisle and lit by the circular windows. On the south side the arcade is only half as high as that on the north and has four bays of shallow elliptical arches on octagonal piers without capitals – the whole looking rather like the elevation of a bridge. The south aisle is a mere passage with a lean-to roof, but there are pairs of big windows above: indeed the clerestorey is as high as the arcade below it. An equally unorthodox timber roof covers the nave, with a form of king-post in the middle, but seemingly boxed in at the sides – a clever device to reduce the apparent width of the roof span. 9a

164. St Ninian's Wynd Church, Crown Street (W. G. Rowan, 1888-9).†

9a The 'boxing-in' in fact only partly conceals a hammerbeam construction. It may have been suggested by a rare medieval example as at Framlingham (Suffolk) or perhaps by Philip Webb's St Martin's, Brampton (Cumberland).

165. St Andrew's East Church, Alexandra Parade (James Miller, 1904). **166.** (opposite) Queen's Cross Church, Garscube Road (C. R. Mackintosh, 1899).

Compared with this extraordinary building, Bodley's St Bride's, Hyndland Road of 1904 is orthodoxy itself, **161**. It is an episcopalian church and follows the plan established in England in the 1860s of a large hall with narrow aisles and no chancel, the sanctuary being divided from the nave only by a low wall. The design, based on late thirteenth-century precedents, is very tasteful and scholarly. (The west end, which goes in for much reticulated tracery, and the sturdy tower were built by H. O. Tarbolton in 1915.) 9b

Mackintosh's St Cuthbert's and Queen's Cross (866 Garscube Road, 1897–9) – his only Gothic building and his only church – naturally moves much farther from medieval origins, **166**. Indeed it is only Gothic in a rather stretched sense, for of course Mackintosh gives his imagination rein. The result can hardly be called really successful: in detail it is fascinating and unpredictable; and this detail looks in places like a try-out for his competition design for Liverpool Cathedral. But there are many conflicting and apparently arbitrary motifs, and a confusion of scales. The most interesting features are the big, strongly buttressed porch at the south-east corner, which clearly has affinities with the entrance of the Art School, and the tower, with its pronounced batter, for which the inspiration has been shown to come from the uncompleted medieval church at Merriot, Somerset. 9c

Equally free is the best of James Miller's churches, St Andrew's East (681 Alexandra Parade, 1904), **165**. This is, broadly speaking, Tudor in style, but has an unusual and striking west front. Two substantial towers stand well out from the main wall. They are square in plan until near the top, where they become polygonal; but the buttresses grow into small square turrets which keep the polygons in a tight grasp. The towers are joined near the top by a large bridge, whose nearly semicircular arch casts a deep shadow on the wall and window underneath. Since the front face of this bridge is more or less flush with those of the towers, one may have the alternative impression of a virtually flat front with an immensely deep arched recess in the centre. The window tracery, and likewise the small square cupola, are rather too small in scale for this toughly conceived composition. The idea may have come from Craigston Castle, Aberdeenshire, though a closer predecessor was Henry Wilson's unexecuted design for the front of St. Andrew's Boscombe; the towers are indebted for detail to a design by C. E. Mallows for a church at Bedford. (The small adjoining hall was built five years before the church by James Salmon.) 9d

Finally there is a series of agreeable small churches by H. E..Clifford, of which the best are perhaps Carntyne St Michael (Edrom Street, 1902)† and Cathcart Old (as late as 1928): both are low-built and sturdy with squat towers. Another, Titwood, has recently been successfully moved to a quite new site in Pollok. 9e

Yet one other small group of churches must come in here, for, though not strictly Gothic, they have the same kind of archaeological roots. These are the neo-Romanesque ones, which include one done in a Scots-German manner by P. M. Chalmers, who was a notable authority on medieval architecture. Not surprisingly his churches are correct and scholarly in detail; but the style has not often been found appealing and does not seem an appropriate choice for dark climates. The best of Chalmers's churches is probably St Margaret's Episcopal (351 Kilmarnock Road, 1912), a double-ender in the German manner, with a tall apse at each end, and a nearly free-

9b Stylistically the church is a reversion to a manner which Bodley had largely given up by the 1870s. It is, however, to virtually the same design as the exactly contemporary St Chad's, Burton-upon-Trent.
9c A wholly inadequate account of this extraordinary and fascinating building. For a brief amends see pp.267ff.
9d And ultimately perhaps to Basil Champney's Rylands Library, Manchester.
9e For St John's Renfield and St Margaret's Knightswood see p.269.

standing and unexpectedly high tower. Much more interesting and inventive is St Ninian's Wynd Church by W. G. Rowan (498 Crown Street, 1888), which has a west tower which must surely be unique, **164**. It is nearly square in plan, with square-capped turrets at the outer corners above massive clasping buttresses. But the outer face of the tower itself incorporates in miniature the characteristic west front of big Norman abbey churches such as St Martin de Boscherville; for the buttresses look like small individual towers, and the space between them is gabled. The aisles thus begin well back from the 'façade', and the angles are filled – rather unfortunately, I think – with polygonal porches. The detailed inspiration comes indeed largely from Normandy, where the pyramidal caps and the repeated blank arcading are so frequent, but also, doubtless, from the contemporary practice in America of H. H. Richardson, whose work, at least in illustration, Rowan must have known well. The idea of linking church and manse may well have come direct from Richardson's Trinity Church, Boston, with its adjoining and related vicarage. The Medical Mission Hall is indeed much more a part of the building than something merely associated with it, and links the church to the next-door tenement very happily. I do not myself find the Glasgow church so attractive as the Boston one, partly because it is built of very dark red stone (now further darkened by smoke); and it seems, even by Romanesque standards, to have unnecessarily small windows (those in the mission hall are larger). But it shares with Richardson's work the relative freedom from strict archaeological correctness which has allowed rein for the architect's imagination to conceive a genuinely new variation on old motifs.

[P.S. This chapter is at fault in leaving out Glasgow's contribution to the 'Arts and Crafts Gothic' of the turn of the century. As early as 1887–9 Burnet had adapted his 'low look' to church architecture in two churches in Arran,[10] the first of a line stretching through to the 1930s. The prompting may have come from Norman Shaw who, following his conversion to late English Perpendicular, had produced a small number of refined but relaxed and spreading church designs by no means confined to exactitudes of revivalism. But though Burnet, like Shaw, used squat sturdy towers topped by small pyramids, his have typically a Scottish weightiness marked especially by corbelled drums at the top angles; and he mixes his 'styles' remarkably: the church at Brechin ranges from neo-Norman through Early English to late Tudor. The one example in Glasgow – Broomhill Congregational in Victoria Park (1900–08) – is a little more orthodox but has the same low profile, broad eaves, square-headed windows, delightful octangular staircase unit and a half-timbered porch which was a feature of the series and was taken on by Rowan for his St Margaret's (1900–01) far out to the east in Tolcross. The very squat tower of this church, strongly reinforced by angle buttresses, is more Shavian than Burnet's: its pyramid comes down with wide eaves like a hat.[11] The double-gabled 'transept' looks like a happy late inspiration, and indeed the whole church has an intimate villagey air suggesting improvisation or growth with its community: one of those seemingly artless designs that appear to have just happened. In fact it grows out of earlier Perpendicular churches by Rowan (Pollokshields Glencairn of 1891 and Cathcart South 1893) built after he had given up the Romanesque of St Ninian's Wynd; yet Strathbungo already (1886) mixes Romanesque not with English Perpendicular but with the tough late Scottish Gothic, recognizing affinities of sturdy proportion between the two styles.]

10 [See David Walker in Alastair Service, *Edwardian Architecture and its Origins*, 1975, pp.197–9. The look was first tried out in a house in Loch Ard in 1886.]

11 [Cf. Shaw's Meerbrook (Staffs), designed 1868 (see Andrew Saint, *Richard Norman Shaw*, 1976, pl.204); Burnet's churches might be compared with All Saints', Richard's Castle (Salop) 1889–93 (*ibid.*, pl.219).]

Chapter 9   **Tenements**

I have not so far found much opportunity to write of tenements. Yet Glasgow is a city of tenements: it is they which set the character of most of its streets; and Glasgow is the only city in Scotland to have developed a distinctive tenement architecture. There can be no particular responsibility for this. On the whole the well-known architects did not build tenements, or if they did the fact is not recorded. In the few cases where a great name can confidently be attached to a range of tenements, what we always have is a personal variation on a general Glasgow theme: Queen's Park Terrace is, when one looks at it closely, clearly Thomson's; but it is Thomson's variation of a basic form used throughout the city, and very largely by builders who are now, and perhaps always were, anonymous and who rarely had architectural ambitions.[1]

Until the middle of the nineteenth century, tenements possibly marked a class distinction in Glasgow; but with the great growth of the city westwards and southwards, it gradually became accepted that middle-class people could own a flat in a tenement without social stigma. However, the middle-class tenement usually has only three storeys against the common four of the rest (perhaps a relic of the three-storey tradition of terraces of individual houses, doubtless also a recognition of the fag of climbing four flights of stairs); and the middle-class flat-dweller goes through a door from the street, rather than a mere hole in the wall.

It is hardly possible to treat tenement architecture chronologically. The main point is that in the early nineteenth century a generic style was developed which was to serve the city as staple for nearly 100 years. The basic inspiration or model was the tough, simplified late Georgian of the Edinburgh and Glasgow terraces, a model itself not wholly distinguishable as an influence from the urban vernacular of a considerably earlier period. And there are three-storey ranges in Hillhead, near St George's Cross and elsewhere, which have outwardly little to distinguish them from terraces of individual houses. They are usually rather plainer, with normally no central emphasis, and the end pavilions only slightly higher or with a larger cornice. But the four-storey ranges,[2] which form the great bulk of the tenements, pose quite a new problem of scale. Georgian houses achieve their sense of rest and poise by a subtle gradation of window sizes: normally, in a three-storey house the tallest windows are on the first floor (where the main rooms are), the next size on the ground floor, the smallest on the top: examples can be seen in almost all the early nineteenth-century terraces of Glasgow: Blythswood Square is as good a place to look as any. By this arrangement the building seems to stand easily and lightly, but firmly, on the ground. The differences in size are not necessarily very great, though they are often emphasized by a heavy cornice, occasionally by pediments, on the first floor; but they are vital for the balance of the façade. If they are neglected the building looks top-heavy. The principle can, with care, be extended to four storeys, as was the rule in Dublin in the eighteenth century, and in much of London as well. In this case, the largest windows remain on the first floor,

[1] Wilson's tenements on Garnethill have an occasional detail which may tell the tale of their authorship, but he was extremely self-effacing. [Two exceptionally well-detailed terraces of tenements face one another in Hill Street. Peel Terrace (1841–2) is four-storeyed with the shallow window pediments favoured by David Hamilton. Breadalbane Terrace (1845 & 1855) is a storey lower and picks up the alternating-pediment theme in bolder relief. Both terraces have now been restored.]

[2] Occasionally five storeys in some late examples.

the ground and second are nearly the same size, the top are now quite small, sometimes less than half as deep as those on the first floor. But where the building is not a house but flats, it becomes hard to square the internal arrangements with such a variety of window sizes on the façade: either the first floor becomes absurdly high, or the third floor too low, or both. If, on the other hand, the windows are regularized while keeping an upright 'Georgian' shape, as in many flats built between the wars in London and elsewhere, the result, particularly in a block of five storeys, is lumpish and top-heavy.

The problem then is to design the façade so that the window gradations *appear* to satisfy the conditions under which the façade looks at rest and has a sense of poise, without unduly distorting the rooms behind. The job is a little easier in Glasgow than it would be in England, because of the tradition of rooms abnormally high by English standards: 12 feet is common, 14 not unusual. The top floor can thus be reasonably high and well lit without the first becoming grotesquely high. But the architects' chief – and more subtle – device was to give special emphasis to the first floor by adding a heavy cornice or series of pediments, sometimes ornamented, sometimes separated from the windows beneath by thin blank panels: the eye reads the window, panel and pediment as one unit, and of course a considerably taller one than

167. Franklin Terrace, Argyle Street (built before 1851).

the window itself. The second-floor windows have a lighter and plainer cornice, the top none at all – merely a pause before the crowning, not usually heavy, cornice of the whole building is reached. By means of this variation in the stonework, a change of balance is suggested which is much greater than would be determined by the quite small, often hardly perceptible, differences in window size alone. Tenements all over the city adopt this device, some naturally more skilfully than others. The most fascinating and individual variant is undoubtedly Thomson's Queen's Park Terrace (355–429 Eglinton Street).[3]

So much for the question of vertical balance. A greater problem, and one which took longer to solve, was the avoidance of horizontal monotony: a very real problem, since Glasgow streets are often long, straight and on the south side flat, and many of the ranges of tenements continue unbroken for extremely long stretches – how to avoid the boredom very quickly induced by an almost endless repetition of evenly spaced windows along a flat façade. Many of the Glasgow tenements of the 1830s and 1840s are rather dull, as a result of a failure to settle, or even perhaps to be aware of, this problem. It had in fact appeared a good deal earlier than this, south of the river in the then fashionable streets of large houses like Abbotsford Place. Here, though the detail is refined, the great length of the ranges is somewhat

168. Pollok Street, Kingston (c.1880), a characteristically assured tenement design.

[3] See p.141.

daunting, and an attempt to avoid monotony by slightly recessing part of the façade is not altogether successful.[4] (Yet a single feature can sometimes have a very powerful effect, like that near the west end of Argyle Street, where the unbroken range of tenements called Franklin Terrace is miraculously brought to life by the single tree which gets its precarious living out of the mud of the front area, **167**.) Even Queen's Park Terrace may seem a bit monotonous, if one lets one's eye move slowly along its length: it should be taken in altogether, in perspective, so that the overall proportions tell. A trouble with some other tenements is that they are so long that it is hardly possible to say that they have, visually, proportions at all: the length simply goes off into the distance.

The Glasgow solution was one which could hardly have suggested itself while Georgian influence was still dominant. It was to keep the basic window shape, but to abandon the principle of even spacing – an eclectic and essentially Victorian gesture. A good simple example is Granby Terrace at the north end of Hillhead Street (west side), **169**, which has a division of groups of windows into $1+3+3+1$, $1+3+3+1$, etc., the single windows being on the stairs (and hence above the street doors), the trios marking off the width of each flat.[5] Later designers were bolder and adapted a device used with such bravado by Hamilton on the Western Club, keeping the

[4] Very long straight façades are common in eighteenth-century Dublin: they are lighter and livelier than the Glasgow examples, partly because of the free use of wrought iron for balconies and railings, partly because the window reveals (which tell significantly in perspective) are invariably marked by being painted in colours which contrast with that of the brick and emphasize the verticals. Even so there are occasional miscalculations: see the (rebuilt) façade of Summer Hill.

[5] The architect was William Clarke (of Clarke & Bell), who was one of the earliest occupiers. It was built in 1856.

169. Granby Terrace, Hillhead Street (William Clarke, 1856).

basic window shape (it became occasionally somewhat narrower) but linking the windows together under a single cornice or lintel, with only mullions between. By judiciously mixing these double or triple window-units with the more orthodox single ones, a restful but not monotonous façade could be contrived even on very long ranges – restful chiefly because the actual windows remained all the same size, though the combinations varied. Triplicated windows occur from time to time in Georgian buildings, for example in Bath, where they became an almost regular feature. They crop up intermittently in the early nineteenth century: they became dominant in the design of Benjamin Wyatt's Lancaster House, St James's. But the device seems hardly to have been used really intensively before the 1840s, when Barry and others took it up. Hamilton was perhaps the only architect of this period to make so bold a use of it as to turn an incipiently classical building into something entirely different. And only in Glasgow, where the lights were regularly all the same size, did it initiate a whole new sub-style of architecture. The windows in couples seem to be a Glasgow invention and are more certainly Victorian, for a classically influenced architect would find it hard to accept the essential duality that they imply: they have to be used with care and in such a way as to oblige the eye always to read the pairs as single units. Examples of this type of tenement are all over the city – indeed they 5a

170. The west end of Bath Street (1850-3), whose superb scale is enhanced by the delicate curve of the street. The foreground stretch was needlessly destroyed in advance of the ring road. The church is Emmett's St Matthew Blythswood as it was before the mutilation of its spire.

5a Coupled windows do occur in Georgian buildings and seem to have been something of a trademark of Nathaniel Ireson of Wincanton (Somerset) in and near which town examples are fairly numerous. Later in the century they crop up in Bath.

are probably the commonest of all, though some are very indifferently handled. Among the best on a straight frontage is Pollok Street, **168**, where a rhythm of 2 + 1 + 1 + 1 + 1 + 2 alternates with 3 + 2 + 2 + 3 and other variations; the effect is pleasant and relaxed with no straining after effect. Another excellent range, enhanced by the curve of the street, is near the west end of Bath Street (north side),† where triplicated windows are introduced as punctuations between groups of single ones, **170**.

Probably some time in the 1880s a more emphatic kind of punctuation became general. Canted bay windows had been used intermittently in Glasgow before – by Wilson on Park Terrace, by Rochead in Buckingham Terrace, by James Thomson in Dowanhill, by Alexander Thomson in Westbourne Terrace. Now they became the fashion, and one which was quickly abused and done to death. Some builders, however, were modest and restrained in their use of bays, and the result is admirable background architecture, quiet and unobtrusive. A nice example is on the north side of Kent Road, where oriels running up the three upper storeys come in pairs, with six bays of flat wall in between, **171**. At the west end of Sauchiehall Street is a long range in which four-storey bays are combined with flat stretches in which single and coupled windows are both involved. At the bottom of Millbrae Road is a much more complicated one, which starts with a canted bay, then four single windows, flat and rather widely spaced, then the corner into Millbrae Crescent, which is managed by a convex quadrant with three separate windows, this time close together, then a short stretch of blank wall, a single window, another canted bay, two pairs of coupled windows, flat, and finally a third bay. The extraordinary thing is that such a melange should produce so pleasing an effect; but then it is all done with restraint and a sense of good breeding.

The same, alas, can hardly be said of many of the tenements of the very late nineteenth century which now ring the centre of the city. Bows were in

5b

189

as well as bays, and these were on the whole handled with far less skill. Often bows and bays are combined, without much sense of how the two might go together; and by this time Glasgow's grey or biscuit-coloured ashlar was giving way to the purplish red sandstone imported from Ayrshire and Dumfries. The large buildings (now often up to five storeys) were cumbrous and ugly, and were made worse and more confusing by the apparent delight which builders took in using together stone blocks of very different tones: the masonry, even when flat, is thus anything but restful. For a fascinating and melancholy example, see Springhill Gardens, looking across Pollokshaws Road to Queen's Park.

Tenement building virtually came to an end with the nineteenth century. Among the few later blocks, that by H. E. Clifford at the corner of Shields and Terregles Roads has been widely admired; but in truth it is clumsy in inception and coarse in execution – as can be seen by comparing it with the contemporary and in some ways similar work of Leonard Stokes, of which Glasgow has one characteristic example in the Western Telephone Exchange (24 Highburgh Road, 1907). The tenements, with all their virtues and drawbacks, were the creation of private landlords; and, at any rate after 1918, none was found who could or would go on building on this scale. From that time the tenements have been called flats – a word carrying no social stigma – and, in the suburbs or the centre, have been the direct responsibility of the Corporation, either by itself or with the help of Sir Robert Matthew and Sir Basil Spence. But that is another, and not specifically Glaswegian story.[6]

[A postscript is due to the work of the City Improvement Trust unfairly maligned by historians (including the present authors) for the wholesale destruction of the remains of seventeenth-century Glasgow in the later nineteenth – something for which the city architect, John Carrick, was certainly not to blame. Most of the work belongs rather to social than to architectural history; but recent cleaning and restoration of Carrick's tenements in Saltmarket (built by the Trust itself in 1886 when the cleared site found none to take up the feus) has shown what decent buildings they are. Crow-step gables and scrolly pediments make small gestures of tribute to the old houses they replaced. Though the flats were mostly of one or two rooms, Honeyman and others objected that such buildings did nothing to solve the problems of housing the really poor – simply pushing the worst slums a few yards further out. But the Trust persevered, and much of the present (or recently past) appearance of High Street and Townhead is due to them. The High Street quadrants north of George Street, done by Burnet and Boston (really designed by William Boston; Frank Burnet was no relation of his famous namesake) in 1900–01 pick up Carrick's gables, though the Renaissance details are less in evidence and the familiar Glasgow bows more so. J. J. Burnet was a perhaps rather unlikely contributor to work of this kind. The best of his tenements for the Workmen's Dwellings Company (Greenhead Court of 1897–9) had elevations which were again a refinement on Carrick's theme but (like almost all of their kind) very utilitarian backs dominated by the access balconies. With the slightly earlier Cathedral Court Greenhead Court was demolished in 1971.[7]]

5c

5c For which see below, p.263n.
6 One range of tenements deserves a special mention here – the longest and one of the best that I know. This is the serpentine St Vincent Crescent, built, with its extension into Minerva Street, by Kirkland in about 1855, 72. It is immense, over half a mile long with only one gap, but the great sweep of the crescent controls what would otherwise be a grotesque stretch of continuous wall. And the detail is very fine indeed – especially the curved corner where Minerva Street meets Argyle Street: the ground floor is arcaded, and above this a row of Ionic pilasters rises through two floors to an elaborately moulded cornice. It is rare for tenements to be treated with such fastidious care. (Another delightful block is across the road from this one at the corner of Finnieston Street: it suddenly breaks out into a large graceful bow, with a row of close-set round-headed windows at the top under a balustrade. Also of about 1855.)†
7 [For the City Improvement Trust see Worsdall, op. cit., esp. pp.91–3, and the same author's Victorian City, 1982, p.109; for Burnet's work with the Workmen's Dwellings Company, see The Tenement, pp.112–17.]

By the end of the third quarter of the nineteenth century Glasgow was as supremely self-confident as ever in its history and seemed to be riding on the crest of a permanently advancing prosperity. The year 1878, therefore, came as an extreme shock, and even today a reminder of it has power to disturb. For a vital element in the city's mercantile and manufacturing success had been the trust placed in the country's banks. Of these the City of Glasgow was the youngest and most enterprising. In 1878 it stopped payment; since it was an unlimited company, all the shareholders were liable for its debts. Most of them were local people, and most were ruined. 'Those whose fortunes survived paid up to 2750 per cent. Depression swept over the wintry city. Factories closed, buildings stood half-completed. The directors were tried for fraud and imprisoned.'[1] Even Glaswegians—habitually so sure of themselves—had serious doubts about the future.

[1] J. M. Reid, *Glasgow*, p.120.

173. The staircase hall of the Municipal Chambers (William Young, 1883–8). A Treppenhaus on a super-Bavarian scale.

174. (left). Municipal Chambers: the
fine baroque arches across John Street
(Watson, Salmond and Gray, 1923).
175. (right) The Municipal Chambers
(William Young, 1883–8).

Yet within an astonishingly short time the city had extricated itself from the worst effects. Shipbuilding, which had not been firmly established before the 1860s, was the first to recover, and quickly became the most prominent, and has remained the most famous, of all the industries of the Clyde. Within a decade of the bank failure Glasgow was confident enough in its strength not only to build a great new palace for its own government, but to stage the first of its short series of international exhibitions. The City Chambers in George Square were actually begun in 1883, and there is nothing in this swaggeringly opulent building to suggest hesitation or doubt, though it was the outcome of one of the most frustrating architectural competitions ever held, **175**. A previous abortive competition left a legacy of diagram plans by John Carrick, which evidently fixed the basic outline and saddled the competitors with the demand for an awkward ratio between height of tower and height and breadth of main façade, which hamstrung the best of them. On sheer individual merit the competition should have been won by George Washington Browne, but popular taste was not ready for so subtle and economical a treatment of Renaissance detail; and it is questionable whether his design would have made much impact on the more deeply modelled Glasgow townscape. T. L. Watson also managed the tower well but in a Waterhouse-*Rundbogen* style, doubtless aimed at the assessor Charles Barry's occasional Romanesque adventures but hopelessly alien to Glasgow. *Ancien régime* classicism turned up in several designs, and so, more successfully, did the French Renaissance. Among these, Burnet's had tall roofs and a central cupola instead of a tower, which presumably put him out of the running; Leiper's tower was wholly unrelated to his otherwise skilful sixteenth-century-type façade; Sellars's French fell academically short of the rest, but he redeemed his design by replacing a feeble tower by a dome after the manner of the Institut in Paris, which like Burnet's cupola departed from the conditions. On the whole the eventual winner, William Young, a London

Scot, deserved his success: he alone seems to have managed a satisfactory solution of the problem of the tower in relation to the façade; and his design, if not the most tasteful, was certainly the grandest that fitted the rules; and moreover it has shown that it wears well in the Glasgow scene. **1a**

Young's great tower, with its banded masonry surmounted by sumptuous Renaissance details and a rather Thomsonesque cupola must be, in sum, without serious precedent, though it may be seen as a Renaissance reworking, stage by stage, of St Vincent Street. The rest of his building contains an amazing amalgam of styles – French, Flemish, Venetian, with Flemish the dominant influence. J. M. Reid is doubtless right that 'the sense of wealth in the place is too insistent', as if the Corporation had set itself to demonstrate as dramatically as possible that Glasgow had recovered from 1878. The vast staircase hall, using rich materials with a lavishness previously unparalleled in the city, makes the point even more emphatically than the main front, **173**. Yet for all the extravagance, for all the crowding of details as if Young could never let a square inch of wall alone, the building undoubtedly has an air – a swagger air, it is true, yet the massing is handsome, and the corner towers give a splendid lift to the façade. Furthermore – a difficult thing in so large a building – the details are in principle satisfactory in scale in relation to the whole: it is over-ornate but not fiddly, the grand civic gesture *par excellence*. **1b**

176. (above) **The Clyde Trust Building, Robertson Street** (J. J. Burnet, 1883, the nearer section 1905).
177. (right) **Central Station Hotel** (R. R. Anderson, 1884).

1a The winner of the first competition, George Corson, had his design ruled out on grounds of cost; yet for the second, in which Barry was joined as joint assessor by Carrick (as City Architect), the allowance was raised from £150,000 to £250,000 – £30,000 more than even Barry's estimate of the cost of Corson's design. The final cost was £540,000. See Colin Cunningham, *Victorian and Edwardian Town Halls*, 1981, pp.108 and 280-1.
1b Something which Waterhouse, working on a similar scale at Manchester, surely doesn't achieve. Perhaps it isn't so easy in Gothic. For further analysis of Young's building see Cunningham, *op. cit.*, pp.138 & 154.

(The use of a giant order on the side façades is a serious failing; seen from George Street it ruins the fine scale of the main façade. It seems to be the result of an undue desire for architectural truth: the order is meant to express externally the scale of the rooms within.)[2]

The three exhibitions (held in 1888, 1901 and 1911) have also left their physical mark on the city – this time at the west end, on the edge of Kelvingrove Park. For the proceeds of the first paid for the Art Galleries, which were ready in time for the second, at the same time as Kelvin Hall was provided as a permanent centre for exhibitions. These are buildings to make the sensitive Glaswegian wince; for while at sunset the wild silhouette of the Art Galleries can have a romantic appeal when one can no longer see the excruciating detail, Kelvin Hall is appallingly dreary, particularly when seen from the University, whence its huge featureless roof is prominent. Having regard to the quantity of architectural talent in Glasgow at the time, these two buildings are a disgrace; and it is all the more to be regretted that for the great international occasions which the exhibitions turned out to be, neither Burnet (who had designed the Edinburgh International Exhibition of 1886) nor Campbell nor Mackintosh nor Salmon was given the chance to show the world what Glasgow could do. For in the last decades of the century, not only did Glasgow recover commercially; the great series of architects, which,

2a

178. The Pearce Institute, Govan (R. R. Anderson, 1903–05).

[2] The later extensions to the east are by Watson, Salmond and Gray, designed in 1913, again in competition, but not built until 1923. They are rather solemn and much less exuberant than Young's work, François Mansart in detail, but Burnet-inspired in fenestration, and are linked to it by the outstandingly fine arches across John Street, **174**; baroque in spirit, with a semi-circular arch enclosed within a giant aedicule consisting of a segmental open pediment carried on coupled Ionic columns.

2a The art gallery we have (1892–1900) is the result of a competition assessed by Waterhouse and won for no obvious reason by Sir John W. Simpson. Almost any of the published designs would have been better, those by Honeyman and by Keppie and Mackintosh much better. But Simpson was shrewd enough to enlist the collaboration of the great George Frampton, who in turn drew in Derwent Wood: the outcome was the most eloquent sculpture in the city, rivalled only by Harry Bates's magisterially expressive Roberts memorial in Park Terrace – Glasgow's noblest equestrian statue by far – by Hamo Thornycroft's harrowing portrait of Gladstone in George Square, by Alfred Gilbert's mysterious and haunting monument to William Graham in the cathedral, and perhaps by Wood's tortured angels on the British Linen Bank in Govan.

179. (left) The 'Glasgow Herald' Building, Mitchell Street (John Keppie and C. R. Mackintosh, 1893). 180. (right) The Fine Arts Institute, Sauchiehall Street (J. J. Burnet, 1878-9); demolished after a fire in 1967. The frieze was by John Mossman. On the right the former Manchester House, as reconstructed by Keppie in 1896, with some details from a student design by Mackintosh: demolished 1972, but the cupola is to be set up in Prince's Square, Buchanan Street.

as one looks back, may have seemed to weaken and almost die with Thomson's death, was reborn into a generation quite as remarkable as any before it.

When Thomson died in 1875, the classical tradition, of which he was in a special sense the culminating representative, as good as died with him. It is difficult to feel that his true originality was at all properly understood by his immediate successors. Those who continued to work in a classical idiom tended to make up for a lack of real imaginative life in their designs by an increased attention to correctness of detail. A great architect who inherits a tradition is never content simply to live within it: it must continue to grow as a living force in his personality and become his own style at the same time as it is an integrated part of a continuing tradition. If the tradition is vital, and if an architect feels it as a living force, it will feed and help to expand his own native genius, which then expresses itself in a particular personal response to the tradition. This is what one sees happening in Thomson's greatest work: 'classical' prototypes can perhaps usually be found, at any rate in his residential terraces, but always they are absorbed into a fresh vision of how the classical tradition could continue to live in that place at that time. And this is emphatically what one cannot feel about the classically motivated buildings of the 1880s. Alexander Skirving, T. L. Watson and Hugh Barclay were respectable figures (Barclay, I think, something more); but all their churches suggest some lack of conviction of their own character; they have a backward-looking air, of remembering past glories, clinging to the vestiges of a tradition which has gone cold, and which their architects can no longer have felt as something living within them.

By the 1880s in fact most of Thomson's successors had decided that the post-classical style had no future. In truth they had little of their own to give it; and for men like Campbell Douglas or the weaker-minded David Barclay to fly in the face of much literary pressure was mere financial stupidity: the coincidence of the Bank Crash with the end of the Neo-Greek must

181. The fantastic silhouette of J. J. Burnet's Charing Cross Mansions, Sauchiehall Street (1891).

have been more than accidental. Sellars, whose handsome City of Glasgow Bank must have kept alive painful memories, lived until 1888, but overwork and too much delegation had blunted his powers until just before his death, when he gave signs of a new trend, first with his Georgianesque Couper Institute, Cathcart (1887) and then with his Anderson Medical School (56 Dumbarton Road), whose rather clumsy sculptured façade in Italianish-cum- Scots Renaissance brings Sellars closer to the work of Rowand Anderson than to anything identifiable with the real Glasgow tradition. Anderson himself is a curiously isolated figure in the architectural history of Glasgow, though he is the author of one of the city's most visited buildings, the Central Station, or rather the hotel part of it, which dominates the corner of Gordon Street and Hope Street with its magnificent tower which seems to join the Scandinavian seventeenth and twentieth centuries together, **177**. Anderson is, one feels, consistently – indeed self-consciously – Scots in all his main work in Glasgow. Yet on examination the details of his buildings prove to be closer to the cosmopolitan origins of the Scots seventeenth century than the Scots seventeenth century ever was. Thus, in addition to its Swedish tower, the Central has windows from the early Florentine Renaissance, others which look English Jacobean, and gables which appear to have come over from Amsterdam. The details are all observed with fastidiously minute

2b

182. The Athenaeum, St George's Place (J. J. Burnet, 1886), now part of the Royal Scottish Academy of Music.

2b A most unfortunate omission from the first edition was of Sellars' building of 1883-4 for Wylie and Lochhead at 45 Buchanan Street (now part of Fraser's). Though the general conception is derived from its predecessor on the site, William Lochhead's building of 1855 which was burnt in 1883 (see **93(e)**), Sellars encased the iron columns in ornate terracotta in accordance with current American fire-proofing practice. The building is most remarkable for its spectacular four-storey top-lit saloon, looking, with its boldly exposed iron galleries, like a particularly swagger arcade.

183. Athenaeum Theatre, Buchanan Street (J. J. Burnet, and J. A. Campbell, 1891) now part of the Royal Scottish Academy of Music: photograph taken soon after building.
184. (opposite). Atlantic Chambers (J. J. Burnet, 1899): the photograph shows the rich modelling of the façade but not the idiosyncratic top storey.

[3] Anderson significantly opposed the idea of a Minister of Fine Art or anything of the kind. In 1889 he held that 'architecture in this country was in a more vigorous and healthy condition than in any other country in Europe' and that this was to be 'entirely attributed to its freedom from State control . . . He held therefore to free trade in art as in everything else'. (From the National Association for the Advancement of Art, Edinburgh.) The relevance of this to Anderson's own imports seems clear. One other revivalist building of about the same date which is worth more than casual attention is the Clydesdale Bank, 91 Buchanan Street, designed by George Washington Browne in 1896 as a tea room for Miss Cranston. Its exquisitely detailed façade is the most appealing example in the city of the short-lived revival of the François I idiom, though the general impression is reminiscent of the 'Pont Street' Dutch of Stevenson and George. See further p.258n.

attention; and the truly remarkable thing about the result is that Anderson is able to work such diverse elements together with no trace of architectural indigestion and get a Scots feeling into the building as a whole – which, while it means that it strikes a somewhat foreign air in Glasgow, is proof total of his consummate mastery of style.

With the Central Station, Anderson's two best buildings in Glasgow are the Pollokshaws Burgh Buildings of 1897 and above all the Pearce Institute (840 Govan Road) of 1903–5. The scrupulous, but intensely self-conscious character of Anderson's revivalism in the Pearce Institute offers, for all the charm of the building, a specially clear example of the difference between continuing or re-creating a tradition and merely reviving one, 178. The main façade of the building is nearly symmetrical, with a two-storeyed block in the middle (windows, gablets and balcony as in the more ambitious town-buildings of the early seventeenth century) and a larger and higher block at either end. But the departures from symmetry are very telling: whereas the eastern end is baronial, with crow-steps, smallish windows and a chimney growing out of the apex of the gable, the other is entirely Renaissance in character, very showy with niches and other adornments on the façade, a huge mullioned and transomed window surmounted by heraldic sculpture, supporting pilasters and an elaborate shaped gable giving an overall serpentine effect. The side elevations continue the story of these two different styles – the eastern straightforward and nearly utilitarian, the western lavishly ornamented with more big windows, an octagonal tower with ogee dome, and even buttresses. Moreover the smaller and simpler eastern windows have, as it were, been touched up with Renaissance details, and one larger one (in a later mode) inserted – for all the world as if what we had were actually an early building enlarged and sophisticated by a later change of taste. So Anderson has not merely revived one style of the past (or two styles side by side): he has imitated the *appearance* of a really old building which has been modernized at a period between its first being built and the present. When one studies the refinement of detail of the Pearce Institute and observes the fastidious care which has gone into its creation, it is impossible not to take pleasure in it. For all that, I cannot feel that stylistically it is greatly more than a rather elaborate and academic practical joke. No wonder, in such a context, that Burnet was not interested in style.[3]

When Sellars died, his chief draughtsman, Keppie, left Campbell Douglas and went into partnership with Honeyman. But Keppie was in no sense an original mind, and by this time Honeyman had done all his own best work. The firm produced little of note until 1893 (the *Glasgow Herald* offices in Mitchell Street, 179), by which time Mackintosh, who had joined a year or two earlier, was coming to be the dominant figure. Meanwhile Sellars's mantle fell on J. J. Burnet, who was to become much the best-known Glasgow architect of his time, with a very widespread practice and a reputation that dwarfed Mackintosh's, at any rate in Britain, though it is now in partial eclipse.

Burnet was born in 1857 and went (perhaps after some apprenticeship in his father's firm, to which he returned in 1877) to the Ecole des Beaux-Arts, which was at that time a magnet for aspiring architects from all over the world and led to something like an international style deriving from the French Second-Empire Renaissance. Burnet's first building after his return

to Glasgow was the Fine Arts Institute of 1879, **180** (171 Sauchiehall Street, later part of Pettigrew and Stephen's store, and recently demolished after a fire). It had become difficult to judge the proportions of this attractive and dignified building, owing to the crude and unrelated shop front which cut off the upper storeys from the ground. It was clearly classical in basic inspiration but the classicism is very unlike the native idiom. Giant columns are high up on the façade (as they were with Sellars), but they now appear more as unusually deep surface detail on a nearly plain wall than as essential supports of an entablature; and they are in couples, a device more baroque than classical (and stemming ultimately from the French seventeenth century). But Burnet's building had nothing of the extreme restlessness of neo-baroque buildings elsewhere. His detailing is extremely scholarly and makes extensive use of figure sculpture, especially in the pediment and the frieze (by John Mossman) – again something relatively new in Glasgow[4] and perhaps not yet, at this time, fully assimilated.

The Clyde Navigation Trust Building (at the corner of Broomielaw and Robertson Street) and the first part of the Athenaeum (in St George's Place), both of which date from 1886, again make much use of figure-sculpture, and this time are distinctly restless. For all his superior Beaux-Arts training Burnet had eclectic tastes and was not above introducing some Sellars-like

[4] But see the floral pediment of Elgin Place by Burnet's father (1856: cf. p.160 above). Clydesdale Bank (1870) and Lanarkshire House (1876) both have figures.
[But the younger Burnet may have had a hand in Lanarkshire House during the vacations of 1875 and 1876.]

185. McGeoch's West Campbell Street (J. J. Burnet, 1905).†

186. (left) 200 St Vincent Street (J. J. Burnet, c.1927); sculpture has since been added to the façade.
187. (right) Wallace Scott Factory, Spean Street, Cathcart (J. J. Burnet, 1913); a photograph taken before recent mutilation.

5 In 1886 a Venetian campanile was intended: Jules Lessore made a dreamy water-colour of it.
5a This account is inaccurate and inadequate: the off-centre pediment is on the Robertson Street elevation and the asymmetry must stem initially from a failure to acquire enough land to the north. Had this façade been completed, the corner drum would have appeared (like the elder Burnet's Merchants House tower) rather as a quasi-independent adjunct to a symmetrical façade. The stylistic mixture on the earlier section is as rich as Anderson's, though of a quite different kind, with a rusticated Palladian ground-floor arcade and first-floor windows whose pediments are also (distantly) Palladian. Yet their frames project almost like oriels, and the pediments, each with a blocked 'attic' of its own, most disconcertingly rise above the level of the bases of the columns of the giant order above. Beaux-Arts influence is strong in this temple front, yet the large second-floor windows look back into the early French Renaissance.

details into the Clyde Trust, **176**. This is a vigorous, indeed almost aggressive, design, not now satisfactory as a whole since the Broomielaw façade is evidently unfinished and ends abruptly: the 'central' pediment with its giant high-up Corinthian columns is almost at one end. (The asymmetry resulted from the addition in 1905 of the baroque cornerpiece, with more giant columns, this time coupled, and a calm and delightful cupola in the tradition of the English baroque of the early eighteenth century.[5]) The Clyde Trust has unusually high storeys, and the largest windows are not on the first but the second, which increases the apparent scale, as does the heavy rustication of the two lower floors. The columns stand rather unhappily on the rusticated stone beneath. The Athenaeum, **182**, is very different – small, unassertive and carefully symmetrical (though it is in fact more or less impossible to see the whole façade from full face). While its general appearance may seem calm enough, the details, with hints of uncertainties in scale and in floor levels produced by a rather mannered use of different window shapes and half-cornices, are not restful. Mannerist also are the four attached Ionic columns on the main storey, each of whose capitals supports no continuous entablature, but (after a square dosseret) a piece of the cornice which juts out like a square hat and in turn carries a sculptured figure. The idea for this colonnade, with its round-headed windows between the columns, surely comes from Honeyman's Barony North Church, the details ultimately from Gibbs; Honeyman gets a lighter effect, because his figures stand free of all masonry against the sky, whereas Burnet's stand back against a solid parapet.

The backwash of the Bank disaster doubtless deprived Burnet of a good many commissions in the 1880s; and by the end of the decade most of the academic purity seems to have gone out of his style. Elaborate bay windows and other protruberances were now fashionable, and although Burnet handled them with his usual skill, the effect was certainly busy when compared either with his earlier work or with that of Charles McKim in America (who had preceded Burnet at the Beaux-Arts by some years). Charing Cross Mansions (corner of Sauchiehall Street and St George's Road, 1891) shows clearly this phase of Burnet's work, **181**. Because of a difficult building line, which prevents the whole frontage being seen at once, the design was divided into two sections determined by the main viewpoints; one a symmetrical quadrant masking the obtuse angle of the two streets, the other asymmetrical with a big circular corner tower which carries the design into Renfrew Street. It is an immense and rather restless amassing of formal components; and, as ever, the dreadful shop fronts make an irritating and irrelevant distraction in an already very involved building. The *grande horloge*, with its resplendent setting of elaborate sculpture, ought to be a real unifying feature, leading to the proud galleried cupola. But it is now neglected and handless, its gilding soured with grime. The third floor has its windows set in recessed panels behind a continuous arcade with elliptical arches – the first appearance in Burnet's work of the Thomson eaves gallery. The rest is pretty confusing (the confusion made worse by one's normally having to look across a sea of traffic), especially the jumbled roofline, where the chimneys get mixed up with the very French-looking truncated pyramids at the corners.[6] At the end of the decade Burnet is still using a very mixed bag of features in Waterloo

[6] Burnet may have been encouraged to introduce this kind of French motif by Wilson's Park Terrace (see above, p.94). [Charing Cross Mansions and the adjoining Albany Chambers have now been restored and the clock again tells the time, but the shops remain as bad as ever. Further consideration confirms that there really is much too much going on on the complex façades, yet the design is unquestionably a fascinating and inventive one.]

188. The Banking Hall of the Glasgow Savings Bank in Ingram Street (J. J. Burnet, 1894).

Chambers (15-23 Waterloo Street, 1899). The building is narrower but taller than Charing Cross Mansions, and would have been two storeys higher still had the fire authorities not demanded a reduction. In certain respects Waterloo Chambers is even more involved than Charing Cross, the dominant accents being strangely intermixed. On the two lower floors the centrepiece is very narrow and is flanked by strongly emphasized horizontal lines. On the four floors above, the central section is much wider and its horizontally insistent balcony thus overlaps those of the side pieces below. Near the top of the centre, two pairs of huge columns rest on the pediments of aedicules crammed between bay windows: they support a heavy balcony (once again less wide than that at third floor level but still wider than the ground floor centre), above which is a simplified eaves gallery. The strong horizontal bands are an heroic attempt to unify a façade containing a multitude of different planes; but if the design is successful it is only narrowly so and depends on an acceptance of a multitude of incidents and boldness of relief as a substitute for clarity and logic.

The eaves gallery appears again in Burnet buildings in Edinburgh (Forsyth's and 80 George Street) and also in Atlantic Chambers (43–47 Hope Street), which though dating from the same year as Waterloo Chambers is much cleaner and bolder, **184**. There are now no conflicting accents, the bay

6a R. D. Sandilands, another Beaux-Arts student, reproduced the central feature of Waterloo Chambers, the Ionic grand order with Doric entablature, at the Parish Council offices, 266 George Street. The source is the so-called Temple of Empedocles at Selinus (Sicily), a hellenistic building reconstructed in J. I. Hittorff's *La restitution du temple d'Empédocle à Sélinonte* (1851), evidently a source for Beaux-Arts experiments: see R. Middleton, *The Beaux-Arts and 19th-Century French Architecture* (1982), p.176 and pl.III. For Sandilands' Govan Town Hall (1897–1901), see p.263.

189. The Ingram Street Savings Bank, drawn by Alexander McGibbon before 1898 when Burnet added the galleried top storey (cf. 188) to his father's rather tame building of 1865-6.

6a

windows are fewer and more simply treated, the horizontals unbroken until the very top, and the eaves gallery becomes the unifying feature with fat columns of its own and a big overhanging cornice broken by a bold central chimney.

During the 1890s Burnet's firm was also pioneering the vertically accented buildings which became a common feature as individual Georgian houses were demolished and their narrow sites re-used for buildings two or three times as high. The crucial design here is the second part of the Athenaeum (now the north building of the Royal Scottish Academy of Music, 179 Buchanan Street), **183**. Like Charing Cross Mansions, it was begun in 1891, but it is utterly unlike them in almost every respect. With its great height on a very narrow frontage, its sweeping lines and strong emphasis on the vertical articulation of the windows, the Athenaeum is well worthy of comparison with contemporary American work. Moreover, though the narrow frontage might have encouraged a readily recognizable formal balance, the elaborately contrived symmetry of Waterloo Chambers and Charing Cross is entirely absent. Indeed the Athenaeum is insistently, wilfully, asymmetrical, consisting of two tall sections side by side, which, though about the same height, do not from the exterior even appear to have the same number of storeys. The left-hand section projects slightly in front of its

6b

6b The rear elevation with strips of oriel bays through four and five storeys is close to contemporary work in Chicago.

190. Elder Library, Govan (J. J. Burnet, 1902).

partner and has a flattish bay window on three storeys, roughly level with which on the right are two very narrow tall panels with windows like arrow slits not quite on a level with one another. And where the left-hand unit ends with a gable above a large semicircular window, the right hand has a flurry of small openings side by side and then, above an elementary cornice, an odd octagonal cupola. The detail in this extraordinary design comes from all over the place – some still Renaissance, some faintly Flemish, some distinctly Scottish, the frieze Greek. Yet – no doubt because of the dominance of the verticals – there is paradoxically less confusion about the Athenaeum design than about Charing Cross or Waterloo Chambers. One could hardly deduce Burnet's later Glasgow work from it; but, looking back, it is just possible to see how McGeoch's and even the Kodak Building derive from its basic principles by a process of the elimination of all arbitrary detail.[7]

Burnet's work in Glasgow reaches a climax in the huge cliff of McGeoch's warehouse at the corner of Cadogan and West Campbell Streets (1905), **185.**† Here the interest in vertical articulation of the façade achieves its triumph, and provides a nearly perfect expression of the constructional techniques which Burnet was likewise pioneering. Here he can properly be seen as the heir of Thomson. For the great vertical window-strips of McGeoch's are the logical outcome of the experiments that Thomson began in Dunlop Street; and from the exposed iron frame of the Buck's Head to the internal steel one of Kodak the principle is basically the same.[8] But there is another potent influence at work – that of Louis Sullivan, whose work Burnet had seen on his visit to America in 1896 (a visit which is also traceable in the high blocks, presumably designed soon after his return, which show particularly the influence of Burnham and Root in Chicago – see especially the Monadnock Block which must also have made its mark on Campbell:[9] Burnet must have spent much of his time in America studying the new steel-framed structures). Probably the Wainwright Building in St Louis is closest of Sullivan's work,

[7] The separate contributions of the partners in Burnet, Son and Campbell have not been properly sorted out. The independent-minded J. A. Campbell was possibly responsible for much of the Athenaeum, though, as in the Barony Church, Burnet has always been given the credit. The two are said to have collaborated only in competition designs. The arch and bay window design perhaps owes something to the tower of the Central Hotel.

[8] Burnet's earlier tall buildings also have steel frames, but their front walls are load-bearing above the first floor level: this accords with contemporary American practice for buildings of fewer than ten storeys.

[9] See below, p.210. Later there was collaboration of some kind between Burnham and Burnet in the design of Selfridge's in London (1908–9). See the comment by Goodhart-Rendel on p.261 of *Architectural Review*, October 1965. The American *Architectural Record* was studied in the best Glasgow offices.

192. (left) **Northern Insurance Building, St Vincent Street** (J. A. Campbell, 1908).
193. (right) **157–167 Hope Street** (J. A. Campbell, 1902).
194. (opposite) **The back of the Northern Insurance Building, with its towering bays of steel-framed windows.**

both in the massive masonry of the ground and mezzanine storeys and in the vertical window strips, to their Glasgow equivalents. Of course Burnet's building is nothing like so high as the American examples, but it has a correspondingly greater massiveness, enhanced by the tower of chimneys at each corner, their height emphasized by the pairs of very tall recessed panels which recall the vertical strips of the Athenaeum. McGeoch's is altogether an exceptionally clearly thought-out building, in which each section or feature is cogently related to the rest: note, for example, how the balcony at second-floor level overruns into the corner towers and so links the upper part of the main façade with the vertical frame of the towers; the tower windows (with pediments the same shape as that of the main door) make a vertical link from the balcony into the towers. All the stonework is unusually sharply cut, giving strong clear contrast of light and shade; and there is very little sculpture to take away from the severe lines of the masonry: that over the main doorway (by Phyllis Archibald) stands out by its very isolation. McGeoch's has not, perhaps, the compelling logic of Sullivan's work at its best, nor of Burnet's own greatest achievement, Kodak House in Kingsway, London. In particular, the treatment of the most prominent corner seems to me a weak point in the design: the semi-cylindrical drum of windows is slightly too 'graceful' for so strong a design, and the chamfered top storey, with its queer gablet, looks a little arty, as well as being unhappily crowded between the close-set chimneys. Perhaps Burnet set himself an insoluble problem at this corner. For all that, McGeoch's marks an impressive moment of the functional tradition in Britain, when the satisfaction to be gained from the

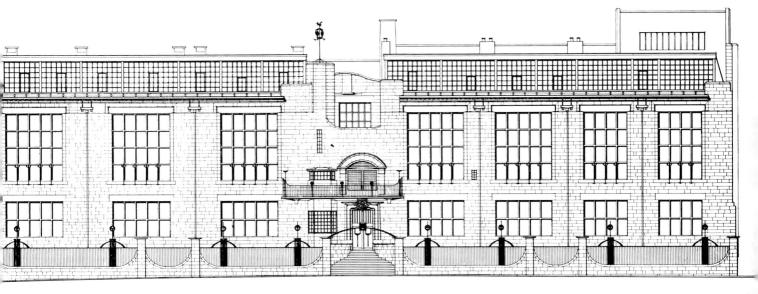

195. (left) The entrance of the School of Art (C. R. Mackintosh, 1897).
196. (above) Elevation of the North Front of the Art School. Drawn by H. C. Ferguson.

straightforward and uncompromising expression of constructional materials was being rediscovered – historically noteworthy as one of the first buildings to make use of reinforced-concrete slabs cast *in situ*, architecturally for its impressive statement of its function in conveying a sense of great strength and reliability.

McGeoch's is the high-water mark of Burnet in Glasgow: of its type the city has nothing finer. But its great virtues should not be allowed to obscure those of later buildings which may not be so obviously striking. One that is now almost impossible to appreciate is the former Wallace Scott factory in Spean Street, Cathcart, which was a later re-working of the principal features of McGeoch's (about 1912), and was the closest that Burnet came in Scotland to the logical conclusion of the line of thought worked out in the Kodak Building, **187**. Alas, it and its astonishing Delhi-like garden layout have recently been disgracefully mutilated by the Electricity Board who now occupy it. Much later Burnet came back from London to design another big office-block in the centre of the city: this is No.200 St Vincent Street (*c.*1927), almost his last work of any kind, **186**. It has little of the daring of McGeoch's, but is in its stolid way masterly – a plain nearly cubical block with massive Richardsonian arches over the two bottom floors and a completely regular rectangular pattern of oblong windows on the five floors above; the dentel-moulded cornice is broken only near the front two corners by the solid masonry rising into chimney towers. It is a design at the farthest remove from Waterloo Chambers, making its effect by complete simplicity and straightforwardness. (For this reason the sculpture, added to the façade some time after the building was finished, seems to me unfortunate.) 9a

Finally there are several smaller buildings of Burnet's in which he was much less experimental than in his big ones and allowed his fancy a free rein over various traditional styles. The domed single-storey banking hall, which stands in front of his father's Savings Bank at 177 Ingram Street, **188**, was built in 1895 shortly before the younger man added the colonnaded top floor to the main building. The banking hall uses Roman Baroque motifs with great gusto: each feature is crowned with a broken segmental pediment, sometimes inside a similar aedicule. The pediments contain cartouches, and that of the aedicule of the main entrance is broken by a smaller aedicule which has a

9a The deliberate astylar restraint of this building is in notable contrast with the big-boned American classicism favoured at the same time by James Miller (Bank of Scotland, 110–20 St Vincent Street) and E. G. Wylie (Scottish Legal Building, 95 Bothwell Street).

197. The west end of the Art School (1907).

9b The device is adapted from the mid-seventeenth-century doorcase of St Mary's, Oxford.

10 This design is very clearly the mark of Burnet's having subscribed in 1901 to Belcher and Macartney's *Later Renaissance Architecture in England*.

11 See for example Bruce Price's house on 56th Street, New York City and E. Townsend Mix's Globe Building, Minneapolis, 1891. (Schuyler, *American Architecture*, pp.243 and 145.)

12 The Phoenix Insurance Building, once thought to be a late work of Campbell's, is in fact entirely the work of his partner, A. D. Hislop. It was built in 1913 in the monumental Americanized neo-classic which had just then come in, and is the first building in Glasgow in which the giant order of columns on the two lowest floors is used functionally.

[The Edinburgh Life has been rebuilt behind the façade and its rear elevation destroyed.]

13 As with Burnet's tall buildings the front walls are load-bearing above the first floor level.

triangular pediment standing on twisted columns. The dome itself is like a tiny version of St Peter's. The corners are broken by slightly recessed convex quadrants (like huge quarter-columns) which rise into sculpture above the line of the main parapet. Not a building of charm (and in this respect different from Lutyens's little bank in Piccadilly, London, which might seem to invite comparison); on the contrary it takes its baroque formulas with solemn seriousness and makes a very good job of them.

Much simpler and probably more appealing are the library and cottage hospital (both 1902–3) which the shipbuilder Elder gave to Govan. The hospital, in Drumoyne Road, **191**, is an academic essay in the Wren style (of, say, Morden College, Blackheath)[10] only straying from detailed fidelity to the originals in the lower-floor windows, which seem to have arrived via Philip Webb, and in the unexpectedly harsh contrast between the quoins and the stone of the walls. The Elder Library (228a Langlands Road) is freer, a singularly graceful combination of elements from French and Austrian Baroque, recalling the contemporary work of E. A. Rickards, **190**. The main feature of its single-storey façade is a serpentine veranda on coupled Tuscan columns topped by a relaxed widely spaced balustrade and a small dome. This really is a building of both elegance and charm, a remarkably calm departure from the concentrated energy of the big blocks in the city centre.

John A. Campbell, who died rather young in 1909, had much in common with Burnet, in whose firm he was for a time a partner. Indeed, as has already been mentioned, it is hard at times to determine who should have the credit. Clearly Campbell was also a pioneer of the vertical articulation of tall buildings: see his Dundas House, 164–168 Buchanan Street (1898), whose arch and bay window theme is very close to that of the Athenaeum and likewise has American parallels,[11] and offices at 71 Robertson Street, 1899 – the year of Atlantic Chambers, with which Campbell's building has much in common including an eaves gallery; yet Robertson Street is indisputably Campbell's, for the partnership had been dissolved in 1897. Much of his work is outside Glasgow, including a large number of houses at Bridge of Weir, where he had a weekend bachelor establishment of his own; but there are three major commercial buildings in the city. Two of these are Insurance Offices, both in St Vincent Street – the Edinburgh Life, No.124 (1906) and the Northern, Nos.86–90 (1908).[12] The design of the main façade of these buildings suggests at first a milder, less authoritative Burnet. Their fenestration is conventional, but the soaring lines of the vertical features are very powerful on the Northern, **192**. It is, however, the backs which are likely to be found of the greatest interest today. Like most buildings in central Glasgow, these back onto narrow lanes, where light is difficult – a serious matter in an office building used all day. Campbell's answer was straightforwardly practical, but also startlingly ahead of his time. Using the steel frame on which all his large buildings are constructed,[13] he reduced the wall-space to a minimum, producing an almost entirely glass façade, **194**. The window space is much increased by the use of steel casements with extremely thin glazing bars, and further by breaking up the façade into a series of flattish canted bays which run almost the whole height of the building. (This last was a device used by Burnet on the rear elevation of Atlantic Chambers at the east end of Cadogan Street; but Burnet has far more masonry and far less glass and still uses sash windows. The red brick rear elevation of the younger Salmon's Mercantile Chambers, with close-packed soaring bay windows, is the immediate prototype.)

From the street, the most impressive of Campbell's Glasgow buildings is the large and somewhat earlier block on the south-west corner of Hope Street and West George Street (1902), **193**. This is larger than McGeoch's and has more swagger, but less native strength. At the angles Campbell has the canted strips of bay windows which he later used on the Northern; with their splayed corners they lack the sharpness and toughness of the corner towers of McGeoch's; and there is far less deliberate strengthening on the ground floor, which may seem a little weak. There is no explicit articulation of the windows on the main part of the façade, though three bays in the centre project – so that the design as a whole may seem less coherent and logical than Burnet's. Nevertheless, for so large a building, the poise and even gracefulness are remarkable. The top floors, to which the powerful lines of the bay window strips lead the eye directly, are particularly impressive. Campbell realized, as so many twentieth-century architects have not, that if a building is to look satisfying, it must present a recognizably logical appearance: one of the great problems of tall buildings is why they should ever stop, and one of the great problems of the architect to provide an aes-

198. The north front of the Art School: the east portion 1897, the west 1907.
199. (p.212) The library of the Art School (1907): note how the curved details soften the harsh rectangularity.
200. (p.213) Art School: the east staircase, inserted c.1907: the shallow oriel was originally external.

thetically convincing answer on his façade. Above a balustraded balcony, Campbell links his two top storeys in a continuous arcade, recessing the windows so that the arches are what count: almost the effect is of a gigantic eaves gallery; a continuous balcony runs underneath. We then read the two uppermost floors as a single unit – naturally a larger one than those below; and this, together with the wide eaves, brings the building convincingly to a stop at the point where the architect's sense of proportion tells him it should.[14]

Of all the Glasgow architects of the generation which, for one reason or another, came to an end with the first world war, much the most famous today is Charles Rennie Mackintosh. It was not always so; and even now he is perhaps rather famous than well known. For while his name has an honoured place in the histories of the 'Modern Movement', there must still be relatively few people who are really as closely aware of his buildings as of many by much lesser men. Even today – as in his own time – Mackintosh seems to be better appreciated by visitors from the Continent than by his fellow-countrymen. Now it is, I think, true – for all that his work seems to anticipate so much in the architectural development of this century – that Mackintosh is most accurately seen as one of the great isolated geniuses of architecture. Though his early interests and his graphic work link him with

[14] The strong horizontal line near the top is repeated in the much smaller Edinburgh Life, but in the Northern Campbell allows his verticals to shoot skyward without interruption.
[15] [See Service, *Edwardian Architecture and its Origins*, pp.478–9, and Margaret Richardson, *Architects of the Arts and Crafts Movement* (1983), pl.88.]

201. The board room in the Art School (1906).

202. Willow Tea-room: interior before spoliation.

16 See Hitchcock, *Architecture: 19th and 20th Centuries*, p.298.
17 A likely contemporary debt of Mackintosh's which has not so far been explored is to the work of J. M. Maclaren, whose very remarkable farmhouse at Fortingall, Perthshire (1889) not only anticipates the simple, direct lines of Mackintosh's houses, but also contains an oriel feature somewhat reminiscent of the earlier Art School work. If Mackintosh went to Fortingall, he would also have seen the equally sympathetic Fortingall Hotel (1891) by Dunn and Watson. Again, the top of the *Glasgow Herald* tower is a very bold development of the corner turret of Maclaren's High School at Stirling.
18 Goodhart-Rendel did not share this opinion: 'much of Mackintosh was rather a fraud, compared with Plumet, Olbrich or Behrens' (N. PEVSNER, 'Goodhart-Rendel's Roll Call', *Architectural Review*, October 1965, p.262). Plumet is presumably here for his decorative interiors: it is hard to see in what way Mackintosh's were more 'fraudulent'. As to Olbrich, there seems to me something freakish – and now very dated – about the design of the famous Hochzeitsturm in Darmstadt, his only building which might be compared with Mackintosh's major work. Of the three only Behrens seems to me in the same class as Mackintosh; and it is worth noting that his individual style did not really prove itself before about 1909. [Pevsner's article is reprinted in Service, *op. cit.*; see p.477 etc.]

the *art nouveau* movement (to which his wife was evidently more strongly and lastingly inclined), as an architect he has little in common with the practitioners of the continental *art nouveau*, with Horta and van de Velde. The sinuous curves, the tendrils and cabbagey things that, in Horta's buildings and in some of the interiors of Sullivan's, make decoration seem more important than their basic form – these are virtually unknown in Mackintosh's architecture, though familiar in his interior decoration of existing buildings not his own. Even the first part of the Art School, designed in 1896 (when Mackintosh was 28, four years after Horta 'began' the *art nouveau* movement) is almost without curves of any kind. And where a contemporary architect like Frantz Jourdain covers the bold iron frame of a shop in Paris not only with decorative metalwork but also with panels of polychrome faience, Mackintosh leaves his great windows entirely, almost ruthlessly, unadorned.

Parallels have been found between Mackintosh and some of his English contemporaries – in particular Harrison Townsend, whose Whitechapel Art Gallery has an asymmetrically heavy stonework front somewhat reminiscent of the main entrance of the Art School, **195**, and C. F. A. Voysey, the designer of many country houses which may have a bit of the precisely calculated but seemingly easy-going calm and simplicity of Mackintosh's admirable houses at Helensburgh and Kilmacolm. The name of the now-forgotten Halsey Ricardo should more particularly be mentioned. An excellent small block of offices, once in Great George Street, London, but long demolished, has many characteristic Mackintosh features as early as 1888 – small leaded panes, a flat bow window set into the thickness of the wall, another recessed under a flat arch.[15] This makes Voysey seem somewhat more remote, though the studio windows of the Art School are reputed to have been derived from a Voysey project.[16] But the houses of the two architects probably have not a great deal in common, except perhaps for a certain discomfort deriving largely from the furniture. Those of Ernest Newton are outwardly near to Mackintosh's, though as English as Mackintosh's are Scottish. For, as has often been pointed out, Mackintosh's identifiable sources are essentially Scottish. Where the houses owe something to the small lairds' houses of the sixteenth and seventeenth centuries,[17] the long rambling south façade of the Art School has a romantic affinity to the cliff walls of medieval and later castles like Linlithgow and Huntly, a connexion also suggested by the east end with its snecked rubble walling and irregular fenestration. Nevertheless, Mackintosh's finest work is that of a completely original creator, drawing nothing from period revivals or from the fashions of the time.[18] The austere north face of the Art School, **198**, takes a certain personal quality from the fantastic masonry of the main entrance, where Mackintosh's favourite small-paned windows appear for the first time, from the idiosyncratic details of the ironwork and from the slight asymmetry of the whole, which of course can never be seen from head-on. Yet this façade has in its essential conception that feature which I have suggested is characteristic of the best of Thomson – as indeed of all great art – a degree of impersonality, a certain detachment in which the artist refuses any temptation to express directly anything of his personal situation or predicament, answering only the demands of the particular occasion. Even so, the work is not merely functional in the loose sense of the word that is generally assumed to be understood. Professor Pevsner has drawn attention to the special kind of experience made possible through those very personal details noted above: referring to the ironwork members jutting out from the lower part of the main windows, he observes: 'The quality equally eloquent in the balls and stalks is Mackintosh's intense feeling for spatial values. Our eyes have to pass through the first layer of space, indicated by the stalks and balls before arriving at the solid stone front of the building. The same transparency of pure space will be found in all Mackintosh's principal works.'[19] And these same stalks and balls give, for all their relative tininess, a remarkable buoyancy to the exceptionally severe rectangularity of the great windows.[20]

The western section of the Art School, begun in 1907, is generally (and I think rightly) considered Mackintosh's greatest piece of design. In the total impression of the west front, **197**, there is much more that one can quickly identify as characteristic Mackintosh than on the north. Yet once again one is not aware of anything intrusively personal. The *tour de force* of the three great oriels rising almost sheer for 65 feet (the delicately immense library windows occupying 25) is something essentially without parallel in Glasgow, or indeed anywhere else at the time. Though they may appear superficially something like the oriel bays used by Campbell and Salmon, the relationship between the volumes they create is entirely new. The fineness of the window details, and the great size of the windows themselves, give an astonishing

203. Willow Tea-room, Sauchiehall Street (C. R. Mackintosh, 1903), recently restored and now a jeweller's shop.

19 *Pioneers of Modern Design* (Penguin edition, Harmondsworth, 1960), pp.166–7.
20 The north front, though of course designed as a whole, was built in two parts in 1897–9 and 1907, since to begin with there was only enough money for the east end – a fortunate thing, as it turned out, for it gave Mackintosh the opportunity to completely redesign the library block. [It is worth comparing Halsey Ricardo's unpremiated competition design for Oxford Town Hall (1892): see Davey, *Arts and Crafts Architecture* (1980), pl.133, or Service, *Edwardian Architecture* (1977), pl.47.]

204. Martyrs Public School, Barony Street, Townhead (C. R. Mackintosh, 1895). The Gothic building beyond is Osmund Cooke's St. Mungo's Retreat (1890-2).

204. Martyrs Public School, Barony Street, Townhead (C. R. Mackintosh, 1895). The Gothic building beyond is Osmund Cooke's St. Mungo's Retreat (1890-2).

lightness to the vast block of masonry. The great height of the building, emphasized already by the steep fall of land to the south, is further dramatized by the soaring upthrust of the uninterrupted vertical lines. (It is chiefly Mackintosh's wonderful feeling for the site which makes the building sit so well in the Glasgow scene, however isolated it is in the general history of the city's architecture – an effect soon to be spoiled and perhaps destroyed altogether by the much higher new block of the Art School to the north of Renfrew Street, a peculiarly callous treatment of a great building: the architects are Keppie, Henderson & Partners – descendants of Mackintosh's old firm – but the blame must lie essentially on the urge to realize land values in monetary terms above all.) I think it is fair to say that the very cleanness, the complete lack of fuss, the directness and clearness of vision that Mackintosh brought to his simultaneous solution of a number of difficult visual and functional problems, are things which probably no other architect of his time could have achieved; and they are what give even the inescapably personal idiom of the west end its curiously dateless quality. It is entirely without any sense of the modish. 20a

Of the interiors the library is justly renowned, 199. As with the most beautiful of Mackintosh's tea-rooms, it is apparently impossible to speak of this without using metaphors drawn from music. Professor Pevsner describes the effect of the library as 'an overwhelmingly full polyphony of abstract form'.21 Be that as it may, it is a room which, like the interiors of the great Gothic churches, never presents a static impression. It is not designed to be experienced from one point only, but depends for its total effect on the varying perspectives obtained as one moves through a volume contained by the complicated enclosure of the walls: an experience in time. Much of the detail – particularly the way in which the galleries do not reach the vertical columns that support them so that horizontal beams have to carry their weight 3 feet farther out into the centre of the room – may seem merely wilful. Yet

205. (left) Mercantile Chambers, Bothwell Street (James Salmon, junior, 1898).
206. (right) Scotland Street School, Kingston (C. R. Mackintosh, 1904).
207. (opposite) One of the great staircase towers of Scotland Street School.

21a The attempt in 1969–70 to restore the Ingram Street tearoom as a restaurant was aborted by the complexities of late twentieth-century regulations. So much would have been destroyed that it was decided to dismantle the fittings for future re-erection. No place has yet been found for this either at the School of Art or at the New Hunterian or at the new Burrell Gallery in Pollok Park; but some of the furniture can now be seen at the Hill House, Helensburgh.

apart from the fact that the interplay of lines and volumes is extremely fascinating in itself, Mackintosh has managed by this device to increase the width, and therefore the usefulness, of the spaces under the galleries, without crowding the upper part of the central space and thereby considerably darkening the whole room.

One criticism that can, I think, be brought against the Art School is of the disturbing effect, when looking from the north-west, of seeing the north and west façades together. I find the change of scale in the details disconcerting – from a few huge windows to a row of relatively small ones, from panes over 5 feet high to panes only 9 inches square. From this angle, the north front remains overwhelmingly powerful, while the west loses a good deal of its strength in the conjunction – an effect enhanced by the colossal eaves above which the sheer wall of the west front does not perhaps rise high enough to counteract the deep shadow produced by the eaves even when (as almost always) the north front is in shade. From a higher position the effect is much reduced, for not only does one see less of the dark underside of the eaves, but the long attic storey of the north front – invisible from street level – provides, with the intermediate-sized panes of its continuous glazing, a link between the two scales. Alas, this is a view that few people ever see.

Mackintosh's reputation virtually rests on a single building. The other things in Glasgow with which he was connected are rather disappointing after the Art School. All the famous tea-rooms are now either destroyed or mutilated. The only two that can now give any impression of what they were once like are the Ingram Street, Nos.215–217, now a store and showroom for novelties which almost hide what of Mackintosh remains, and that at 217 Sauchiehall Street (now part of Daly's shop), for which Mackintosh designed the individual, though not entirely successful, façade, **203**, and which, inside, was perhaps the most attractive of them all – close in feeling to the Art School library, though less uncompromising in its detail, **202**. The fan-

tastic plaster frieze happily remains among bridal scenery; and the whole building could easily and should certainly be restored. Of the work done by Honeyman's firm after Mackintosh joined, it is not easy to tell how much is due to him. He certainly worked on the *Glasgow Herald* building in Mitchell Street, on the *Daily Record* office, and on the Martyrs Public School (11 Barony Street, 1895), though none of these (except for the rear elevation of the *Daily Record*) would draw attention to their architect without other evidence. The strange octagonal tower of the *Glasgow Herald* was drawn by Mackintosh and is presumably largely his invention, though inspired by J. M. Maclaren; of the rest, the lower storeys are Mackintosh's; the upper are said to be Keppie's and were re-used by him in Sauchiehall Street in 1904:[22] it is all surprisingly vigorous and unfussy. The Martyrs School is a notably sturdy block, plain and rectangular, its principal windows still basically Georgian in shape, **204**. But the staircase windows tell a different story; so perhaps do the tall square chimney and the balustrade: the influence of Burnet seems clear. The Queen's Cross Church (866 Garscube Road, 1899) must be mainly Mackintosh's, but is rather unhappily Gothic-inspired.[22a]

There remains the majestic and powerful Scotland Street School (Kingston) of 1904, **206**. The great feature here is the pair of circular staircases, enclosed in cylinders almost entirely of glass, with thin masonry mullions

208. (above) **Anderston Savings Bank** (James Salmon, junior, 1899).
209. (right) **Anderston Savings Bank: doorway with sculpture by Albert Hodge.**

21b The Willow has now been separated from the rest of Daly's, the façade (in the design of which, incidentally, Mackintosh's invention was constricted by the need to retain some of the old façade at the upper levels) has now been expertly restored and much of the missing interiors replaced under the supervision of Geoffrey Wimpenny (of Keppie, Henderson & Partners). Regrettably, the staircase – one of the finest features – has had to be enclosed to satisfy fire regulations.
22 According to the late A. G. Henderson. But the drawings when last seen were reported to be wholly in Mackintosh's hand. [Keppie may have suggested the outline, but the preliminary drawings are all in Mackintosh's hand too. Keppie, who was no great inventor, often re-used ideas they had worked out together in the 1890s.]
22a A foolish remark: see pp.267ff.

running all the way up and transoms only near the top and bottom, **207**. These are very spacious and light (important since the building faces north) and foreshadow the somewhat similar glass cylinder produced by Gropius in 1914. The ironwork is again excellent, and the symmetrical composition handsomely balanced; the main block, with its rather uneasily spaced windows, is rather less compelling, and not so attractive as the Martyrs School: it seems not beyond the powers of a lesser man. The general plan, however, with the block of classrooms between the staircases, and cloak-rooms at each end, is standard board school practice of the time. No doubt Mackintosh was required to conform: it is the design of the windows which is, in the circumstances, pedestrian. The cloakrooms with their stepped back upper storeys are, however, conspicuously successful: they act visually like buttresses to the great staircase towers.[23]

Mackintosh was under 40 when he designed the second part of the Art School. It was his crowning achievement, and it was to all intents and purposes his last.

Of Mackintosh's contemporaries the nearest to him in spirit was James Salmon. The two were indeed friends, and Salmon (when he has been looked at at all) has usually been dismissed as a mere hanger-on of Mackintosh,

210. Salmon's perspective sketch for 'The Hatrack'. It is not known if the right-hand elevation was built: it is now hidden by a tall block to the east. The building as executed shows several changes in fenestration (cf. fig.189). The tall gabled building on the left is a Commercial Bank branch by Sydney Mitchell (1888), now, with its small Georgian neighbour, demolished.

[23] The school would probably have been more successful in white stone. Red stone seems to need more relief than there is at Scotland Street: Burnet knew perfectly how to handle it at McGeoch's. Mackintosh intended small-paned classroom windows, but the authorities seem to have insisted on the usual pattern, greatly to the detriment of the design.

copying the master's ideas in a more timid form. This is both quite unfair and extremely misleading. Salmon was one of the few really original architects of his time in this country, a genuinely creative mind, with two of Glasgow's most remarkable buildings to his credit. Interestingly enough, it is one of these, 142 St Vincent Street, nicknamed 'The Hatrack', which gives Salmon if anyone the best right to be called Glasgow's architect of the *art nouveau*. His contact with continental *art nouveau* was in fact far closer than Mackintosh's.

Salmon (who was called the Wee Troot because of his size) was the third generation of an architectural family, his grandfather and namesake being the architect of Arthur's Warehouse in Miller Street.[24] His father, W. Forrest Salmon, sent him to Leiper, where he worked for a time under W. J. Anderson. In about 1895 he joined his father, who was himself no architect but a first-class job-getter, whose work had greatly improved on the arrival of J. Gaff Gillespie as draughtsman in the early nineties. Gillespie is said to have designed the rather wild Renaissance Temperance League Building, 106–108 Hope Street (1894, now the Woolwich Equitable). In the later work of the [24a] firm it is not easy to distinguish Gillespie's hand from the younger Salmon's. Forrest Salmon remained in the firm until he died in 1911: he was the 'commercial traveller' and latterly was never seen with a pencil in his hand.

James Salmon, junior, seems to have begun as a rather self-conscious stylist, thinking of architecture largely in terms of decoration (he continued to make lavish use of the work of his sculptor friends). Among his early buildings, the most interesting in the centre is Mercantile Chambers, Bothwell Street, **205**, an elaborate seven-storey commercial building designed about 1896, whose vertical bay window strips are joined by *force majeure* by an arcade of large windows on the fifth floor and a very clumsy attic. The prominent gables, one at each end, high up, do not help the design towards unity; but the ground-floor arcade is an attractive feature and has luckily not yet been mutilated, though some box-like excrescences have recently grown out of the top one. This upper arcade above the firm horizontal line of a cornice may have given Campbell an idea for the Hope Street building. The rear elevation has already been mentioned as an influence on Campbell. The Anderston Savings Bank, 752–6 Argyle Street (1899), **208**, is a much smaller building full of idiosyncratic detail including much applied *art nouveau* decoration, particularly round the doorway (sculpted by Albert Hodge), **209**. The design seems to keep promising symmetrical aspects and then just failing to fulfil them. It is balanced about one corner which has an irregular octagonal tower, whose 'cornice' is on alternate sides lifted into a sharp little gablet; above this a dome, like an upturned fritillary with a stalk on top, holds its own surprisingly well among a crowd of tall chimneys mostly plain and rising straight out of the wall, one issuing into a trio of columns carrying a cornice like a tray with three diminutive pots on top. This inventive and unconventional building, full of wayward charm, was long under sentence of death for standing among the desert spaces of Anderston; but happily its value to the new development has been officially recognized and a pardon granted.

The British Linen Bank (816–818 Govan Road), also of 1899, is a considerably simplified version of the Anderston theme, with relatively orthodox fenestration but a highly original openwork crown on top of the corner and some lively *art nouveau* sculpture on the ground floor. Attractive though the

[24] See above, p.109.
[24a] Perhaps it *is* a little wild: there is certainly plenty of incident, especially on the narrow main frontage to Hope Street (what did the Temperance League think?). But the details are of high quality, and the building, unlike its self-important neighbours, is of admirably discreet manners and considerable charm. It is not given to all office buildings to raise a smile of pleasure. Moreover, sculpture and architecture are designed in entire harmony with one another.

211. ·The Hatrack', 142 St Vincent Street (James Salmon, junior, 1899).

detail is, it would hardly have made Salmon into a major architect. But the turn of the century brought a dramatic change in his attitude to architecture. 142 St Vincent Street (1899–1902), **211**, is one of the most remarkable buildings in Glasgow, ten storeys high (including basement and attic), only three bays wide, and narrow bays at that: a fascinating essay in how to get light into a building with a tall, narrow frontage. It has recently been called Gaudiesque, and Beardsleyesque features had indeed appeared in Mercantile chambers; but the exuberantly rippling front, with the stonework whittled away to nearly nothing, has nothing of the delight in sinuous, arbitrary curves, the elimination of angles, the attempt to make a building imitate natural forms, that mark Gaudí's mature work. Salmon's building, in fact, for all the deliberate refusal to make any two storeys identical, is sane and indeed logical: it has strong vertical lines, and the eye is drawn upwards along the continuous bay windows of the outer bays; separate storeys are sharply demarcated but not so as to cut the building into layers; and the top, even with its weird octagonal fantasy, seems proper and fitting (the jolly crowning pinnacle has unfortunately been taken down). And if the enjoyment of variety for its own sake and the continuously undulating façade bring the building as close as Britain gets in its architecture to *art nouveau*, it is certainly a northern – indeed a Glasgow – version of the style. What at first sight seems wilful

24b

212. (above) **The lift hall of 'The Hatrack'.**
213. (right) **Napier House, Govan (W. J. Anderson, 1899). The top floor at the right hand chimney is a clumsy later addition.**

24b The sculpture at Mercantile Chambers, at Govan and probably also at St Vincent Street was by Francis Derwent Wood who clearly had a considerable influence on Salmon & Gillespie from 1897.

214. Lion Chambers, Hope Street (James Salmon, junior, 1906).
215. (opposite) The rippling glass wall of the north front of Lion Chambers.

25 Cf. Campbell's Northern Assurance Building (p.210 above).
26 28 November 1906; quoted in *Architects' Journal*, 6 May 1964, p.1018. Hennebique had used this system for factories in the early 1890s.
[Structurally 'The Hatrack' is also adventurous – cantilevered (in steel) off two rows of iron columns to reduce the side walls to minimum thickness and so increase floorspace: something of a precursor therefore of Lion Chambers.]
26a Anderson brought his knowledge of Italy to bear on this building, which looks like a late medieval Veronese palazzo which has had Renaissance arcades applied to the façades.
27 See above, p.180.

and arbitrary turns out in fact to be an imaginative and sensitive solution of a difficult problem. And perhaps one might not be so inclined to say 'art nouveau' were it not for what little decorative detail Salmon allows himself – the strange semi-cylindrical lantern over the main door with its curved abstract design in the glass, the arched head of the main first-floor window, the bulging barrel-shaped balconies near the top, above all the ironwork of the lift hall, 212, which shows distinctly the influence of Mackintosh's designs in iron and paint. A sketch of the building made in 1899 shows a fascinating side elevation rather in the Art School vein. This – if it was ever built – is now hidden by later work to the east, 210.

Salmon's last major work in Glasgow is Lion Chambers, 170–172 Hope Street, designed about 1905 with Gillespie, who soon after, on Forrest Salmon's death, left the partnership, and set up on his own, 214. It is less exciting to look at than the St Vincent Street building, and here one may feel that there is something arbitrary about the patterns on the main façade, though they may have been suggested by the tall Burnet and Campbell buildings in Buchanan Street. In particular the gable at the south-west corner seems unrelated either to the large semicircular window underneath or to the polygonal dome next to it. But both the north-west angle and the main windows on the Hope Street front (four reducing to two reducing to one, as one goes up) are adroitly handled; and the façade to the extremely narrow West Regent Lane to the north is as masterly as anything Salmon ever did, 215: a rippling glass wall going up eight storeys, the broadly canted bay windows allowing in as much light as possible and producing an entrancing, and quite light-hearted, effect as one looks up to the cornice 90 feet above.[25] Furthermore Lion Chambers is historically very important as it marked the first use in Glasgow of the Hennebique system, the earliest to make possible the construction of very tall buildings with a reinforced-concrete frame. The building is also entirely faced in reinforced concrete, allowing for much thinner walls than would be necessary when using masonry, particularly if – as here – a great deal of glass is also needed. According to the *Builders' Journal*[26] 'the outer walls are four inches thick only – a significant fact; for, if the thickness prescribed by the Building Act had been enforced, the rooms would have been too small for useful occupation'. The engineer was L. G. Mouchel.

Several lesser figures of this period deserve brief mention. W. J. Anderson also experimented with concrete (without designed reinforcement) in his Orient Boarding House (now the Ozalid, McPhater Street, Cowcaddens)[26a] and Napier House, in Govan, and as a result of an accident at the latter, shortened his days in doing so. Napier House, 213, is very wilful in its window shapes, and although it has sixteenth-century references, is really in a very personal form of *art nouveau*. Fairly close in feeling to Mackintosh is the work of Duncan and Alan McNaughtan. Their Tolcross Park Church and Royston School, Royston Road (1906), are very refined, though without structural innovations. The McNaughtans did not pursue the style after Mackintosh left Glasgow. P. M. Chalmers, chiefly known as a church architect,[27] designed the Neptune Building, 470 Argyle Street, 216 (unfortunately now lost in the Anderston redevelopment) in a refreshingly non-period style which, though perhaps influenced by Salmon and Mackintosh, is not closely related to that of any of his contemporaries. 118 Howard Street is by J.

216. Neptune Building, Argyle Street
(P. M. Chalmers, 1905; demolished
1966).
217. (opposite) The corner of
Buchanan Street and St Vincent
Street, with the National Bank
(J. M. Dick Peddie, 1900) and the
Carron Building beyond (James
Boucher, 1884).

Gibb Morton (c.1904), with a finely moulded front quite close to continental *art nouveau*, though obviously influenced by Burnet and Campbell. It has one of the worst modern ground floors in Glasgow. J. M. Dick Peddie designed the dignified National Commercial Bank at the corner of Buchanan and St Vincent Streets in 1899, **217**. The general outline is as sober as those of his contemporaries were lively and unpredictable. The wide corner bays with their tall coupled columns give great strength to a fastidiously detailed design. His offices for the Scottish Provident Institution (17–29 St Vincent Place, 1906) are less attractive: the French Second Empire Renaissance in an unusually stiffly academic form.

William Leiper has been referred to for his churches,[28] but he is also responsible for one of central Glasgow's most prominent, but, as it seems to me, most confusing, buildings, the rather flashily exotic Sun Insurance Office at the corner of Renfield and West George Streets (1892–94). This building sufficiently impressed the French for it to be given a silver medal at the Paris Exhibition of 1900, no doubt on account of the predominantly François I inspiration of a majority of its staggering display of mixed details. This fact may not much recommend it to present taste, but it finds its admirers in high places, and is indeed one of the few buildings in the city about which the authors of this book have been unable to come to a common opinion. Leiper's other big commercial building is another matter – Templeton's Carpet Factory on Glasgow Green, also of 1889, **219**. This is a great spreading façade of gaudy Paduan Gothic, in red terra-cotta with multicoloured glazed brickwork and faience on the upper storeys (below a parade of Guelfic battlements). The occasion of this weird *tour de force* was a decision of the firm who 'as patrons of the arts, resolved not alone in the interests of the workers, but also of the citizens, to erect instead of the ordinary and common factory something of permanent architectural interest and beauty'. It is arguable that the colours are not exactly selected to tone in with the Glasgow scene; but nevertheless Templeton's is a delightfully gay – almost irresponsible – piece which brings a puckish but innocent glee to the art of decoration.[29] W. H. McNab, Leiper's hero-worshipping junior partner, wrote of it after his master's death: 'in point of design and as a piece of architecture and specimen of decorative brickwork nothing finer, in the opinion of competent critics, is to be found outside of Italy'.[30] Leiper was a shy, retiring bachelor, nearly all of whose later work is at or near Helensburgh, where there is a large series of villas, some in the François I idiom in which he seemed to feel most at home, but some showing strongly the influence of Webb, Shaw and the Arts-and-Crafts movement.

This introduction to Glasgow's architecture proposes to halt at the first world war. By this time Campbell was dead, and Burnet had transferred both his practice and his chief interest to London, where, after the great Kodak building, he produced (alone or in partnership) a series of lavish and fairly ostentatious office buildings and only rarely (as in the Edward VII Gallery at the British Museum, completed in 1914) returned to something like his own purity. Salmon's partnership with Gillespie was dissolved in 1913, and neither partner produced anything of note afterwards, though Salmon did not die until 1924. As for Mackintosh, he too gave up Glasgow, exasperated, as it seems, by the city's philistinism; he too took to London, but, unlike Burnet, remained unhonoured, indeed unknown and in con-

28a

28 See p.173.
28a I now find my dislike of this building hard to account for: see further, p.259.
29 [These adjectives seem hard now to justify: though Templeton's may involve a dash of snook-cocking, Leiper's fastidious and learned attention to detail is too wholehearted to suggest an uncharacteristic frivolity or pleasure in whimsy. Indeed it has an almost solemn air, though Leiper will have enjoyed the irony of turning an Italian Gothic palace into a factory without having to damage any of the real ones.]
30 [R.I.B.A. Journal 1916. W. F. McGibbon made interesting variations on Italian Gothic themes with his Florentine towers at Scotstoun Mills, Partick (1898) and 118 Tradeston Street (1900), **197**.]

218. ICI Warehouse, Tradeston Street
(W. F. McGibbon, 1900): a variation on
the Bargello in Florence and perhaps
influenced by Templeton's.
219. (opposite) Templeton's Carpet
Factory, Glasgow Green (William
Leiper, 1889): for a full enjoyment the
building needs its colour.

31 [See Howarth, *Charles Rennie Mackintosh and
the Modern Movement* (1952, new ed. 1977),
Robert Macleod, *Charles Rennie Mackintosh*
(1968, new ed., 1983) and Andrew McLaren
Young's catalogue to the centenary
exhibition at the Edinburgh Festival of 1968.
It would be wrong to leave Gillespie without
mention of his outstandingly resourceful
house at 12 University Gardens (1900), which
makes really clever domestic use of the
octagonal tower feature *within* the façade: its
magnificent interior shows very strongly the
influence of Mackintosh.]
32 Wylie's large glass shop façade at the
corner of Rose and Sauchiehall Streets is
a refreshingly individual contribution
during a general architectural slump.
33 One reason is undoubtedly the casualness
with which important commissions were
handed out. The very large Peddie-inspired
Scottish C.W.S. warehouse at No. 71
Morrison Street (begun in 1919) is the work
of James Ferrigan, who, though he had
been with Keppie and worked with
Mackintosh, was at the time simply an
assistant in the Co-operative Surveying
Department. Luckily Ferrigan made a decent
job.

sequence unemployed. He died in 1928, having spent his last twenty years with hardly a commission; as with some other great architects before him, to gain an impression of his stature, one has to take into account many unfulfilled projects.[31]

So good architecture in Glasgow virtually ends with the war. Such worthy work as was done later is mainly that of men who had established their reputations well before; but this is hardly worth listing. Others, including W. H. McNab and A. D. Hislop, who made their names only just before 1914, found no worthwhile opportunities; and the only considerable architect to appear in the 1920s was E. G. Wylie, whose work (for example the Scottish Legal Life Building, Bothwell Street, 1927) was usually in the American classical vein introduced by A. D. Hislop before the war and later much exploited by James Miller.[32] Miller himself, the most prominent Glasgow architect of the period between the wars, was in fact very much of an older generation, only a year younger than Burnet and eight older than Mackintosh. His pre-war buildings show some individuality – for example, Lowther Terrace, Great Western Road (1907) – but are not usually very attractive. Some of them are indeed worse than this, notably the crushingly dominant Royal Infirmary, for which Miller was given the commission after a disagreement between the directors and the assessors of a competition won by H. E. Clifford. Miller's large office blocks of the 1920s and 1930s have found some recent admirers; but he fitted in too complacently to the opulent philistinism that drove Mackintosh out, and his style degenerated very badly in his later years when he attempted to 'modernize' classical detail. Nor would the most ardent admirer claim that a period represented at its best by the Union Bank (Renfield and St Vincent Streets) is a very distinguished one. It is an extraordinary and depressing fact that a generation of architects taught by such distinguished men as W. J. Anderson, Eugene Bourdon and Alexander McGibbon, and growing up when Mackintosh, Burnet, Salmon and Campbell were at the height of their powers, should have produced nothing at all. Glasgow's record between the wars is as dismal as anywhere in the country.[33]

Of architecture since the second world war, it is difficult to say much at this stage – not because I think that criticism and analysis of new buildings should be delayed, but because so much is at present only half-built that it is almost impossible to assess the probable effect on the Glasgow scene of so many large new buildings. One thing that can be said now is that relatively little of the new work – and that little generally speaking on a small scale (for example J. Coia's little school building looking on to Glasgow Green) – can be said to have a distinctly Glaswegian flavour. For all their differences, the great series of architects of the nineteenth and early twentieth centuries made between them something that can definitely be identified as a Glasgow way: not that many of the buildings would necessarily be quite out of place elsewhere, but the composite effect of them all is to produce an entirely distinctive and unmistakable city scene. This was no doubt largely the result of the definite localness of most Glasgow architects: there was so much to do in the city that they saw little call to go outside; at the same time those who commissioned new work found little call to go outside either. Buildings like the City Chambers are comparative rarities – even there the architect, though a Londoner, was also a Scot. Now things are very different. Glasgow has become part of the international scene, and its architects work in an

34 The work of Derek Stephenson (Royal Exchange Assurance House, 320 St Vincent Street, 1964) may be singled out not only for its architectural dignity and refinement, but for the architect's sensitive feeling for the Glasgow landscape, natural or man-made. It is most fortunate for Glasgow that Mr Stephenson has been chosen as the architect for the vitally important site in Bothwell Street immediately below St Vincent Street Church. His exciting design is like the redemption of a promise in which one had abandoned hope.
[Too optimistic alas: Stephenson's building impertinently interferes with Thomson's, hiding its podium behind a new and totally unnecessary stylobate. For a few further thoughts on recent building in the city see pp.273–6.]

essentially international idiom, of which the local variations seem at present insignificant. The only major exception to this generalization is in the quantities of hideous housing estates which ring the city: the four-storey tenements in particular have a notably Scottish ugliness about them. As for the buildings in the city centre, whatever their merits considered in isolation, extremely few, it seems to me, really take into account the character of the city where they are to stand and often to dominate.[34] This character is tough, but it is not indestructible. The great danger today is that, where rebuilding has to be done so fast and on so large a scale, the city may become visually anonymous. There is a vital lesson to be learnt from the equally fast and huge building programmes of the nineteenth century.

Chapter 11   Glasgow's Townscape

Hills matter more in Glasgow than in any other large city in the country; and hills, more than anything, determine the special character of Glasgow's townscape. A plan of the centre of the city looks like that of countless American towns – a regular square or rectangular grid covering a large area with almost no interruptions. What the plan does not show (or only very indirectly by the contour lines) is the three-dimensional effect. North of the river it is only in the area of the old merchant city, on either side of Trongate, that the ground is level. Especially to the west and north, the streets climb steeply; some that are so straight on plan climb and descend twice, sometimes very steeply indeed, so that – even if one ignores the buildings – the character of no two of them would be the same.

The lie of the land being what it is, Glasgow north of the Clyde could hardly help being an exciting place. But there cannot be townscape unless there is an essentially urban design to take advantage of the natural land formation. Many splendid effects of townscape are more or less accidental; and I do not propose here to distinguish the accidental from the deliberate, though Glasgow probably has more of the latter kind than most cities, and some are very obviously intentional, like the placing of the Royal Exchange on the axis of Ingram Street.[1] What is clear is that architects and builders, whether consciously or not, have taken advantage of the contrasting characteristics of different sites in the city to create localities with a sharply individual feel. Note, for example, how the close and intimate character of the merchant city, with its generally narrow streets and absence of outward views, contrasts with the much greater openness of Blythswood Hill; or how different is the friendly casualness of Partickhill from the patrician air of Woodlands Hill. (The ability to create these localities gives Glasgow one distinct advantage over San Francisco, which also imposes a rectangular grid on an exceptionally hilly site, much more consistently in fact and without leaving room for the quiet enclaves of which Glasgow has so many. Another important difference between the two cities is in the width of the streets. In San Francisco they tend to be all of the same width or nearly so, so that all have an appearance of equal importance; in Glasgow they vary greatly, and the wide and obviously more important streets not only mark off different localities from one another, but also loosely unite them by drawing into themselves the shops which serve all the abutting areas.)

A grid plan can result in a very dreary place indeed, especially where the streets go on almost indefinitely and have no natural or man-made features to block the outward views. The only flat part of Glasgow's central grid – between George Street and the river, between Buchanan Street and High Street – avoids this potential dreariness very easily. For one thing the streets are narrow, perspectives are therefore sharp, and buildings easily dominate, even where the traffic is thick. And in all directions there are natural barriers, hills on three sides (quite steep to the north), the river to the south. The river, being necessarily flat, would not in fact act as a visual barrier; and the visual stop to the south of Trongate is actually provided – for the few streets

[1] Perhaps, since the Cunninghame Mansion was sited on the axis of Ingram Street (laid out in the previous year) to obtain an uninterrupted outlook, one should say that the decision to incorporate the mansion into the new Exchange cannot be separated from the choice of a commanding site for an important civic building.

231

221. Ingram Street about 1829 with the Ramshorn Church in the foreground (Thomas Rickman, 1824–6) and the Royal Exchange at the far end. (From Swan's 'Views')

222. The Royal Exchange seen from Ingram Street: no longer dominant, it still ends the street admirably.

223. (above left) Royal Exchange
Square seen through one of the arches
from Royal Bank Place: at the end, the
British Linen Bank by David and
James Hamilton (c.1840),† with a now
decapitated top storey by James
Salmon, junior, or J. G. Gillespie
(c.1905).

224. (above right) St George's Church
seen from George Street: the Church
is now surrounded by large buildings
and its fine lines impaired (cf. fig.45).
The buildings on the left have all now
been demolished.

225. (right) Virginia Court: a
characteristic scene in the old
merchant city. The small enclosure
gains much of its charm from the
incidental details of ironwork and
cobbles.

that run through – mainly by the St Enoch railway viaduct. Elsewhere, too, the effect of natural barriers is reinforced by man-made stops, giving an agreeable sense of enclosure, of the intimacy I mentioned, **223**. Ingram Street comes to a formal halt at its west end with the portico and cupola of the Royal Exchange, **221**, which ought to be symmetrically framed by smaller buildings (the one on the south-east corner of Ingram and Queen Streets is too large, **222**); at the east end of the street, the rise to High Street performs the same function less formally. Of the streets south of Ingram Street none has a direct view out, so that one can never forget that one is *in* a place, **225**. Only two streets cross Ingram Street at all: the others all meet it in a T-piece. Of the two that do, Miller Street only goes one block farther north and is formally stopped by the great column in the centre of George Square (and now by the huge new block of the Stow College as well); while the other is Queen Street, itself the closure of Ingram Street, stopped at present by the supremely graceful arch of the station: if that goes will something equally fine be found to take its place? North of Ingram Street, there must be special mention of John Street for its powerfully dramatic tunnelling under the great arches at the back of the City Chambers. In this part of the city – as indeed all over it – much care seems to have been taken over the placing of the more important and socially significant buildings, **224**. Hutcheson's Hospital, **226**, and the Ram-

1a No longer: the railway has entirely gone, and the space left is currently desert land.

226. Hutcheson Street looking towards Hutcheson's Hospital.

227. George Square, with the College of Building from Hanover Street. The 1825 terrace at the far side of the square has now gone, but Robert Mathieson's post office palazzo of 1875-6 remains.

shorn Church each have a semi-formal approach in a street which stops in front, though curiously the frontispiece of the City and County Buildings lacks any vantage point; nevertheless the columned centre of its long west side is exactly on the axis of Garth Street, which is made quite grand by the placing at its other end of the principal front of the Trades House. And of course the City Chambers were given the grandest position of all by the great open space of George Square.

But George Square is the beginning of a new view of city building, at least in Glasgow, **227**. The pleasant character of the merchant city seems to have come about less through a sense of conscious civic design than from a desire simply to produce a workmanlike, sensible place, with some feeling of civic decorum and of the relative fitness of things. The two squares laid out in the 1780s at the west end of the old town mark the beginning of a new approach. George Square must originally have been too large for the buildings surrounding it, which were nowhere of more than three storeys. Today, with prodigiously large buildings on three sides, a tower above it to the north, and the ostentation of the City Chambers to the east, the dignity of the square itself is unimpaired. What *is* unfortunate is that the central space has become so cluttered. David Rhind's splendid column cannot any longer be the focal point it should; it is not the impressive array of municipal statuary that has done the real damage (though Burnet is not to be congratulated on his Cenotaph), but the irritating and fiddly flowerbeds and above all the timber information bureau – natty, up-to-the-minute (a number of minutes ago) and mean.

George Square still feels like a continuation of the old city – indeed its layout antedates most of the present buildings to the east. The 'new town' west of Buchanan Street is something entirely new and different. Even though some streets from the George Square area continue across Buchanan Street, one becomes conscious of a change of scale, a much more open feel (partly

because one is quickly on a hill above the old town, partly because the buildings are smaller in relation to the street widths), and above all of the opportunities given by a quite different site. At the start of the new venture, little advantage seems to have been taken of the dramatic possibilities of Blythswood Hill, **230**. The new town was entirely residential and seems to have been without churches of its own. So there were no large or high buildings to give vertical accent or punctuation. But, particularly from the south, the extremely steep slope of the hill gives the buildings higher up a much greater prominence than they would otherwise have. Later architects have taken advantage of this, and some important buildings gain enormously from a dramatic placing. Thomson's church is the most notable – its steeple the dominant feature from either direction in St Vincent Street, and the whole church standing magisterially above as one looks up from Bothwell Street (a fine effect soon to be changed to the 'surprise view' in Derek Stephenson's big new scheme). Furthermore, the hill really gives three-dimensional shape to the fiercely geometrical layout of the streets, which build across one another, especially from the south, like a series of gigantic steps, so steeply do the streets rise, **228**. With buildings high up given a greater emphasis by their height, an accent is created, defining at once the scale of the street and its place in a larger complex: the vertical presence of the

229. Looking along the Kelvin to the Stevenson Memorial Church and the cliffs of North Kelvin.

230. St Vincent Street about 1829
(From Swan's 'Views'). The exquisite
house in the foreground stood at the
corner of Wellington Street, and has
only lately been demolished.

buildings thus helps to establish the extreme formality of the plan, which, unlike many geometrical layouts which can be appreciated only on paper or from the air, really makes itself felt on the ground.

Does Blythswood Square sitting on the top of the great scheme seem something of a disappointment after this build-up? I do not think so. Admittedly there is nothing showy about it: only four quiet rows of houses. It is only about half the size of George Square, and so the smaller buildings are in scale; together they make a fine, restful composition, perhaps a little spoiled by the density of the shrubbery in the middle which makes it impossible to see the square as a whole, and certainly by the dismal fence. Perhaps too it is a little too windy, too exposed: some containment at any rate is lost by there being two streets coming in at each corner, though as these quickly disappear downhill, probably less space leaks out than it otherwise would.[2] And the sweep downhill of some of these streets is splendid – especially West George Street, swinging straight down from the top to come to a halt at the impassive bulk of St George's Church.[3]

One more excellent townscape effect to be noted in this area is the west end of Bath Street. Bath Street is flatter than most of the streets on Blythswood Hill, and also a little wider: with its three-storey terraces that rarely have to be stepped as do those farther south, it has a less busy and less urgent air than, say, West George Street. But as Bath Street goes steadily downhill towards North Street, a new accent is introduced by the steeples of two churches[4] and the very solid eastward-facing portico of a third; the scale changes, the three-storey terraces give way to a great range of four-storey tenements, punctuated once only by the narrow gap of Newton Street, which marks and intensifies the effect of the superbly graduated curve, as the street bends very slightly to the south, **170**. Seen, say, from the corner of Holland Street, this curve is just enough to bring the north side of Bath Street round to conceal its meeting with North Street: clearly this is the

[2] A building badly out of scale has recently gone up immediately to the north-west in Douglas Street: it very nearly wrecks the west aspect of the square.

[3] At one time there was a scheme to move the church to 'a more convenient position ... with a view to the opening up of George Street'. Luckily this deplorable proposal came to nothing. But from the point of view of someone looking down West George Street to the church, it is a pity that the roof line has been allowed to become so broken by very high buildings. Something of the sweep of the street is thereby lost.

[4] One of these has a spire, the other an octagon: the latter has recently been demolished.

conclusion of a great architectural progression, and the curve, while enhancing the effect of the magnificently judged scale – a poised proportion between height and width both of great dignity and elegance – prepares for the formal ending of the street straightforwardly but without abruptness, allowing it to contain itself. When such sureness of proportion is combined with such subtlety in perceiving the effect of slight changes of direction and emphasis, we can speak of an architectural planning that comes near to genius – whether or not the genius was conscious of what it had achieved. [4a]

If Blythswood Hill is open and almost relaxed, Garnethill is close and perhaps a little stiff. Here the hill is even steeper, especially to the north and south, but with one exception it has not been used to produce a specially dramatic townscape. The exception is the greatest thing of its kind in the city: looking across Sauchiehall Street and up Scott Street and up and up to the great vertically accented cliff of the west end of the Art School, **231**. This is architecture with a sense of drama played to the utmost: it is not something which any city can afford to attempt more than rarely, for the drama would be lost by repetition; and such effects depend greatly on a general sense of restful horizontals to set them off. It would be disastrous if – as seems quite possible – the valley of Sauchiehall Street gets filled up with high buildings of its own. Almost anywhere in Glasgow a miscellaneous col-

231. (above) Looking down on the valley of Sauchiehall Street from the Art School.
232. (right) The curve of Park Terrace above Kelvingrove.

[4a] Alas, all this is no more: what stops the west end of Bath Street now is the canyon of the motorway – visibly nothing and the ravager of qualities of city building and design which the late twentieth century seems utterly unable to approach.

233. (left) A characteristic scene in Partickhill, the perfect combination of house, wall and trees.
234. (right) A lane on Partickhill; Glasgow has an old tradition of pedestrian ways that are much to be prized.

lection of towers will eliminate much of the fine visual effect of the hills, as anyone who has witnessed the 'modernization' of San Francisco would immediately agree: at this point it would be simply ruinous.[5]

One of the great pleasures of walking about Glasgow, at least on a Sunday, comes from the rapid changes of scene, both physical and social, which one meets almost without preparation. Cross Sauchiehall Street from Blythswood Hill into Garnethill, and one is in a different world, socially and visually; go from Sauchiehall Street to Great Western Road and one discovers immediately the difference between a *street* – something in a town, part of its essential fabric – and a *road* – something that goes somewhere, leads out of the town.[6] The areas on either side of Sauchiehall Street belong to the street: it is their meeting place, common ground to them both. Great Western Road, on the other hand, divides: it does not join. This is especially true west of Kelvin Bridge, where the terraces become the façades of those almost entirely self-contained enclaves which are so characteristic of Glasgow; and this is in itself a distinct and interesting kind of townscape, as one moves between long buildings that look down at but do not take part in the street scene. Then, as one penetrates into Hillhead or into something utterly different like the queerly remote-feeling North Kelvin, **229**, one experiences what it is to move into a locality – inescapably a Glasgow locality but much more than a mere section of an amorphous mass. Though a street in Hillhead may look superficially like one in Belmont, the general feel of each locality is quite its own. It is difficult to *say* why in particular cases. Why, for example, is Hamilton Drive obviously not a street in Hillhead? In Hillhead the roadways themselves are narrower, though the houses may be as far apart; the houses appear a little smaller on the whole; there are more trees in the street: such small things add up to a character peculiarly the property of one quite small place – something, I am sure, that many people who know their Glasgow must be constantly aware of, even if not on the

[5] The effect of the new Art School tower north of Renfrew Street may be equally lamentable; see above p.217.
[6] Sauchiehall Street used to be Sauchyhall Road, but was appropriately renamed when it was absorbed into the city. Not all the names are necessarily so apt: New City Road is a real metropolitan street [*was:* it has now vanished totally under the ruthless ring road]. Hawthorn Street can never have been part of anything.

235. The Park Towers seen from Sauchiehall Street about 1890.

235. The Park Towers seen from Sauchiehall Street about 1890.

surface of their consciousness.[7] And it is something which, so far as I can tell, the new housing estates entirely lack. How does one tell Castlemilk from Drumchapel if these subtle distinctions are not maintained?

One special effect of this kind I should like to identify – the curious islands of Partickhill and Dowanhill (not wholly distinguished one from the other), for here one meets one of the rare examples of a really successful mixed development: rows of tenements suddenly giving way to a much more loosely planned collection of villas set among trees, and interspersed with terraces. I recommend particularly the walk up Lawrence Street with its seemly terraces into the trees and houses of Partickhill Road, **233, 234**, noting in passing the astonishing view down precipitous Gardner Street to the shipyards; then back, across Hyndland Road again, up to Crown Road South and round the remarkable convex crescent of Crown Circus, **75**, up into Prince Albert Road, where the rather severe Princes Terrace is suddenly supplanted by the villas of Sydenham Road. How is it that this charming place makes such different buildings belong together and avoids the uneasy effect of hostility, or just plain unrelatedness, that one finds in so many modern mixed developments of flats and houses? Three things are, I think, important. In the first place, the villas, though obviously smaller than the terraces, are on something like the same scale, solidly and substantially built; secondly all the buildings are of approximately the same material, a vital unifying factor for any mixed area of this kind; thirdly, and perhaps most important, the scale is set as much by the trees as by the buildings. Partickhill and Dowanhill are full of big trees, in private and public gardens and along the streets; and nowhere do the buildings dominate the trees, except in occasional set-pieces (like Crown Circus) which we recognize as such. What we have in fact is a garden suburb, or perhaps better a park suburb (for the all-important trees belong to the public view as much as to the private) of the best kind; Partickhill and Dowanhill make up, I think, an almost uniquely successful example.

[7] As one further example, compare Queen's and Belmont Crescents – similar in plan, yet in feel very different. Whereas Queen's is intimate and turned on itself, Belmont is almost lordly. The scale is larger and the high block in the middle makes it somewhat more ambitious.
[7a] Sadly Partickhill has lately suffered grievously from haphazard demolition and rebuilding, Dowanhill rather less so, though it is not unscathed.

7a

236. The University from Park Terrace.

The townscape of Glasgow is endlessly varied. Some of the best effects are entirely casual and haphazard, as when one walks up dingy, run-down Ann Street and finds oneself suddenly among the wharves of Port Dundas, with its air of slow, remote business, little bridges over the canal and men with whippets on the towpath. Some again have a romantic formality, as when the handsome, wide Victoria Road comes to a stop at its south end not with a church or a civic building but with the tree-covered hills of Queen's Park. (An extremely pleasant feature of Victoria Road is its unusually wide pavements, which allow people to congregate easily and hence give it the feeling of a place to be in rather than just a road to move along.) Some effects again are entirely formal, though in no immediately obvious way. My last description is of one of these – without doubt the most impressive piece of architectural planning in Glasgow, and indeed one of the finest anywhere in the country.

7b

Woodlands Hill is well known to Glaswegians: the view of the 'contrasting but surprisingly congruous' Park Towers seen across Sauchiehall Street is one of the city's sights, **235**. Yet the subtle use made of changes of direction in the streets and of the varying contours of the hill is not always appreciated. The whole scheme can, and should, be explored from several different directions. I propose starting from Charing Cross, for this offers, I think, the most

7b See map D (p.338).

237. The Park Towers from Park Circus.

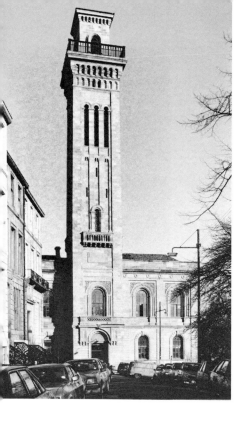

fascinating object-lessons and the most surprises, the most enigmatic and alluring changes of direction, and allows one best to see how the genius of Charles Wilson knitted together the work of at least three other architects to make a completely unified composite design.[8]

Woodside Crescent, then, **240**, takes one up the gentlest slope of the hill, starting straight, then curving through a quadrant, still uphill, till there is room for Woodside Terrace to lie level along the east-west contour, looking down across the shrubs to Woodside Place at the bottom. There are plenty of incidental effects to enjoy here: the high central block of Woodside Crescent which terminates the view from Woodside Place, the articulating of the curve by the prominent pair of porches on the house in the middle of the quadrant; the emphatic way in which the large house at the top of the rise announces the end of the Crescent, the start of the terrace – an effect now rather lost as the trees have grown somewhat too high; the punctuation of Woodside Terrace by the quite fierce row of Doric porches, **64**. Woodside Terrace is split half way along, the gap being the unexpectedly broad, flat opening which leads into the middle of the trees of Lynedoch Crescent, **241**, the gentle, feminine design which, with its garden, takes up most of one side of Lynedoch Street, the only street that climbs straight up the hill. To the right, though the street falls steadily away, the building line

8a

238. (above) **The towers of the Free Church College from Woodlands Terrace.**
239. (right) **The towers from Lynedoch Crescent.**

[8] Rochead's Park Church was built about two years after Wilson's work was designed, but clearly Wilson took into account the future placing of the church, even if he could not calculate its precise effect on the skyline. The church is now in danger: as the Hill is now all offices, it has no congregation and the site is valuable. It is not specially distinguished architecture, but scenically it is very precious. The tower, at any rate, is a necessary part of the townscape sequence of Woodlands Hill; and if the body of the church goes, it is vital that the replacement should be on the same modest scale and should not interrupt, still less attempt to dominate, Wilson's processional design.
[8a] The bottom of Woodside Crescent has gone, as has the body (but not the all-important tower) of Park Church.

240. Looking through the severe Doric porches of Woodside Terrace towards Woodside Crescent.

does not, thus making a fine, crisp boundary to the whole scheme of the hill. In the other direction, at the top of Lynedoch Street, one is faced with the prominent tower of Rochead's Park Church, **237**, not quite on the axis of the street but obliging one to go either left (and so round the side of the hill) or half-right into Park Circus Place, the broad processional approach to Wilson's Park Circus, **68**. Like the Circus at Bath, this was probably not intended to have as many or as large trees in the middle as at present, for the shape can now be fully appreciated only from the air. (Unlike in the loose and informal arrangements of, say, Partickhill, large trees in a formal scheme can be a drawback – which is not to say that they should be replaced by frilly suburban shrubs, but rather that they should be regularly pruned, *not lopped*, to keep them the right size and shape for their place.) I have discussed the architectural character of Wilson's work elsewhere:[9] enough here to draw attention to the great spaciousness achieved by drawing out the circus into an oval, and flattening the centrepiece of the north-east side, which, with its two carefully judged projections, is given just enough emphasis to bring the quadrants on either side into a single design.

The climbs have all along been steady and gentle: it is therefore all the more surprise to the newcomer (and still a gratifying experience to one who knows it well) to find that the continuation of the processional way leads

241. Lynedoch Crescent from the north.

[9] See above pp.92ff.

one suddenly to the edge of a rocky cliff, with the rolling park well below and the University on another height a few hundred yards away, **236**. The convex complement to the concave curves of Park Circus is Park Terrace and can only be seen as a whole from among the trees of the park, **232**; it is hardly designed to be looked on as a formal composition in its own right. The southern arm of Park Terrace curves round to become Woodlands Terrace (mainly the work of John Baird No.1), narrower and less flamboyant, which suddenly reveals the campanile of Wilson's crowning work on the hill, the Free Church College, **238**. One has passed the front of this already, but it makes its best effect either from here or from the north in Lynedoch Crescent, **239**. At the beginning of Woodlands Terrace, however, there is another surprise, this time a processional stairway leading down to the level of the park, **243**, at the bottom of which one finds oneself in the comparatively plain Park Gardens, which leads eastwards now quite low down the hill, to Baird's admirable Claremont Terrace, a very shallow crescent lying back into the hill, nicely unified by the curve of the crescent itself and by the projecting ends of the terraces which flank it, **67**. And so back to Woodside Terrace. Or one may go farther downhill among the trees which are almost an extension of the park, so much do they close one in, hanging over the cobbled path[10] – the 'street' I have in mind is charmingly called Clairmont Pass, **242**.

[10] These cobbles are a small but important part of the attractiveness of such a scene: they give variety of texture to the floor, whereas tarmac or asphalt is quite dead. It is a great pity that the pleasant patterns made by the combination of setts and smooth runs of stone for cartwheels have now vanished from the hilly streets of the centre.

Apart from the excellence of the architecture, three things stand out about Woodlands Hill – the imaginative use of the site to make possible a fresh kind of urban experience, the amount of variety in layout and street-shape in a small area, and, this notwithstanding, the unity of place which links so many designs together into one composite design.

As in many other planned cities of the eighteenth and nineteenth centuries, a great deal of Glasgow is designed as a series of sequences, or is at least best appreciated as such: it is the sequences which count as units, not individual houses; and these sequences make their effect as wholes, which can be spoiled by quite small changes, if these are made insensitively. Even the colossal half-mile sweep of St Vincent Crescent is a single design, to be tampered with only at the peril of the whole work. There is far too much evidence in Glasgow that this vital point is not understood, or if understood is ignored by those in a position to make or allow changes. Many years ago the proportions of Carlton Place were wrecked by the loss of one end pavilion and its replacement by a block out of scale with the terraces. More recently the same thing has happened to Somerset Place, where a new pavilion which is a weak substitute for the old upsets the balance mainly through the coarseness of its detail. Another palace-fronted terrace in Bath Street has been

244. A pattern of Glasgow railings.

badly damaged by two windows having been cut deep into its bold cornice. In Berkeley Street, a lamentable new building totally spoils one side of the street, its coarsely insistent horizontals ruining the pattern of verticals in the terrace, *all* its floor levels contradicting those of its neighbours. In Woodside Terrace smaller changes have been almost equally damaging: two top-storey windows have been replaced by a horizontal 'picture-window' and at the same time the cornice above has been removed – a change disturbing the whole terrace, which has been further damaged by the loss of some of the railings and by the substitution of clumsy brick, or imitation stone, walls, and by the addition of red tiles on the steps. Even paint, if chosen injudiciously, can have an appalling effect, as in Moray Place, where, at the time of writing, one house has a liberal coating of bright yellow which destroys the unity of the terrace nearly as effectively as a structural alteration. It may be tiresome to have to come to some agreement with one's neighbours about such things as the colour of one's front door; but it is a small price to pay for the privilege of living in a piece of great architecture.

In the streets which are not carefully unified designs obviously much more variation is possible. Yet even here, the character and interest of the street can easily be changed and – if new buildings are insensitive – spoiled. The most delicate problem of this kind is Buchanan Street. It has a splendid sweep

245. A typically sharp Glasgow corner in Maryhill Road: the end block manages the awkward site consummately and may be by Alexander Thomson.
All in this picture have of course now been destroyed.
246. (overleaf) The Necropolis from Cathedral Square: the end of many famous Glaswegians.

247. The great sweep of Buchanan
Street, perhaps the finest group of
mixed nineteenth-century architecture
in Britain, containing the work of
Burnet and Campbell, A. N. Paterson,
Stark, Burnet senior, Hamilton,
Dick Peddie, and Boucher.

to the south which at one time used to come to a very satisfactory halt in
St Enoch's Square, where the simple but comely steeple and portico of the
church were there to bring it to a formal close. James Miller's toy underground station is entirely too small and whimsical a design to be a satisfactory terminus to so large-scale a street. Farther north the roof line is
gradually disintegrating, and the character of the street with it. But the west
side is still Glasgow's best stretch of mixed urban architecture, the best
mixed nineteenth- and early twentieth-century group in the whole country, 247.
From the fine Edwardian Renaissance of Dick Peddie's bank on the corner
of St Vincent Street to the high building of the Athenaeum there is astonishing variety and an astonishingly high quality throughout: the group includes the Western Club, the Stock Exchange, the Tron Church and its
square with the earlier piece of the Athenaeum and the Faculty of Procurators, the sturdy and superbly well-detailed old Liberal Club (A. N. Paterson,
1909), and finally the Athenaeum Theatre itself. Buchanan Street still has
more buildings of high quality than any other street in the city, and this
range is unique; but it is already losing some of its character, not yet through
changes in the outer fabric of the buildings that make it up, but through the
unfortunate predominance of buildings nearby. Not long ago the steeple of
the Tron Church used to be the principal accent of the street – as it should be:
now it is gradually receding into subordinance, as high buildings go up
around. For high buildings count in the town scene much more than the
street in which they stand; and it is hardly possible now to get an impression
of what Royal Exchange Place was like before it was dominated by the ugly
high backs of St Vincent Place. [11]

If Glasgow matters architecturally, it matters not only as a collection of fine
buildings, but as a great city. The effect of Glasgow, as the effect of some of
its best integrated parts, is cumulative. Take away a range of tenements here
and there and the effect may only be local; but too much removal and the
city will suddenly be a different place. And in particular, if the general pattern of three- and four-storey streets which the terraces, business blocks and
tenements have given the city is generally abandoned in favour of the currently fashionable high point blocks, it is hard to see how even the local
character of small areas will remain. Glasgow has as much architectural
character as any city in the kingdom; in addition it has real metropolitan
scale in far larger proportion that most cities – essentially the tenements see
to this. The character is in the main an excellent one; but it is not indefinitely strong. It will not survive a massacre of the buildings which define it,
and the preservation of isolated special monuments is not enough. If we want
Glasgow to remain Glasgow, we must, as Pope told us, consult the genius
of the place in all. In Glasgow it is still not too late; but the genius must be
consulted now.

[11] [The pedestrianizing of the lower section of
Buchanan Street (as of part of Sauchiehall
Street) has been an enormous gain for those
with a feeling for the Glasgow scene: not
only does it allow one to enjoy the buildings
safely and at leisure. but the new varied
floors unite them as the tarmac once divided,
and the trees slightly but perceptibly soften
the severity of the streetscape.]

Chapter 12

Afterword

248. 140 St Vincent Street (Burnet & Boston, 1898).

This final chapter includes a few second thoughts on buildings already (but inadequately or inaccurately) referred to in the main text, and notes on a miscellany of items accidentally omitted from the first edition. But its largest job is briefly to survey a highly characteristic field of Glasgow architecture whose qualities we certainly undervalued.

The Free Style

It is a custom of those who organize pet shows, after providing individually for every known breed, to add one more category, called 'any other variety' in which any animal not otherwise identified may find a home. A section on 'free-style architecture' – particularly in a chapter avowedly given over to second thoughts in a book that concerns itself much with architectural styles – may appear just such an undiscriminating catch-all. Yet the buildings to be discussed here – for all their heterogeneity, for all the sometimes bizarre amassing of features on a single façade – do form a recognizable class. They are moreover, if only because of their very bulk, the buildings which, even after the vast changes of the last twenty years, do most to define the character of the centre of Glasgow. A few have already been described, for Burnet and Campbell, and perhaps the younger Salmon, were free-stylists much of the time and strongly influenced lesser architects whose work it has taken time and the aesthetic weariness induced by too much blank curtain-walling to teach us to appreciate again.[1] For the most obvious, and from the point of view of the street scene, the most important characteristic of these buildings is the variety and deep modelling of their three-dimensional façades. Perhaps there are too many of them competing for attention close together, and undeniably the result of a craving for variety is often an excess of rich detail and a stylistic muddle; yet the detail itself is almost never without interest, there is hardly a building in this very considerable collection that is not worth pondering, and their combined contribution to the Glasgow townscape is enormous and of incalculable value. One's gaze doesn't *slide* along the walls of Hope Street or Buchanan Street: it is constantly alerted, arrested by projections and recessions, drawn up and down by marked verticals, made to pause on features that articulate a huge façade and give it scale – linking that of the human to buildings fifteen or twenty times one's own height. These buildings are, most of them, very big – six-, seven- or eight-storey offices profiting from the boom of the post-depression years and the falling-in of leases, built sometimes on commission from banks or insurance companies or merchants, sometimes as speculations – and they gave the streets of central Glasgow a new proportion and their architects a new kind of problem in designing façades.[2] Much of this architecture is indeed façade-mongering, and the styles adopted may have very little evident connexion either with the building's working plan or with the purpose it was to fulfil.[3]

The job was to maintain both interest and coherence over a huge area of wall with quantities of windows lighting similar-sized rooms. Interest was

[1] But Sam Lambert, in the special number of the *Architects' Journal* devoted to Glasgow as long ago as 1965, had in fact shown the way.
[2] The availability of new structural methods was an essential prerequisite of the new scale; much was learnt from contemporary American practice, though neither Glasgow nor any other city in Britain went near the heights then becoming common in Chicago and New York.

very often achieved, coherence less commonly. Contrast, for example, the approach of Clarke and Bell to their former shipping offices at 15–25 Bothwell Street[4] with James Thomson's block in West George Street built for William Connal. Clarke and Bell's work is thoroughly sensible and almost styleless, logically repeating a simple window form over the whole of a nearly flat façade: good background architecture, but on the dry side, and a street of such buildings would be very dull. Connal's, on the other hand (1898–1900), has a façade (plainly conceived in two parts) which overwhelms one with piled-up Renaissance motifs, in which no two floors are the same and only the first and second are treated even similarly, **256**. The left-hand section starts (above the now irrecoverable ground floor) with duple windows divided by terms, which derive from the mid-sixteenth-century Heinrichsbau at Heidelberg castle. These give way to 'two-bay aedicules', with central column, a technically corrupt form which was very popular in late nineteenth-century Glasgow.[5] Each level so far has had its own small order (each of a different form), but suddenly we come up against tortuous Corinthian capitals a dozen times bigger than any we have so far met: they stand on top of curious ladder-like strips which separate the bays through three storeys and which we now learn to interpret as disproportionately lanky pilasters.[6] The clash of scales is abrupt and violent, and almost equally so is that between the aedicules and trios of arched windows (the central smaller than the outer) which come immediately above: two has given way to three, which for the main top storey gives way to two and a half; for a row of five windows alternating with pilasters supported on corbelled heads runs across all this part of the façade: we are thus obliged to accept that $2 + 2 = 3 + 3 = 5$. At last there is a cornice, and then an attic with yet another order within an elaborate shaped gable. It is a pity that this façade is joined to a slightly wider and more mechanically detailed one to the right, for on its own it might compel a kind of logic out of the heterogeneity by the sheer force of the upward thrust of the verticals.

Such a design seems to have arisen through a process of free association among remembered or studied elements of the continental Renaissance. Italian influence had of course been strong for decades: it was now joined by French in different forms (Sun Life, Hope Street; Manchester House, Sauchiehall Street[7]), German (91 Buchanan Street; Citizen Building, St Vincent Place) and Flemish (116 Hope Street, which borrows from Antwerp town hall) – often, as at Connal's, together in the same building. As well as the two-bay aedicules, shaped gables were popular, swan's-neck pediments and all possible varieties of French and Italian orders. At the same time more distinctively Glaswegian features regularly appear, most notably vertical bay-window strips, balconies (or sometimes eaves galleries) pulling the design together horizontally, and a tendency to glaze directly to structural members.[8] Buildings with a single street frontage are often asymmetrical in detail within a basically symmetrical layout[9] – perhaps on occasion to try to conquer the uncomfortable duality which seems to have resulted from developing two adjacent narrow sites, by treating the façade as if it belonged to two independent but related buildings. T. L. Watson's admirably detailed (and well-preserved) Citizen Building (designed 1885), **249** is particularly instructive here: though some features are continuous across the whole double frontage, others stop half-way, and those that run on do so across a wide strip of masonry suggesting a party-wall (with one gable on each side).

3 The entrancing tea-room designed by George Washington Browne at 91 Buchanan Street (1895–6) has nevertheless a delicacy and charm as well as an exceptionally fastidious care for detail which seem altogether appropriate, despite the formidable reputation of Miss Cranston. The source, pace what was said above (p.198n), is less François I than the north German Renaissance of such buildings as the town hall at Bremen; and Washington Browne's house would slip almost without comment into a street in Hamelin or Lemgo.

4 *c*.1890: the designer was presumably the younger George Bell.

5 It can be regarded as a derivative of a standard Renaissance window-form capped by a pediment and perhaps first appears complete in the Cour de l'oval at Fontainebleau in 1528.

6 These also seem to be adapted from Heidelberg. Even more extravagant versions appear on the same firm's Liverpool, London and Globe (see below, p.262).

7 See p.195, **180** above. French too had been around earlier, though less commonly: see, e.g., the roofs of Park Terrace, **72**.

8 For bay-window strips see, e.g., Burnet & Boston's Castle Chambers, 57 Renfield Street (1898) or the same firm's 140 St Vincent Street (also 1898, with additionally an eaves gallery); for the linking balcony see David Barclay's 48 Bothwell Street (*c*.1893) or Clarke & Bell's 102–14 Union Street (*c*.1894). Sellars' terracotta façade for Wylie & Lochhead, with its early North Italian Renaissance elements (see above p.197n) and his façade in Trongate with a central bow are in some respects portents of the style, as are his gablet tops at the *Glasgow Herald* and City of Glasgow Bank, which anticipate a silhouette much favoured in the 1890s.

9 See, e.g., R. A. Bryden's Ocean Chambers, 190 West George Street (1900); Bryden was a partner in Clarke & Bell's firm from the 1870s to 1890s.

249. Citizen Building, St Vincent Place (T. L. Watson, designed 1885).
250. Sun Life Building, West George Street and Renfield Street (William Leiper, 1889).

249. Citizen Building, St Vincent Place (T. L. Watson, designed 1885).
250. Sun Life Building, West George Street and Renfield Street (William Leiper, 1889).

[10] Occasionally the corner feature may just be a piece of whimsy, as in the drum topped with a golden onion which enlivened a dreary stretch of Govan Road on Bruce and Hay's now destroyed Rutland House of 1896 (see Worsdall, *The City that Disappeared*, p.125); or – still to be seen on the building in Waterloo Street now belonging to the Distillers' Company but designed by James Chalmers in 1897 for Wright & Greig – the fantasy of an octagon flush with the façades (so the effect low down is of a chamfered corner) whose top undulates, bulging out under a wavy coping into corbelled turrets and barley-sugar-columned balconies all sprouting miniature cannon. Mr Worsdall (*Victorian City*, p.70) describes this engaging piece of nonsense, which elsewhere has empty niches and an inaccessible porticoed balcony, as 'wholly functional'. One function, he reports, was to advertise the firm's most famous product via a statue of Rhoderick Dhu over the door

[11] See above, p.222 and **208**.

[12] Leiper's own drawing reproduced by Mr Worsdall (*Victorian City*, p.63) makes the octagon appear top-heavy and lop-sided.

At the former Reid and Todd's (202 Sauchiehall Street, by James Thomson, 1902) the main front appears at first sight symmetrical, but minor changes on the upper floors and major ones in the attic reveal that the right-hand bay is treated as if it were an addition set a few inches back; the other two bays then turn out to be nearly identical with those on the façade to the incoming street: the building is in fact pivoted about the corner, and the change to the outer bays is really to emphasize its corneriness.

There are many corners in the tight grid of central Glasgow, and they provide many opportunities for a favourite Glasgow device – the cylindrical or octagonal tower which may be used as no more than added emphasis to an exposed angle, but in the most interesting examples enables the whole building to be designed (not usually symmetrically) about the corner.[10] On a smallish scale this has already been illustrated in Salmon's Anderston savings bank.[11] On the scale of the big office blocks none does it better than one of the earliest – Leiper's Sun Life (West George and Renfield Streets, 1889), **250**, where the domed octagon achieves just the right degree of dominance by projecting fairly boldly and being given a plainer wall treatment than the façades, which are richly pilastered and columned.[12] John Hutchison obviously studied Leiper's building for his Norwich Union in

251. St George's Mansions (Burnet & Boston, 1900).

252. North British Rubber, 60 Buchanan Street (Robert Thomson, 1898).

253. Chip-carving on the Scottish Legal building, Wilson Street (Alexander Skirving, 1889).

254. Liverpool, London & Globe Insurance, 116 Hope Street (James Thomson, 1898).

255. Cumming & Smith's, Sauchiehall Street (David Barclay, 1892).

256. Connal's, West George Street (James Thomson, 1898-1900).

13 But see Burnet & Boston's 140 St Vincent Street, p.263 below. Details on the Norwich Union seem heavily in debt to Salmon's then recently completed Mercantile Chambers (**205**); the portholes at the top are a nice variation. The designer was in fact T. Ramsay, who had replaced Andrew Black as Hutchison's chief assistant in 1891 (see n.24 below).

14 Carruthers became a partner in the firm in 1901. It seems certain that he was responsible for most of Burnet & Boston's more interesting and adventurous work from the late 1890s onwards.

15 Again designed by Carruthers.

16 On the long side-elevations there are even bays in pairs which have triangular and segmental pediments side by side.

17 The aediculed canted bays, strong balcony and arched windows here and elsewhere in Burnet & Boston derive from the unconnected J. J. Burnet; and St George's Mansions once admirably complemented the curved frontage of the great man's Charing Cross Mansions across the road, but now a motorway footbridge spoils the view. With the Glasgow approach to corner sites compare Waterhouse's for his Prudential building in Clare Street, Bristol (see Crick, *Victorian Buildings in Bristol* (1975), pl.65; and Gomme, Jenner & Little, *Bristol: an Architectural History* (1979), p.389 and pl.307); or again his Prudential in St Andrew's Square, Edinburgh (1892–5), where the top stage of the corner octagon is turned so that its angles rest on the centre-points of the sides of the main octagon. The Glasgow Prudential (48–50 West Regent Street, 1890) does not show Waterhouse at his most distinctive or distinguished – a tired-looking pile of predictable sub-Renaissance detail in the manner of his building for Caius College, Cambridge, slightly fussed up by 'baronial' turrets at the corner. The gablets in the roof are too small to act as more than irritations, and the inevitable glazed brick for the main walls is unhappy in central Glasgow.

18 See above pp.223ff.

19 The effective architect of both buildings was Andrew Wilson, evidently a clever draughtsman who quickly drops into oblivion. The functional advantages of a canted bay are two-fold: it adds floor space and attracts light from a wide angle. Both are negated by recessing the bay, and the conflict of motives presented by recessing and projecting simultaneously is essentially mannerist – a term which could be widely used of this architecture.

20 The whole vertical sequence is repeated several times on the long façade to the narrow side lane.

Hope Street (1898), which likewise has its main entrance on the angle: he uses a round drum, well-proportioned but inclined to compete too much in the same forms with the rest of the building (and the right-hand façade is weakly abbreviated – such designs are difficult when the two frontages are of very different lengths[13]). At Burnet and Boston's Castle Chambers (Renfield Street 1898, designed by James Carruthers, then an assistant[14]), despite a handsome top storey, the octagon isn't really big enough to bring the energetic activity of the façades into order, and the interesting figures by Ernest Gillick tucked under the overhangs at the corner almost pass unnoticed. All this architecture is of course highly sculpturesque – too much so perhaps for individual figures to tell. Quite the best of Burnet and Boston's corner schemes – indeed their most rewarding contribution to the Glasgow streetscape – is the gusset between Woodlands and St George's Roads – St George's Mansions, **251**, built for the Police Board in 1900.[15] The angle is acute, and the building cuts it with a tall two-bay façade framed by corbelled drums: it breaks all the rules, being hopelessly dualistic, split down the middle by one of a set of three pilasters that stand on nothing; there are five Ionic orders of unrelated scales, splayed pilasters on the angles under the corbelling, triangular pediments with concave sides, broken segmental pediments, round arches, again all on different scales.[16] Yet amazingly it works and even reduces the predictably poor shopfronts to insignificance: the strong uprights – especially bay-window strips – lead the eye through the balcony to arched windows and up to the crown of the iron-balustraded roof; the turrets clamp the façade very satisfactorily, and the boldly bracketed cornice pulls it all together. Grasp the nettle firmly . . .[17]

A distinctive group of buildings have tower-like elevations on a very narrow frontage. The plots on which smallish houses had been built early in the nineteenth century were often owned or leased individually; but even a frontage thirty feet wide is very valuable in a city centre street if you can build both high and deep. How Salmon did this at the Hatrack and Lion Chambers has been told already.[18] Those buildings are, with Burnet and Campbell's Athenaeum Theatre, undoubtedly the best of their kind. But the extra storeys which had transformed part of William Spence's warehouse at 16 Buchanan Street into an appealingly simple grid-fronted tower had long anticipated them. And Burnet's approach was followed in two very striking buildings by Robert Thomson, who developed the Athenaeum motif, of a canted bay-window strip set into a recess under an arch, into the whole principle of his façades.[19] The offices for North British Rubber (60 Buchanan Street, 1898), **252**, are indeed a variation on the left-hand half of the Athenaeum façade, in an opulent fruity style in which, above four fairly restrained storeys, a great wide arch decorated with consoles engulfs the bays, below a balcony which swells forward in a serpentine curve.[20] Above again is a round-headed window under a deep hood within an extravagantly crow-stepped gable, each step adorned with tiny machicolations. The former *Daily Record* office (67 Hope Street, 1899) is a two-bay version: the canted strips each have their own recess and arch, but a single swelling balcony unites them below a kind of triumphal arch topped by an even fancier gable. On both buildings tall narrow polygonal projections at the outer angles tie the top storey convincingly into the lower walls: in Buchanan Street they are hollowed out into niches with statues, in Hope Street figures sit on brackets at the bottom.

One could hardly say that there is a history to this architectural explosion: it was all over so quickly, and so much happened within a few years that phases, influences and developments were inextricably mixed. The first sign perhaps came in 1877 with Peddie and Kinnear's vast hotel and arcade building in Hope Street, because, though the detail is mostly Greek, the inflated scale, with so much up in the Frenchy roof, marks the start of buildings determined by the range of lifts rather than stairs – with which the old palazzo formula could not cope. In the early 1880s Bruce and Hay began their series of lumpish piles with mechanical Ionic orders and much incised detail;[21] then a giant free Ionic with elaborate chip-carving came into the city centre with Alexander Skirving's Scottish Legal Insurance building in Wilson Street (1889), the first large office building to use the rich red sandstone which then suddenly became everyone's choice. Skirving is still Greek-Thomsonizing between the big columns, and though the modelling doesn't seem to count for much from some angles, seen against the sun the incised carving comes into its own and is rather fine, **253**. James Thomson, whose firm of Baird and Thomson came to have the largest practice in the city, punctuated his classico-Italianate style with French pavilions but was still doing old-fashioned Barryesque Renaissance at the Clydesdale Bank, Argyle Street in 1892; and as late as 1909 his sons James Baird and William Aitken added a huge columnar top-hamper to their father's reticent Standard Life in Gordon Street built nineteen years earlier.[22] By this time the sons had long provided most of the firm's life, and it must have been they who brought in the flamboyant Flemish or German mannerism already referred to: one can almost see them taking over as one goes up the elevations of 202 Sauchiehall Street, but already by 1898 the colossal alloverishness of the Liverpool, London and Globe (116 Hope Street), **254**, which represents an extreme departure from their father's ponderous Italian, must be theirs alone. This vast pile is also a building to make one wonder rather than admire; but it's more fun than Bruce and Hay even though the mass of small-scale detail never begins to make a design.

David Barclay's warehouse and office work, done after the death of his talented elder brother, is a generally more coherent version of this manner, though 'coherent' may not be the obvious word for the long and somewhat lax three-part row in Bothwell Street for the Central Thread Agency (36–62: 1891–8), which relies rather too much on the repetition of incident. But the big block of 1892 in Sauchiehall Street for Cumming and Smith (and now called the Savoy Centre, **255**) is splendidly disciplined without any loss of richness. It uses the arch-and-canted-bay theme almost as early as Burnet, but here five times over to articulate a long façade which is horizontally united by a continuous columnar eaves gallery: the pedimented end pavilions (of one bay each) are flanked by narrow window strips which, most intelligently bringing the big plain pilasters closer together, add weight to the ends: for all the energetic in-and-out movement of the bays the overall frame is indeed neo-classical and makes one suspect that Hugh Barclay may have had a hand in it before he died.[23] Colin Menzies' Argyle Chambers, built in 1904 over the Buchanan Street entrance to the arcade, follows Barclay's manner but is coarser and showier, as if the architect couldn't let well alone. Burnet and Boston's large office block further up the street (116–28: 1898–1902) by contrast relies nearly entirely on one feature endlessly repeated – it is all over aedicules; their best work in the city centre is

[21] Their gigantic warehouse for the Scottish C.W.S. at 95 Morrison Street, Kingston (1897) is the apotheosis of this manner, equipped with giant order through the upper floors, tower and dome and immense mansarded corner pavilions – a building, as *Glasgow at a Glance* puts it, to evoke wonder rather than pleasure. Its precursor was an almost equally ambitious block with a central tower at 216 Wallace Street (1888–92), for the same client.

[22] Italian of a different kind – indirectly Genoese – was the unfortunately lost former Corn Exchange in Hope Street by David Barclay's pupil W. Forsyth McGibbon (1894), one of the earliest and best of the numerous paraphrases of Belcher and Pite's Institute of Chartered Accountants in Moorgate Place, London, which had set the architectural world by the ears on its completion a year before. (See Worsdall, *The City that Disappeared*, p.55.)

[23] For very size Barclay's Royal College of Science & Technology in George Street (1901–5, now the University of Strathclyde) must be mentioned: it is in a coarse, though boldly moulded Italianate, somewhat reminiscent of the work of William Gingell in Bristol. Equally gargantuan is James Miller's Caledonian Chambers, Union Street (1903) packed out with rather fruitless baroque detail which shows Miller searching for a style in the years before he fell in with American classicism (see n.48 below).

257. 26-30 St Enoch Square c.1880. On the right the Royal Bank of Scotland, 22 St Enoch Square (A. N. Paterson, 1906).

[24] Hutchison's chief assistant Andrew Black is said to have been largely responsible, and the details were drawn by Mackintosh. It was built in 1889, gutted in 1904 and immediately rebuilt. By 'direct glazing' here, we mean glazing between columns or pilasters without intervening wall or window frames.
[25] No.16: see above p.261.
[26] Plain in another way is the elegant Western Telephone Exchange in Highburgh Road (1907), one of three in Scotland designed for the National Telephone Company by Leonard Stokes (the others are Rose Street, Edinburgh and Aberdeen). Its two principal elevations have straightforward Georgian sash-windows relieved by pairs of oriel bays surmounted by quietly Vanbrughesque parapets pierced by arches: the elements are very simple but treated with all Stokes's fastidious delicacy: note the neat handling of the minute projection of the fenestrated sections, which, contrasting in colour as well as scale of modelling with the rusticated corners, contrive to suggest the insertion of an older elevation within a new building.
[27] See above p.203n.

the Hatrack's neighbour at the corner of St Vincent and Hope Streets (1898), **248**, which has one of the most vigorously moulded of all the façades, a fine corner octagon almost all window, good strong linking horizontals and a sensitively introduced tower of plain ashlar to give repose between two different kinds of display: it has perhaps a touch of later Norman Shaw as well as much of J. A. Campbell.

Occasionally among the wealth of Renaissance columns and pediments and gables the Glasgow fascination with direct glazing gives a 'proto-modern' character to a façade or part of one: it is even there in the middle of the Hope Street frontage of the Liverpool, London and Globe; and it really defines the whole appearance of, for example, Hutchison's Wylie Hill's at 20 Buchanan Street:[24] only a few sub-classical details and the curious French pavilion in the roof depart from the maximum of utilitarian plainness. This severity was perhaps inspired by that of its elegant neighbour[25] and had been anticipated by the remarkably shaven mullions of 26–30 St Enoch Square, **257**. This is of c. 1880, comfortably ahead of Lethaby's famous Eagle Insurance Office in Birmingham with which it shares a logical approach to fenestration within a completely plain grid relaxed only for a small amount of fantasy in the arcaded Romanesque pediment and flanking dormers. For a chaste Beaux-Arts solution to the problem of tall and relatively narrow frontages one can turn to its neighbour the Royal Bank, **257**, by A. N. Paterson whose solution is more orthodox but carefully studied, and similarly concentrates the detail at the top floors. Paterson also hit on just the right scale of detail at the Liberal Club (1909) in Buchanan Street, whose reticent Renaissance elegance gives true grace to its sturdy cube. It is a remarkable achievement to have designed a building which both makes a sympathetic but unsubdued neighbour to the Athenaeum Theatre and boldly shapes the corner of St George's Place without overwhelming the church. Though as late as 1907 Eric Sutherland produced at 260 Clyde Street a streamlined version of Atlantic Chambers, this was the swansong: by then the steam had gone out of the free style, and Glasgow really had no Edwardian baroque.

J. A. Laird's large and gaunt warehouse at 12–20 Ingram Street (1910) has something of the same pleasure in plainness as the Royal Bank building, though it is less comely. In fact the plain style was now briefly taking over,[26] as witness the austere flat façades of Thomson and Sandilands' towering building for the City Improvement Trust, Albion Street (1903–11), which gets near to being a curtain-wall job, with pilasters in the lowest possible relief, a very subdued central pediment and only the fine domed corner octagon reminding one seriously of its baroque ancestry – an ancestry which had included Sandilands' own richly vigorous parish council offices at 266 George Street (1900–02) whose coupled Ionic order with Doric entablature is stolen from that of Burnet's Waterloo Chambers.[27] The idea of clamping the façade between 'pylons' – in this case based on the arch-and-bay-window motif – likewise derives from Burnet. Sandilands had been apprenticed to the unmemorable Alexander Petrie but went to the Beaux-Arts in 1880, staying for five years – two longer than any other Glasgow architect. Quite the most impressive result was Govan town hall (1897–1901), **258**, externally the purest Beaux-Arts building in the city, with an excellently composed façade, restrained in detail yet with plenty of forceful accents, the mansarded corner pavilions very cleverly proportioned to the slightly lower pedimented portico at the centre and to the large dome above. The pavilions have an

258. Govan Town Hall (Robert Sandi-lands, 1897-1901).

[28] See above pp.198, 210, 222ff. But the town hall could do with cleaning. The relations between its principal features may be compared with those on the City Chambers; it is in fact a miniature synthesis of the better Beaux-Arts designs for the City Chambers competition. Inside, the Govan building has a predominantly free-style character with only touches of Beaux-Arts. (Almost contemporary but very different is the Scottish Renaissance mansion built by Sandilands for John Morrison in Sherbrooke Avenue, Pollok-shields (1896): it is now the Sherbrooke Hotel – Worsdall, *Victorian City*, p.112.) A further Beaux-Arts-inspired building in Govan is John Keppie's headquarters for the Fairfield Shipbuilding Co., now Glasgow Shipbuilders (1890). The centrepiece (see Worsdall, *op. cit.* p.130) is heavily indebted to Burnet's Clyde Trust, *see* **176**, clearly French in derivation, but it seems that Keppie was anxious above all to emulate the superior polish that Burnet had brought from Paris to Glasgow.

[29] See Denholm, *History of Glasgow* (3rd edn 1804), p.214; Oakley, *The Second City* (1967), p.37. For the Dunlop Street theatre see Oakley, p.140 and Worsdall, *The City that Disappeared*, pp.144-5.

Ionic order in antis, completing, so to speak, that of the portico: they are mimicked by miniature pavilions flanking the pediment, whose order is finally taken off by an open tabernacle before the drum of the dome. Occasional Glasgow details pertly comment on the formal classical display – especially the cheeky tall chimney stacks sandwiching the dome like the stiff arms in a child's drawing. Govan, a Cinderella burgh if ever there were one, is nevertheless singularly fortunate in its public buildings.[28]

Theatres are a natural for the free style, though in this case not an indigenous one. Glasgow once had many, in many styles, some architecturally humdrum, some much more adventurous. There are not many left, but at least one is among the best.

The first Theatre Royal was built in Queen Street in 1804: David Hamilton was the architect, and for his exterior he chose a style probably suggested by Adam's Assembly Rooms, with a bold display of free-standing columns above a rusticated arcade.[29] It burned down in 1829, and its name was taken a few years later for a building in Dunlop Street which had antedated that in Queen Street, was reconstructed by William Spence in 1839–40 and survived until another fire in 1863, but even then was rebuilt incorporating the old façade which at the time was a quite stylish piece of mannerism, likewise with columns on the first floor but arranged as two aedicules about a plainer centre: there were five niches, with Shakespeare in pride of place. In 1869 (when the southern part of Dunlop Street was absorbed into St Enoch station) the elder George Bell converted the Coliseum music hall

259. Alhambra Theatre, Wellington & Waterloo Streets (John James Burnet, 1910-11).†

into a new Theatre Royal at the top of Hope Street. This was duly burnt in 1879, and a new auditorium, designed by Charles Phipps, the leading theatre architect of mid-Victorian Britain, was inserted. It burned in 1895, but its successor, again by Phipps, has been luckier and is now, after extensive restoration and the provision of an extremely clever foyer by Derek Sugden,[30] the home of Scottish Opera. Phipps's theatre – a less expensive prototype of the same architect's Her Majesty's Theatre in Haymarket, London – has three tiers of boxes-cum-galleries, the lowest swinging out in serpentine curves: juicy Corinthian columns, fluted on the top half only, flank the boxes nearest the stage, but otherwise the decor is quite chaste – chiefly a kind of strapwork along the gallery fronts and round the proscenium arch.

Phipps was duly upstaged by the egregious Frank Matcham, of whose three Glasgow theatres the Empire (1895–7, extraordinarily evocative inside of cynical *fin-de-siècle* optimism, full of sensuous and suggestive forms and imagery) went in 1963, and the Coliseum (1905) has had its interior torn out; but the King's (Bath Street, 1904) survives. This richly characteristic building, designed as a first-run provincial theatre for shows aimed at London, is wonderfully sumptuous, more august and less extravagant than Matcham's exactly contemporary London Coliseum: the side walls of the gallery overhang in rows of great shell-hoods supported on Corinthian columns. The Matcham trademark of serpentine broken pediments[31] appears here not only over the boxes but atop the proscenium arch as well. Every feature, classical as its origins are, has free decoration added – swags of fruit between all the

[30] The foyer is a cuboid three bays square, two storeys high, the upper walls filled with arches, either open or mirrored, giving an intriguing *trompe-l'œil* impression of halls beyond halls. The work of restoration was done in 1974–5.

[31] See Glasstone, *Victorian and Edwardian Theatres* (1975), p.121 and pls.175–6; Glasstone reports that Matcham had patented his own system of curvilinear cantilevers for balconies slung between parallel walls. For the Empire see Brian Walker (ed.), *Frank Matcham, Theatre Architect* (1980), pp.85–6.

brackets of the main cornice, drops of flowers on the columns.

Matcham's pupil Bertie Crewe did two theatres: the Palace in Gorbals Street has deplorably been destroyed: it had an astonishing Anglo-Indian interior with elephant heads on the columns between the lower boxes, and above them buxom half-dressed caryatids single-handedly holding up dome-topped tabernacles with most insouciant gestures. The Pavilion in Renfield Street (1902–4) has a less striking, somewhat French, interior, but is remarkable outside for two strongly contrasting façades – the entrance front full of lavish baroque carving under three big segmental pediments, richly moulded to catch the sun, the north symmetrical between pyramid-capped towers, all in much lower relief and stylistically in a manner which, especially in the top storey and parapet, contrives to suggest Voysey or the early Holden.[32] The north-east tower turns the corner and cleverly unites the two dissimilar designs by overlapping a section of the east front. Both façades are clad, and all the carving and moulding executed, in faience, properly biscuit-coloured but now for some reason painted over.

The Citizens' Theatre in Gorbals Street (1878 and formerly the Royal Princess's) still just about keeps its rich but sober interior by Campbell Douglas – the deep cove to the ceiling gives a fine domical effect – but when the adjoining tenements were demolished in the 1970s, the façade, lacking lateral supports, unsurprisingly fell into the street.[33] Fallen altogether is another of Glasgow's splendours – the Alhambra, **259**, J. J. Burnet's only theatre, built in 1910–11, destroyed in 1970 (buildings in this country are beginning to have the short lives characteristic of America). Alhambras were of their nature Moorish, but Burnet's only concession to the exotic were the topee-topped turrets in banded red and white at the corners of an aggressively square-shouldered entrance elevation. Uncompromisingly unmoulded window slits in pairs emphasized verticality at the sides, but the central feature was a kind of picture-frame window of a type much imitated in the 1930s for cinema façades. The balcony high up under a heavy cornice was an echo of Burnet's favourite eaves gallery. The huge interior, constructed on American lines, had some sparse Louis XVI decor but its character was chiefly determined by streamlined curves which are likewise prophetic of cinema architecture: it represented a wholesale rejection of the opulent baroque of Matcham and was entirely in line with Burnet's mood at the time of Kodak House and the Wallace Scott factory.[34]

In some respects it is a small step – architecturally and even in atmosphere – from the theatres to the earlier and better-known of two Roman Catholic churches designed by the Belgian architect C. J. Ménart:[35] St Aloysius Garnethill (1908–10) is also spatially the more complex of the two and yet at the same time the more conventional – a big cruciform baroque church inspired more by the London Oratory than directly by Rome.[36] Green marble pilasters with gilt capitals are everywhere, between, rather than carrying, the nave arches: there is much entablature above the capitals as well as a frieze between them. The exterior is again sumptuously Italianate, with a three-bay pedimented west front, but the nearly free-standing tower has a touch of the Athenaeum Theatre. The church of the Sacred Heart (in Old Dalmarnock Road, Bridgeton, 1912, **260**) is plainly a much cheaper job – obviously for a working-class parish: its stern dark red exterior, with unadorned walls below and huge thermal windows above, suggests a piece of industrial

[32] Note also the theatre's name in large art-nouveau letters.
[33] It had originally been the portico of the Union Bank in Ingram Street and was adapted for the new setting by Douglas's partner, Sellars.
[34] See above p.209 and **187**; also D. M. Walker in Service, *Edwardian Architecture and its Origins*, pp.207 and 210f. One Glasgow cinema is worth at least a footnote – the Cosmo in Rose Street, by the younger W. J. Anderson (1939), strongly, though belatedly, influenced by Dutch work of the 1920s and alone in Glasgow in that respect: severe brick walls on a steel frame and only a stepped tower at the upper end to make any concession to popular cinema design. For cinemas generally see T. Louden's inclusive and engaging *Cinemas of a Cinema City* (1983).
[35] Ménart was in practice in Perth with a certain Jarvie. His work there is notably Burnetian and suggests that he had worked with Burnet at some time.
[36] Note, e.g., the coffered tunnel vault between the big dome at the crossing and the small one in the nave. The high altar was perhaps inspired by the magnificent late seventeenth-century Brescian Lady Altar at Brompton.

architecture, or it might actually *be* a public bath. What a contrast when one goes inside: the interior is brilliantly lit without dazzle (the light is all from above), a huge single hall with mere passageways outside its colonnades, which alternate two free-standing marble columns with two fluted square pillars joined over a doorcase by a section of wall: a curious and intricate rhythm echoed and simplified in the clerestorey where the mullions of each thermal window correspond to the columns below and the solid between them to the pillared sections of wall. The segmental concrete vault is boxed in at each side to the width of the chancel arch (but the 'chancel' is really only a deep recess at the (ritual) east end, whose design suggests a Romanized version of the effect G. E. Street sought for in Gothic, concentrating attention on the sanctuary by physically narrowing the field of vision). There is possibly too much going on in this interior – every stretch of wall having some sculptured or painted feature – and too many changes of colour (though the range is kept within bounds); but altogether a thoroughly intelligent and original design, answering a clear programme within a limited budget but without sacrificing warmth, geniality and a sense of welcome.

Among other late churches the account of Queen's Cross must be revised and amplified. Thomas Howarth concedes that, viewed from the south, the church 'appears to have been conceived in two completely separate parts . . . as though the architect had been forced to use semi-traditional motives for the first part, and had completed the southern half in his own way . . . the external form was sacrificed for internal effect'.[37] The external form in fact graphically expresses the internal, for the two-storey left-hand half of the façade contains the west gallery (lit by the large upper windows) and the right-hand bay includes the south gallery stairs. The continuity of the cleverly conceived aisle passage linking the two entrance vestibules is clearly visible in the line of the eave low down in the recessed central section, whose highly characteristic version of a flying buttress points to the main element of the roof construction. That perhaps sounds like a sophistical defence of artistic muddle by means of aesthetic theory – and one which we have in any case outgrown, haven't we? But is the exterior a muddle? Doesn't Mackintosh

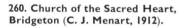

260. Church of the Sacred Heart, Bridgeton (C. J. Menart, 1912).

[37] Howarth, *Charles Rennie Mackintosh and the Modern Movement*, pp.145f.

relate his variant window forms rather well? Doesn't the heroic idiosyncrasy of the south-east bay answer the blunt statement of the tower with a vertical assertion of a different kind but quite as powerful – more powerful indeed than Mackintosh's own drawing[38] indicates? And above all, doesn't the rich modelling of the façade, which even on a dull day leaves deep shadows, create a dramatic interaction, a kind of conceptual overlapping from one volume to another and so mark the church as distinctively a part of the Glasgow street scene? The cross-gables aren't accidental oddities – Mackintosh has observed that they are characteristic features of the city's Victorian churches: his peculiar skill is in rethinking such traditional elements and absorbing them into his own personal idiom alongside others that have no precedent.

Mackintosh was of course a tiro at church design and never had a chance to build another: it is hardly surprising that he uses traditional motifs (his links with other traditions are now widely acknowledged) – most obviously the main windows whose Perpendicular character is not seriously disturbed by the heart- and egg-shaped devices he worked in. Moreover, he had a difficult corner site with no room to spare. So had Norman Shaw for his Harrow mission church in Latimer Road, Hammersmith (1887–9)[39] whose boldly simple interior surely gave Mackintosh his model – that of a large uninterrupted open hall with a huge timber barrel vault pierced by ties at the level of the tops of exterior buttresses. (Hence the significance of Mackintosh's one visible buttress – the others are absorbed into the cross-walls of the two-storey sections.) The tie-beams, which form the base of the framework of the principals, are in each case – to cope with the considerable span (about fifty feet at Queen's Cross) – of rolled steel: hence the absence of king-posts. Shaw's are encased in wood, Mackintosh's are bare, with the

[38] *Ibid.*, pl.70.
[39] See Saint, *Richard Norman Shaw* (1976), pl.218.

261. St John Renfield, Beaconsfield Road, Kelvinside (James Taylor Thomson, 1927-30).

rivets plainly showing. Pugin would have found the church stylistically as well as liturgically abhorrent; but it follows his principle of 'constructional truth' very closely. Most of the furnishing has survived: the pulpit is an unmistakable piece – a working-out in three-dimensional woodwork of motifs used by Mackintosh and his wife for flat decorative panels in paint, glass and ceramics: Mackintosh reinvented them a year or two later for bed-room furniture at the Hill House.

The originality of Queen's Cross can be immediately recognized by comparing it with two very late medieval-inspired churches built in the 1920s for wealthy suburban congregations in the west. St John Renfield (Beaconsfield Road, Kelvinside, **261**), by James Taylor Thomson, 1927–30, has an upstanding Pearsonesque profile – tall, cruciform, with an ornate flèche at the crossing – and Bodleyish arts-and-crafts tracery. The transepts are very short, the aisles very plain and low, so that there is room for a row of fine high clerestorey windows. The plan (a rational redressing of Gothic for Presbyterian worship) and overall proportions take much from Sellars' Belhaven;[40] but the almost blank chancel, the free handling of the tracery – note the west window with enormous buttress-like mullions reminiscent of late Paley and Austin but also of the window form invented by Henry Wilson at St Peter's, Ealing in 1892[41] – the general absence of moulding especially at the coping, and the random coursing: all point to the date. St Margaret's, Knightswood (1929–32), Robert Lorimer's only building in Glasgow and in fact only in sketch form at the time of his death, is simpler – a plain rectangle with tall narrow round-headed windows and a few of the bluff vernacular touches characteristic of Lorimer. Its only real feature is the thin west tower with crowstepped saddleback roof, prompted no doubt by reminiscences of Lübeck and the Baltic, its height emphasized by a long strip of stone pro-jecting from the west face: again the stonework has random coursing; small windows have art-nouveau heads.

Three Bridges

Glasgow's oldest surviving bridge crosses the White Cart Water in the grounds of Pollok House – a simple balustraded segmental arch, hand-somely executed enough to have been attributed to John Adam, though with nothing of the heroic boldness of the Adams' great arch at Dalkeith. It was built, soon after the house, in 1757–58.[42] Incomparably more interesting is the Kelvin Aqueduct, **262**, built by the engineer Robert Whitworth to carry the Forth-Clyde canal over the river valley – when completed in 1790 the largest in Britain, 445 feet long. It has four arches of fifty feet span divided by what look like cutwaters but are in fact buttresses (only one pier stands in the river itself), designed to counteract the outward thrust of the parapet walls at their weakest point; for the walls are in plan (seen from the outside) concave over each arch, and consecutive segments meet over the piers. Deep rustication in the stonework of the voussoirs, spandrels and buttresses combines with the plain ashlar of the upper walls to give an impression of formidable strength.[43]

In extreme contrast is a bridge equally little known though it spans the Clyde – near the elbow in the middle of Glasgow Green. This is Glasgow's other suspension bridge, St Andrew's, built by Neil Robson in 1854, with architectural details said to have been supplied by Carrick's assistant Charles O'Neill.[44] As against the gigantic neo-Greek of its greater brother, St

[40] See p.175 and **158** above. Something may also have come from the planed-off Bodleian Gothic practised in America by R. A. Cram and Bertram Goodhue. Cf. also Giles Gilbert Scott's Liverpool Cathedral.

[41] And cribbed by Caröe five years later for St David's, Exeter.

[42] See Hume, *Industrial Archaeology of Glasgow* (1974), pl.69 and Kinchin, *Pollok House* (1983), p.15. The bridge is not unlike those built just previously at Inveraray by John Adam and Roger Morris and Adam's at Dumfries House.

[43] See further Ted Ruddock, *Arch Bridges and their Builders* (1979), pp.128f. A few simple arches, carrying the canal over roads, also survive from Whitworth's time.

[44] Worsdall, *The Victorian City*, p.122, and Hume, *op. cit.*, pl.71. It was always a foot-bridge and was built originally to enable workers from Bridgeton and Camlachie to get to their factories in Hutchesontown.

Andrew's has small neatly dressed pylons which look like baldacchinos – rectangles of Corinthian columns carrying full entablatures and shallow pyramidal hats, all in cast iron, the quite dainty Roman conjoining oddly with the straightforward engineering of the flat-link chains passing through holes in the frieze.

Between the Wars and Onwards

To the handful of inter-war buildings already briefly characterized may be added a few more to confirm the impression they give of a classicism not surrendered nor remembered with conviction, a modernism too cautious to draw attention to itself by more than coy miniature gestures. A. G. Henderson's awkwardly high-waisted Bank of Scotland (235 Sauchiehall Street, 1931) has dropped the stylar treatment of the lower floors that James Miller still used in his Union Bank (110 St Vincent Street)[45] but clings rather weakly to elementary Greek detail proportionately too small to be more than a minor irritant. That is not a fault to be found with E. G. Wylie's very large Scottish Legal building (95 Bothwell Street, 1927), which is really Selfridges squared off, it features a glazed four-storeyed pilastrade on each main façade framed by conventional fenestration, and still looks very cold. McInnes Gardner's Electricity Board offices in Waterloo Street (again of 1927) show the stylistic uncertainty graphically. Overall it suggests a fussier version of Burnet's 200 St Vincent Street[46] by an architect who can't let well alone. On the first floor he is still harking back (with architraves and cornices) to a window-form of at latest the 1870s.[47] But after two storeys of mere rectangular holes the top has parodies of squat fluted pilasters inserted as panels between long horizontal windows. Henderson's store for Watt Bros at the corner of Rose and Bath Streets (1929) stalks with more swagger into the moderne and in so doing slicks up all its vestigial classicism; yet between the giant order of capital-less half- or quarter-columns appear only tinny-looking prow-shaped window-strips – apologies for bays, decked out with feeble pressed detail. One has only to cross Sauchiehall Street to the splendid

[45] See p.228 above. Miller's design turns out to have been a blatant plagiarism of York & Sawyer's Guaranty Trust building, 140 Broadway, New York, illustrated in the *Architectural Review U.S.A.*, ii.7 (1913), a copy of which was lent by A. G. Lochhead to Richard Gunn, Miller's chief draughtsman, in time for the 1924 competition.
[46] See **186** above.
[47] Cf. Horatio Bromhead's delightful Crown Halls, Sauchiehall Street (1871), crowded with as many sashes as will go into the available wall. The irregularity of fenestration of Gardner's building suggests that it was designed in two parts: the elevation to Blythswood Street is crassly mishandled. Gardner had been with James Miller, much of the time working on ship interiors in which he later had a large business on his own.

263. The Dental Hospital, Renfrew
Street (E. G. Wylie, 1928-31).

263. The Dental Hospital, Renfrew
Street (E. G. Wylie, 1928-31).

Barclay warehouse[48] to see where the overall formula comes from and to
register the relative vacuity of so much twentieth-century effort.

A far more intelligent façade is that of Wylie's Dental Hospital in Renfrew
Street (1928–31), 263. Like its near-neighbour the Art School it faces north –
and uphill: so almost the whole wall must be of glass; but what one sees first
is the powerful grid of projecting uprights and recessed horizontals. Bold
mullions carry the eye up three storeys to a light cornice; then the attic
repeats the pattern, but the mullions are much lighter and the cornice a little
heavier: so now it is the horizontals that tell. But the continuing lines of the
mullions (picking up the verticals after a broad band of masonry) ensure that
the attic is visibly the top of *this* building, not simply a horizontal laid above
something to which it is not related. The masonry strip functions visually
like the sub-attic cornice on baroque houses and the vertical strips which join
it one bay in from each end like pilasters, though (with the possible exception
of dentils at the top) the building is without direct classical reference. The
outermost bays are wider than the rest, giving a visual logic to their *being*
the outermost, though the whole main façade is then clamped within a
pair of masonry towers – a good (vestigially neo-classical?) idea, but they
aren't well composed, lacking (especially at the top) a clear relation to the
façade between. The formula, which essentially repeats that of the Scottish
Legal, is a simplification of the Burnet idea of a colonnade stretched between
pylons, with the columns reduced to mullions. Kodak House and the
Wallace Scott factory must have been a major inspiration, with a dash of
Holden in the towers (a most difficult architect to assimilate). The decorative
panels in the horizontals, perhaps a little brutally in view of the building's
function, suggest rows of forceps. Such a thoughtful working-out of a
modern façade in terms still of a classical sense of balance is in amazing
contrast to a building almost directly behind – that stunning moment in
Sauchiehall Street where all the jazz-modern stops are pulled out to produce
the Beresford Hotel (Weddel & Inglis, 1937: now a hostel of Strathclyde
University, 264): violently exhibitionist with harsh bright verticals like a

super-cinema sprung up to thrice the normal height. It is deliberately, insistently alien, kicking all the old Glasgow manners in the teeth, a strident eye-catcher from a brash bypass world, monument to an age which vanished almost as soon as it was born: no wonder Glaswegians have such an affection for it: it must of course be most jealously preserved.

What a change to the rational hush of Hughes and Waugh's reading room in University Avenue (1939), just above Wellington church, from which it differs as much and as politely as from the university it serves: a building which modestly and sensibly goes about its business, using a traditional circular plan well lit by vertical window strips, showing its date in the deliberate avoidance of moulding on its pallid brick walls, but straightforward enough to do comfortably without identifiable style. It has nothing notice-ably Glaswegian to offer – in this respect unlike Hughes's fine university chemistry building, first planned in 1936, whose staircase towers, with their wholly glazed convex walls braced only by the thinnest of mullions irresist-ibly send one back for a long look at Scotland Street: Mackintosh seen through the eyes of Erich Mendelsohn.

Jack Coia's two inter-war churches strike a quite individual note. The longitudinal plan of Ménart's Sacred Heart, with the ritual east end treated as a sanctuary which the congregation stop short of at the communion rail, would have given even this distinctive church a familiar traditional feeling. Coia, by contrast, at his earliest church, St Anne's, Whitevale Street, Dennistoun (1933), **265**, breaks with this and all other traditional plans. The entrance front

264. Beresford Hotel, Sauchiehall Street
(Weddel & Inglis, 1937).

265. A gable on St Anne's church, Dennistoun (J. A. Coia, 1933).

gives little away: pedimented attic leant on by bulbous consoles, triple-arched entrance, a façade of bare brick like that of a Roman baroque church which never achieved its intended marble facing.[49] But the side elevations are very fresh: they have two tall round-headed windows going right up into semicircular gables whose deeply rubbed tops make a kind of brick ruff. Eastward of these is a shallow transept with a large polygonal gable. One enters a narthex quite cut off from the church and must move right or left into what appears to be a corridor all round the building; but it turns into the 'aisles' – aisles which vanish at each window and then start again. The sanctuary (level with the transepts) is marked architecturally only by a square of groined plastering, the rest being covered by a plain tunnel vault. There is exposed brickwork throughout the interior, creating a no-nonsense atmosphere which anticipates that of Catholic churches later in the century. The scale, however, is small, and the church feels trim and neat.[50]

St Columba's, Hopehill Road, Woodside of 1937 is quite another thing: a great barrack of a church, lying humped like a gigantic disconsolate cat in a bleak waste surrounded by regenerated tenements already beginning to look seedy – a sure indication that merely reconstituting buildings is not enough if the rest of the environment is left desolate. In place of a tower the church has a *Westwerk*, a broad shallow mass of brickwork almost without features, flanked by much lower round-ended transepts. Low aisles, extremely severe deep-set rectangular clerestorey windows, and then an enormous gambrel roof; petite polygonal apse. There is nothing subtle about this exterior: it goes all out to deliver a once-for-all knock-out blow, and the interior does it again. It is in principle similar to that of St Mary's, Shirehampton, Bristol, by Percival Hartland Thomas (1929),[51] and it looks as if Coia had studied that church, though his is much higher and not so insistent a lesson in modernism. Transverse portal frames twisted into pointed arches carry the roof and articulate the nave, coming down into wall-piers which are pierced for the aisles and carry longitudinal concrete beams below the clerestorey. Again subtlety isn't in it – there is nothing here to discover by degrees or patient exploration – but it makes a powerful statement, of a religio-aesthetic creed which (like the building) may now make us uncomfortable.

Harold Hughes's work for the University bridges the war. And here once again, as in our first edition, we stop short. The post-war architecture of Glasgow is a subject at once too big and too small. There has on the one hand been so much building – as much during the last fifteen years as in any fifty before. Yet it is still, regretfully, our view that its contribution to the city's architecture has been minimal. Whatever the faults of the buildings we have discussed in this chapter they are nearly all recognizably Glaswegian; whatever the merits of such buildings as the Boyd Orr at the University or the Charing Cross redevelopment or Langside College (or indeed, from before the war, Owen Williams's much-praised *Glasgow Herald* in Albion Street), they might just as well – whether or not designed by Glasgow architects (most of them are not) – be in Leeds, or London, or Los Angeles. The story is as it was in 1968, only of course much more so; and there are sadly few opportunities to record an impression that architects are responding to Glasgow. Since a sense of Glasgow as a city of extraordinary and brilliant individuality has all along been what seemed to us of the greatest worth and what we especially wanted to convey, this is a disheartening conclusion –

[49] This façade sorts oddly with the untraditional inventiveness behind: perhaps the clients insisted on a more familiar type of front.
[50] The presbytery alongside has a brick ruff of its own and a spectacular display of sculpture.
[51] See Gomme, Jenner & Little, *op. cit.*, pp.419f. and pl.333.

all too familiar to observers of the twentieth-century urban scene. And lest this closing impression should be *merely* disheartening we end, with some pleasure, by referring to a small handful of recent designs that really do seem to incorporate an awareness of the characteristic fabric of the city.

King, Main and Ellison had the unnerving task in 1977 of building, for Scottish Amicable Life, next to the Hatrack in St Vincent Street, as individual a building as even Glasgow has to show.[52] The site is difficult, sloping on two adjacent façades, long but shallow – and would have drawn from an unimaginative team mere acres of curtain wall. The building has indeed much glass: on a bright day the north-facing buildings opposite are lit up in brilliant reflected sunlight. But the façade breaks forward and back; tall granite strips articulate the divisions between large glazed oriels: the architects have seen that Glasgow is a city of verticals.[53] Not that verticals will do on their own: the repeated thin ribs of Leslie Norton's Scottish Life House (4 St Vincent Street, 1968) create no co-ordinating principle, and there is nothing else to tie the design together or give it proportion: it is simply façade-making by the yard or hundred yards. The Amicable Life on the other hand has regulated the proportions of its bays by the measure of those that Glasgow has made so much its own. Perhaps the top is a little weak (tops so often seem to present non-traditionalist architects with insoluble difficulties); and one may wonder whether the proportion of void to solid will ever entirely assimilate itself to a stone-built street; but for all the relative novelty of its cladding, this is a building which belongs in the historic city. G. D. Lodge's Clydesdale Bank extension (1981) at the corner of Buchanan and West George Streets (what a challenging site!) is hardly the obvious offshoot of John Burnet's bank on to which it backs:[54] the form of its two adjoining façades has been likened to that of the famous Gardner's in Jamaica Street,[55] though in truth the new building has nothing of the subtle gradations of scale and detail of the old, or of its grave patrician dignity; its mansard-type attic looks perhaps towards the unhappy top-hamper of the Ca d'Oro: lacking any ghost of a cornice or overhang it is somewhat weakly recessive, especially at the all-important corner, where, with a kind of look-no-hands mannerism, Lodge puts only the thinnest of steel glazing bars. Such a site is not the place for tricks of this kind.[56] Still, it is a building which combines some vigour with refinement and even elegance, and it has taken note of the kind of adventurous experimenting that Baird and his followers made into an expressly Glaswegian contribution to the new architecture of their time.[57]

Perhaps Gillespie, Kidd and Coia had an easier job slipping their little British Airways office into one of the traditional narrow sites (at 85 Buchanan Street, 1970): it is the very size of the big sites which can defeat an architect's artistic integrity or his respect for the setting and his neighbours; moreover the overall shape of this front was bound to be upright – a very useful foundation on which to work. However that may be, the copper-clad grid standing out in front of the glass makes a graceful and ingenious variation on Glaswegian themes. It is in fact flat, but the chamfered corners of each opening hint at the canted bays which in one form or another are still all around. The treatment of the top, creating an appearance of a 'cornice' by briefly recessing the wall-face above the topmost horizontal of the grid, is, in the Glasgow of recent years, almost uniquely successful.[58]

At a great remove in setting and function comes Glasgow's most popular building for many decades – Barry Gasson's home for the Burrell collection

[52] See **211** above.

[53] Contrast the painful effect of the insistent horizontals on T. P. Bennett's Bank of Scotland, Queen Street (1971) – across from the Royal Exchange at a particularly sensitive spot. Seifert's Charing Cross offices of 1975 are equally and similarly insensitive.

[54] See **140** above.

[55] See above pp.114–15.

[56] Contrast the visibly reliable corner stanchion at Gardner's, **91**; for the Ca d'Oro, see **138**.

[57] As with many glass-walled buildings this one acts as a mirror: the visual effect incorporates as well the opposite side of the street; especially on bright days what one notices even before the bank's own shape are the crazily undulating pink reflexions of the Stock Exchange and St George's. The building seems to us altogether superior to its brutalist neighbour, Walter Underwood's Bank of England, 21 West George Street (1981), which is too low, too dogmatic, and lacks gradations of scale; yet this too recognizes the need to articulate a fundamentally horizontal design by stressed verticals: only the heavy concrete attic doesn't work like the eaves galleries and balconies of the free style to tie in verticals as well as bringing them to a halt.

[58] It is a pity, though, that this building, with such a fastidious feeling for the street as a whole, pointedly cold-shoulders the little house next door, to which its other, and equally contrasting neighbour, Washington Browne's tea-room, accommodates itself with perfect good manners. Incidentally, the copper facing has darkened handsomely over the past decade and a half to tone with its as yet uncleaned neighbour to the south: how ironic if it soon stands out as a dark building among pale ones!

in Pollok Park. Looked at as a piece of 'pure architecture', as its own monument, it is, in its unassertive reticence, nestling into the woods like a huge glass marquee, both undemonstrative and no more essentially Glaswegian than that other great Glasgow greenhouse, the Kibble Palace.[59] But it is not itself designed or thought of as a piece of sculpture, and criticisms of its undramatic exterior from those who hold that a building must make an unambiguous statement or be part of an identifiable architectural lineage are off the point. Its extraordinary success in making a home for the extremely multifarious collection paradoxically militates against its being judged fairly in 'architectural' terms. The home is not just an envelope, however complex (to reflect the very different conditions needed for studying and safeguarding objects so different in size and materials): it was a stroke of genius to incorporate major architectural fragments into the construction of the building so that the collection itself in part defines its environment. The planning, with its set of intersecting cross-routes within the perimeter walk, its opportunities for views down from the mezzanine as well as up from the floor, constantly offers suggestions for new ways to interpret the collection, making, as Gasson himself has said, for 'juxtapositions that are both intentional and a surprise'. The varieties of enclosure within the larger envelope make one of its greatest pleasures – varieties of volume, colour, texture and lighting which nevertheless always encourage concentration on the exhibit at the moment when attention should be narrowed on to it; and the larger exhibits become features of the building as well as objects within it. Significantly perhaps, the more conventional 'museum rooms' seem the least interesting: the period rooms are simply white cuboids, anonymous backgrounds for objects which have no other evident physical relationship (though the Bridgwater ceiling is indeed acting as itself above one); and the Hutton Castle rooms, not themselves outstanding for their fixtures, are stubbornly alien elements however they ensure Burrell's continuing presence in his new home. Perhaps, too, nothing else quite equals the opening progression through the entrance tunnel across the Hutton courtyard, under the Hornby arch (all the more sumptuously striking for the plain wall of its setting) and out into the trees: for that is what it feels like – in summer at least – so powerfully does the uninterrupted forest backdrop determine the character of the open avenue into which one turns, walking between the polished concrete columns standing like so many tree trunks among the sculpture and the showcases. There are houses such as Holkham or the Hill House for which all the furniture and fitments have been purpose-made, conceived as the *Gesamtkunstwerk* from the start, or those like Wightwick which have through time gradually filled with the character and personal interests of a builder or owner. The new Burrell is a unique kind of fusion, making a work of art out of an existing and very miscellaneous collection by setting it into the natural and human environment in a distinctive and highly individual way.[60]

And finally some tenements. The old tenements have fallen in their tens of thousands, and in their place have risen point blocks and slabs in what are optimistically called landscaped areas. Landscape, not townscape: there are no streets in the new Hutchesontown or Cowcaddens, and the blocks are too high for the inhabitants to use streets if they had them. A piece of new townscape has however been made among the new pink brick tenements of Woodside – buildings which deserve the honourable old name. Boswell,

[59] See above p.92n.
[60] For a widely illustrated survey of the Burrell gallery, with discussions of technical and other aspects of the building, see the special number of the *Architects' Journal*, 19 October 1983.

Mitchell and Johnston, who began the scheme in the early 1970s, worked out a formula which enables even eight-storey ranges to reflect and recreate the deeply modelled walls of Glasgow. They do in fact use again the old canted bays, in pairs of storeys worked into plain walling flush with the fronts of the bays to create alternating overhangs: the effect is once again of a truly three-dimensional façade, vigorous and lively. It is of course only one formula and, repeated without variation in detail and layout, could become as monotonous as the blandest curtain wall. There is some sign in Woodside that this too has been recognized: will it be borne in mind when the time comes to replace the purpose-built slums of the last twenty years?

Chronological table

The following table is a brief chronological resumé of the main events in the more recent architectural history of Glasgow; it is diagrammatic, and more detailed information must be sought in the narrative chapters and the appendices. The dates at which buildings appear in column four are those of the design or at which building began: completion may be up to several years later. The date at which an architect's name appears in column two is calculated as the mid-point between his twentieth birthday and his death, except where (as indicated by an asterisk) this would – usually because of marked precocity – be grossly misleading, or cannot at present be discovered for certain. In these cases a date has been chosen to represent the mid-point of the architect's career as a designer. (Thus, for instance, Mackintosh's date is half-way between the first and second designs for the Art School, a few years earlier than the formula date, by which time his career was virtually at an end.) The date in brackets after the architect's name in this column is that of birth.

Date	Floruit	Died	Buildings	Events
1750			St Andrew's by the Green (Hunter)	Glasgow Ship Bank founded
1764		Dreghorn		
1768			St Andrew's Square (laid out) St Enoch's Square (first feus)	Firth-Clyde Canal begun (completed 1790)
1770	R. Adam (1728)			Monkland Canal begun (completed 1790)
1772	J. Adam (1730)		Jamaica Bridge	
1773				Dredging of Clyde begins
1776				American Declaration of Independence
1777				Failure of Buchanans
1780			St Enoch's Church (Jaffrey)	
1782				Tontine Hotel opened
1783				First British Chamber of Commerce, Glasgow. First Turkey-red dye-works
1784			Spreull's Land	
1786			St Andrew's Square (houses)	First great cotton mill (New Lanark)
1787			George Square	First ironworks in Glasgow
1788			Grammar School (later Anderson's College, Craig)	First London–Glasgow mail coach
1789				French Revolution
1790			Candleriggs (present buildings)	
1791			Trades House (R. Adam)	Census: Glasgow 67,000

Date	Floruit	Died	Buildings	Events
1792		R. Adam	Old Infirmary (R. & J. Adam)	
1794		J. Adam		Outbreak of French Revolutionary War
1796			Assembly Rooms (J. & W. Adam)	Anderson College founded
1802			Hutcheson's Hospital (Hamilton) Carlton Place (Nicholson)	
1804			Houldsworth's Mill (Boulton & Watt)	
1807	*Stark		St George's Church (Stark) Justiciary Court House (Stark) North British Station Hotel (as terrace of houses)	
1809			Lunatic Asylum (Stark)	Glasgow Banking Co. founded
1811				Census: Glasgow 101,000
1812				Kirkman Finlay elected M.P. for Glasgow burghs. 'Comet' steamboat on the Clyde
1813		Stark		
1815	Nicholson (1765) *Brash		St Andrew's Catholic Church (Gillespie Graham)	End of Napoleonic War
1816	D. Hamilton (1768)			
1819			Tobacco Exchange	
1820				Weavers' Strikes
1823			Blythswood Square (Brash)	
1825			Abbotsford Place	
1826				Monkland & Kirkintilloch Railway
1827			Argyle Arcade (Baird) St Enoch's Church (Hamilton) Royal Bank of Scotland (Elliot)	
1828				Neilson invents hot blast furnaces Iron foundries established in Glasgow
1830			Royal Exchange Square (Elliot, Hamilton & J. Smith)	Glasgow Union Banking Co. founded
1831			Woodside Crescent (G. Smith)	Census: Glasgow 202,000
1833			Athol Place	
1837			Newton Place (G. Smith)	
1838	J. Bryce (1805)			City of Glasgow Bank founded
1839	Baird (1798)		Royal Crescent (A. Taylor)	
1840			Custom House (G. L. Taylor) Queen's Crescent (J. Bryce)	
1841			Western Club (Hamilton)	

Date	Floruit	Died	Buildings	Events
1842			Claremont House (Baird)	Edinburgh–Glasgow Railway
1843		D. Hamilton		
1844	J. Hamilton (c.1807)	Nicholson	City & County Buildings (Clarke & Bell)	
1845	G. Smith (1793)		Kirklee Terrace (Wilson)	
1846	J. Smith (1808)			
1847	Wilson (1810)			
1848		Wylson	Canada Court (Wylson)	Famine Riots
1849			St Matthew, Blythswood (Emmet) 3–11 Dunlop St. (Thomson) 81 Miller St. (Salmon, sen.) St Vincent Crescent (Kirkland)	
1850	D. Bryce (1803)		Royal Bank Building (Wilson) Wylie & Lochhead's (Argyle St.)	
1851		J. Bryce	Victoria Bridge (Walker)	Great Exhibition (London)
1852	Rhind (1801)		'The Knowe' (Thomson)	
1854			Kelvingrove Park (Wilson & Paxton) National Commerical Bank (Rhind) 37–51 Miller St. (Kirkland) Royal Faculty of Procurators (Wilson)	Archibald Maclellan Gallery bequest to Glasgow
1855	Spence (?1806)		Grosvenor Terrace (Rochead) Park Area (Wilson) Iron Building, Jamaica St. (Baird) Wylie & Lochhead's (Buchanan St.)	Glasgow Bill (water from Loch Katrine)
1856	Rochead (1814) Thomson (1817)		Elgin Place Church (Burnet, sen.) Free Church College (Wilson) Caledonia Road Church (Thomson) 25–25a Mansionhouse Road (Thomson)	
1857	Salmon, sen. (1805)		Queen's Rooms (Wilson) Walmer Crescent (Thomson)	
1858			Crown Circus (J. Thomson) St Vincent St. Church (Thomson) Randolph Elder Engine Works (Spence)	Faculty of Old College abolished; University Court controls finance and policy
1859		Baird	No.1 Moray Place (Thomson) John St. Church (Rochead) Grosvenor Building (Thomson) Queen's Park Terrace (Thomson)	
1860			Cairney Building (Thomson)	
1861	*Clarke *Bell, No.1		Mechanics' Institute (Salmon)	Census: Glasgow 395,000 1861–65, American Civil War Cotton slump
1862		J. Hamilton	Lansdowne Church (Honeyman)	
1863		J. Smith Wilson	Buck's Head Building (Thomson)	

Date	Floruit	Died	Buildings	Events
1865	Carrick (1819)		Grecian Building (Thomson)	
1866		Cousland	University (Scott)	City Improvement Act
1868	Burnet, sen. (1814) Peddie, sen. (1824)		Queen's Park Church (Thomson)	
1869	Gildard (1822)		Northpark Terrace (Thomson) Great Western Terrace (Thomson) Bank of Scotland (Rochead)	
1870	H. Barclay (1828)		Clydesdale Bank (Burnet, sen.)	
1871	*Boucher		Westbourne Terrace (Thomson) Egyptian Halls (Thomson) St Mary's Episcopal Cathedral (Scott)	University moves to Gilmorehill
1872	Kinnear (1830)		Ca d'Oro (Honeyman)	
1873			St Andrew's Halls (Sellars)	
1874		Billings	Bank of Scotland Buildings, George Square (Sellars)	
1875		Thomson	St Enoch Station (Fowler & Blair) Glasgow Stock Exchange (Burnet, sen.)	
1876	Sellars (1843)	D. Bryce	Lanarkshire House (Burnet, sen.)	
1877		G. Smith	Kelvinside Academy (Sellars) Belhaven Church (Sellars) City of Glasgow Bank (Sellars)	
1878		Rochead	Queen St. Station (Carswell) Barony North Church (Honeyman) Fine Art Institute (Burnet, jun.) Camphill Church (Leiper)	Failure of City of Glasgow Bank
1879	Douglas (1828)		21–31 Buchanan St. (Spence) Kelvingrove Church (Sellars)	
1880	Stevenson (1831) J. Thomson (1835)		Westbourne Free Church (Honeyman)	
1881				Census: Glasgow 511,000
1882	Honeyman (1831) Turnbull (?1839)			
1883		Rhind Spence	City Chambers (Young) Wellington Church (Watson)	
1884			Central Station Hotel (R. Anderson)	
1886			Barony Church (Burnet & Campbell) St George's-in-the-Fields (Barclay) Athenaeum (Burnet, jun.)	
1887	R. R. Anderson (1834) Leiper (1839)	Bell, No.1		
1888		Salmon, sen. Sellars	Anderson's College of Medicine (Sellars)	First Glasgow International Exhibition

Date	Floruit	Died	Buildings	Events
1889			Templeton's Carpet Factory (Leiper)	
1890		Carrick		
1891	W. J. Anderson (1863) D. Barclay (1846)		Athenaeum Theatre (Burnet & Campbell) Charing Cross Mansions (Burnet & Campbell)	Art Galleries Competition
1892		H. Barclay		
1893	*Keppie (1863)		Glasgow Herald Building (Keppie & Mackintosh)	First Municipal electricity service County Status
1894	Campbell (1859)			
1895	*Burnet, jun. (1859) Bell, No.2 (1854) Rowan (?1846) Watson (?1850)	Gildard	Langside Hill Church (Skirving) Martyrs School (Mackintosh)	Glasgow Corporation Act
1896			Savings Bank Hall (Burnet, jun.)	
1897			Mercantile Chambers (Salmon, jun.) Argyle Tea Room (Mackintosh & Walton) School of Art, E. section (Mackintosh) Queen's Cross Church (Mackintosh)	
1898			Napier House (W. J. Anderson) 166–8 Buchanan Street (Campbell)	
1899			142–4 St Vincent St. (Salmon, jun.) Atlantic Chambers (Burnet, jun.)	
1900	*Salmon, jun. (1874)	W. J. Anderson	Stevenson Memorial Church (Stevenson)	
1901	Chalmers (1859)	Burnet, sen.		Census: Glasgow 761,000 Second Glasgow International Exhibition
1902	*Mackintosh (1868)		157–167 Hope St. (Campbell)	
1903			Sauchiehall St. Tea Room (Mackintosh) Pearce Institute (R. R. Anderson)	
1904			Scotland St. School (Mackintosh)	
1905		J. Thomson	McGeoch's (Burnet, jun.)	
1906			Lion Chambers (Salmon, jun.)	
1907			School of Art, W. section (Mackintosh)	
1908			Northern Assurance Building (Campbell) Liberal Club (Paterson)	
1909		Campbell		
1910	*Clifford *Paterson (1862)	Douglas		
1911				Third Glasgow International Exhibition
1912			Phoenix Assurance Building (Hislop)	
1913	Miller (1860)			
1914		Honeyman		

dr. = draughtsman.
pup. = pupil.
▼ indicates that the architect was a pupil of the one immediately above. The plain vertical lines indicate continuation of the same firm or of a given architect's practice.
The broken lines indicate a change of appointment during an architect's career.
Architects whose names are shown in parentheses were employed in the practice to which they are attributed. The names of firms and partnerships are shown without parentheses.

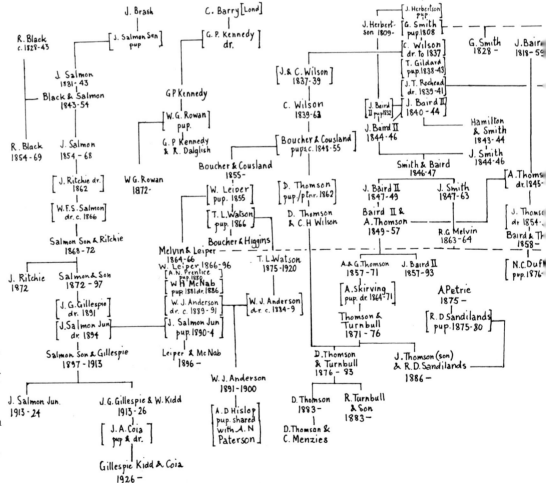

Genealogical Tree

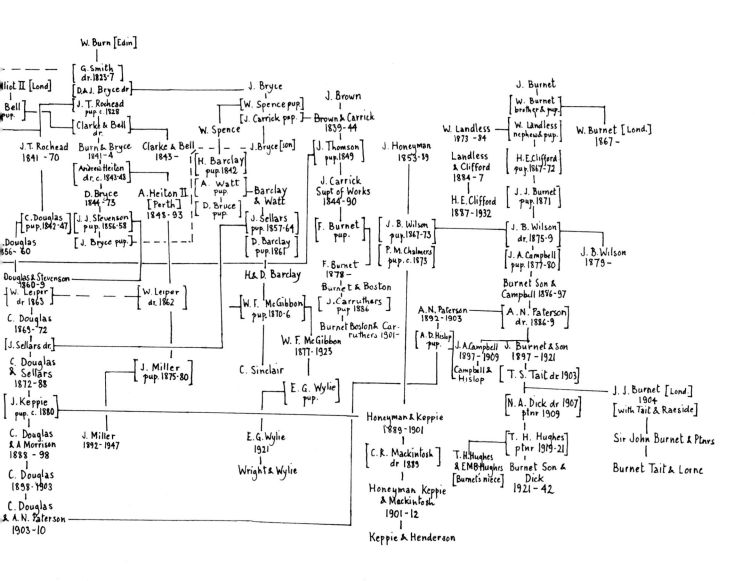

The principal Glasgow architects and their buildings

This list is not exhaustive; its aim is both to suggest the range of a given architect's work and to give some indication of how it developed chronologically. Only buildings in Glasgow have been included in the case of those architects like the Adams, whose main work lies outside the city; but in a few cases, where an architect is remembered chiefly for his work in Glasgow, buildings elsewhere have occasionally been noted. *Dates are in many cases approximate only and normally refer to the beginning rather than the completion of the building.* An asterisk before the name of a building indicates that the attribution is not certain; (S) after the name indicates that the building is on the south side; the numbers in bold refer to the listing by streets given in the list of buildings of architectural interest, which begins on page 305, and to the maps (pp. 330–8). References to the text and illustrations are in parentheses.

Adam, Robert (1728–92) and James (1732–94)

The Adams seem to have spent little time in Glasgow, and that during the last years of their lives. All their work in the city dates from the 1790s, and it is virtually impossible to distinguish their individual contributions. The work was supervised by their nephew, John Robertson, John Paterson, and probably David Hamilton.

1790
*52 Charlotte Street, **171**
*57–59 Charlotte Street, **168**
*60 Wilson Street, **812**. (p.62, fig.41)
*David Dale's House, Charlotte Street. Demolished, c.1950, **173**. (p.61)

1791 Trades House, 85–91 Glassford Street (Robert), **272**. (pp.54, 65, 82, 235, fig.42)

1792 Royal Infirmary, Cathedral Square. Demolished 1912. (pp.18, 61, 65, figs.38–9)
Assembly Rooms, Ingram Street. Built c.1796, demolished c.1889, **381**; centrepiece rebuilt as McLennan Arch, Glasgow Green, 1893, **172**. (pp.60–1, 264, fig.37)
Barony Church, Cathedral Square (executed by John Robertson). Demolished c.1890. The drawing survives at the Soane Museum, **159**. (pp.64n, 155, fig.38)

1793 College Houses, 169–177 and 179–185 High Street (James), **332–3**. Demolished. (p.69, fig.40)

1794 Tron Kirk, 71 Trongate (James), **685**. Now a theatre. (pp.47, 62)
*16–18 Blackfriars Street, **80**. Restored 1986.

Adam, William (1689–1748)

No buildings by William Adam remain in the city itself. But one former country house is now within the boundaries.

1732 Old College: Library, **335**. Demolished c.1880.

1737 Pollok House, 2060 Pollokshaws Road, Pollok. Built 1747–52, probably by John Adam. Terraces and pavilions by R. R. Anderson, 1890 onwards. (S) **957**. (pp.65–7, 269, fig.43)

Anderson, (Sir) Robert Rowand (1834–1921)

Anderson practised only occasionally in Glasgow; but his few buildings all show academic detailing of a high order. The Central Station is an essential part of the city's townscape.

1884 Govan Old Parish Church, 868 Govan Road (S), **901**
Central Station Hotel, Gordon Street, **282**. (p.197, 205n, fig.177)

1890 and later Additions to Pollok House, 2060 Pollokshaws Road, Pollok (S), **957**. (p.67, fig.43)

1897 Pollokshaws Burgh Buildings, 2025 Pollokshaws Road, Pollokshaws (S), **955**. (p.198)

1903 Pearce Institute, 840 Govan Road, Govan (S), **900**. (p.198, fig.178)

Anderson, William James (1863/4–1900)

Anderson was apprenticed to Gillespie of St Andrews and spent time in Dundee before coming to Glasgow early in the 1880s. According to his own account, he had by 1889 assisted both T. L. Watson and William Leiper, in whose office James Salmon, jun., worked under him. In 1887 he won the Thomson Travelling Scholarship. In 1894 he was appointed Director of the Department of Architecture at the Glasgow School of Art, and probably encouraged Francis Newbery to choose a modern design. During the construction of his last building, Napier House, the fifth floor fell, killing five men. Anderson was not then in charge; and it seems that the client had used inadequate centring and that the concrete was badly mixed. The jury, without technical evidence on these points, blamed the structural engineer, but Anderson felt equally responsible, took it very much to heart and worried himself to death. He published *Architectural Studies in Italy* in 1890, *The Architecture of the Renaissance in Italy* in 1896, and *The Architecture of Greece and Rome*, finished after his death by Phené Spiers.

1885	Citizen Office, 24 St Vincent Place (with T. L. Watson), **590** (p.258, fig. 249)
	Sun Life Building, 117–121 West George Street (with William Leiper), **757**. (p.226)
1892	Orient House, 16 McPhater Street, Cowcaddens, **439**. (pp.224, 259, fig. 250)
1893	21 Sherbrooke Avenue, Pollokshields (S), **982**
1899	Napier House, 640–646 Govan Road, Govan (S), **898**. (p.224, fig.213)

Baird, John ('no.1') (1798–1859)

Baird was born at Dalmuir and apprenticed to one Shepherd who died in 1818, leaving the 20-year-old Baird in charge. Little information is available about his later life, which, to judge by the number of more or less well authenticated works, must have been fully occupied in designing. Baird's brother Anthony was also an architect, but later became a chartered accountant. John Baird's portrait, by Macnee, hangs in the Glasgow Art Gallery. He was no relation to John Baird No.2.

1821	Greyfriars Church, 186 Albion Street, **6**. (p.114n). Demolished c.1969.
1823	Wellington Church, Wellington Street, Blythswood. Demolished 1909, **744**. (p.114n)
	*St John's Chapel of Ease, 598 Gallowgate, Calton, **243**
1827	Argyle Arcade, 98–102 Argyle Street, **14**. (p.114, fig.88)
1833	*Athol Place, 181–199 Bath Street, Blythswood, **39**. (p.78)
	*Athol Place, 182–200 Bath Street, Blythswood, **46**. (p.78)
1834	Cambridge Street Church, 154–156 Cambridge Street, Garnethill, **148**. Altered 1846 and 1868. Demolished c.1975.
1839	Anderston Old Parish Church, Heddle Place, Anderston, **329**. Demolished 1967.
1840	Somerset Place, Sauchiehall Street, **657**. End block rebuilt 1962. (pp.88, 250)
1842	Claremont House, 7–8 Claremont Terrace, Woodlands, **179**. (p.92)
	Erskine U.P. Church, 43 South Portland Street, Laurieston (S), **985**. Demolished.
1845	Proposals for rebuilding University on Woodlands Hill.
1847	Claremont Terrace, Woodlands, **179**. Wings added to Claremont House. (pp.92, 249, figs.67, 242)
1849	Woodlands Terrace, Woodlands, **823**. (p.249, fig.238)
1854	118–128 Brunswick Street, **112**. Façades by R. W. Billings.
	1–3a Hanover Street, **328**. Demolished 1968.
	34–38 Buchanan Street incorporating his earlier Prince's Square (1840), **130**. (p.114n)
1855	Gardner's, 36 Jamaica Street, **389**. (pp.114–5, 274, figs.91, 92, 93d)

Barclay, Hugh (1828–1892) and David (1846–1917)

Hugh Barclay was a pupil of William Spence. He later became James Sellars's master; and the two architects remained close friends until Sellars died. (According to Colin Sinclair, David Barclay's successor, they even had some working association, but no-one remembers this now.) Hugh and David together built a large number of schools; but it seems clear from the sharp decline in the quality of the firm's work after Hugh's death, that he did most of the earlier work and was the more talented designer.

1857	Colosseum, 60–66 Jamaica Street (with A. Watt). Ground floor mutilated. **391**. (p.118, fig.93g)
1858	Ewing Place Church, Waterloo Street (with A. Watt). Demolished. (fig.147), **739**
1878	Partick Academy, 75 Peel Street, Partick, **512**. Demolished.
	Glasgow Academy, Colebrook Street, Belmont, **199**. (p.163)
1882	Abbotsford Public School, 131 Abbotsford Place, Laurieston (S), **832**
	Pollokshields Secondary School, 241 Albert Drive, Pollokshields (S), **838**
1883	Rutland Crescent Public School, 8 Rutland Crescent, Plantation (S), **974**. (pp.163–4). Demolished.
1884	Hillhead High School, Cecil Street, Hillhead, **166**
1886	St George's-in-the-Fields Church, St George's Road, Woodside, **581**. (pp.163, 165, fig.145)
1887	Govanhill Public School, 27 Annette Street, Govanhill (S), **844**. (p.163, fig.146)

1891	Central Thread Agency, 36–62 Bothwell Street, **93** (p.262)
1892	Warehouse, 128–152 Sauchiehall Street, **648** (pp.260, 262, fig.255)
1897	Cunninghame Church, 45–47 Thistle Street, Hutchesontown (S), **989**. Demolished.
1898	106–114 Argyle Street, **15**: remodelling.
1901	Royal College of Science & Technology, George St, **262** (p.262n)

Billings, Robert William (1813–1874)

It is curious that so sensitive and exquisite a draughtsman (see Chapters 1 and 2) should have designed such brutally detailed buildings. A good story relates how the young Rowand Anderson taxed him about his castellated waterworks in North London. 'What would you have me make it look like?' 'Why, a waterworks of course.' 'Can you tell me what a waterworks is like?' 'No, but you might invent one.' But Billings was unconvinced and said firmly that he must have a model from which to work. His two Glasgow buildings are both baronial, of a kind.

1854	118–128 Brunswick Street, **112**. Façades only; plans by John Baird No.1.
1860	102–104 Brunswick Street, **109**

Boucher, James (c.1832–1906/7) and **Cousland, James** (c.1833–1866)

Both were apprenticed to Charles Wilson in the 1850s. They lived in semi-detached houses in Pollokshields designed by themselves, **976**. Cousland's health was upset by an accident at St George's and he died young. Boucher was closely associated with the Macfarlanes of Saracen Ironworks. From c.1876 he was in partnership with Henry Higgins.

1857	Renfield Free Church, 291 Bath Street, Blythswood, **55**. Demolished 1967.
1858	35–37 St Andrew's Drive Pollokshields (S), **976**. Demolished 1968.
1864	St George's, Berkeley and Elderslie Streets, Sandyford, **232**. Demolished 1964.
1872	22 Park Circus, Woodlands Hill, interior, **492**
1875	Wm Teacher's, 14–18 St Enoch Square, **568**
1875	Arthur's 223–9 Ingram Street, **371**
1877	998 Great Western Road, Kelvinside, **317**. (p.122n)
1884	Carron Building, 123–129 Buchanan Street, **123**. (figs.217, 247)

Brash, John (d. 1838/9)

Brash is known only by a few plain classical churches and Blythswood Square where he may only have been executant.

1806	Tolcross Central Church of Scotland, 1088 Tolcross Road, Tolcross, **683**. (p.75)
1819	McMillan Calton Church of Scotland, 290–302 London Road, Calton, **431**. (p.75). Demolished.
1823	Blythswood Square, Blythswood, east, west and south sides, **82–84**. (pp.75–8, 183, 238, fig.53)
1829	Blythswood Square, Blythswood, north side, **81**. (pp.74n, 75–8)

Bryce, David (1803–1876)

Best known for his country houses, most of which are baronial, and for work in Edinburgh. There are two characteristic works in Glasgow. His pupils included J. T. Rochead and J. J. Stevenson.

1848	Tolcross House, 591 Tolcross Road, Tolcross, **682**
1868	Scottish Widows' Fund Building, 112–114 West George Street, **773**. Originally the Junior Conservative Club. Altered.

Bryce, John (c.1805–1851)

Younger and more classically-minded brother of David Bryce. He settled in Glasgow in the 1820s, where his largest job was the Duke Street Reformatory, a big classic affair now demolished; its appearance is only known from poorish engravings. The two brothers built together speculatively in Garnethill. Among John Bryce's pupils were John Carrick and William Spence.

1833	Necropolis, Cathedral Square, **164**. Jews' Enclosure, Catacombs, Egyptian Vaults.
1840	Queen's Crescent, St George's, **532–3**. (pp.101, 242n, fig.74)
1849	55–71 Ashley Street, St George's, **25**
	4–26 Bothwell Street, Blythswood, **92**. With Alexander Kirkland. (p.111)
1850	West Princes Street, St George's, **794–6**

Burnet, Frank (1848–1923), **Boston, William** (1861–1937) and **Carruthers, James** (1872–?)

Burnet began business in 1878 after seven years in the office of John Carrick, thereby acquiring experience with the City Improvement Trust which was to prove useful later: his other clients were drawn largely from the licensed trade. In 1901

Carruthers, first a pupil and then an assistant, became a partner for some years. In the period 1898–1913 they worked in a manner close to that of J. J. Burnet to whom Frank Burnet was not, however, related.

1898	St Vincent Chambers, 41 St Vincent Place and 114–128 Buchanan Street, **136**
1898	Castle Chambers, 57 Renfield Street and 51–57 West Regent Street, **538**. (pp.258n, 261)
1898	140–142 St Vincent Street and 153–5 Hope Street, **613**. (pp.258n, 263, fig.248)
1900	St George's Mansions, 63–89 St George's Road and 2–48 and 50–68 Woodlands Road, **578** and **822**. (fig.251)
1900	231–287 and 250–284 High Street, **331**. (p.190)
1900	133–58 Stockwell Street, **677**
1905	Gordon Chambers, 80–94 Mitchell Street, **466**
1913	91–95 West George Street and 53 West Nile Street, **756**
1923	175–9 Trongate and 1–33 Stockwell Street, **691**

Burnet, John (sen.) (1814–1901)

Burnet's reputation has been eclipsed by that of his more famous and more powerful son. In fact he seems to have been a reticent man: though he was Glasgow correspondent of the Dictionary of the Architectural Publication Society, he barely mentions himself. He was born at Craighead House, Kirk of Shotts, the son of a lieutenant of Militia, and educated at Dunipace Parish School. He became successively a carpenter, clerk of works, and in 1844 architect. His first known job was the now demolished Free Church at Alloa, whose near-identical twin (not authenticated on paper) survives at Clackmannan, small and Italianate. Burnet's early work is modestly classical in the manner established by Baird, George Smith and others. Later, though the influence of various phases of the Italian Renaissance is almost always observable, his designs became much more independent and resourceful. He was at the height of his powers in the 1870s; he was elected Fellow of the R.I.B.A. in 1876, and from 1876 to 1878 was President of the Glasgow Institute of Architects. His son joined the firm in 1877, and by 1889 Burnet sen. was semi-retired. His work is almost always marked by a refined fastidiousness of detail.

1847	Fitzroy Place, Sauchiehall Street, Kelvingrove, **643**. (p.88)
1854	61–63 Miller Street, **452**. (fig.84)
1856	Elgin Place Congregational Church, 240 Bath Street, Blythswood, **48**. (pp.78, 160–1, 163, 164, 200n, figs.143–4)
1857	1–3 Bridge Street, Laurieston (S), **849**
1858	Alexander's (now Ladywell) School, 94 Duke Street, **221**
1865	Savings Bank, 99 Glassford Street, **273**. (p.209)
1870	Clydesdale Bank, 30 St Vincent Place, **591**. (pp.159–60, 200n, 274, fig.140)
	Former Union Bank, 115–117 St Vincent Street, **600**
1871	Glasgow Eye Infirmary, 174 Berkeley Street, Charing Cross, **78**. Demolished.
1874	Merchants' House, 30 George Square, **253**. Top storeys by J. J. Burnet. (pp.157–8, fig.137)
	Woodlands Parish Church (now St Jude's Free Presbyterian), Woodlands Gate, Woodlands, **820**. (fig.70)
1875	Glasgow Stock Exchange, 63–75 West George Street, **753**. East section. (pp.160, 178, 255, figs.163,247)
1876	Cleveden Crescent, Kelvinside, **180**. (pp.92n, 160–1, fig.141)
	Hutcheson's Boys Grammar School, 211 Crown Street, Gorbals (S), **870**. Remodelling and east block. Destroyed 1969–70.
	Lanarkshire House, 191 Ingram Street, **369**. North façade. (pp.158–9, 200n, fig.136)

Burnet, (Sir) John James (1857–1938)

Son of John Burnet, sen., and nephew of William Burnet of London. At the age of seventeen he went to the Ecole des Beaux Arts in Paris, studying in the atelier of Jean Louis Pascal and working in the office of François Rolland. In 1877 he returned to his father's firm and immediately gained prominence with Pascal-inspired designs. In 1886 J. A. Campbell who had earlier been a pupil became a partner in the firm which for the next 12 years was called Burnet Son and Campbell; during this period it is frequently difficult to distinguish the work of the two younger partners. Burnet travelled extensively on the continent in 1895, studying museum design, and in 1896 made the first of several visits to the United States to study hospital and laboratory design, visits which had an immediate and very marked effect on his work.

Burnet, (Sir) John James (1857–1938)
(continued)

In 1903 Burnet was selected to design the Edward VII Gallery at the British Museum and this soon decided him to move his main office from Glasgow to London, where Thomas S. Tait (who had joined him in 1903) and David Raeside became partners, the firm becoming first Sir John Burnet and Partners, later Burnet, Tait and Lorne. In 1909, the Parisian trained Norman Aitken Dick, on the completion of two years as a senior assistant, became a partner in the Glasgow office which took the style of Burnet, Son and Dick from 1921. Tait gradually took over the principal designing in London from 1911 onwards, though until his retirement in 1935 Burnet continued to supervise his staff daily and produced beautiful small-scale sketches of designs in progress. Except at Adelaide House most of the purity of Burnet's earlier work is missing in the lengthy series of opulent office designs which the firm produced in London between the wars, although the effect of his association with H. P. Nénot in the design of the League of Nations Building at Geneva is evident in Tait's St Andrew's House in Edinburgh. Burnet was knighted in 1914. Goodhart-Rendel described him as 'a Frenchified Scotsman, extraordinarily nice, with a tremendous love of order and system. He never lost hold of the essentials and thought no-one in England knew anything about them. He used to say that nothing ought to be done without a decision behind it. He had no interest in style as such. He really was a great man' (*Architectural Review*, October 1965, p.261).

1878   Fine Art Institute, 171 Sauchiehall Street, **661**. Ground floor despoiled; gutted 1964, demolished 1967. (p.200, fig.180)

1883   Clyde Navigation Trust, 16 Robertson Street, Broomielaw, **549**. North section. (pp.200–201, 264n, fig.176)

1886   Barony Church, 1 Castle Street, **155**. With J. A. Campbell. (pp.175–7, figs.159–60)
        Athenaeum, 60 West George Street, **769**. (pp.200–1, 255, fig.182)
        International Exhibition, Edinburgh: lay-out and buildings.

1887   Women's Union, (now John McIntyre Building) University of Glasgow, Hillhead, **713**

1891   Charing Cross Mansions, 2–30 St George's Road, Charing Cross, **582**. (pp.95, 202, 204–5, 261n, fig.181)
        Athenaeum Theatre, 179 Buchanan Street, **125**. With J. A. Campbell. (pp.204–5, 210, 255, 261, 263, figs.183, 247)

1894   Glasgow Stock Exchange, 63–75 West George Street, **753**: w. section. (p.178, fig.163)
        Pathology Buildings, Western Infirmary.
        Savings Bank of Glasgow, 99 Glassford Street, **273**: Banking Hall. (pp.209–10, figs.188–9)

1895   Women's Union, University of Glasgow, Hillhead, **713**: extensions.

1896   2–10 University Gardens, Hillhead, **714**

1897   Albany Chambers, 528–534 Sauchiehall Street, **655**
        Kelvinside Railway Station, 1051 Great Western Road, Kelvinside, **305**
        347–353 Renfrew Street, **546**

1898   Royal Faculty of Physicians and Surgeons, 232–242 St Vincent Street, **617**. Interiors. (p.74)
        Savings Bank of Glasgow, 99 Glassford Street, **273**: Top storeys of main block. (p.209, fig.188)

1899   Tron Church, Chisholm Street, **175**. Screen wall.
        Royal Mental Hospital, 1055 Great Western Road, Kelvinside, **306**. Lodge, gates and screen wall.
        Atlantic Chambers, 43–47 Hope Street, **348**. (pp.203–4, fig.184)
        Waterloo Chambers, 15–23 Waterloo Street, **735**. (pp.202–3, 204–5, 209, 263)
        218–220 St Vincent Street, **616**: Alterations.
        15–27 Saltmarket, **625**

c.1900   2 Park Gardens Lane, Woodlands Hill, **498**
        University of Glasgow, Hillhead, **713**: Botany and Engineering Buildings. With J. Oldrid Scott, who was probably responsible for their general appearance.
        15–17 Hope Street, **346**
        Trinity Broomhill Congregational Church, Victoria Park Gardens South, Broomhill, **726**

1902   Bakery, 5–7 Newton Street, Charing Cross, **473**. Demolished 1965.
        Elder Cottage Hospital and Nurses' Home, Drumoyne Road and Langlands Road, Govan (S), **910**. (p.210, fig.191)
        Elder Library, 228a Langlands Road, Govan (S), **909**. (p.210, fig.190)

1904	British Museum, London: Edward VII Gallery. (p.226)
1905	Clyde Navigation Trust, 16 Robertson Street, Broomielaw, **549**: southern section. (pp.200–201, fig.176)
	McGeoch's, 28 West Campbell Street, Blythswood, **751**: (pp.205–9, 211, fig.185). Demolished 1971.
1906	Royal Mental Hospital, 1055 Great Western Road, Kelvinside, **306**: extensions.
1907	Forsyth's, 30 Princes Street, Edinburgh. (p.203)
	Merchants' House, 30 George Square, **253**: two upper storeys. (p.158)
1910	Alhambra Theatre, 43 Wellington Street, Blythswood, **743**. Demolished 1971. (p.266, fig.259)
	Tennant Mansion, 195 West George Street, **788**: alterations and extension. Demolished c.1968.
1911	Royal Hospital for Sick Children, Dalnair Street, Kelvinhaugh, **215**. Demolished, 1967–8.
	Kodak House, Kingsway, London. (pp.205, 206, 209, 226)
1913	Wallace Scott Factory, 42 Spean Street, Cathcart (S), **986**. Mutilated. (p.209, fig.187)
1914	Laurieston Renwick Church, 35 Cumberland Street, Laurieston (S), **872**: hall.
1920	Alhambra Theatre, 43 Wellington Street, Blythswood, **743**: western section.
1922	Cenotaph, George Square, **257**. (p.235)
	University of Glasgow: Zoology Building, **713**
1923	University of Glasgow, Hillhead, **713**: chapel. (p.177n)
1927	200 St Vincent Street, Blythswood, **615** (p.209, 270, fig.186)

Campbell, John Archibald (1859–1909)

Campbell's early life is obscure, but he was apprenticed to Burnet and Son from 1877 to 1880, after which he followed the younger Burnet to the Atelier Pascal at the Ecole des Beaux Arts in Paris, returning to Glasgow in 1883. From 1886 to 1897 he was a partner in his old firm, which thus became Burnet, Son and Campbell. He was in independent practice from 1897 until shortly before his death, when he took A. D. Hislop into partnership. He was Tite Prizeman in 1885, elected F.R.I.B.A. in 1895. Apart from his work in Glasgow, he built a number of houses in the surrounding counties, particularly at Bridge of Weir, where he had a very large and handsome weekend house of his own. Campbell's bachelor life seems to have been hospitable; he both lived and worked hard.

1886	Barony Church, 1 Castle Street, **155**. With J. J. Burnet. (pp.175–7, figs.159, 160)
1888	Shawlands Old Parish Church, 1120 Pollokshaws Road, Shawlands (S), **956**. (p.177, fig.157)
1891	Athenaeum Theatre, 179 Buchanan Street, **769**. With J. J. Burnet. (pp.204–5, 210, 255, figs.183, 247)
1898	Britannia Building, 164–168 Buchanan Street, **138**. (p.210)
1899	71–75 Robertson Street, Broomielaw, **548**. (p.210)
1900	3 and 7–23 Kirklee Road, Kelvinside, **416–7**
1902	157–167 Hope Street, **351**. (pp.211, 214, fig.193)
1904	United Kingdom Provident Building, 122–126 St Vincent Street, **611**. (p.210, 214n). Gutted 1981.
1905	50 Argyle Street, **13**
1908	Northern Assurance Building, 84–94 St Vincent Street, **608**. (pp.210–11, 214, 224n, figs.192, 194)

Carrick, John (1819–1890)

Carrick was born at Denny, but the family moved to Glasgow when he was four. He was articled to John Bryce in 1831, worked as a draughtsman for John Herbertson and spent a short time in England before returning to Glasgow to form a partnership with James Brown (d.1878) in 1839. They engaged in speculative building at the west end to their own and others' designs. In 1844 Carrick was appointed Superintendent of Streets (with one clerk and an office in the South Prison), which in time developed into Master of Works and City Architect, which offices, through the City Improvement Trust, had a great and generally deleterious effect on the old parts of the city. The partnership was dissolved in 1854, Carrick by this time having ceased all private practice. His style hardly altered during his long career, though the details vary in later years according to the draughtsman employed on the working drawings.

| 1840 | Somerset Place, Sauchiehall Street, **642**. Built to John Baird's design. (pp.88, 250) |
| 1841 | Old Corn Exchange. Remodelled 1858; demolished 1894, **357** |

1842	Sandyford Place, Sauchiehall Street, **642**. (p.88)
	Renfield Street Church. Accredited to James Brown, **542**. Demolished 1963. (p.173n, fig.153)
1859	Western Police (later Social Security) Building, Cranston Street, Cranstonhill, **206**. Demolished 1971.
1875	Deadmeat Market, 13–46 Graham Square.
1877	Yate Street Police Office, 976 Gallowgate, **247**
	Abercromby Model Lodging House, 324 Abercromby Street, Calton. Demolished 1982.
1884	Gorbals Public Baths, 140–154 Gorbals Street, Gorbals (S), **890**
1885	City Hall, 85–91 Albion Street, **2**: Candleriggs front.
1890	Northern Police Office, 19–27 Maitland Street, Cowcaddens, **442**. Destroyed 1972.

Chalmers, Peter Macgregor (1859–1922)

Chalmers, who was a pupil of Honeyman, was perhaps too much of a scholar to be a genuinely original architect. His historical studies (in particular *A Scots Medieval Architect*) remain very interesting; and he had a notable and on the whole successful brush with the formidable MacGibbon and Ross over Melrose Abbey and Glasgow Cathedral. Mrs Chalmers was also in the architectural business and is said to have ruled her husband with a rod of iron. Chalmers was one of the leading Glasgow church builders of his time, designing almost entirely in Romanesque. He rebuilt the nave of Iona Cathedral. The very original Neptune Building was perhaps his most distinguished design, and its loss is deplorable.

1897	St Kenneth's Church, St Kenneth's Drive, Govan (S), **977**. Demolished 1981.
1902	St Margaret's Church, 110 Polmadie Road, Polmadie (S), **960**
1905	Neptune Building, 470 Argyle Street, Anderston, **21**. Demolished 1966. (p.224, fig.216)
1906	Dennistoun Parish Church, 169–71 Armadale Street, Dennistoun, **24**. Demolished.
1911	Whiteinch-Jordanvale Parish Church, Squire Street, Whiteinch, **674**
1912	St Margaret's Episcopal Church, 351 Kilmarnock Road, Newlands (S), **908**. (p.180)
1915	Holy Trinity Parish Church, 80 Merrylee Road, Merrylee (S), **921**. Unfinished.

Clarke, William (1809–89), Bell, George (no.1, 1814–87; no.2, 1854–1915), Bryden, Robert Alexander, (1841–1906), Craigie, James Hoey, (d.1930)

Bell the elder was a pupil of Archibald Elliot the younger but moved to William Burn's office where he met Clarke who had been articled to David Bryce. In 1842 they won the competition for the City and County Buildings, thereby establishing a practice in Glasgow. Their earliest works are refined neo-Greek or neo-Tudor, moving into refined Italianate and a rather crude early pointed later. By the 1880s their work had become free Renaissance. In the early-mid 1890's the younger Bell took Bryden into partnership, and on his departure, Craigie, whose repertoire encompassed neo-Greek, German Baroque and art nouveau. Otherwise it is difficult to associate much of their work with individual partners.

1842	City and County Buildings, 40–50 Wilson Street, southern and western (old Merchants' House) sections, **811**. (pp.54, 62, 72, 83n, 104–5, 235; figs.41, 77, 79)
1853	102–104 St Vincent Street, **609**
1856	Granby Terrace, 2–28 Hillhead Street, Hillhead, **343**. (pp.101; fig.169).
1871	City and County Buildings, northern section to Ingram Street, **811**
1873	Fish Market, 64–76 Clyde Street **188**. (p.122n)
	Johnston Memorial Church, 524 Springburn Road, Springburn, **673**. Demolished.
1886	42–50 Gordon Street, **285**
c.1890	15–25 Bothwell Street, **87**. (p.258)
1899	42 Jamaica Street, **390**
1907	Grosvenor Buildings, 72–80 Gordon Street, upper floors and interiors (recently destroyed), **286**
1910	Justiciary Courthouses, Jocelyn Square, Saltmarket, **627**. (p.70). Reconstruction.

Clifford, Henry Edward (1852–1932)

Clifford was a pupil of Burnet Senior and was briefly in partnership with J. J. Burnet's cousin, William Landless. He won the competition for the Royal Infirmary in 1901, but the commission was given to James Miller. He flirted briefly with art nouveau around 1900, but is best known for his sturdy late gothic churches and domestic work, the latter figuring much in Muthesius' *Das Englische Haus*.

1893	Pollokshields Burgh Hall, 72 Glencairn Drive, Pollokshields (S), **887**
1894	Titwood Church, Pollokshields. Demolished and re-erected as St James's Church, 165 Meiklerigg Crescent, Pollok, 1953–4 (S), **920**. (p.180)

1895	44–84 Terregles Avenue, Pollokshields (S), **988**. (p.190)
1899	Newlands South Church, 2 Langside Drive, Newlands (S), **913**: hall
1900	Stoneleigh, 48 Cleveden Drive, Kelvinside, **182**
1901	64–6 Cadogan Street, Blythswood. In the swim of the time. **146**. Demolished 1972.
1902	Newlands South Church, 2 Langside Drive, Newlands (S), **913**: church.
	St Michael's Parish Church, 50 Edrom Street, Carntyne, **231**. (p.180). Demolished.
	398 Albert Drive, Pollokshields (S), **841**
	17–57 Fotheringhay Road, Crossmyloof (S), **884**
1903	31 Dalziel Drive, Pollokshields (S), **876**
1910	Education Offices, 127–129 Bath Street, Blythswood, **37**
1927	Cathcart Old Parish Church, Carmunnock Road, Cathcart (S), **858**. (p.180)

Douglas, Campbell (1828–1910)

Campbell Douglas is another man to whom it is difficult to attach a clear architectural personality. He had a large number of distinguished partners and assistants during his long career, and it is possible that he was more an entrepreneur of architecture than an original architect himself. His last partner, A. N. Paterson, considered, however, that he had a share in the design of most of the buildings now attributed to Sellars. Douglas was apprenticed to J. T. Rochead from 1842 to 1847, left for John Dobson's, Newcastle, and returned to Glasgow in 1856. Between 1860 and 1869 he was in partnership with J. J. Stevenson, and the firm produced many houses and churches. Sellars joined him in 1870 or 1872, though he may have been a junior slightly earlier: the firm then became Campbell Douglas and Sellars, and turned out an enormous quantity of work before Sellars's death in 1888, including as many as fifty-three churches. Douglas worked alone for some time after a short-lived partnership with Alexander Morrison, but was joined by Paterson in 1903. His assistants included William Leiper, George Washington Browne, William Flockhart, John Keppie and J. M. Brydon. He is said to have been a very generous man, with a hearty joyous nature. See further under James Sellars. But the following seem almost certainly to be by Douglas himself.

1859	Briggate Free Church. Gothic. Demolished.
1861	McDonald Mission Church, Maitland Street, Cowcaddens. Gothic. Demolished.
1865	Townhead Parish Church, 176 Royston Hill, **561**
1872	Queen's Park High Church, Queen's Drive, Queen's Park (S), **964**. James Sellars may have had a hand in this, (p.174, fig.156)
	Wesleyan Church, 14 Claremont Street, Charing Cross, **178**. With J. Sellars. Demolished 1979.
	Cowcaddens Church, 30–34 McPhater Street, Cowcaddens, **440**. With James Sellars.
1878	Blackfriars Church, 9 Wester Craigs, Dennistoun, **752**. With J. Sellars.
	Citizens' Theatre, 121–129 Gorbals Street, Gorbals (S), **889**. Façade demolished *c.*1975. (p.266)
1896	Discharged Prisoners' Aid Society, 28–32 Cathedral Square, **162**

Dreghorn, Allan (1706–64)

Dreghorn was a merchant with iron, lead and joinery interests, and as an architect probably relied much on his master-masons and sculptors. He worked with James Craig on the Town Hall, and the two also produced a design for the College Library, which was however rejected in favour of that by William Adam. Dreghorn was Baillie of Glasgow in 1741, and was the first person in the city to keep a four-wheeled carriage. His son Robert, known as Bob Dragon, is said to have been 'the ugliest man in Glasgow, and also the most profligate Debauchee of his time' (*Glasghu Facies*, p.1099).

1737	Town Hall, Trongate; with James Craig. Extended 1758–60, remodelled as Tontine Hotel 1781; **700**. Demolished 1911. (pp.52–3, 57, 60, 71n, figs.28–9)
1739	St Andrew's Church, St Andrew's Square, **564**, with Mungo Naismith. (pp.58–60, figs.35–6)
1752	Dreghorn Mansion, 130 Clyde Street, **195**. Incorporated in warehouse 1857, destroyed 1980. (p.50)

Gildard, Thomas (1822–95) and MacFarlane, R. H. M., (d. 1862)

Gildard was a pupil of the Hamiltons from 1838–43 but spent most of his life as the senior assistant of his friend John Carrick. In the mid 1850s he formed a briefly successful partnership with his brother-in-law MacFarlane, but returned to Carrick following his early death. Through handling the Dean of Guild Court business and acting as correspondent for several of the building journals, he knew all his architect contemporaries. Late in life he wrote manuscript memoirs of them, with fuller length biographies of Carrick and Thomson, which are now in the Mitchell Library.

1856   Belgrave Terrace, Great Western Road, Hillhead, **295**

1857   Britannia Music Hall, 115 Trongate, **687**, ground floor altered (p.109n)

Graham, James Gillespie (1776–1855)

Only two works are recorded in Glasgow, both (originally) churches, though very different in style. With George Meikle Kemp he was also responsible for the abortive design for the new west front of the cathedral (pp.28–9) and in 1820 for feuing in Blythswood.

1814   St Andrew's Catholic Chapel, 172 Clyde Street, **189**. Enlarged 1870 and 1890–2 and now the cathedral. (pp.170–2)

1819   George Street Church, 14 West George Street, **789**. Demolished 1975.

Hamilton, David (1768–1843) and James (c.1807–1862)

Very little is known of the life of the elder Hamilton, except that he was educated as a carpenter or mason and apparently turned to architecture only in early middle age. But he must have had some contact with the Adam family, for he made many copies of unpublished Adam drawings to which he would not normally have had access. And the extraordinary assurance of his earliest recorded building suggests that it must have been preceded by others in which he had a large hand. David's son William was a fine draughtsman and water-colourist and took a short but active part in the business before his early death (c.1827). John Hamilton seems to have been in charge of the marble business which traded as David Hamilton and Sons; James seems to have been more continuously active in the partnership than his brothers. He was 'tall and remarkably handsome, somewhat of an Italian cast ... his long black hair was rolling in ringlets'. He was in partnership, after his father's death, with his brother-in-law, James Smith. The business was, however, sequestrated as early as 1844 and James Hamilton then retired, though he probably helped behind the scenes in Smith's office.

1802   Hutcheson's Hospital, 158 Ingram Street, **158**. (pp.45n, 54, 81–2, 234, figs.55, 226)

1804   Queen Street Theatre. Burnt down 1827. **525**. (p.264)

1806   Gorbals John Knox Parish Church, 35 Carlton Place (S), **857**. Never fully completed. Spire later mutilated. (pp.81–2). Demolished 1973.

      Nelson Monument, Glasgow Green, **267**

1813   Crawford Priory, Fife.

1814   Tolbooth rebuilt. **698**. (p.44, figs.28–9). Demolished c.1921

1819   St John's Established Church, 313 Bell Street, **67**. Demolished. (p.170)

1821   Castle Toward, Argyll.

1822   Hamilton Palace, Lanarkshire. Demolished. (p.81)

1823   Aitkenhead House, King's Park (S), **859**: wings. The house itself possibly an earlier work of Hamilton (1806).

1827   St Enoch's Church, St Enoch Square, **574**. Body of church rebuilt; now demolished. (p.82)

      Royal Exchange, Royal Exchange Square, **559**, incorporating Cunninghame Mansion. (pp.50, 54, 82–3, 231, 234, figs.56, 221–3)

1830   Royal Exchange Square, **556–7**: with James Smith; based on a design by Archibald Elliott the younger. (pp.83–4, 143, 255, figs.56, 223)

1834   *151–157 Queen Street, **521**. (pp.84n, 143, 150, figs.57, 128a)

1835   Cleland Testimonial Building, 235–249 Buchanan Street, **126**

      St Paul's Church. Demolished.

      *Castlemilk House, **847**: bridge. (S)

      Houses of Parliament, London: competition design, awarded third prize. (pp.11, 81n)

1837   Normal School, 6–8 New City Road, Cowcaddens, **472**: (p.81n)

1838   Mosesfield House, Springburn Park, Springburn, **72**

1839   Hutcheson's Boys Grammar School, 211 Crown Street, Gorbals (S), **870**. (p.81n)

      British Linen Bank, 110–18 Queen Street, **528**. Upper storeys by J. Salmon jun. and J. G. Gillespie. Demolished 1968. (fig.223)

1841   Western Club, 147 Buchanan Street, **124**. (pp.84–6, 94, 186, 255, figs. 59, 247)

      Clydesdale Bank, Queen Street, **526**. Demolished 1962. (p.118)

1842   Union Bank, Ingram Street, **369**. Façade demolished 1877. Columns re-used at Citizens' Theatre, Gorbals Street, Gorbals (S), **889**. (p.158, 266n)

Honeyman, John (1831–1914)

Honeyman was originally intended for the Church, but soon gave up his studies, and was then articled to Alexander Munro. By 1854 he was already practising alone in Glasgow. He was an authority on medieval architecture, having made measured drawings of many medieval buildings in England. This gave him an intimate knowledge of gothic, which is revealed not only in his own gothic churches, but in his detailed study of Glasgow Cathedral, to which he was for a long time architect. He restored Linlithgow Church and the cathedrals of Brechin and Iona. Outside Glasgow he designed churches at Edinburgh, Greenock and Perth. John Keppie joined Honeyman in 1889, and the firm was then Honeyman & Keppie. C. R. Mackintosh joined as draughtsman in the same year, and his influence is from then on increasingly marked. Honeyman was elected A.R.S.A. in 1892 and R.S.A. in 1896. He retired in 1901 to enable Mackintosh to become a partner. His work in Glasgow, as elsewhere, is always refined and sure, in whatever style he was at the time working.

1862 St Andrew's Parish Church Halls, Charlotte Street, Glasgow Green, **169**

Lansdowne Church, 416–420 Great Western Road, Woodside, **308**. (pp. 155, 172–3, fig. 152)

1864 Trinity Congregational Church, (now Henry Wood Hall) 71 Claremont Street, Charing Cross, **177**.

24–30 Jamaica Street, **388**

1866 Barony Free Church, 45–53 Castle Street, **155**. (p. 175). Demolished.

1870 Admiral Street Wesleyan Church, 20–24 Admiral Street, Kingston (S), **837**

1872 Ca d'Oro, 41–55 Gordon Street, **281**. Top storeys by J. G. Gillespie. (pp. 156–7, figs. 93i, 138)

Craigie Hall, 6 Rowan Road, Dumbreck (S), **970**

1874 Burnbank School, 40–60 Henderson Street, Woodside, **330**. (pp. 177–8). Burnt down 1983.

1875 Candlish Memorial Church of Scotland, 513 Cathcart Road, Govanhill (S), **860**

1878 Barony North Church, 14–20 Cathedral Square, **161** (pp. 155–7, 201, fig. 135)

1880 Westbourne Church of Scotland, 52 Westbourne Gardens, Kelvinside, **750**. (pp. 156, 159, fig. 139)

Keppie, John (1862–1945)

Keppie was a pupil of Campbell Douglas & Sellars, despatched to J. L. Pascal's *atelier* for one year only in 1883. On Sellars's death he left to become Honeyman's partner. His earliest work derives from Sellars and the Beaux Arts, but he was soon working closely with Mackintosh, continuing to adopt the free Renaissance style they evolved in the 1890s until A. Graham Henderson took over almost all the design work from about 1912.

1888 Anderson College of Medicine, 56 Dumbarton Road, Kelvinhaugh, **224**. Completed after Sellars's death by Keppie, who probably designed much of the detail. (pp. 155, 197)

1890 Fairfield Shipbuilding Offices, **902**. Entirely in Sellars's early vein with Beaux Arts detail. (p. 264n)

1892 Craigie Hall, 6 Rowan Road, Dumbreck (S), **970**: additions. With C. R. Mackintosh.

1893 Glasgow Herald Building, 60–76 Mitchell Street, **465**. With C. R. Mackintosh. (pp. 198, 220, fig. 179)

1895 Northpark House, Queen Margaret Drive, Belmont, **529**: annexe (Queen Margaret College). With C. R. Mackintosh. Encapsulated.

Martyrs Public School, 11 Barony Street, Townhead, **35**. With C. R. Mackintosh. (p. 220, fig. 204)

1906 307–333 Hope Street, **352**.

1908 Savings Bank, 1456 Gallowgate, Camlachie, **244**. (fig. 220)

Kirkland, Alexander (1824–92)

One of the most mysterious figures in 19th-century Glasgow. He would seem to have been not so much an architect as an engineer of some vision manipulating the architectural talents of others, notably in his ambitious developments for James Scott of Kelly at Bothwell Street and Finnieston. Stylistically his work encompassed neo-Greek, austere classical and Venetian, the two last the result of collaboration with John Bryce and the assistance of James Hamilton respectively. After failing to establish himself as a civil engineer in London he emigrated to Jefferson, Wisconsin, in 1868 as liquor merchant, moving in 1871 to Chicago where he finally established himself as a successful public figure by becoming Commissioner of Public Buildings in 1879. He died at Portland, Oregon.

1849	2–26 Bothwell Street, **92**. With John Bryce. (p.111)
1850	1–9 Corunna Street, Anderston, **201**
	31–70 St Vincent Crescent, Finnieston, **583** (pp.99–101, 111, 190n, 250, fig.72)
1851	Suspension Bridge from Carlton Place to Clyde Street, **194**. With George Martin, engineer. (pp.73, 111, fig.86)
1853	*953–971 Argyle Street, Anderston, **22**. Demolished.
	1–21 Minerva Street, Anderston, **463**. (p.109n, fig.172). Demolished.
1854	Eagle Buildings, 205–229 Bothwell Street, Blythswood, **91**. Perhaps with G. H. Russell. (p.111)
	37–51 Miller Street, **459**. (pp.111, 159, fig.85) Demolished.
1855	2–12 Corunna Street, Anderston, **202**
	19–30 St Vincent Crescent, Finnieston, **584**. (pp.99–101, 111, 190n, 250, fig.72)
	26–32 Minerva Street, Anderston, **461**. (fig.172)
1856	8–20 Minerva Street, Anderston, **462**. (fig.172)
1882	County Building, Chicago. Illinois. With Egan. Demolished 1909.

Leiper, William (1839–1916)

Leiper was a pupil of Boucher & Cousland, leaving for London in 1860 to gain experience in the offices of J. L. Pearson and William White. On his return he worked briefly for Campbell Douglas and the Perth architect Andrew Heiton, to whom he seems to have imparted a similar enthusiasm for Early French gothic, before commencing a short-lived partnership with R. G. Melvin. His success in the Dowanhill competition immediately challenged Honeyman's position as the city's leading Gothicist and for his first twenty years he was in the vanguard of the Anglo-Japanese manner, working closely in conjunction with the decorative artist Daniel Cottier. In the late 1870s he briefly gave up architecture and took to painting in Paris. Most of his work was domestic, particularly in Helensburgh where he himself had a sizable bachelor house, and from the 1880s onwards was markedly influenced by Norman Shaw (a list is given in *JRIBA* 1916). From 1881 he was assisted by W. Hunter McNab who became a partner in 1896. His work in Glasgow itself was intermittent and consisted mainly of church work.

1865	Dowanhill Church of Scotland, 98 Hyndland Street, Dowanhill, **366** (pp.172, 173)
1866	Dumbarton Burgh Halls and Library, Dumbarton.
1872	Partick Burgh Hall, Burgh Hall Street, Partick, **142** (p.155)
1875	Belmont and Hillhead Parish Church, Saltoun Street, Dowanhill, **629**: general scheme of design said to be Leiper's. (pp.174–5, fig.155)
1878	Camphill Church of Scotland, Balvicar Drive, Queen's Park (S), **846**. (pp.173–4, fig.154)
1885	Domira, 47 Partickhill Road, **510**: Addition. Demolished 1983.
1886	Hyndland Parish Church, 79 Hyndland Road, Hyndland, **365**. spire unfinished.
1889	Templeton's Carpet Factory, 62 Templeton Street, Glasgow Green, **681**. (p.226, fig.219)
1892	Sun Life Assurance Building, 147–151 West George Street, **757**. (p.226, 258–9, fig.250)
1903	St James's (now St Columba's), Kilmacolm, Renfrewshire.

McGibbon, William Forsyth (1856–1923)

McGibbon was apprenticed to the Barclays and commenced business on his own account very early. Church work was the mainstay of his career, but the Corn Exchange showed awareness of the latest trends in London while the effectively profiled brick Italian castellated of his industrial buildings showed how resourceful he could be on a limited budget.

1882	Pollokshields East Church, 60 Leslie Street (S), **915**. Destroyed 1983. (p.175n)
1886	Old Girls' High School, Buccleuch Street, Garnethill: addition, **114**
c.1887	Allerley, 229 Nithsdale Road, Pollokshields (S) (for himself) **935**
1894	Sherbrooke-St Gilbert's Church, Nithsdale Road, Pollokshields (S) **940**. (p.175n)
1895	Corn Exchange, 81 Hope Street, **357**. Demolished. (p.262n)
1896	Shettleston Old Church, 99 Killin Street, Shettleston, **410**
1898	Scotstoun Mills, Scotstounmill Road, Partick: riverside block, **665**. Demolished.
1900	118 Tradeston Street (S), **991**. (p.226n, fig.218)

Mackintosh, Charles Rennie (1868–1928)

Mackintosh, the son of a Police Superintendent, determined to become an architect very early in life. Habits of walking and sketching gave him knowledge of vernacular architecture in Scotland; and in 1884 he was apprenticed to John Hutchison. At the same time he began taking classes at the Glasgow School of Art and in 1890 won the Thomson travelling scholarship and went to France and Italy. He joined Honeyman and Keppie as draughtsman in 1889, and his influence is immediately noticeable. Soon afterwards Mackintosh met Herbert McNair and the sisters Frances and Margaret Macdonald. 'The Four' as the group called themselves exhibited together in craft work and graphic design, all very much in the style of art nouveau, to which Margaret Macdonald, later Mackintosh's wife, remained faithful. In 1896 Mackintosh (in the guise of Honeyman and Keppie) won the limited competition for the new Art School. At this stage only the eastern section could be built. For the next few years Mackintosh and his wife were much occupied with interior designs, though he got commissions for two country houses. In 1901 he became a partner in his firm; and in 1907 the redesigned western section of the Art School was begun. This peak of his career was virtually its end. In 1913 he suddenly left Glasgow, following disappointment over the Jordanhill Training College competition. He settled in London, where he devoted himself mainly to textile design. After the war he spent a good deal of time in the south of France and painted a series of striking watercolours. As an architect he gained only a few minor commissions during the last fifteen years of his life. A large quantity of his furniture has survived in private and public collections.

See further Thomas Howarth, *Charles Rennie Mackintosh and the Modern Movement*; N. Pevsner, *Pioneers of Modern Design*; R Billcliffe, *Charles Rennie Mackintosh, The Complete Furniture, Furniture Drawings and Interior Designs*.

1890	140–142 Balgrayhill Road, Springburn
1893	Glasgow Herald Building, 60–76 Mitchell Street, **465**; J. Keppie in charge. (pp.198, 220, fig.179)
1895	Northpark House, Queen Margaret Drive, Belmont, **529**: annexe; with J. Keppie.
	Martyrs Public School, 11 Barony Street, Townhead, **35**: with J. Keppie. (p.220, fig.204)
1896	Buchanan Street Tea-Room: decoration. Effaced. **121**
1897	Glasgow School of Art, 167 Renfrew Street, Garnethill, **543**; eastern section. (pp.167, 215–6, figs.195–6, 198, 200)
1897	Argyle Tea-Room: interiors. **15** Gutted
1898	St Cuthbert's and Queen's Cross Church, 866 Garscube Road, Woodside, **248** (pp.180, 220, 267–9, fig.166)
	Ruchill Parish Church, 24 Ruchill Street, Ruchill: hall, **563**
	Exhibition hall: project for Glasgow Exhibition of 1901.
	233 St Vincent Street, **605**: interior work
1900	Tea-Room, 205–217 Ingram Street, **370**: interiors now dismantled and stored. (p.218)
	Daily Record Office, 106–108 Hope Street, **353**: rear section with façades to Renfield Lane and St Vincent Lane. (pp.210–11, 220)
1900	Windyhill, Kilmacolm, Renfrewshire. (p.215)
1902	The Hill House, Helensburgh, Dunbartonshire. (p.215)
	Liverpool Cathedral: competition design (unpremiated).
1903	Willow Tea-Room, 217 Sauchihall Street, façade restored; interior largely restored, 1978–80. (pp.218–20, figs.202–3)
1904	Scotland Street Public School, 225 Scotland Street, Kingston (S), **633**. (pp.220–1, figs.206–7)
1906	78 Southpark Avenue, Hillhead: interiors. House demolished; interiors rebuilt
1907	Glasgow School of Art, 167 Renfrew Street, Garnethill, **543**: western section. (pp.216–8, 239, figs.197–9, 231)
	Ingram Street Tearoom **370**: Oak Room. Dismantled.
1908	5 Blythswood Square, Blythswood. **81**: doorway. (p.75)
1911	Tea-Room, 205–217 Ingram Street, **370**: Cloister and Chinese rooms. Dismantled.
1916	78 Derngate, Northampton: remodelling.
1920	Squire Studio, Glebe Place, Chelsea.

Miller, James (1860–1947)

Miller was a pupil of Andrew Heiton of Perth and rose rapidly in the civil engineering department of the Caledonian Railway, becoming known to its directors, the most powerful business men in the city. Clifford's competition win for the Royal Infirmary was overthrown for him. From 1903 onwards he became the most persistent creator of massive mercantile monuments in the city, at first neo-baroque but from 1920 onwards American classic. In these later years he was assisted by Richard Gunn.

1893	Belmont Parish Church, 121 Great George Street, Hillhead, **292**
1896	St Enoch's Underground Station, St Enoch Square, **573** (pp.56, 255)
1898	Lancaster Crescent, Kelvinside, **314**
1903	Caledonian Chambers, 75–101 Union Street, **704**. (p.262n)
1904	9–10 Lowther Terrace, Great Western Road, Kelvinside, **313** (p.228)
	St Andrew's East Church, 681–685 Alexandra Parade, Dennistoun, **7** (p.180, fig.165)
1907	Central Station, **282** Hope Street façade : extensions.
1925	Union Bank, 110–120 St Vincent Street, **610**. (p.228, 270n)

Nicholson, Peter (1765–1844)

Little is known of Nicholson's work in Glasgow, where he appears to have lived between 1800 and 1808. He designed several houses in the city, all of which seem to have disappeared, built a timber bridge over the Clyde, and made additions to the Old College. He practised in Edinburgh and the north of England, wrote voluminously on building, was a ceaseless and inventive experimenter, had an architectural son called Michael Angelo, and was the grandfather of Alexander Thomson's wife.

1802	40–61 Carlton Place, Laurieston (S), **855**, including Laurieston House (no.51). One pavilion destroyed. (pp.72–3, 78, 250, figs.48–50)
1813	65–85 Carlton Place, Laurieston (S), **856**. One pavilion destroyed. (pp.72–3, 250)

Paterson, Alexander Nisbet (1862–1947)

A fastidious, comfortably off and retiring architect, whose best work is too little known. He was at the Atelier Pascal from 1883 to 1886, when he joined Burnet, Son & Campbell. Later he went to Col. Edis and Aston Webb. He was the partner and friend of Campbell Douglas in the latter's late years, from 1903 to 1910.

1903	Barr & Stroud's, 920 Crow Road, Partick.
1906	National Bank, 22–24 St Enoch Square, **569**. (p.263, fig.257)
1909	Liberal Club, 54 West George Street, **768**. Now part of Royal Scottish Academy of Music. (pp.255, 263, fig.247)
1925	Muirend Savings Bank, 443 Clarkston Road, Muirend (S), **861**. With D. M. Stoddart.

Peddie, John Dick (1824–91) and Kinnear, Charles George Hood (1830–94)

Peddie is said to have been the Italian and Kinnear the baronial partner. The firm worked easily in both styles, and added Romanesque, and ecclesiologists' and early German Gothic for good measure.

1856	Pollok Street Church, 3–5 Pollok Street, Kingston (S), **950**. Italian.
1857	Trinity Duke Street Church (now Kirkhaven) 176 Duke Street, **223**
1872	City of Glasgow Assurance, 28a Renfield Street. Demolished.
1875	20–40 Gordon Street, **284**. Pilastraded.
1877	91–115 Hope Street, **350**. Second Empire style. (p.262)

Peddie, John More Dick (1853–1921)

This scholarly Edinburgh architect, son of J. D. Peddie, designed only two buildings in Glasgow, both solid and with a high academic finish.

1900	National Bank, 47 St Vincent Street, **592**. (pp.226, 255, figs.217, 247)
1904	Scottish Provident Building, 17–29 St Vincent Place, **586**. (p.226)

Rhind, David (1801–1883)

Another Edinburgh architect who made only occasional visits to Glasgow. Yet the Commercial Bank is one of his finest achievements.

1838	Scott Monument, George Square, **257**. (p.235, fig.227)
1854	Commercial Bank, 8–16 Gordon Street, **283** (pp. 120–1, fig.95)

Rochead, John Thomas (1814–1878)

Rochead was born in Edinburgh and was a pupil of David Bryce. In 1837 he went to Doncaster, where for two years he was a draughtsman in the firm of Hurst and Moffatt. He then returned to Scotland, settling in Glasgow as chief draughtsman to David and James Hamilton. By 1841 he was practising on his own, and continued to do so until 1870, when he went back to Edinburgh where he lived until his death. Campbell Douglas was a pupil.

1840	Catholic Cathedral, Belfast : first prize in competition. Not built.
1841	Western Club, 147 Buchanan Street, **124** : details drawn by Rochead. (pp.84–6, 94, fig.59)
1849	Kew Terrace, Great Western Road, Kelvinside, **298**. (p.91). After James Brown.
1852	Buckingham Terrace, Great Western Road, Belmont, **310** : eastern half. (p.189)

1855	Grosvenor Terrace, Great Western Road, Kelvinside, **297**. (pp.91–2, fig.63)
	74–92 Trongate
1858	Buckingham Terrace, Great Western Road, Belmont, **310**: western half. (p.189)
	Park Church, Lynedoch Place, Woodlands Hill, **496**. (pp.172, 247, figs.65, 70, 235, 237). Tower only survives.
1859	John Street Church, 37 Cochrane Street, **196**. (p.92n, fig.137)
1869	Northpark House, Queen Margaret Drive, Belmont, **529**. Completed by J. Honeyman. (p.92n)

Rowan, William Gardner (1845–1924)

Rowan was a pupil of George Penrose Kennedy, an ex-assistant of Barry's. He was on his own as an architect-engineer from 1872, and some time afterwards formed a partnership with J. McKissack, which was dissolved in about 1890. He is best remembered for his churches, which are often exquisitely detailed, though he rarely had opportunities to design on a large scale. He was at first a follower of Thomson, but later worked mainly in Gothic.

1877	Pollokshields West Church, 614 Shields Road, Pollokshields (S), **984**
1883	St John's Methodist Church, 18–20 Sauchiehall Street, Tower altered 1958.
1886	Queen's Park Baptist Church, 178 Queen's Drive, Queen's Park (S), **966**
	Strathbungo Church, 601–605 Pollokshaws Road, Strathbungo (S), **953**
1888	St Ninian's Wynd Church and Mission, 498–500 Crown Street, Gorbals (S), **869**. (p.182, fig.164). Demolished.
1891	Baptist Church (former Pollokshields–Glencairn Church), 67 Glencairn Drive, Pollokshields (S), **886**
1900	St Margaret's Church, 179 Braidfauld Street, Tolcross, **95**
1902	Eastbank Church, Old Shettleston Road, Shettleston, **488**

Salmon, James, sen. (1805–1888)

Salmon's father died early. He was apprenticed to John Brash and was in business on his own by 1830 in a basement. In 1843 he formed a partnership with Robert Black (1800–69), architect of the demolished City of Glasgow Bank in Virginia Street, the Exchange courts and Adelaide Place. The partnership was dissolved in about 1854 and from 1862–72 Salmon was assisted, from 1868 as a partner, by James Ritchie, who appears to have been associated with the polychrome French gothic and rundbogen phase in Salmon's work. His son W. Forrest Salmon (1843–1911) returned from G. G. Scott's about 1866 but his experience there is hardly obvious in the commonplace work of the later 1870s and 80s. Salmon was a man of wide interests, a Liberal, a Free Kirker who conducted Bible classes, and a poet (who wrote a pastoral comedy called *Gowandean*). He became a member of the Town Council in 1860 and was a Convener of Parks and Galleries, promoting the first extension of Kelvingrove. He lived in his own suburb of Dennistoun, but seems not to have been widely loved. *The Baillie* caricatured him as Mr. Pecksniff: 'a moral man, a grave man, a man of noble sentiments and speech ... Perhaps there never was a more moral man than Mr. Pecksniff, fuller of virtuous precept than a copy book ... He was just the person who would have improved the city, and his circumstances, by contriving to enrich it with a suburb [Dennistoun] and to draw all the plans himself in order to prevent important work from falling into improper hands ... Aware of the uprightness and integrity of his motives, he would, if he were a commissioner or a member of a prison board, employ himself as architect without any of the hesitation which less eminently respectable persons might feel out of deference to the proprietors [Duke Street Prison] ... This is not the character of an ancient Roman, but it is such as we poor moderns are bound to admire'.

1848	St Mark's Free Church, Main (now Argyle) Street, Anderston.
1849	St Matthew's Free Church, Bath Street, Blythswood, **58**. Demolished. (p.170n, figs.70, 151)
	Arthur's Warehouse, 81 Miller Street, **453**. (p.109, fig.84)
1852	Catholic Apostolic Church, 340–362 McAslin Street, Townhead, **437**. Based on a sketch by Pugin. (p.170)
1853	Lanarkshire House, 191 Ingram Street, **369**: south wing. Interiors destroyed.
1861	Mechanics Institute, 38 Bath Street, Blythswood, **44**. (p.145, fig.122)
1866	Langside College, **961**. Built as Deaf and Dumb Institute.

Salmon James, jun. (1873–1924)

Son of W. F. Salmon, and grandson of James, senior. He was apprenticed first to his father and then to William Leiper, returning in 1895. Forrest Salmon, though active until his death, was the firm's commercial traveller, rather than an architect. The other designer was J. G. Gillespie (1870–1926), the firm being called Salmon, Son & Gillespie. It is difficult to separate the work of the two partners, and it may be that Gillespie should be given much of the credit. Unlike his grandfather, Salmon was much admired by *The Baillie*, which published a laudatory account of him in 1918, long after his best work had been done. 'He has strong views and expresses them fearlessly. In fact, he might be ready to call himself a social and municipal Bolshevik and smile all the more if some chuckle-headed people were shocked at the announcement. He has no special religion, which of course means that he possesses the necessary touch of paganism to make a broad human churchman ... He will tell you that he believes in the existence of the Glasgow School of Art, the Fine Art Institute, the Art Club and the Corporation, but thinks they imperfectly realize what they exist for ... He says "he thinks Glasgow so ugly that the more there is the more's the pity", and he declares himself "annoyed that nobody else is proud enough of it to be ashamed of it" ... He believes that "the continual efforts by officials to destroy our finest buildings are due to the hope that their own will be the best left, but thinks this would entail too much destruction" ... He considers that the glorified jobbing gardener has had too free a hand with the public parks and wants to see an opportunity given to an architect who has seen real gardens'.

1897	Mercantile Chambers, 39–69 Bothwell Street, Blythswood, **88**. (pp.211, 222, fig.205)
1899	Anderston Savings Bank, 752–756 Argyle Street, Anderston, **19**. (p.222, figs.208–9)
	British Linen Bank, 816 Govan Road, Govan (S), **899**. (pp.222–3)
	St Andrew's East Parish Church, 681–685 Alexandra Parade, Dennistoun, **7**: hall only.
	'The Hatrack', 142–144 St Vincent Street, **614**. Finial removed. (pp.222–4, 261, figs.210, 211, 212)
1900	British Linen Bank, 162–170 Gorbals Street, Gorbals (S) **891**
	12 University Gardens, Hillhead, **715**. By J. G. Gillespie.
1902	Lloyd Morris Memorial Church, 155–157 Rutherglen Road, Hutchesontown (S), **972**
1905	British Linen Bank, 110–118 Queen Street, **528**: upper storeys. (fig.223). Demolished.
1905	Lion Chambers, 172 Hope Street, **355**. (p.224, 261, figs.214–15)
	Catholic Apostolic Church, 340–362 McAslin Street, Townhead, **437**: north aisle and narthex. Demolished.
1908	Stirling Municipal Buildings (Gillespie). Competition win.
1914	Dalmarnock Congregational Church, 231 Dalmarnock Road, Dalmarnock, **214**: modifications to church by J. C. MacKellar.
1924	Redlands Hospital for Women, 11 Lancaster Crescent, Kelvinside, **315**: attics and rear addition.

Scott, (Sir) George Gilbert (1810–1878) and John Oldrid (1841–1913)

The elder Scott did two buildings in Glasgow, both of which were completed by his younger son, John Oldrid Scott. Oldrid Scott also worked in the city on his own account in association with J. J. Burnet.

1866	University of Glasgow, Gilmorehill, **713**: main building by G. G. Scott; spire and central range by J. O. Scott, 1878–84; spire 1887 to modified design. (pp.46–7, 169–70, 177, 249, figs.148, 150, 236)
1870	St Mary's Episcopal Cathedral, Great Western Road, Woodside, **307**: by G. G. Scott; spire by J. O. Scott, 1893. (p.169)
1900	University of Glasgow, Gilmorehill, **713**: Botany Building; by J. O. Scott, in association with J. J. Burnet.

Sellars, James (1843–1888)

Sellars was the son of a house-factor. He was apprenticed in 1857 to Hugh Barclay and stayed there until 1864, when he joined James Hamilton No.2. He left in 1867, and his movements are obscure for a few years. He joined Campbell Douglas in or about 1870, after J. J. Stevenson had left for London. In that year Sellars won the first abortive Stewart Fountain competition and in January 1871 the second. Campbell Douglas made him a partner shortly thereafter. In 1872 he went to France – one of two trips abroad – experimenting with late 16th-century French from 1874 onwards. He was badly overworked in the 1880s; in 1887 he won the 1888 Exhibition competition and was ordered to proceed at once. Douglas was ill, and Sellars had to work until after midnight every night. Not until all was settled financially did he leave for the Western Highlands on holiday; but a poisoned foot developed gangrene and he died.

1872	Queen's Park High Church, Queen's Drive, Queen's Park (S), **964**. Probably by Campbell Douglas, though perhaps with Sellars assisting. (p.174, fig.156)

1873 St Andrew's Halls, Berkeley Street, Charing Cross, **77**. Rebuilt as part of Mitchell Library 1973–80 after being gutted by fire 1962. (pp.153–4, 156, fig.133)

St Enoch's, Overnewton, Finnieston. Crown tower. Destroyed.

97–113 Berkeley Street, Charing Cross, **75**

1874 Bank of Scotland Chambers, 24 George Square **252**. (pp.157–8, fig.137)

1875 Belmont and Hillhead Parish Church, Saltoun Street, Dowanhill, **629**. Perhaps based on a scheme by William Leiper. (pp.174–5, fig.155)

1877 Kelvinside Academy, Bellshaugh Road, Kelvinside, **68**. (pp.153, fig.130)

City of Glasgow Bank, Glassford Street, **277**. Never completed; demolished 1959. (pp.153, 155, 197, 258n, fig.132).

Tower Building, 156–160 Buchanan Street, **137**

Belhaven Church, 29 Dundonald Road, Dowanhill, **227**. Now St Luke's Greek Orthodox Cathedral. (pp.175, 269, fig.158)

Gilmorehill Church of Scotland, 9 University Avenue, Hillhead, **711**. Unfinished.

Queen Insurance Office, St George's Place, **786**. Demolished. (pp.114, 153, 155, fig.131)

1878 Milton Street School, 69 Milton Street, Cowcaddens, **460**

Finnieston (later Kelvingrove) Parish Church, 41 Derby Street, Kelvingrove, **216**. (pp.155, 157, fig.134)

1879 New Club, 144–146 West George Street, **776**. (p.155)

Glasgow Herald Building, 63–69 Buchanan Street. **119** (p.258n).

1880 Lambhill Cemetery, Balmore Road, Lambhill, **31**: gateway and lodges.

Wylie & Lochhead's Factory, Kent Road, Charing Cross, **406**

1882 252–256 Paisley Road West, Plantation (S), **947**

Victoria Infirmary, Grange Road, Langside (S), **905**. Built 1888–90.

Dispensary for Sick Children, 9–11 West Graham Street, Garnethill, **790**

1883 Wylie & Lochhead's (now Fraser's) 45 Buchanan Street, **117**. (pp.197n, 258n)

1887 Couper Institute, 86 Clarkson Road, Cathcart (S), **862**. (p.197)

1888 Anderson College of Medicine, 56 Dumbarton Road, Kelvinhaugh, **224**. Finished by John Keppie. (pp.155, 197)

Smith, George (1793–1877)

Smith was born in Aberdeen and was apprenticed to David Hamilton, working on the engineering of Union Street there. He struggled hard to establish himself in Aberdeen, advertising his travels and running a drawing academy, but by 1823 was glad to become William Burn's principal clerk. In business on his own in Edinburgh from 1827, he was nevertheless the first to establish a distinctive Glasgow style in the terraces of the West End.

1831 Woodside Crescent, Woodlands Hill, **826**. (pp.92, 245, fig.240)

1835 1–11 Woodside Terrace, Woodlands Hill, **828**. (pp.92, 245, figs.64, 240)

1837 Newton Place, Sauchiehall Street, Charing Cross, **656**. (p.88)

1838 Woodside Place, Woodlands Hill, **827**. (p.245)

1842 12–21 Woodside Terrace, Woodlands Hill, **829**. (pp.92, 245, fig.64)

1845 Lynedoch Crescent, Woodlands Hill, **433**. (pp.92, 245, figs.65, 241)

1–19 Lynedoch Street, Woodlands Hill, **434**. (pp.92, 245)

Smith, James (1808–1863)

Smith was born at Alloa of crofting stock, though his father was a builder and built the parish church there in 1817–19 to the designs of Gillespie Graham. In 1826 the family moved to Glasgow, where Smith senior became the contractor for the Royal Bank and built much of Royal Exchange Square. They owned most of the north side, which was left on their hands and then let. In 1837 James Smith took over from his father as both architect and builder and, having married David Hamilton's daughter, formed a partnership with his son James on David's death in 1843. In 1844 the business was sequestrated, but after enforced sales, Smith survived and James Hamilton withdrew. A partnership with John Baird No.2 was then formed, but did not last. Smith's last years were financially very successful (he became a director of North British Insurance) but were clouded by the murder trial of his daughter Madeleine. He moved from Helensburgh to Bridge of Allan to avoid sightseers, and again to Polmont, where he died.

1830 Royal Exchange Square, **556–7**: north side. With David Hamilton and A. Elliot II. (pp.83–4, 143, 255, figs.56, 223)

299

	1837 Victoria Baths, 106–108 West Nile Street, **793**. Now offices.
	1840 Collegiate School, Garnethill. Demolished.
	1855 McLellan Galleries, 254–290 Sauchiehall Street, **650**. Front building only.
	1863 Stirling's Library, 48–56 Miller Street, **455**. Now a warehouse. (p.125n, fig.99)
	Bellahouston Parish Church.

Spence, William (?1806–1883)

Rather a shadowy figure in Glasgow. He was assistant to John Bryce, but was working on his own by 1837. He designed a number of theatres, all now destroyed; and his remaining buildings are chronologically widely spread; but all show an adventurous and resourceful mind. Hugh Barclay was a pupil. Spence retired to Helensburgh, where he died.

1854 *Paisleys' Warehouse, 72 Jamaica Street, **392**. (pp.115, 148, fig.94)
1858 Randolph & Elder's Engine Factory, 13–23 Tradeston Street, Tradeston (S), **992**. (p.107, figs.82, 83). Demolished.
1873 116–120 Argyle Street and 12–14 Buchanan Street, **16** and **127**.
1879 21–31 Buchanan Street, **115**. (p.112, fig.87)

Stark, William (1770–1813)

Little is known of Stark's early life, except that he was born in Dunfermline and was in St Petersburg in 1798. He spent several years in Glasgow and died in Edinburgh, where in his last years he had been Playfair's master, and may hence be described as the originator of neo-Greek in Scotland. He made a study of the design of mental hospitals ('Remarks on the Construction of Public Hospitals for the Cure of Mental Derangement'); and, apart from his own lost masterpiece in Glasgow, two hospitals were built according to his designs – at Dundee (on an H-plan, 1812) and at Gloucester (by John Collingwood, 1822–3). He was also responsible for the restoration of the chancel of Glasgow Cathedral and the insertion of the now removed galleries.

1804 Hunterian Museum, Old College, **335**. Demolished. (p.70)
1807 St George's Tron Church, St George's Place, **577**. (pp.69–70, 113n, 238, 255, figs.45, 224, 247)
Justiciary Court House, Saltmarket, **627**. Rebuilt 1910, except for entrance portico. (p.70, fig.46)
1809 Lunatic Asylum, Bell's Park, **502**. Demolished. (pp.70–1, fig.47)
1810 Saline Church, Fife.
1812 Muirkirk Old Church, Ayrshire.
Signet Library, Edinburgh: interiors. Upper (originally Advocates) completed by R. Reid.

Stevenson, John James (1831–1908)

Stevenson, like several other Glasgow architects, started as a theological student; a visit to Italy changed his mind, and he became David Bryce's pupil (1856–8). For two years he worked in Gilbert Scott's office in London, then in 1860 returned to Scotland and joined Campbell Douglas (Campbell Douglas and Stevenson). The partnership lasted until 1869, when Stevenson went again to London, where he went into partnership with E. R. Robson, architect to the School Board. He built his own house in Bayswater in 1872 in the Queen Anne style, of which he was a pioneer. He made occasional visits to design buildings in Glasgow, and was responsible for churches at Gilmerton (1880), Crieff (1881), Perth (1883), Fairlie (1894) and Stirling (1900). He built many houses in England and did some university work at Oxford. In 1880 he published *House Architecture*. He was a relative of the engineer Stevensons and of the novelist. His office was the Scotsman's stepping-stone to London.

1862 Former Kelvinside Parish Church, 731–735 Great Western Road, Kelvinside, **296**. (p.174)
1890 67–79 St Vincent Street, **595**. The date is conjectural. (p.160n, fig.96)
1900 Kelvin Stevenson Church, Belmont Street, Belmont, **71**. (pp.178–9, figs.162, 229)

Thomson, Alexander (1817–1875)

'Greek' Thomson was the seventeenth of twenty children of John Thomson (d.1824), of piously strict Covenanting stock. The family moved from Stirlingshire about 1800, but not until after John's death were the children 'exposed to the dangers and temptations of life in the City' by a move into Glasgow itself, where, nevertheless, the family joined the congregation of the United Secession Church in Gordon Street, on the site of which Thomson's own office was later built (originally as a speculative venture). Alexander was employed in a writer's office, where he attracted the attention of Robert Foote, who then took him on as apprentice. Foote was compelled by illness to retire in 1836, when Thomson went as assistant to John Baird No. 1, and was his chief draughtsman from 1845 to 1849. During this period he married the daughter of Michael Angelo Nicholson (son of Peter Nicholson, q.v.), whose other daughter married John Baird No. 2, with whom Thomson formed the firm of Baird and Thomson, which lasted from 1849 to 1857. In 1856, the year in which the Thomsons moved into a new suburb south of the city, where so much of his most important work was done, his brother George joined the firm, not himself as a designing architect. From 1857 to 1871 it was called A. and G. Thomson. During the last two years of his life, he was in partnership with Robert Turnbull (Thomson and Turnbull). Thomson was widely revered by his contemporaries and became President of the Glasgow Institute of Architects in 1871. He violently attacked Scott's design for the University, for which he may himself have submitted sketch plans. But his own published statements were rare – the most important being the Haldane Lectures of 1874. He rarely left Scotland and never Britain. An ex-assistant, Clunas, described him as 'unassuming ... considerate and even affectionate', alternating in mood between 'dreamy unrest' and bursts of productivity when 'urged on by the idea that was moving him'. Much was on the drawing board awaiting lower prices when Thomson died. Since Turnbull was, by his own admission, no designer, some at least of his work must be largely based on Thomson schemes.

1851	Design for Blairs, Howard Street. Not built. (pp.127, 147, 149, figs.93b, 126)
1852	'The Knowe', 201 Albert Drive, Pollokshields (S), **839**. (pp.125, 134–5)
1853	Blairs, 36–38 Howard Street, **361**. Demolished 1967. (p.143)
1856	Hutchesontown and Caledonia Road Church, 1 Caledonia Road, Hutchesontown (S), **853**. Gutted 1965. (pp.98n, 128–31, 135, figs.105, 106)
	25/25a Mansionhouse Road, Langside (S), **916**. (pp.124, 127, 130, 132, 135–6, figs.100, 101, 109, 110c)
	Holmwood, Netherlee Road, Cathcart (S), **930**. (pp.127, 134–6, 145, fig.111)
	Pollok School, 2097 Pollokshaws Road, Pollokshaws (S), **959**: annexe. Demolished 1968. (pp.132, 134n, fig.110f)
1857	190–192 Hospital Street, Hutchesontown (S), **906**. Linked with **853**. Demolished 1967.
	37–39 Cathcart Road, Hutchesontown (S), **861**. Linked with **853**. (p.134n)
	Walmer Crescent, Paisley Road West, Ibrox (S), **995**. (pp.125–6, 139–40, 149, fig.117)
	Queen's Park Terrace, 355–429 Eglinton Street, Laurieston (S), **882**. (pp.141–2, 145, 183, 185–6, fig.118). Demolished.
1858	*307 Eglinton Street, Laurieston (S), **881**. Demolished.
	United Presbyterian Church, 265 St Vincent Street, Blythswood, **606**. (pp.129, 131–4, 140, 145n, 149, 237, figs.107, 108)
	99–107 West Nile Street, **792**. Date conjectural.
1859	Chalmers Free Church, 42–50 Ballater Street, Hutchesontown (S), **845**. Demolished. (p.126n)
	1–10 Moray Place, Strathbungo (S), **925**. Perhaps designed in 1857. (pp.102, 123, 137–9, 140, 251, figs.115, 116)
	126–132 (later 172) Sauchiehall Street: Washington Hotel. Demolished. (fig.128d)
1860	249–259 St Vincent Street, Blythswood, **623**. Linked with **606**. Demolished 1967. (p.131, fig.108)
	*600–614 Eglinton Street, Port Eglinton (S), **880**
	Cairney Building, Bath Street, Blythswood, **56**. Demolished. (pp.128, 145, 147–52, figs.122, 128i)
c.1860	12–24 Norfolk Street, Gorbals (S), **942**
1863	Buck's Head Building, 63 Argyle Street, 10, and 1–11 Dunlop Street, **228**. (pp.114n, 127, 145–7, 150–2, 205, figs.121, 123–4, 128h). Partly demolished.
	*487–91 Eglinton Street, Laurieston (S), **883**. Demolished.
1864	Grosvenor Building, 68–80 Gordon Street, **286**. Designed 1859. Built 1861, burnt and rebuilt 1864. Top storeys by J. H. Craigie, 1907. (pp.143–7, 150–1, figs.125, 128e)
	*11–17 Moray Place, Strathbungo (S), **926**
1865	27–53 Oakfield Avenue, Hillhead, **482**. (pp.101, 126, 140n)
	Grecian Building, 336–356 Sauchiehall Street, **651**. Ground floor destroyed. (pp.147, 149–152, figs.127, 128f)
1866	Northpark Terrace, 35–51 Hamilton Drive, Belmont, **325**. (pp.102, 126–7, 140, fig.119)

Thomson, Alexander (1817–1875)   1867 Queen's Park United Presbyterian Church, Queen's Park (S). Burnt down 1943.
(continued)   (pp.125–9, 134n, figs.102–104), **914**
                                      Great Western Terrace, Great Western Road, Kelvinside, **300**. (pp.92, 123, 126, 136–7,
                                          149, figs.113, 114)
                               c.1869 Lilybank House, Bute Gardens, Hillhead, **143**: extensive additions. Date conjectural.
                                1870 202 Nithsdale Road, Pollokshields (S), **939**. (p.133, fig.110e)
                                1871 Blackies' Printing Works, 17 Stanhope Street, Townhead, **675**. Demolished. (p.148n)
                                      Egyptian Halls, 84–100 Union Street, **708**. Ground floor partly reinstated. (pp.128,
                                          148–52, fig.128g, 129)
                                      Westbourne Terrace, 21–39 Hyndland Road, Kelvinside, **363**. (pp.123, 126, 140–3,
                                          189, fig.120)
                                      200 Nithsdale Road, Pollokshields (S), **938**. (pp.135–6, 149, fig.112)
                                1872 *485–503 Govan Road, Govan (S), **896**. Demolished.
                                      Stairway from Kelvinside Terrace West to Queen Margaret Road, North Kelvin, **404**
                                      Cowcaddens Cross Building, 110–120 Cowcaddens Street, Cowcaddens, **203**. (p.148n).
                                          Demolished.
                                1873 84–112 Nithsdale Road, Strathbungo (S), **937**. Finished by R. Turnbull (p.140n)
                                      *36–40 Pollok Street, Kingston (S), **952**.
                                1875 87–97 Bath Street, Blythswood, **53**. (pp.149, 152). Demolished.
                                      *32–68 Gorbals Street, Gorbals (S), **893**. Demolished. (pp.142–3)
                                      265–289 Allison Street, Govanhill (S), **843**
                                      148 Bath Street, Blythswood: reconstruction of Alexandra Hotel. **57**. Demolished.

Thomson, James (1835–1905)   Thomson (no relation of his famous namesake) was a pupil of James Brown. He joined
                                      John Baird No.1 as draughtsman, and became a partner shortly before Baird's death,
                                      thereafter continuing the firm as Baird and Thomson until his own death. His best
                                      patrons were the ironmasters. His early work is pure Italianate, but goes free in
                                      mid-career; later, with his sons James Baird Thomson (d.1917) and William Aitken
                                      Thomson (d.1947) he developed a style derived from the early German Renaissance.
                                      His practice was perhaps the largest in the city.
                                1858 Crown Circus, Downhill, **209**. (pp.92n, 102, 242, fig.75)
                                1860 138–140 West George Street, Blythswood. Remodelled later.
                                      166–168 West George Street, Blythswood.
                                1863 217–221 Argyle Street, **11**, (fig.93h)
                                1866 Belhaven Terrace East, Great Western Road, Kelvinside, **299**
                                1869 Merryflats Poorhouse and Asylum, Govan. Notable for its huge size.
                                1870 Belhaven Terrace West, Great Western Road, Kelvinside, **299**
                                      1–14 Crown Gardens, Downhill, **210**
                                      1–12 Prince's Terrace, Prince Albert Road, Downhill, **515**. (pp.102n, 242)
                                1873 3–11 Crown Terrace, Downhill, **212**
                                1875 5–8 Queen's Gardens, Downhill, **534**
                                      244 St Vincent Street, Blythswood, **618**
                                1878 Glasgow High School, Buccleuch Street, Garnethill, **114**
                                1890 Standard Life Building, 82–92 Gordon Street, **287** (p.262, fig.125). See also 1898.
                                1897 Lancashire Building, 133 West George Street, Blythswood, **758**
                                1898 Standard Life Building, Gordon Street, **287**: reconstruction (p.262)
                                      London, Liverpool and Globe Building, 116 Hope Street, **354** (258, 262–3, fig.254)
                                1899 Connal's, 34–8 West George Street, **766** (p.258, fig.256)
                                1902 202–212 Sauchiehall Street, **649** (pp.259, 262)

Thomson, John (1859–1933) and   Thomson was the elder son of Alexander Thomson, to whose successor Robert
Sandilands, Robert Douglas (c.1860–1913) Turnbull he was apprenticed just after his father's death. From 1881 he studied under R
                                      Phené Spiers at the R A schools in London and for a time worked for William Flockhart.
                                      Refused re-admission to his fathers' firm, in 1886 he formed a partnership with
                                      Sandilands, who had just returned from the Ecole des Beaux Arts, where he had studied
                                      under Guadet, 1880–5, following an apprenticeship with Alexander Petrie. Within a
                                      couple of years Sandilands had made the firm's reputation by winning the Gartloch
                                      Asylum competition, the first of the several major competition wins on which the firm's
                                      prosperity largely depended.

1895	St James School, Green Street, Calton.
1896	11 Sherbrooke Avenue, Pollokshields (S), **981**. (p.264n)
1897	Royal Insurance Building, 106–112 Buchanan Street **135**.
	Govan Burgh Buildings, 401 Govan Road (S), **895**. (p.263, fig.258)
1900	Parish Council Offices, 266 George Street, **260**. (p.263)
	Stobhill Hospital, Balornock Road, Stobhill, **33**
1903–12	Buildings in Albion Street, Bell Street and Trongate for City Improvement Trust, **5**, **64** and **693**. (p.263)
1910	Hutcheson's Girls' School, Kingarth Street (S)
1923	New Bridgegate Church, 69–87 Dixon Road (S), Polmadie, **878**.

Turnbull, Robert (?1839–1905)

Partner of Alexander Thomson (Thomson & Turnbull), 1873–5. Turnbull was 'outdoor man' rather than architect, and in 1876 a new firm of Thomson & Turnbull was formed, the other partner being David Thomson (no relation), who had earlier been a partner of Charles Wilson. In 1883 the firm became R. Turnbull and Son when David Thomson withdrew and Alexander T. Turnbull became a partner.

1876	*2–38 Millbrae Crescent, Langside (S), **922**
1877	18–76 Nithsdale Road, Strathbungo (S), **936**
	*471–485 Scotland Street, Kingston (S), **979**. Demolished.
	*40–46 Millbrae Crescent, Langside (S), **923**
1878	*336–338 Albert Drive, Pollokshields (S), **840**
1879	Cockburn Hotel, 135–143 Bath Street, Blythswood, **54**. Incorporating parts of houses previously on the site. Demolished.
1880	Salisbury Quadrant, 52–58 Nithsdale Street, Strathbungo, **941**
	*Winton House, 9 Winton Drive, Kelvinside, **818**
	*Hawarden Terrace, 51–59 Partrickhill Road, Partickhill, **505**. (pp.102)
1888	84–112 Nithsdale Road, Strathbungo (S), **937**. Begun by Alexander Thomson. (p.140n)

Watson, Thomas Lennox (?1850–1920)

Watson was apprenticed to James Boucher 1866–71 leaving for London as an assistant to Waterhouse. He was for a short time in partnership with Henry Mitchell, but seems mainly to have worked on his own, though he had distinguished apprentices and assistants, including W. J. Anderson. He was President of the Glasgow Institute of Architects in 1895, and had eclectic interests, which included designing the interiors of expensive yachts (his brother G. L. was a naval architect). He proposed a High Level Bridge over the Clyde, an idea which found little favour until our own time, and had an argument with Chalmers over the lower church of Glasgow Cathedral (see p.37n)

1875	Adelaide Place Baptist Church, 209 Bath Street, Blythswood, **42**. (p.78n)
1883	Wellington Church, University Avenue, Hillhead, **712**. (pp.161–3, fig.142)
	Hillhead Baptist Church, 41 Creswell Street, Hillhead, **207**
1889	Citizen Building, 24 St Vincent Place, **590**. With W. J. Anderson. (p.258, fig.249)
1894	Adelphi Terrace School, 85 Adelphi Street, Gorbals (S), **836**

Wilson, Charles (1810–1863)

The least known of the major Glasgow architects of the 19th century. Wilson was the son of a builder, and was apprenticed to D. and J. Hamilton in 1827. From about 1833 to 1837 he was the Hamiltons' chief draughtsman. In 1837 he left to form a firm apparently with his brother (J. and C. Wilson, Architects and Builders): their father seems to have had no hand in this, though he probably insisted on the elder brother's initial coming first, despite his not being very active. In 1839 the firm became Charles Wilson's and remained so until his death. David Thomson was a partner at the end of Wilson's life, and afterwards joined Charles Heath Wilson (no relation): see Chapter 4, note 8, p.93. Wilson was a shy and retiring man, but had a very extensive practice, though almost entirely within Glasgow. He was President of the Glasgow Institute of Architects. He visited Paris in 1841, and French influence is thereafter plain.

1837	Hutchesontown Church, Hospital Street, Hutchesontown (S). Demolished.
1839	Strathbungo Church, 601–605 Pollokshaws Road, Strathbungo (S), **953**. Largely demolished, 1885, but parts incorporated into the present church by W. G. Rowan.
1840	Curator's House, Botanic Gardens, Kelvinside, **311**
1841	Royal Mental Hospital, 1055 Great Western Road, Kelvinside, **306**. Tudorish.
1845	Kirklee Terrace, Great Western Road, Kelvinside, **312**. (pp.91, 140n, fig.62)

247 St Vincent Street, Blythswood, **622**. Demolished 1967.

1846 Glasgow High School, Elmbank Street, Charing Cross, **237**. Only the frontage remains. Built as Glasgow Academy. (p.99n)

Argyle Free Church, 14 Oswald Street, **489**. Demolished.

Greenhead House, Greenhead Street, Calton, **322**. Now Fairfield Centre.

*Breadalbane Terrace, 97–113b Hill Street, Garnethill, **339**

*102–112 Hill Street, Garnethill, **341**

1847 144–152 Buchanan Street, **140**. Demolished c.1978.

Free Church, Rothesay, Bute.

1848 Alexander's Mill, Duke Street, **222**. Now Great Eastern Hotel. (p.106n)

Southern Necropolis, 316 Caledonia Road, Hutchesontown, **854**: gateway.

Shandon House, Gareloch, Dunbartonshire.

Free Church, Rutherglen, Lanarkshire.

1850 Royal Bank Building, 92–100 Buchanan Street, **134**. Interior rebuilt 1966. (pp.93, 94n, 118–20, fig.90)

1853 515–543 Sauchiehall Street, Charing Cross, **640** (p.94n)

901–3 Sauchiehall Street, Kelvingrove, **645**

1854 Royal Faculty of Procurators, 62–8 West George Street, **770**. (pp.11n, 93, 121–2, 255, fig.97)

Kelvingrove Park, Kelvingrove: layout, with Joseph Paxton. (pp.92, 249, fig.70)

Stairway from Park Terrace to Park Gardens, Woodlands Hill, **501**. (p.249, fig.243)

1855 Park Quadrant, Woodlands Hill, **499**

Woodlands Hill: layout of whole scheme. (pp.92, 247)

22–24 Woodlands Terrace, Woodlands Hill, **824**. (p.95)

1–6 Park Gardens, Woodlands Hill, **497**

Park Terrace, Woodlands Hill, **500** (pp.92n, 94–5, 189, 202n, 249, 258n, figs.70, 232)

1856 Free Church College, Lynedoch Street, Woodlands Hill, **435**. Now Trinity College (pp.95–9, 249, figs.70, 71, 235, 237–9)

1857 1–16 Park Circus, Woodlands Hill, **491**. (pp.93–4, 247, figs.68–70)

Queen's Rooms, 1 La Belle Place, Woodlands Hill, **420**. Now Christian Science Church. Fenestration altered. (pp.98–9, 164, fig.73)

2–5 La Belle Place, Woodlands Hill, **421**. (p.99, fig.73)

*Clairmont Gardens, Woodlands Hill, **176**

1860 *1055–1065 Sauchiehall Street, Kelvingrove

1861 18–29 Park Circus, Woodlands Hill, **492–3**. Designed c.1855. (pp.93, 247)

1862 Great Western Hotel, Oban, Argyllshire.

1872 Park Circus Place, Woodlands Hill, **494**., Designed c.1855. (p.247, fig.70, 237)

Wylie, Edward Grigg (c.1885–1954)

Wylie was apprenticed to W. F. McGibbon. He was appointed a lecturer at Glasgow School of Architecture in 1912, and became closely identified with the ideas and teaching of its Beaux Arts professor, Eugène Bourdon. In 1921 he won the competition for the new Hillhead High School, shortly thereafter forming a short-lived partnership with Alexander Wright who had practised in Canada. In 1927 they won the competition for the Scottish Legal Life Building in Bothwell Street with a design by Wylie, which is also said to be a reflection of Bourdon's teaching. Burnet observed that he should have been its architect (whether he meant that it was good enough to have been designed by him, or that he would have done it better no one dared ask) and in the first ten years Wylie must certainly have been as much influenced by Burnet as by Bourdon. In the 1930s he became consultant architect to the Scottish Industrial Estates for which he designed many factories in a manner derived from the 1938 Exhibition.

1921 Hillhead High School, Southpark and Oakfield Avenues, Hillhead. Not built until 1929.

1924 55 Mitre Road, Partick: Burnetian villa.

1927 Scottish Legal Life Building, 95 Bothwell Street, **90**. (p.270)

1927 250 Sauchiehall Street, alterations for Margaret Hunter, new wing to Rose Street, **553**

1928 Dental Hospital, 203–217 Renfrew Street, **544**. (p.271, fig.263)

Buildings of architectural interest listed by streets

Numbering sequence
Numbers printed in bold refer to references on the maps on pp.330–8.

This list includes all buildings mentioned in the text (and numerous others) built or designed before 1939. Destroyed buildings, marked by a dagger, are grouped at the end of each street entry. References to the text and illustrations are in parentheses. Buildings at street corners are normally indexed under one of the intersecting streets only; and it may sometimes be necessary to consult the map to check where an entry is to be found. In each street the two sides are listed separately, odd numbers first. Where no district is given, the street is (or starts) in the city centre.

A. Glasgow north of the river

Albert Bridge	**1**	Bridge over Clyde: three Gothic cast-iron spans. By Bell & Miller, 1870–71 (p.112n)
Albion Street	**2**	85–91: City Hall & Bazaar. Bazaar formed by J. Cleland, *c.*1817; City Hall by George Murray, 1840 (reconstructed internally 1852); further additions, including frontage at 60–104 Candleriggs, by John Carrick, 1885. Notable two-tier glass-roofed market hall. S. addition, 13–31 Bell Street, by J. A. T. Houston, 1907.
	3	131–141: warehouse. By H. E. Clifford, 1906. Modern movement style.
	4	163: *Glasgow Herald* building (former *Daily Express*). By Sir E. Owen Williams, 1936. Glass curtain walling on r.c. frame. (p.273)
	5	2–58: offices for City Improvement Trust. By Thomson & Sandilands, 1903–11 (p.263)
	†6	[186: Greyfriars & Alexandra Parade church. By John Baird no.1, 1821. Destroyed *c.*1968 (p.114n)]
Alexandra Parade, *Dennistoun*	**7**	681–5: St Andrew's East church & hall. Church by James Miller, 1904; hall by James Salmon, 1899. (p.180, fig.165)
Annfield Place, *Dennistoun*	**8**	1–16: terrace of houses, *c.*1850. Two-storey late classical.
Argyle Street, *City to Finnieston*	**9**	1–3: 4-storey house block, *c.*1763.
	10	63: Buck's Head Building. By Alexander Thomson, with R. McConnel, iron-founder, 1863. (pp.114n, 145–7, 150–2, 205, figs.123–4, 128h)
	11	217–21: offices & shops. By James Thomson, with R. McConnel, ironfounder, 1863. Cast-iron frontage. (fig.93h)
	12	1175–1263: Franklin Terrace: tenements, before 1851. (p.186, fig.167)
	13	50: office block with shops. By J. A. Campbell, 1905. Narrow 8-storey corner building.
	14	98–102: Argyle Arcade. By John Baird no.1, 1827. Argyle Street frontage probably earlier. (p.114, fig 88)
	15	106–114: offices & shops. Remodelled by H. & D. Barclay, 1898–9. Four storeys with bargeboarded gables. Interior work by George Walton & C. R. Mackintosh (for Miss Cranston), now largely destroyed. 18th-cent. rear elevation survives.
	16	116–20: warehouse. By William Spence, 1873. Renaissance.
	17	134–56: warehouse & offices. By Horatio Bromhead, 1900–03. Return continuation of 21–31 Buchanan Street (**115**).
	18	344: Clydesdale Bank. By James Thomson, 1892. Recently reduced. Corinthian. (p.262)
	19	752–6: Anderston Savings Bank, now Savings Bank administration building. By James Salmon jun. & J. Gaff Gillespie, 1899. Sculpture by Albert Hodge and Johan Keller (pp.222, 259, figs.208–9)
	†20	[5–11: 4-storey house block, *c.*1763. Cf.**9**.]
	†21	[470–8: Neptune Building. By P. Macgregor Chalmers, 1905. Destroyed 1966. (p.224, fig.216)]
	†22	[953–7: tenement block, *c.*1853. Ascribed to Alexander Kirkland. Destroyed 1972. (p.190n.)]
	†23	[Shawfield Mansion. By Colen Campbell, 1712. Destroyed 1793. (p.51, fig.27)]
Armadale Street, *Dennistoun*	**†24**	[169–71: Dennistoun parish church. By P. M. Chalmers, 1906–7. Romanesque.]

Ashley Street, *St George's*	25	55–71: terrace of tenements. By John Bryce, 1849–51. 3 storeys with good late Georgian detail. Partly demolished.
	26	44: former Albany Academy. By H. & D. Barclay, 1875.
Athole Gardens, *Dowanhill*	27	1–20: terrace of houses, c.1878–80. Bay-windowed with Thomsonesque detail.
Bain Street, *Calton*	28	26–42: former clay-pipe factory. By Matthew Forsyth, 1876. 3-part composition with lower centre; Palladian & other detail.
Balliol Street, *St George's*	29	3–29: terrace of tenements, c.1850. Similar to **25** & **30**.
	30	10–30: terrace of tenements, c.1850. Similar to **25** & **29**.
Balmore Road, *Lambhill*	31	1035: gateway & lodges to Lambhill Cemetery. By James Sellars, 1880.
	32	21–25 Canal Bank, Lambhill Bridge: warehouse, c.1790.
Balornock Road, *Stobhill*	33	Stobhill Hospital. By Thomson & Sandilands, 1900–04. Brick, with Colcutt-type tower.
Banavie Road, *Partickhill*	34	1–37: terrace of 2-storey houses, c.1850.
Barony Street, *Townhead*	35	11: former Martyrs Public School. By C. R. Mackintosh, 1895. (p.220, fig.204)
Bath Street, *Blythswood*	36	81: house, c.1805. 2 storeys + basement.
	37	127–9: Education offices. By H. E. Clifford, 1910–11. Influence of J. M. Dick Peddie.
	38	145–73: terrace of houses, c.1830.
	39	181–99 (Athol Place): terrace of houses. Perhaps by John Baird no.1, begun 1833. Interior work at no.185 by Keppie & Mackintosh. (p.78) Cf.**46**
	40	201–5 (Adelaide Place): incomplete terrace of houses. By Robert Black, begun 1839. Cf. **47**.
	41	207: former Philosophical Institute. By T. L. Watson, 1875.
	42	209: Adelaide Place Baptist church. By T. L. Watson, 1875. (p.78n)
	43	279: clinic (former U.P. church). By D. Sturrock, 1874. Late classical.
	44	38: former Mechanics' Institute. By James Salmon 1861. Top floors by Arthur Hamilton, c.1910. (p.145, fig.122)
	45	152–78: terrace of houses, c.1830.
	46	182–200 (Athol Place): terrace of houses answering to **39**. Probably by John Baird no.1. Domed rear wing to no.200 by John Keppie. (p.78)
	47	202–18 (Adelaide Place): terrace of houses. By Robert Black, begun 1839. (pp.78, 250f., fig 54)
	48	240: restaurant (formerly Elgin Place Congregational church). By John Burnet, sen., 1856. (pp.78, 160f., 163f., 200, figs.143f.)
	49	256½: St Stephen's Renfield (formerly Blythswood Independent) church. By J. T. Emmett, 1849–52. Details altered & spire mutilated 1968. (p.170, figs 70, 149, 170)
	50	264: corner tenement, c.1849; art-nouveau ground floor pub by William Reid, 1903–4.
	51	268–318: terraces of tenements, 1850–3. Western section demolished c.1970. (pp.189, 238f., fig.170)
	52	King's Theatre. By Frank Matcham, 1901–4. (p. 265)
	†53	[87–97: office block. By Alexander Thomson, 1875–6. Destroyed 1970. (pp.149, 152)]
	†54	[135–43: Cockburn Hotel. By David Thomson & Robert Turnbull, c.1879–81 incorporating house on site. Destroyed 1970.]
	†55	[291: Renfield Free Church (later City Temple). By Boucher & Cousland. Gothic. Destroyed 1967.]
	†56	[42: Cairney Building. By Alexander Thomson, 1860. (pp.128, 145, 147–52, figs 122, 128)]
	†57	[140–52, Pettigrew & Stephen's department store. E section by A. Graham Henderson, 1922 (sculpture by Benno Schotz); W section the former Alexandra Hotel, reconstructed by Alexander Thomson, 1875. Destroyed 1973–4.]
	†58	[St Matthew's church. By James Salmon, 1849. Destroyed c.1954. (p.170n, figs.70, 151)]
Beaconsfield Road, *Kelvinside*	59	22: St John's Renfield church. By James Taylor Thomson, 1929–31; glass by Douglas Strachan. (p.269, fig.261)
Beaumont Gate, *Hyndland*	60	1–18: tenement with bows & art-nouveau glass. By David Barclay, c.1900.
Beith Street, *Partick*	61	Partick fire station. By James Miller, 1905. Brick & stone Wrenaissance.
Belgrave Terrace, *Hillhead*		See Great Western Road.
Belhaven Terrace, *Kelvinside*		See Great Western Road.
Bell Street	62	51: commercial building with market to rear. By A. B. Macdonald, 1902. 5 storeys.
	63	6–20: commercial building. By Campbell Reid & Wingate, 1914–21. 6 storeys.

Bell Street (continued)	64	26–36: commercial buildings for City Improvement Trust. By Thomson & Sandilands, c.1910. 6 storeys.
	65	Bell Street railway warehouse, 1889. (p.106)
	66	118–126: warehouse, c.1880, perhaps based on a design by Alexander Thomson.
	†67	[St John's church. By David Hamilton, 1819. Destroyed c.1960. (p.170)]
Bellshaugh Road, *Kelvinside*	68	Kelvinside Academy. By James Sellars, 1877–9. (p.153, fig.130)
Belmont Crescent, *Belmont*	69	1–20: terrace of houses, 1869–70. Partly demolished. (pp.92n, 102, 242n, fig.76)
Belmont Street, *Belmont*	70	Belmont Bridge, 1870. High semi-elliptical arch.
	71	Kelvin-Stevenson Memorial church. By J. J. Stevenson, 1900–02. (pp.178f, figs.162, 229)
Benmore Street, *Springburn*	72	Mosesfield House (with Springburn Park). By David Hamilton, 1838. Minimal Elizabethan.
Bentinck Street, *Kelvingrove*	73	34–58: tenement, c.1878. Shallow bays and deep eaves.
Berkeley Street, *Sandyford*	74	53–91: terrace of houses, c.1860. Similar to **76**.
	75	97–113: industrial workshops. By Campbell Douglas & Sellars, 1870–3.
	76	42–84: terrace of houses, c.1860. Similar to **74**. No.72 rebuilt, c.1965. (p.251)
	77	Mitchell Library extension (formerly St Andrew's Halls). By James Sellars, 1873–7. Gutted 1962, rebuilt retaining façade only, 1973–80. (pp.153f, 156, fig.133)
	†78	[174: Glasgow Eye Infirmary. By John Burnet, sen., 1871–4. Gothic. Destroyed c.1970.]
Bishop Court, *Blythswood*	†79	[McLeod's warehouse (originally Bishop Garden cotton mill), 1826. Extensive use of glass. Destroyed 1966.]
Blackfriars Street	80	16–18: house (now offices). Perhaps by Robert & John Adam, c.1790. Doric columns remain at ground floor, top floor & pediment reinstated 1986.
Blythswood Square, *Blythswood*	81	1–7: terrace of houses (now offices). By John Brash, c.1829, perhaps after a design by Gillespie Graham. Doorway at no.5 by C. R. Mackintosh, 1908. (pp.75–8, 183, 232)
	82	8–13: terrace of houses (now Royal Scottish Automobile Club). By John Brash, as **81**. Central porch & interiors by James Miller, 1923. (pp.75–8, 183, 232, fig.53)
	83	14–20: terrace of houses (now offices). As **81**. (pp.75–8, 183, 232)
	84	21–26: terrace of houses (now offices). As **81**. Notable interior at no.26. (pp.75–8, 183, 232)
Blythswood Street, *Blythswood*	85	107: small office building, c.1870. Thomsonesque fenestration.
	86	[110: house, c.1830.]
Bothwell Street, *Blythswood*	87	15–25: former shipping offices. By Clarke & Bell, c.1890. (p.258)
	88	39–69: Mercantile Chambers. By James Salmon, jun., 1897–8. (pp.211, 222, 261n, fig.205)
	89	75: offices. By Clarke & Bell, c.1895. Similar to **87**.
	90	95: Scottish Legal building. By Edward Grigg Wylie (of Wright & Wylie), 1927. (p.270)
	91	205–29: Eagle Buildings (formerly Bothwell Circus). By Alexander Kirkland, 1854. Gutted. (p.111)
	91a	2–26: offices. By Alexander Kirkland & John Bryce, 1849. Interior rebuilt 1978. (p.111)
	92	30: Royal Bank of Scotland. By James Miller, 1934. Classico-modern.
	93	36–62: Central Thread Agency offices. By David Barclay, 1891–1901. Three-part design in crowded baroque-cum-renaissance. (pp.258n, 262)
	†94	[64–100: Christian Institute. By John McLeod 1878–9 & R. A. Bryden, 1895–8. Gargantuan romanesque. Destroyed 1980.]
Braidfauld Street, *Tolcross*	95	St Margaret's church. By W. G. Rowan, 1900–01. (p.182)
Bridgegate	96	141: Merchants' Steeple, 1665. Surviving fragment of former Merchants' Hall. Now within former Fishmarket (see **188**). (pp.44f.)
	97	128–36: tenements. By N. S. Macdonald, 1905. Baroque in the manner of Burnet & Campbell.
	†98	[Campbell of Blythswood's Mansion, c.1660. (p.43)]
Bridgeton Cross, *Bridgeton*	99	42: savings bank. By D. Bennet Dobson, 1903. Idiosyncratic baroque.
	100	Olympia theatre. By George Arthur, with Frank Matcham, 1910.
Broomhill Avenue, *Broomhill*	101	2–24: terrace of tenements, c.1870. In the manner of Charles Wilson.
Broomhill Drive, *Broomhill*	102	218–30: Balshagray parish church. By Stewart & Paterson, 1907–12. Curvilinear Gothic.
Broomhill Terrace, *Broomhill*	103	19–33: terrace of tenements, c.1870. Similar to **101**.
Broomielaw	104	2–12: warehouse. By Alexander Skirving, 1883. Corinthian.
	105	70–74: office block, c.1840. Now ships' store.

Broomielaw (continued)	†**106**	[150: Sailors' home. By J. T. Rochead, 1855–6. Italianate with circular corner tower. Destroyed 1971.]
Brown Street, *Broomielaw*	†**107**	[27: office building. By W. F. McGibbon, *c.*1910. American inspiration. Destroyed 1985.]
Brunswick Street	**108**	63: commercial building, *c.*1800. 3 storeys, plain.
	109	102–4: office block. By R. W. Billings, 1859. Angular baronial.
	110	106: offices, *c.*1770. Plain.
	111	108–10: warehouse, 1883. 5 storeys; pilastered renaissance façade, nearly all glass.
	112	118–28: warehouse. By John Baird no.1 (plans) & R. W. Billings (elevations), 1854. Baronial. Interior rebuilding 1985.
	†**113**	[67–73: commercial building, *c.*1790. 4 storeys, pedimented, with later architraves. Destroyed 1981.]
Buccleuch Street	**114**	Former High School for Girls. By James Thomson, 1878. Italianate with tower. Wing by W. F. MacGibbon, 1886.
Buchanan Street	**115**	21–31: department store (originally Macdonalds'). By William Spence, *c.*1879. (p.112, fig.87)
	116	37: warehouse (originally Kemp's), 1853–4. Top two floors by Boucher & Cousland. (p.115, fig.93c)
	117	45: department store (originally Wylie & Lochhead's). By James Sellars, 1884–5. (pp.197n, 258n)
	118	55–61: house (now offices), *c.*1845. Late classical.
	119	63–9: former *Glasgow Herald* building. By James Sellars, 1879. Ground floor altered. (p.258n)
	120	71–9: offices. By James Thomson, 1880. Arcaded Corinthian.
	121	91: Clydesdale Bank (formerly tea-room). By George Washington Browne, 1896. Interiors by George Walton & C. R. Mackintosh now destroyed. (pp.198n, 258, 274n)
	122	101–111: shops & offices, *c.*1825. Pilastered shop fronts.
	123	123–9: Carron building. By James Boucher, 1884. Astylar Italianate.
	124	147: former Western Club. By David Hamilton, 1841. W additions (now demolished) by John Honeyman, 1871. (pp.84–6, 94, 157n, 186, 255, figs.59, 247)
	125	179: Athenaeum Theatre (now part of Royal Scottish Academy of Music & Dramatic Art). By J. J. Burnet & J. A. Campbell, 1891–3. (pp.204f., 210, 255, 261, 263, figs.183, 247)
	126	235–49: Cleland Testimonial Building. By David & James Hamilton, 1835–6.
	127	12–16: warehouse with superimposed orders. By William Spence, 1873; later section to left designed as tower. (p.261)
	128	20: department store (originally Wylie Hill's). By John Hutchison and Andrew Black, 1889; details drawn by C. R. Mackintosh. Gutted 1904 & rebuilt to same design. (p.263)
	129	28–32: Argyle Chambers. By Colin Menzies, 1904. (p.262)
	130	34–54: Prince of Wales Building (with Prince's Square). By John Baird no.1, 1854. Incorporating earlier square of 1840, roofed over 1986–7. (p.114n)
	131	60–62: offices (originally North British Rubber Coy). By Robert Thomson & Andrew Wilson, 1898. (p.261, fig.252)
	132	66: commercial building. By John Baird no.1, 1851. Free Grecian detail showing affinities with Alexander Thomson.
	133	82–90: offices & shops. By Robert Foote, *c.*1835. Later top floor perhaps by Alexander Thomson.
	134	92–100: Royal Bank building. By Charles Wilson, 1850–1. (pp.93, 94n, 118–20, fig.90)
	135	106–12: Royal Insurance building. By Thomson & Sandilands, 1897–8. Restrained free renaissance.
	136	116–28: office block. By Burnet & Boston, 1898–1902. (p.262)
	137	156–60: Tower Building. By James Sellars, *c.*1877. Altered 1964.
	138	164–8: Britannia Building (formerly Dundas House). By J. A. Campbell, 1898. (p.210)
	†**139**	[45: Wylie & Lochhead's store. By William Lochhead, 1855. Burnt 1883 & replaced by **117**. (pp.115–8, 153, 197n, fig.93e)]
	†**140**	[144–52: offices & shops. By Charles Wilson, 1847. Destroyed *c.*1978.]
	†**141**	[176–80: warehouse & offices, *c.*1880. Elaborate French façade in shallow relief with tile spandrels. Destroyed 1982–3.]
Buckingham Terrace, *Hillhead*		See Great Western Road

Cleveden Drive, *Kelvinside*	**181**	28–40: terrace of houses. By J. C. MacKellar, *c.*1904. Baroque detail; notably elaborate house at no.40.
	182	48: Stoneleigh. By H. E. Clifford, 1900. Lavish neo-Tudor.
	183	50: villa, *c.*1870. Craggy Gothic.
Cleveden Gardens, *Kelvinside*	**184**	15: villa. By A. N. Prentice, 1904. Refined renaissance with cupola.
Cleveden Road, *Kelvinside*	**185**	1: villa. By John Gordon, 1877. Very elaborate interior including vaulted billiard room.
	186	4–8: mansion, *c.*1870. Jacobethan with Louis XV interiors.
	187	16: mansion, *c.*1870. Early renaissance with tower.
Clyde Street	**188**	64–76: former Fishmarket. By Clarke & Bell, 1873. Renaissance with iron galleried halls. (p.122n)
	189	172: St Andrew's R.C. cathedral. By J. Gillespie Graham, 1814–7; internal alterations by Pugin & Pugin, 1871 & 1892. (pp.170–2)
	190	228–46: houses in terrace (now offices). Early 19th-century.
	191	260: office building. By Eric A. Sutherland, *c.*1907. (p.263)
	192	286: house block extending into terrace at rear, *c.*1840.
	193	298–306: former Custom House. By John Taylor, 1840. (p.86, fig.60)
	194	Suspension bridge. By George Martin & Alexander Kirkland, 1851; reconstructed 1871, by Bell & Miller. (pp. 73, 111. fig.86)
	†**195**	[130: Dreghorn mansion. By Allan Dreghorn, 1752; later incorporated in warehouse of 1857. Destroyed *c.*1980. (p.50)]
Cochrane Street	**196**	27: John Street church. By J. T. Rochead, 1859. Derelict. (p.92n, fig.66)
	197	45–57: terrace of offices & flats. Early 19th-century. (p.54)
	†**198**	[15–25: terrace of offices & flats. By J. & W. Carswell, late 18th-century. Plain. Destroyed *c.*1978. (p.54)]
Colebrook Street, *Kelvinbridge*	**199**	Glasgow Academy. By H. & D. Barclay, 1878. (p.163)
College Street	†**200**	[32: house, *c.*1800 with additions of *c.*1850. Destroyed *c.*1977]
Corunna Street, *Finnieston*	**201**	1–9: terrace of tenements. By Alexander Kirkland, *c.*1850.
	202	2–12: terrace of tenements. As **201**, but *c.*1855.
Cowcaddens Street, *Cowcaddens*	†**203**	[110–20: Cowcaddens Cross Buildings. By Alexander Thomson, 1873. Destroyed 1971. (p.148n)]
	†**204**	[Free Normal Seminary (Stow College). By Thomas Burns, 1846. E additions by Campbell Douglas & Stevenson, 1861, matching W addition 1901. Tudor. Destroyed 1973]
Craigpark Street, *Dennistoun*	†**205**	[Regent Place church. By H. & D. Barclay, 1877–8. Italianate with campanile. Burnt 1983]
Cranston Street, *Anderston*	†**206**	[55: police station. By John Carrick, 1857–8. Sumptuous Italianate. Destroyed 1971]
Cranworth Street, *Hillhead*	**207**	30: Hillhead Baptist church. By T. L. Watson, 1883. Neo-Greek of Sellars type.
	208	Western Baths. By Clarke & Bell, 1873. Mixed Gothic & Venetian.
Crown Circus, *Dowanhill*	**209**	3–10: terrace of houses. By James Thomson, *c.*1858. (pp.92n, 102, 242, fig.75)
Crown Road North, *Dowanhill*	**210**	1–14 Crown Gardens. By James Thomson, *c.*1870.
	211	2–8: terrace of houses. By James Thomson, *c.*1870.
Crown Terrace, *Dowanhill*	**212**	3–11: terrace of houses. By James Thomson, *c.*1873.
Dalhousie Street, *Garnethill*	**213**	42–48: terrace of tenements, *c.*1840. Classical.
Dalmarnock Road, *Dalmarnock*	**214**	231: Dalmarnock Congregational church. By J. C. MacKellar, 1911; embellishments by James Salmon, jun., *c.*1914.
Dalnair Street, *Kelvinhaugh*	†**215**	[Royal Hospital for Sick Children. By J. J. Burnet, 1911–14; enlarged by Burnet, Son & Dick, *c.*1923. Destroyed 1967–8]
Derby Street, *Kelvingrove*	**216**	Cava recording studio (formerly Kelvingrove, originally Finnieston, church). By James Sellars, 1878. (pp.155, 157, fig.134)
Devonshire Terrace, *Hyndland*		See Great Western Road.
Dowanhill Street, *Dowanhill*	**217**	91–127: terraces of flats. By David Barclay, *c.*1900. Elaborate glasswork.
Drumover Drive, *Tolcross*	**218**	Tolcross parish church. By Duncan & Alan McNaughtan, 1905. Gothic with 'modern movement' elements. Hall, 1902.
Drury Street	†**219**	[13–15: office block. By Peddie & Kinnear, 1872. Arched recesses. Demolished 1986]
	220	17–21: The Horse Shoe, *c.*1870. 4 storeys with pilastrades & ornate friezes.
Duke Street, *Townhead to Dennistoun*	**221**	94: Ladywell (formerly Alexander's) school. By John Burnet, sen., 1858. Renaissance with slim tower.
	222	100: Great Eastern hotel (formerly Alexander's mill). By Charles Wilson, 1842. Conversions & additions by N. C. Duff, 1909. (p.106n)

George Street (continued)	**261**	280: former tax offices. By W. W. Robertson, 1885. Renaissance with French roofs.
	262	University of Strathclyde (formerly Royal College of Science & Technology). By David Barclay, 1901–05. (p.262n)
	†263	[Glasgow Grammar School (later Andersonian Institute). By James Craig, 1788. Destroyed 1903. (p.60n)]
Gibson Street, *Hillhead*	**264**	40–50: terrace of tenements, *c.*1830.
Gilbert Street, *Kelvinhaugh*	**265**	8–20: Volunteer drill hall. By W. H. McNab, 1901. Free Tudor.
Glasgow Cross	**266**	Tolbooth, 1626. Steeple only remains. (pp.43f., 52, figs.18f., 28)
Glasgow Green	**267**	Nelson Monument. By David Hamilton, 1806.
	268	People's Palace. By A. B. Macdonald, 1894. Renaissance, large winter garden at rear.
Glasgow Street, *Hillhead*	**269**	15–25: terrace of tenements, *c.*1840. 3 storeys, stepped in slope.
	270	8–12: terrace of tenements, *c.*1840. As **269**.
Glassford Street	**271**	61–5: warehouse. By Robertson & Dobbie, 1908. 5 storeys, art-nouveau.
	272	85–91: Trades House. By Robert Adam, 1791–4; interior largely by James Sellars, 1887. (pp.54, 65, 82, 235, fig.42)
	273	99: Savings Bank. By John Burnet, sen., 1865–6; banking hall & top storey by J. J. Burnet, 1894–6 & 1898–9; interior modified 1975. (pp.209f., figs.188f.)
	274	44: warehouse, *c.*1860. Pilastered with 2nd-floor arches.
	275	76: offices (formerly house), *c.*1790. 4 storeys with pedimented gable; late Victorian arched & pilastered pub.
	†276	[31–41: offices & shops, *c.*1800. Plain. Destroyed *c.*1978]
	†277	[City of Glasgow Bank. By James Sellars, 1877. Destroyed 1959. (pp.153, 155, 197, 258n, fig.132)]
Gordon Street	**278**	19: warehouse (formerly restaurant). By James Carruthers, 1931. 5 storeys; pilastered; art deco detail on elevator doors.
	279	23–7: shops & offices, *c.*1815. Classical, plain.
	280	29–35: shops & offices, *c.*1840. Idiosyncratic classical with splayed corner.
	281	41–51: Ca d'Oro (formerly warehouse). By John Honeyman, 1872; mansard storeys by J. G. Gillespie, 1926–7. (pp.156f., 274, figs.93i, 138) See also 122 Union Street.
	282	71–99: Central Station hotel. By R. R. Anderson, 1879–83; additions, extension of trainshed, buildings in concourse by James Miller, 1907. (pp.197, 205n, fig.177)
	283	2–8: Royal Bank. By David Rhind, 1854–7; E section by Sydney Mitchell, 1887; rebuilt internally 1937. (pp.120f., fig.95)
	284	20–40: shops & offices. By Peddie & Kinnear, 1875. 4 storeys, pilastered.
	285	42–50: warehouse. By Clarke & Bell, 1886. 4 storeys; shallow bays & idiosyncratic detail.
	286	72–80: Grosvenor Building. By Alexander Thomson, 1859; burnt & rebuilt 1864; interior (now destroyed) & top floors by J. H. Craigie, 1907. (pp.143–7, 150f., figs.125, 128e)
	287	82–92: Standard Life offices. By James Thomson, 1890. Top storeys by J. B. & W. A. Thomson, 1909. (p.262)
Grafton Square	**†288**	[Pleasant square of classical tenements with one curved angle, 1849–79. Destroyed 1970.]
Great George Street, *Hillhead*	**289**	1–9: terrace of tenements, *c.*1830. 3 storeys, classical.
	290	2: villa, *c.*1830. 2 storeys, classical.
	291	10: villa, *c.*1830. As **290**.
	292	121: Laurelbank school annexe (formerly Belmont parish church). By James Miller, 1893–4. Gothic, using 'Gerona' plan.
Great Western Road, *St George's to Anniesland* S. side	**293**	Kelvinbridge. By Miller & Bell, 1890–1. Iron spans, Gothic detail.
	294	445–59: Caledonian Mansions. By James Miller, 1897. 3½ storeys. Jacobean.
	295	Belgrave Terrace. By Gildard & Macfarlane, 1856. Italianate.
	296	731–5: Bible training institute (former Kelvinside parish church). By J. J. Stevenson, 1862. (p.174)
	297	Grosvenor Terrace. By J. T. Rochead, 1855. (pp.91f., fig.63)
	298	Kew Terrace. By James Brown & J. T. Rochead, 1849. (p.91)
	299	Belhaven Terrace. By James Thomson, 1866–9 & 1870–4.
	300	Great Western Terrace. By Alexander Thomson, 1869. (pp.92, 123, 126, 136f., 149, figs.113f.)
	301	Lancaster Terrace, *c.*1875. Distinctive late classical.
	302	985: Westbourne House, *c.*1873. Italianate villa with tower & bows.

Great Western Road, *St George's to Anniesland* S. side (continued)	303	Devonshire Gardens (1–5), *c*.1877. Houses with French roofs.
	304	Devonshire Terrace (1–9). By James Thomson, 1883. Unfinished.
	305	1051: Former Kelvinside station. By J. J. Burnet, *c*.1897.
	306	1055: Gartnavel Royal Hospital. By Charles Wilson, 1841–3; additions by J. J. Burnet, 1906–14; nurses' home by Norman Dick, 1934–7.
(N side)	307	St Mary's Episcopal cathedral. By George Gilbert Scott, 1870–4; spire completed by J. Oldrid Scott, 1893. (p. 169)
	308	416–20: Lansdowne church. By John Honeyman, 1862–3. (pp.155, 172f., fig.152)
	309	Ruskin Terrace, *c*.1855–8. E half handsome Italianate.
	310	Buckingham Terrace. By J. T. Rochead, 1852 (E half) & 1858. (p.189)
	311	Botanic Gardens. Curator's house, by Charles Wilson, 1840. Kibble Palace, originally built at Coulport *c*.1863, re-erected here 1873. (p.92n)
	312	Kirklee Terrace. By Charles Wilson, 1845. (pp.91, 140n, fig.62)
	313	Lowther Terrace: 8 & 10 by James Miller, *c*.1904; 9 by Sydney Mitchell, *c*.1904.
	314	Lancaster Crescent: 1–9, mixed terrace of houses by Henry Higgins (no.1, 1898), James Miller, (no.2 1898) J. L. Cowan (nos.3–7, 1900) & J. C. MacKellar (nos.8–9, 1901)
	315	Lancaster Crescent: 11, Redlands Hospital. By James Boucher, 1869–71. Renaissance.
	316	994: villa. By John Gordon, *c*. 1877. Classical; Gothic addition by H. O. Tarbolton, 1912.
	317	998: mansion. By James Boucher, 1877. Italianate renaissance. (p.122n)
	318	1000: mansion, *c*.1885. Classical with central tower in style of James Thomson.
	†319	[1014: Red Hall. By T. L. Watson, 1885. Tudor. Destroyed 1968]
Greendyke Street, *Glasgow Green*	320	33–39: warehouse (formerly hide, wool & tallow market). By John Keppie, 1890. Plain classical with giant arcade.
Greenhead Street, *Calton*	321	100–13: terrace of tenements, *c*.1850. Classical.
	322	Fairfield child guidance centre (formerly Greenhead House). By Charles Wilson, 1846.
Grove Street, *St George's*	323	80–84: Grove Street Institute. By Alexander George Thomson, 1865–6. Mildly late classical.
Hamilton Drive, *Belmont*	324	1–33: terrace of houses. By Robert Crawford, 1857–9. Classical.
	325	35–51: North Park Terrace. By Alexander Thomson, begun 1866. (pp.102, 126f., 140, 142, fig.119)
	326	53–63: terrace of houses. By Robert Crawford, 1857–9. As **324**.
Hanover Street	327	5: offices. By James Miller, *c*.1923. American classical.
	†328	[1–3a: warehouse. By John Baird no.1, 1854. Destroyed 1968]
Heddle Place, *Anderston*	†329	[Anderston old church. By John Baird no.1, 1839–40. Classical. Destroyed 1967]
Henderson Street, *Woodside*	†330	[40–60: Burnbank school. By John Honeyman, 1874. Burnt 1983. (pp.177f.)]
High Street	331	Bell o' the Brae: terraces of tenements for City Improvement Trust. By Burnet & Boston, 1900–1. (p.190)
	†332	[169–77: flats & shops. By James Adam, 1793–5; alterations & quadrant by John Carrick, 1872. Destroyed. 1973. (p.62, fig.40)]
	†333	[179–83; flats & shops. By James Adam, 1793–5. As **332** but unaltered. Destroyed 1973. (p.62, fig.40)]
	†334	[Blackfriars church, 13th-century? Destroyed 1670. (pp.42n, 58)]
	†335	[Old College, mid-17th-century & later. Destroyed 1887. Fragmentarily reconstructed in University Avenue, 1888; see (pp.16f., 42n, 43, 45–7, 61f., figs.21–3)]
Highburgh Road, *Partickhill*	336	24: Western telephone exchange. By Leonard Stokes, 1907. (pp.190, 263n)
	337	28–40: tenements. By David Barclay, *c*.1900. With bow windows & art-nouveau glasswork.
Hill Street, *Garnethill*	338	45–7: St Aloysius College. By Archibald Macpherson, 1883, wings 1892. Italian renaissance of unusual design.
	339	97–113b: Breadalbane Terrace: tenements. Perhaps by Charles Wilson, *c*.1845, extended later. (p.183n)
	340	125–35: synagogue. By John McLeod, 1881. Idiosyncratic romanesque.
	341	102–12: Peel Terrace: tenements. By David Hamilton or Charles Wilson, *c*.1845. (p.183n)
Hillhead Street, *Hillhead*	342	53: Florentine House, early 19th-century. Classical villa.
	343	2–28: Granby Terrace: tenements. By William Clarke, 1856. (pp.101, 186, fig.169)
Hillkirk Street, *Springburn*	344	St Aloysius R.C. church. By J. L. Bruce, 1881. Gothic.

Holland Street, *Blythswood*	†345	[14: house, *c.*1830. Classical. Destroyed *c.*1970]
Hope Street	346	15–17: offices. By J. J. Burnet, 1900.
	347	19–23: offices, *c.*1875. Crowded idiosyncratic renaissance.
	348	43–7: Atlantic Chambers. By J. J. Burnet, 1899. (pp.203f, fig.184)
	349	67: former *Daily Record* office. By Robert Thomson & Andrew Wilson, 1899. (p.261)
	350	91–115: offices (former hotel). By Peddie & Kinnear, 1876. (p.262)
	351	157–67: office block. By J. A. Campbell, 1902. (pp.211, 214, fig.193)
	352	307–33: McConnell Building: tenement for City Improvement Trust. By John Keppie, 1906.
	353	106–8: Scottish Temperance League (now offices). By W. F. Salmon & J. G. Gillespie, 1894; rear block by C. R. Mackintosh, 1900. (pp.220,222)
	354	116: Liverpool, London & Globe offices. By James Thomson, 1898–9. (pp.258, 262, 263, fig.254)
	355	172: Lion Chambers. By James Salmon, jun., 1906. (pp.224, 261, figs.214f.)
	356	282: Theatre Royal. By George Bell, 1867, altered later; interior by C. J. Phipps, 1895; restored & new foyer by Derek Sugden, 1974–5. (p.265)
	†357	[81: Corn Exchange. By W. F. McGibbon, 1894. Destroyed 1963. (p.262n)]
Hopehill Road, *Woodside*	357a	St. Columba's R.C. church. By J. Coia, 1931. (p.273)
Horslethill Road, *Kelvinside*	358	1: villa, *c.*1840, enlarged later. Greek Doric.
Howard Street	359	114: warehouse. By A. Balfour, 1903. 6 storeys, red sandstone.
	360	118–20: warehouse. By J. Gibb Morton, 1904. (pp.224–6)
	†361	[36–8: warehouse & shop. By Alexander Thomson, 1853. Destroyed 1967. (p.143)]
Hutchesontown Bridge	†362	[By John Rennie & James Walker, 1829. Destroyed 1864. (p.111n)]
Hyndland Road, *Hyndland*	363	21–39: Westbourne Terrace. By Alexander Thomson, 1871. (pp.123, 126, 140f., 142f., fig.120)
	364	61: St Bride's Episcopal church. By G. F. Bodley, 1903–4 (chancel & E part of nave), & H. O. Tarbolton, 1915–6 (tower & W part of church). (p.180, fig.161)
	365	79: Hyndland parish church. By William Leiper, 1886. Gothic.
Hyndland Street, *Hyndland*	366	Dowanhill church. By William Leiper, 1865–6. (pp.172f.)
India Street, *Charing Cross*	367	6–28: terrace of houses, *c.*1845.
Ingram Street	368	159–61: warehouse, *c.*1860. 4 storeys, Italianate with conch windowheads.
	369	191: Lanarkshire House. Former Union Bank building by David Hamilton, 1841; refronted by John Burnet, sen., 1875–8; banking hall by James Salmon, sen., 1853. (pp.158f., 266n, 200n, fig.136)
	370	205–17: warehouse & offices, *c.*1875; interiors by C. R. Mackintosh & Scott Morton, for Miss Cranston's tea-room, 1900–12, now removed. (p.218)
	371	223–9: warehouse. By James Boucher, 1875. 5 storeys, free renaissance.
	372	12–20: leather works. By J. W. & J. Laird, 1910. (p.263)
	373	54–64: Albion Buildings, *c.*1875. 4 storeys, mixed renaissance and rundbogen.
	374	98: St David's Ramshorn church. By Thomas Rickman, 1824–6. (pp.54, 170, 234f., figs 30, 221)
	375	126–36: commercial building, *c.*1875. 4 storeys with double-windowed bays.
	376	144–52: commercial building, *c.*1840. 3 storeys, severe astylar.
	377	158: Hutcheson's Hospital. By David Hamilton, 1802–5; interior reconstructed by John Baird no.2, 1876. (pp.45n, 54, 81f., 234, figs.55, 226
	378	162–6: commercial building, *c.*1820. Simple astylar, 3 storeys.
	379	174–6: office (formerly Bank of Scotland). By William Burn, 1828. Mutilated.
	†380	[118–22: School of Design. By David Hamilton, *c.*1805, enlarged mid-19th-century. Destroyed 1982.]
	†381	[Assembly Rooms. By Robert & James Adam, 1792; wings by Henry Holland, 1807. Destroyed 1889/1911: centre re-erected as McLennan Arch (see **172**). (pp.60f., 264, fig.37)]
Jamaica Bridge	382	Bridge over Clyde. By Thomas Telford, 1833–6; rebuilt in widened form with modifications, by Blyth & Westland, 1894–9. (p.111n)
Jamaica Street	383	21–5: warehouse & offices, *c.*1875. Pilastered with upper arches.
	384	27–33: warehouse & offices. By James Thomson, 1875. Pilastered.
	385	47–51: Jamaica Chambers, *c.*1855. Severe double-bayed treatment.
	386	2–8: offices, *c.*1830. Severe, plain; glazed top floor & mansard added *c.*1880. Thomsonesque.

North Speirs Wharf, *Port Dundas*	**477**	174: canal office, 1812. Pedimented.
	478	City grain mills & warehouses: extensive 6- & 7-storey range, 1851–70. (p.106n)
	479	256: Port Dundas sugar refinery, 1866. 7-storey classical.
	†480	[158–64: collector's house, c.1790. Destroyed c.1975]
	†481	[170: house, c.1812. Destroyed c.1975]
Oakfield Avenue, *Hillhead*	**482**	41–53: terrace of houses. By Alexander Thomson, c.1865. (pp.101, 126, 140n)
	483	57–69: terrace of houses, c.1868.
	484	70–80: terrace of houses, c.1858–9; additions & alterations at corner house (70 University Avenue) by J. J. Burnet.
Old Dalmarnock Road, *Bridgeton*	**485**	52: church of the Sacred Heart. By C. J. Ménart, 1912. (p.266, fig.260)
	†486	[122: Dalmarnock gas works. By William Spence, 1843. Greco-Egyptian retort house. Destroyed c.1976]
Old Dumbarton Road, *Partick*	**487**	206: Bishop Mills, 1839 & 1853. 4 storeys, plain.
Old Shettleston Road, *Shettleston*	**488**	Eastbank church & hall. By W. G. Rowan, 1902. Gothic.
Oswald Street	**†489**	[14: Argyle Free church (later warehouse). By Charles Wilson, 1846. Romanesque.]
Otago Street, *Hillhead*	**490**	94–106: tenement. By Alexander Thomson, 1874.
Park Circus, *Woodlands Hill*	**491**	1–16: terrace of houses. By Charles Wilson, c.1857–9. (pp.93f., 247, figs.68–70)
	492	18–22: terrace of houses. By Charles Wilson, c.1861–3; no.22 has lavish interior by James Boucher, further elaborated by Salmon & Gillespie. Wood-carving by Derwent Wood. (pp.93, 247)
	493	23–9: terrace of houses. By Charles Wilson, c.1861–3. (pp.93, 247)
Park Circus Place, *Woodlands Hill*	**494**	1–17: terrace of houses. By Charles Wilson, designed 1855–6, built c.1872–3. (p.247, fig.70)
	495	2–8: terrace of houses, c.1872–3. As **494**. (p.247, fig.70)
	496	Park parish church. By J. T. Rochead, 1858. Destroyed; tower remains. (pp.172, 247, figs.65, 70, 235, 237)
Park Gardens, *Woodlands Hill*	**497**	1–6: terrace of houses. By Charles Wilson, c.1855.
Park Gardens Lane, *Woodlands Hill*	**498**	2: flat with garage underneath. By J. J. Burnet, c.1905.
Park Quadrant, *Woodlands Hill*	**499**	1–10: terrace of tenements. By Charles Wilson, c.1855–8.
Park Terrace, *Woodlands Hill*	**500**	1–17: terrace of houses. By Charles Wilson, c.1855. (pp.92n, 94f., 189, 202n, 249, 258n, figs.70, 232)
	501	Stairway to Park Gardens. By Charles Wilson, c.1854–5. (p.249, fig.243)
Parliamentary Road	**502**	[Lunatic Asylum, Bell's Park. By William Stark, 1809. Destroyed 1908 (pp.70, fig.47)]
Parson Street, *Townhead*	**503**	52: St Mungo's R.C. church. By George Goldie, 1869–71. Gothic.
	504	54: St Mungo's monastery. By Fr. Osmund Cooke, 1891–2. Gothic.
Partickhill Road, *Partickhill*	**505**	51–9: Hawarden Terrace. Perhaps by Robert Turnbull, c.1880. Thomsonesque.
	506	71: villa, c.1855. Broad-eaved Italianate, with Thomsonesque detail; clerestoreyed billiard room.
	507	56: villa, 1841. Greek revival with Ionic porch; outbuildings complete. (fig. 233)
	508	64: villa, c.1840. Plain classical with Tuscan porch.
	509	74: villa, c.1860. Rundbogenstil. (p.134n)
	†510	[47: villa, c.1845, Wilsonesque; additions, c.1875 with sumptuous interiors by William Leiper. Destroyed 1983]
Peel Street, *Partick*	**511**	53–63: terrace of tenements. By H. & D. Barclay, 1875.
	†512	[75: Partick Academy. By H. & D. Barclay, c.1878. Destroyed, 1971]
	†513	[70: City Temple. By John Honeyman, 1869. Gothic; interesting plan with stairs beneath apse. Destroyed c.1983]
Prince Albert Road, *Dowanhill*	**514**	2: Holmhurst: villa, c.1855. Wilsonesque Italianate; later heightened.
	515	Prince's Terrace. By James Thomson, c.1870 (pp.102n, 242)
Provanhall Road, *Provan*	**516**	Old Provan Hall. 16th- & mid-18th-century. (p.40)
Queen Street	**517**	3–9: warehouse & shops, c.1800. Plain.
	518	45–67: Hunter Barr warehouse. By David Barclay, 1899.
	519	73–87: South Exchange Court & Royal Exchange Court: offices. By Robert Black, c.1830. Simple classical.
	520	Wellington monument. By Baron Marochetti, 1844. Equestrian bronze.
	521	151–7: offices & shops. By David Hamilton, c.1834. (pp.84n, 143, 150, figs.57, 128a)
	522	18–28: offices. By H. E. Clifford, c.1912.
	523	54–72: Queen Court: warehouses, c.1833. Simple classical with segment-headed windows.

Queen Street (continued)	524	136–48: offices. By James Miller, c.1904–5.
	†525	[Theatre Royal. By David Hamilton, 1804. Destroyed 1829. (p.264)]
	†526	[11–13: Clydesdale Bank. By D. & J. Hamilton, 1840. Destroyed c.1962. (p.118)]
	†527	[74–82: Canada Court. By James Wylson, 1848; doorpiece later. Destroyed 1967. (p.109n)]
	†528	[110–18: British Linen Bank. By D. & J. Hamilton, 1840; upper storeys by Salmon & Gillespie, 1903. Destroyed 1968. (fig.223)]
Queen Margaret Drive, *Kelvinside*	529	North Park House (now Broadcasting House). By J. T. Rochead, 1869–71; completed by John Honeyman; additions by James Miller, 1936 & later. NE portion (former Queen Margaret College) by John Keppie & C. R. Mackintosh, 1895; enclosed in new buildings & largely destroyed 1962. (p.92n)
	530	North Kelvinside church. By J. B. Wilson, begun 1895. Collegiate Perpendicular.
	531	Queen Margaret Bridge. By Thomas Somers, 1926–9. Concrete with neo-classical veneer.
Queen's Crescent, *St. George's*	532	1–9: terrace of houses. By John Bryce, 1840. (pp.101f., 242n, fig.74)
	533	10–18: terrace of houses. By John Bryce, 1840. As **532** (pp.101f., 242n)
Queen's Gardens, *Dowanhill*	534	8–11: fragment of terrace. By James Thomson, c.1870. Astylar classical.
Queen's Place, *Dowanhill*	535	Westdel & Royston: large semi-detached villas, 1890. Jacobean. Interior at Westdel by C. R. Mackintosh 1898, removed to New Hunterian museum at University 1976.
Renfield Street	536	1–11: former Forsyth department store. By Boucher & Cousland, 1856–8; domed corner, top floor & mansard by J. J. Burnet, 1896–1903.
	537	13–17: former Cranston's restaurant & cinema. By James Miller, 1914–6. Tall classical faience façade. Interior altered.
	538	57: Castle Chambers. By Burnet & Boston, 1898 (pp.258n, 261)
	539	121: Pavilion Theatre. By Bertie Crewe, 1902–04. (p.266)
	540	28–36: offices. By James Miller, 1929. American classical.
	541	106–12: offices & shops, c.1870. Severe.
	†542	[Renfield Street church. By James Brown, 1849. Destroyed 1963. (p.173n, fig.153)]
Renfrew Street, *Garnethill*	543	167: Glasgow School of Art. By C. R. Mackintosh, 1897 (E section) & 1907–9 (W section). (pp.167, 215–8, 239, figs.195–201, 231)
	544	203–17: Dental Hospital. By E. G. Wylie, 1928–31. (p.271, fig.263)
	545	231: Garnetbank school. By T. L. Watson, 1905.
	546	347–53: block of flats. By J. J. Burnet, c.1896. Renaissance.
Robertson Street, *Broomielaw*	547	51 (within court): warehouse, c.1800 & 1830. Tall with projecting pedimented front. Noteworthy cast-iron gallery inside engineering shop of 1869.
	548	71–5: offices. By J. A. Campbell, 1899. (pp.210, 226n)
	549	16: Clyde Port Authority (formerly Clyde Navigation Trust). By J. J. Burnet, 1883–6 (N section) & 1905–8 (S section). (pp.200f., 264n, fig.176)
	550	62: offices, By Steele & Balfour, 1905. Baroque.
Rose Street, *Garnethill*	551	23–5: St Aloysius R.C. church. By C. J. Ménart, 1908–10. (p.266)
		12: Cosmo Cinema. By W. J. Anderson II, 1939; interior altered. (p.266n)
	553	Brinkley Studio. By E. G. Wylie, 1927.
Rosevale Street, *Partick*	554	Former St Bride's church. By P. M. Chalmers, 1897. Gothic.
Rottenrow, *Townhead*	†555	[Cathedral Court: tenements. By J. J. Burnet, 1895. Destroyed 1971. (p.190)]
Royal Exchange Square	556	1–29: terrace of shops & offices. By David Hamilton & Robert Black, 1830, based on scheme by Archibald Elliot II. (pp.83f., 143, 255, figs.56, 223)
	557	2–40: terrace of shops & offices. By David Hamilton & James Smith, 1830–9. As **556**. (pp.83f)
	558	Royal Bank of Scotland. By Archibald Elliot II, 1827; interior modernized. (p.83, fig.58)
	559	Royal Exchange (now Stirling's library), 1778; recased & enlarged by David Hamilton, 1827–30; sculpture by James Fillans; front attic by David Thomson, 1880. (pp.50, 54, 82f., 231, 234, figs.56, 221–3)
Royal Terrace, *Kelvingrove*	560	1–20: terrace of houses, 1845 & later.
Royston Hill, *Townhead*	561	176: Townhead parish church. By Campbell Douglas & Stevenson, 1865. Gothic; Cottier glass.
Royston Road, *St Rollox*	562	102: St Rollox (now Royston) school. By Duncan & Alan MacNaughtan, 1906. (p.224)
Ruchill Street, *Ruchill*	563	Ruchill parish church. By N. C. Duff, 1903–5; hall by C R. Mackintosh 1899.

St. Vincent Street, *City to Finnieston* (continued)	**606**	265: St Vincent Street church. By Alexander Thomson, 1858–9. (pp. 129, 131–4, 140, 145n, 149, 237, figs.107f.)
	607	78: former Phoenix building. By A. D. Hislop, 1912–13. (p.210n)
	608	84–94: former Northern Assurance building. By J. A. Campbell, 1908. (pp.210f., 214n, figs.192, 194)
	609	102–4: former insurance buildings, now offices. By Clarke & Bell, 1853. Renaissance, ground floor destroyed.
	610	110–20: Bank of Scotland (former Union Bank). By James Miller, 1925–7, after a design by York & Sawyer. (pp.209n, 228, 270n)
	611	122–8: former United Kingdom Provident building. By J. A. Campbell, 1904. Interior rebuilt 1981–2. (pp.210, 214n)
	612	130–6: shops & offices, 1876. Corinthian upper order: cf.**598**.
	613	140–2: offices. By Burnet & Boston, 1898. (pp.258n, 263, fig.248)
	614	142a–44: offices (the 'Hatrack'). By James Salmon, jun., 1899–1902. Sculpture probably by Derwent Wood (pp.222–4, 261, fig.210–12)
	615	200: Commercial Union (formerly North British & Mercantile) building. By J. J. Burnet, 1927. (pp.209, 270, fig.186)
	616	202–26: terrace of houses, (now offices), 1825–30; nos 218–20 altered by J. J. Burnet, 1899–1900; nos 220–2 altered by James Miller 1932–4 and again since. (p.75)
	617	232–42: terrace of houses, 1825–30. Interior of no.242 altered by J. J. Burnet for Royal Faculty of Physicians & Surgeons.
	618	250: Windsor House: offices (formerly hotel). By James Thomson, 1875; top floor later.
	619	260–80: terrace of houses, *c*.1825. Stepped in slope.
	620	St Columba's Gaelic church. By W. Tennant & F. V. Burke, 1901–4. Rockfaced curvilinear Gothic with spire.
	†621	[175: office (formerly house), *c*.1810, remodelled with Thomsonesque details, *c*.1878. Destroyed 1983.]
	†622	[247: house (latterly office). By Charles Wilson, 1845. Destroyed 1967.]
	†623	[249–59: tenement. By Alexander Thomson, *c*.1865. Destroyed 1967. (p.131, fig.108)]
	†624	[298: house, *c*.1830. Finely detailed windows. Destroyed *c*.1975.]
Saltmarket	**625**	15–27: tenement block. By J. J. Burnet, 1899–1900. Scots renaissance.
	626	109–29: tenements for City Improvement Trust. By John Carrick (1886). (p.190)
	627	Justiciary Court House. By William Stark, 1809–14; rebuilt except for portico by J. H. Craigie, 1910–13, externally approximately in original form. (p.70, fig.46)
	†628	[Silvercraig's Land, late 17th-century. Destroyed *c*.1845. (p.43)]
Saltoun Street, *Dowanhill*	**629**	Kelvinside-Hillhead (formerly Belmont-Hillhead) parish church. By James Sellars, 1875–6. (pp.174f., fig.155)
Sauchiehall Street, *City to Finnieston*	**630**	141–3: shops & offices. By John Keppie, 1904. Baroque with bold dormer aedicules.
	631	147–63: La Scala. By Mitchell & Whitelaw, 1908. Free renaissance top-hamper over glazed lower floors; altered.
	632	199–215: department store. By J. M. Munro, *c*.1904, remodelled from mid-19th-century terrace of tenements.
	633	217: former Cranston Willow tea-room. By C. R. Mackintosh, 1903–4; ground floor recently restored & interior partially reinstated. (p.218–20, figs.202f.)
	634	219–233: terrace of tenements, mid-19th-century, showing original form of **632**.
	635	235: Bank of Scotland. By John Keppie & A. Graham Henderson, 1931. Sculpture by Benno Schotz. (p.270)
	636	269–305: terrace of tenements with shops, *c*.1845.
	637	325–49: terrace of tenements (incomplete at east end), *c*.1850. Distinctive window detail.
	638	373–87: tenement, *c*.1860. Refined Thomsonesque detail.
	639	401–27: tenement, *c*.1860. Bold window detail of Bromhead type.
	640	515–43: tenement. By Charles Wilson, 1853. (p.94n)
	641	Newton Terrace, *c*.1864–5. (p.88)
	642	Sandyford Place. By Brown & Carrick, 1842–56. (p.88)
	643	Fitzroy Place. By John Burnet, sen., 1847. (pp.88f.)
	644	Westminster Terrace, *c*.1854.
	645	901–3: hotel (formerly tenement). By Charles Wilson, 1853.
	646	931–73: Wellesley Terrace, *c*.1858–62.

Sauchiehall Street, *City to Finnieston* (continued)	647	94–102: Crown salerooms. By Horatio Bromhead, 1871. (p.270n)
	648	128–52: warehouse (now Savoy Centre). By H. & D. Barclay, 1892–3; interior rebuilt. (pp.262, 271, fig.255)
	649	202–12: warehouse & shop. By James Thomson, 1902. (p.259, 262)
	650	254–90: McLellan Galleries. By James Smith, 1855; rear building by A. B. Macdonald, 1913–4; corner dome by Burnet & Boston, 1904, whose shopfronts now destroyed.
	651	338–56: Grecian Building. By Alexander Thomson, 1865; partial restoration 1983–4. (pp.147, 149–52, figs.127, 128f.)
	652	396–450: terrace of tenements. By T. L. Watson & Henry Mitchell, 1902 & 1907. Baroque detail of Burnet derivation.
	653	University of Strathclyde hostel (formerly Beresford Hotel). By Weddel & Inglis, 1937–9. (p.271, fig.264)
	654	518: Royal Highland Fusiliers (formerly Annan Gallery). By John Keppie, 1903. Free renaissance with Michelangelesque statuary.
	655	528–34: Albany Chambers. By J. J. Burnet, 1897. (fig.181)
	656	Newton Place. By George Smith, c.1837. (p.88)
	657	Somerset Place. By John Baird no.1, 1840. E pavilion rebuilt 1962. (pp.88, 250)
	658	Royal Crescent. By Alexander Taylor, 1839–49. (p.89, fig.61)
	†659	[Empire Theatre. By Frank Matcham, 1895–7. Destroyed 1963. (p.265)]
	†660	[167: Copeland & Lye's department store. By James Boucher, 1877–80. Corinthian. Destroyed 1973–4.]
	†661	[171: Fine Art Institute. By J. J. Burnet, 1878–80. Destroyed 1967. (p.200, fig.179)]
	†662	[191: Pettigrew & Stephen's department store. By John Keppie, with C. R. Mackintosh, 1896–7, incorporating earlier building; giant order with dome. Destroyed 1973–4. (p.195, 258, fig.180)]
	663	1055–65: tenement block. Style of Charles Wilson, c.1870.
	†664	[Grand Hotel. By James Thomson, 1877–82. Destroyed]
Scotstounmill Road, *Partick*	†665	[Scotstoun flour mills: brick addition by W. F. McGibbon, 1898. Bargello Gothic. Destroyed c.1980]
Skaethorn Road, *Maryhill*	666	Kelvin Aqueduct. By Robert Whitworth, 1787–90. (p.269, fig.262)
South Street, *Scotstoun*	667	North British diesel engine works. By Karl Bernhardt & John Galt, 1912. Influence of Peter Behrens
South Frederick Street	668	16: offices, c.1860. Simple astylar.
Southpark Avenue, *Hillhead*	669	65–73: terrace of houses, c.1840.
	670	64: semi-detached mansions, c.1850. Paired Doric porches.
Southpark Terrace, *Hillhead*	671	Terrace of houses, 1862. Renaissance.
Springburn Road, *Springburn*	672	255: Sighthill Cemetery lodge & gates. By John Stephen, 1839. Egyptian.
	†673	[524: Johnston memorial church. By Clarke & Bell, 1873–4. Corinthian. Destroyed 1972.]
Squire Street, *Whiteinch*	674	Whiteinch-Jordanvale church. By P. M. Chalmers, 1911. Romanesque.
Stanhope Street, *Townhead*	†675	[17: Blackie printing works. By Alexander Thomson, 1871–2. Destroyed 1966. (p.148n)]
Stockwell Street	676	133–58: tenements for City Improvement Trust. By N. S. Macdonald, 1905.
	†677	[28: house. Dated 1678. Destroyed c.1978. (p.43)]
Sydenham Road, *Dowanhill*	678	1: villa, c.1855. Italianate, with stilted arch bow.
	679	4: villa, c.1855. Broad-eaved, with clerestoreyed billiard room. Cf. **506**.
	680	8: villa. By James Thomson no.2, 1859. Very large, Tudor, with fretted bargeboards & verandas.
Templeton Street, *Glasgow Green*	681	62: Templeton Business Centre (formerly carpet factory). Founded 1857; main frontage by William Leiper, 1888–92; large art-deco additions by George A. Boswell, 1928 & 1934. (p.226, fig.219)
Tolcross Road, *Tolcross*	682	591: Tolcross House (within Tolcross Park). By David Bryce, 1848. Baronial; conservatory mid-19th-century.
	683	1088: Tolcross Central church. By John Brash, 1806; steeple 1834–5; refurnished 1858; reroofed 1884; pulpit remodelled 1904. (p.75)
Trongate	684	3–39: tenements for City Improvement Trust. By John Carrick (?), 1877 onwards. Renaissance with French-roofed corners.
	685	71: theatre (formerly Tron Kirk). By James Adam, 1794; steeple 1595 & 1635; arches inserted by John Carrick, 1855. (pp.47, 62, fig.28)

Trongate (continued)	686	97–101: warehouse. By J. T. Rochead, 1849. Pilastered.
	687	109–17: former Britannia music hall. By Gildard & Macfarlane, 1857. (p.109n)
	688	137–9: warehouse. By James Sellars, 1885. Free renaissance with central bow. (p.258n)
	689	151–5: warehouse, c.1860. Tall astylar palazzo front.
	690	167: warehouse, c.1850. Renaissance detail in manner of James Wylson.
	691	175–9: warehouse. By Burnet & Boston, 1923–9. Domed.
	692	2–16: offices. By A. Graham Henderson, 1922 (designed 1913). Concave front intended to be double feature. (fig.19)
	693	18–40: offices. By Thomson & Sandilands, 1912. Of same design as **5**.
	694	42–70: warehouses, shops & offices. By J. T. Rochead, 1854. Baronial.
	695	130–6: warehouse, shops & offices, c.1790. Plain, with arched pend.
	696	138–44: warehouse, c.1875. 3-bay iron façade between non-period masonry pilasters.
	†697	[129–35: Maclellan Building, c.1880. Cast-iron front with Italian renaissance detail. Destroyed c.1970]
	†698	[Tolbooth, 1626; gothicized by David Hamilton 1814. Destroyed 1921. (pp.43f., 52, figs.28f.)]
	†699	[Hutcheson's Hospital, 1641. Destroyed 1794. (pp.45, 50n, 81, fig.20)]
	†700	[Town hall. By Allan Dreghorn, 1737–60; completed by John Craig; adapted for Tontine Hotel by William Hamilton, 1781. Destroyed 1911. (pp.52f., 57, 60, 71n, figs.28f.)]
	†701	[110–44: warehouse, c.1790. Plain, with nepus gable. Destroyed c.1976]
	†702	[182–6: Spreull's Land: offices (former tenement), 1784. Destroyed 1978. (p.53)]
Turnbull Street, *Glasgow Green*	703	33: former St Andrew's Episcopal church. By William Paull & Andrew Hunter, masons, with Thomas Thomson, wright, 1750–2. Interior partly dismantled. (p.60)
Union Street	704	75–95: Caledonian Chambers. By James Miller, 1903; sculpture by Albert Hodge. (p.262n)
	705	101–15: offices & shops. By James Brown, 1850–1.
	706	50–76: warehouse & shops. By William (?) Lochhead, 1855. (p.118, fig. 93f.)
	707	78–82: offices. By James Thomson, c.1880. Cf.**120**.
	708	84–100: Egyptian Halls. By Alexander Thomson, 1871–3. (pp.128, 148f., 150–2, figs.128g, 129)
	709	102–14: offices. By Clarke & Bell, c.1894. (p.258n)
	710	118–20: Ca d'Oro extension. By Gillespie, Kidd & Coia, 1925–7. Tall concrete front.
University Avenue, *Hillhead*	711	9: Gilmorehill Hall (formerly Anderston Free church). James Sellars 1876–8; tower unfinished. Gothic.
	712	Wellington church. By T. L. Watson, 1883–4. (pp.161–3, 272, fig.142)
	713	University of Glasgow. By Gilbert Scott, 1866–72; Bute Hall, 1878–84 & spire, 1887, by J. Oldrid Scott; chapel & western range by Burnet, Son & Dick, 1923–7; Unicorn stair 1690 transferred from Old College; Pearce Lodge rebuilt from Old College façade by A. G. Thomson, 1887; Women's Union (now John McIntyre building) by J. J. Burnet, 1887 & 1895; Anatomy, Botany & Engineering buildings by James Miller, 1905–6; Zoology by Burnet, Son & Dick, 1923; Men's Union by John Arthur & Alan G. MacNaughtan 1927–30; reading room by T. Harold Hughes 1939; Chemistry building by T. H. Hughes & D. S. R. Waugh, 1939–52. (pp. 46f., 169f., 177, 249, 272, figs. 148, 150, 236)
University Gardens, *Hillhead*	714	1–10: terrace of houses. No.1 by Robert Ewan, 1902; nos 2–10 by J. J. Burnet, c.1894–6.
	715	12: house. By J. Gaff Gillespie, 1900. Sculptor, Albert Hodge (p.228n)
	716	14: house. By J. J. Burnet, 1900.
	717	11–25: terrace of houses. By Burnet, Son & Campbell, 1882. Nos 13–25 destroyed 1966.
Victoria Bridge	718	Bridge over Clyde. By James Walker, 1851–4. (p.111n)
Victoria Circus, *Dowanhill*	719	3: Cairndavan, villa, c.1860. Late classical.
	720	4: villa, c.1860. Wilsonesque Italianate.
	721	6: Kensington Tower, villa, c.1860. Large, Italianate.
	722	10: Ramoyle, villa, c.1860. Mixed classical & Italianate.
Victoria Crescent Road, *Dowanhill*	723	2–34: terrace of houses, c.1870–80. Bowed oriels; ingenious use of sloping site.
	724	38–52: terrace of houses, c.1855–60. Late classical.

Victoria Crescent Road, *Dowanhill* (continued)	725	Former chapel of Notre Dame convent. By Pugin & Pugin, 1900; glass by Harry Clarke.
Victoria Park Gardens South, *Broomhill*	726	20: Broomhill Trinity Congregational church & hall. By J. J. Burnet, 1900–08. (p.182)
Virginia Street	727	31–5: Tobacco (later Sugar) Exchange, c.1819; converted to shops & offices; internal court somewhat altered. (p.54, fig.33)
	728	37–53: Virginia Buildings & Virginia Court, c.1817. (p.54, figs.31f., 225)
	729	42: former Gas office. By R. G. Melvin & William Leiper, 1867. Bold palazzo façade incorporated into store 1983–4.
	730	52: house, later offices, c.1795. Turnpike stair in court.
	†731	[73–9: house, latterly offices, c.1800. Destroyed, c.1975.]
	†732	[City of Glasgow Bank. By Robert Black, 1838. Destroyed. (p.276)]
Walls Street	733	24–32: former Gas Department workshops, 1878, 1888 & 1903. Severe Italianate of earlier type.
Washington Street, *Broomielaw*	734	30–42: Buchanan's Bond. By A. Gardner 1897 & H. E. Clifford 1906. Giant arcaded front.
Waterloo Street	735	15–23: Waterloo Chambers. By J. J. Burnet, 1899. (pp.202–5, 209, 263)
	736	75–7: Electricity House. By A. McInnes Gardner, 1927. (p.270)
	737	36–48: Post Office parcels office. By W. T. Oldrieve, 1903–5. Renaissance.
	738	64: Distillers' Company offices. By James Chalmers, 1897. (p.259n)
	†739	[58: Ewing Place church. By Hugh Barclay, 1858. Destroyed 1958. (fig.147)]
Watson Street	740	17–23: warehouse, c.1880. Thomsonesque.
Wellington Street, *Blythswood*	741	9–11: warehouse, c.1880. Giant orders with detail of Thomsonesque derivation.
	742	40–60: Baltic Chambers. By Duncan McNaughtan, 1898–9.
	†743	[43: Alhambra Theatre. By J. J. Burnet, 1910 & 1920. Destroyed 1971. (p.266, fig.259)]
	†744	[Wellington church. By John Baird no.1, 1823. Destroyed 1909. (p.114n)]
	†745	[Wellington arcade. By John Baird no.1, c.1858. Destroyed c.1930. (p.114n)]
Westbourne Gardens, *Kelvinside*	746	1–18: terrace of houses, 1870–3.
	747	20–27: curved terrace of houses, c.1878, probably adapted from a design by Alexander Thomson.
	748	28–41: terrace of houses, c.1878. Free gothic.
	749	49–51: terrace of houses, c.1879. Ionic colonnade; based on a design by Alexander Thomson.
	750	52: Belhaven-Westbourne church. By John Honeyman, 1880 (pp.156, 159, fig.139)
West Campbell Street	†751	[28: McGeoch's Building. By J. J. Burnet, 1905. Destroyed 1971. (pp. 205–9, 211, fig.185)]
Wester Craigs, *Dennistoun*	752	9: Blackfriars parish church. By Campbell Douglas & Sellars, c.1878. German Romanesque; pyramid spire now removed.
West George Street, *City to Blythswood*	753	63–75: Stock Exchange, St George's Place. By John Burnet, sen., 1875–7; W section by J. J. Burnet, 1894–8, 1904; internally rebuilt c.1970. (pp.160, 178, 255, figs.163, 247)
	754	77–81 (St George's Place): offices. By James Boucher, 1875. Italianate. (fig.131)
	755	85: restaurant & offices. By Peddie & Kinnear, 1872. Simple Italianate.
	756	91–5: offices. By Burnet & Boston, c.1913. 7 storeys in manner of J. A. Campbell.
	757	117–21: former Sun Life Building. By William Leiper, 1892–4. Sculptor, W. Birnie Rhind (pp.226, 258, 259, fig.250)
	758	133–7: Pearl Assurance building. By James Thomson, 1897. Mixed renaissance.
	759	139–41: offices, c.1900. Narrow gabled frontage with canted bay.
	760	163–7: Bank of Scotland, c.1870. Renaissance in manner of James Thomson; doorpiece mutilated.
	761	201–3: former Burns-Aiken building. By John McLeod, 1881. Renaissance.
	762	213–21: terraced houses (now offices), c.1825. Roman Doric porches.
	763	223–5: offices (former tenement), c.1830.
	764	239–47: terraced houses (now offices), c.1825. Roman Doric porches.
	765	299–309: terrace of houses (now offices), c.1825–30.
	766	34–8: Connal's: offices. By James Thomson, 1899–1900. (p.258, fig.256)
	767	44–6: offices. By James Thomson, 1871. Renaissance.
	768	54: Liberal Club, St George's Place. By A. N. Paterson, 1909. Now Royal Scottish Academy of Music. (pp.225, 263, fig.247)

West George Street, *City to Blythswood* (continued)	**769**	60: Athenaeum, St George's Place, now R.S.A.M. By J. J. Burnet, 1886. (pp.200f., 225, fig.182)
	770	62–8: Royal Faculty of Procurators, St George's Place. By Charles Wilson, 1854. (pp.11n, 93, 121f., 255, fig.97)
	771	92–6: Royal Bank of Scotland. By James Miller, 1930. Art-deco classical.
	772	104: St George's Chambers, c.1880. Canted bay composition with rundbogenstil top.
	773	112–4: Scottish Widows' Fund. By David Bryce, 1868–9; altered internally by Peddie & Kinnear, 1871; reconstructed by Walter Underwood, 1959.
	774	134–6: Clydesdale Bank. By John Burnet, sen., 1867; ground floor remodelled c.1900.
	775	138–40: Provincial Insurance building. By James Thomson, 1859–60. Top two floors & porches later.
	776	144–6: former New Club, now James Sellars House. By James Sellars, 1879; interior rebuilt. (p.155)
	777	150–4: offices. By James Thomson, c.1873. Renaissance.
	778	158–60: houses, now office, c.1820. Top floor & rear later.
	779	166–8: offices. By Baird & Thomson, 1859–60 in style of 1830.
	780	188–92: Ocean Chambers. By R. A. Bryden, 1900. (p.258n)
	781	196–8: house (now office), c.1830.
	782	204: house (now office), c.1830. Ionic porch; top floor later.
	783	206–24: terrace of houses (now offices), c.1830. Anta doorpieces.
	784	226: house (now office), c.1830. Roman Doric doorpiece.
	785	232–48: terrace of houses (now offices), c.1830.
	†786	[Queen Insurance office, St George's Place. By James Sellars, 1876–7. Destroyed 1904 (pp.114, 153, 155, fig.131)]
	†787	[147–51: Alliance Building, c.1860. Palazzo with crowning sculpture group. Destroyed, c.1968]
	†788	[195: Tennant Mansion. By John Thomson, 1829, enlarged & reconstructed as offices by J. J. Burnet, c.1910. Destroyed c.1968]
	†789	[12–14: West George Street Independent chapel, latterly railway offices. By J. Gillespie Graham, 1819. Roman Doric. Destroyed 1975.]
West Graham Street, *Garnethill*	**790**	9–13: former dispensary for sick children. By James Sellars. 1882–4.
West Nile Street	**791**	19–23: shops & offices. By Burnet & Boston, 1902. Baroque. Designed linked to **595**.
	792	99–107: shops & offices. By Alexander Thomson, c.1858.
	793	106: Victoria Baths (now offices). By James Smith, c.1837.
West Princes Street, *St. George's*	**794**	1–59: terrace of tenements. By John Bryce, 1850–2.
	795	61–127: Queen's Terrace. By John Bryce, 1850–2. Partly destroyed 1970.
	796	2–56: terrace of tenements. By John Bryce, 1850–2.
West Regent Street, *Blythswood*	**797**	61–9: houses, c.1828: Four storeys with consoled doorcases & sculptured heads.
	798	79: house, remodelled as offices by James Salmon, jun., 1903–4.
	799	105–7: offices. Remodelled by Alexander Thomson, 1872.
	800	113–43: terrace of houses (now offices), c.1830–40; some heightened.
	801	4: offices. By J. A. Bell, 1858–60. Baronial.
	802	48–50: former Prudential Assurance building. By Alfred Waterhouse, 1890. (p.261n)
	803	64–88: terrace of houses (now offices), c.1840. Manner of David Hamilton.
	804	98–104: former Masonic building. By J. L. Cowan, 1900–4. Sculpturesque.
	805	126–52: terrace of houses (now offices), c.1830.
	806	158: Deaf & Dumb Institute. By Robert Duncan, 1894; church by Norman Dick, c.1925.
	807	176–86: terrace of houses (now offices). By Robert Scott, 1830–2. Romanesque porches, c.1860.
	808	188: house (now office). By Robert Scott, 1831–2.
Whitevale Street, *Dennistoun*	**809**	St Anne's R.C. church & presbytery. by J. A. Coia, 1933. (p.272, fig.265)
Whittingehame Drive, *Kelvinside*	**810**	11: villa. By John Ednie, 1908. Scots arts-&-crafts, with art-nouveau interiors.
Wilson Street	**811**	40–50: City & County Buildings (later sheriff courthouse). By Clarke & Bell, 1842–4 (S & central sections); 1871 (N section); Ingram Street frontage extended & rebuilt 1892. Sculptor, Walter Buchan. Disused. (pp.54, 62, 72, 83n, 104f., 235, figs.41, 77, 79)
	812	60: warehouse (originally offices), c.1790. Mutilated, with modern attics. (p.62, fig.41)
	813	76–84: former Scots Legal Life building. By Alexander Skirving, 1889. (p.262, fig.253)
	814	Links House: offices. By J. Taylor Thomson, 1932. In manner of Kodak House.
	†815	[20–34: warehouse (originally offices), c.1790. Destroyed 1982. (p.62)]

Wilton Street, *Belmont*	**816**	143–205 : terrace of houses, *c*.1870. Wilsonesque with later additions.
Windsor Terrace, *Woodside*	**†817**	[2–48 : terrace of houses, mid-19th-century. Destroyed *c*.1975]
Winton Drive, *Kelvinside*	**818**	9 : Winton House. Perhaps by R. Turnbull, *c*.1880. Greco-Egyptian. Damaged.
Woodend Drive, *Jordanhill*	**819**	10 : All Saints' Episcopal church. By James Chalmers, 1904. Romanesque.
Woodlands Gate, *Woodlands Hill*	**820**	Woodlands church & hall (now St Jude's Free Presbyterian). By John Burnet, sen., 1874–5. Gothic. (fig.70)
Woodlands Road, *Woodlands*	**821**	287 : Teachers' Centre. By Robert Dalgleish, 1882. Jacobean.
	822	50–68 : tenement. By Burnet & Boston, 1900.
Woodlands Terrace, *Woodlands Hill*	**823**	1–21 : terrace of houses. By John Baird no. 1, 1849–51. (p.249, fig.238)
	824	22–4 : terrace of houses. By Charles Wilson, 1855. (p.95)
	825	Stairway from Clifton Street. By Charles Wilson, *c*.1855.
Woodside Crescent, *Woodlands Hill*	**826**	2–19 : terrace of houses. By George Smith, begun *c*.1831. Lower houses destroyed 1969. (pp.92, 245, fig.240)
Woodside Place, *Woodlands Hill*	**827**	1–28 : terrace of houses. By George Smith, begun *c*.1838. (p.245)
Woodside Terrace, *Woodlands Hill*	**828**	1–11 : terrace of houses. By George Smith, begun 1835. (pp.92, 245, figs.64, 240)
	829	12–21 : terrace of houses. By George Smith, *c*.1842. (pp.92, 245, fig.64)
York Street, *Broomielaw*	**830**	23–31 : bonded warehouse. By Scott, Stephen & Gale, 1841. (p.106n)
	831	74 : warehouse & offices. By Neil C. Duff, 1901. Baroque.

B. Glasgow south of the river

Abbotsford Place, *Laurieston*	**832**	131 : Abbotsford public school. By H. & D. Barclay, 1879; extended 1893.
	†833	[1–53 : terraces of houses & tenements, *c*.1825–38. Destroyed 1972. (pp.73, 185, fig.52)]
	†834	[2–50 : terraces of houses & tenements, *c*.1825–38. As **833**. Destroyed 1972. (pp.73, 185, fig.52)]
Adelphi Street, *Gorbals*	**†835**	[United Co-operative bakery. By Bruce & Hay, 1886–1908. Destroyed 1978. (p.262)]
Adelphi Terrace, *Gorbals*	**836**	85 : Adelphi Terrace school. By T. L. Watson, 1894. Renaissance.
Admiral Street, *Kingston*	**837**	20–24 : Admiral House (formerly Wesleyan church). By John Honeyman, 1870. Renaissance.
Albert Drive, *Pollokshields*	**838**	241 : Pollokshields secondary school. By H. & D. Barclay, 1882.
	839	301 : The Knowe : villa. By Alexander Thomson, 1852–3. (pp.125, 134f.)
	840	336–8 : double villa. Perhaps by R. Turnbull, *c*.1878.
	841	398 : villa. By H. E. Clifford, *c*.1902. Tudor.
	842	Albert Drive church (now R.C.). By J. B. Wilson, 1886. Free renaissance.
Allison Street, *Govanhill*	**843**	265–89 : tenement block. By Alexander Thomson, *c*.1875 ; completed to simpler design by R. Turnbull, 1877.
Annette Street, *Govanhill*	**844**	27 : Govanhill public school. By H. & D. Barclay, 1886. (p.163, fig.146)
Ballater Street, *Gorbals*	**†845**	[42–50 : Chalmers Free church. By Alexander Thomson, 1859. Destroyed 1970. (p.126n)]
Balvicar Drive, *Queen's Park*	**846**	Camphill-Queen's Park church. By William Leiper, 1875–83. (pp.173f., fig.154)
Barlia Terrace, *Castlemilk*	**847**	Castlemilk House, 15th-cent ; remodelled 18th & 19th centuries. Destroyed 1969. Stables (*c*.1800) & bridge (perhaps by D. & J. Hamilton, *c*.1833) remain.
Barrhead Road, *Pollokshaws*	**848**	1554 : East Hurlet, 1763. 2-storey house with single-storey wings.
Bridge Street, *Laurieston*	**849**	1–3 : Bank of Scotland. By John Burnet, sen., 1857. Refined renaissance.
	850	36–54 : former Caledonian station. By James Miller, 1888. François I ; ground floor overlaid.
	†851	[Bridge Street Station. By James Collie, 1840. Greek Doric portico. Destroyed *c*.1952/1971]
Brockburn Road, *Pollok*	**852**	174 : Crookston Castle, 14th-century. (p.39)
Caledonia Road, *Hutchesontown*	**853**	1 : Hutchesontown & Caledonia Road church. By Alexander Thomson, 1856–7. Gutted 1965. (pp.98n, 128–31, 135, figs.105f.)
	854	316 : Southern Necropolis : gate. By Charles Wilson, 1848. Romanesque.
Carlton Place, *Laurieston*	**855**	40–61 : terrace of houses. By Peter Nicholson, 1802–4. Fine plasterwork at nos 51–2. (pp.72f., 78, 250, figs.48–50)
	856	65–84 : terrace of houses. By Peter Nicholson, 1813–18. (pp.72f., 250)
	†857	[34 : Barony of Gorbals church. By David Hamilton, 1806–10. Destroyed 1973. (pp.81f.)]
Carmunnock Road, *Cathcart*	**858**	Cathcart Old church. By H. E. Clifford, 1927–8. Gothic. Graveyard contains 17th-century tombs & the tower & W wall of the former parish church, 1831. (p.180)

Carmunnock Road, *Cathcart* (continued)	859	Aitkenhead House (within King's Park), 1806; wings by David Hamilton, 1823; further additions *c.*1828. Restored as flats, 1985–6.
Cathcart Road, *Hutchesontown & Govanhill*	860	513: Candlish Polmadie church. By John Honeyman, 1875. Gothic.
	†861	[37–9: tenement block. By Alexander Thomson, *c.*1857: design integrated with **853**. Destroyed 1968. (p.134n)]
Clarkston Road, *Cathcart*	861a	443: Muirend savings bank. By A. N. Paterson & D. M. Stoddart, 1925.
	862	86: Couper Institute. By James Sellars, 1887; library wing by J. Houston, 1923–4. Scots renaissance. (p.197)
	863	92: Cathcart South church. By W. G. Rowan, 1892. Gothic. (p.182n)
Coplaw Street, *Govanhill*	864	67–9: Royal Samaritan hospital. By McWhannel & Rogerson, 1894–1931. Scots style with modern-movement features.
Corslet Road, *Darnley*	865	Darnley Mill farm, early 18th-century. Crow-stepped with low circular tower.
Cross Street, *Pollokshaws*	866	1: the Round Toll, *c.*1800. Single-storey tollhouse.
Crossloan Road, *Govan*	867	Elder Park MacGregor memorial church. By James Miller, 1902–4. Gothic.
Crown Street, *Gorbals*	868	357–69: tenement block, *c.*1860. Thomsonesque.
	†869	[498–500: St Ninian's Wynd church & mission. By W. G. Rowan, 1888–9. Demolished. (p.182, fig.164) Sculptor, J. M. Sheriff.]
	†870	[211: Hutcheson's boys grammar school. By David & James Hamilton, 1839–41; E block & tower by John Burnet, sen., 1876. Mixed renaissance. Destroyed 1969–70. (p.81n)]
Cumberland Street, *Laurieston*	871	St Francis R.C. church & friary. By Pugin, Ashlin & Pugin, 1878–81. Very tall Gothic.
	†872	[35: Laurieston Renwick church. By J. Barbour; 1869; hall by J. J. Burnet, 1914. Gothic. Destroyed 1972.]
	†873	[40: house, *c.*1830. Doric porch. Destroyed *c.*1973.]
	†874	[41–51: houses (later tenements), *c.*1830. Destroyed *c.*1973. (p.73)]
Cuthbertson Street, *Govanhill*	875	Cuthbertson school. By James Miller, 1906.
Dalziell Drive, *Pollokshields*	876	31: villa. By H. E. Clifford, *c.*1903.
	867a	30: villa, *c.*1892. Renaissance.
Darnley Street, *Pollokshields*	877	46–50: former printing & publishing offices. By D. Bennet Dobson, 1902, Art-nouveau.
Dixon Road, *Govanhill*	878	69–87: New Bridgegate church. By Thomson & Sandilands, 1923. Curvilinear Gothic.
Eglinton Street, *Laurieston*	879	Coliseum Theatre. By Frank Matcham, 1904; altered 1925 & 1962; façade partly reclad. Derelict. (p.265)
	880	600–614: tenement block. Possibly by Alexander Thomson, *c.*1860.
	†881	[307: tenement. Probably by Alexander Thomson, *c.*1858. Destroyed 1969.]
	†882	[355–428: Queen's Park Terrace: terrace of tenements. By Alexander Thomson. Destroyed 1980. (pp.141f., 145, 183, 185f., fig.118)]
	†883	[487–91: tenement block. Possibly by Alexander Thomson, *c.*1863. Destroyed 1970.]
Fotheringhay Road, *Crossmyloof*	884	17–57: block of tenements. By H. E. Clifford, *c.*1902.
Garmouth Street, *Govan*	†885	[Fairfield public school. By H. & D. Barclay, 1891; N block later. Destroyed 1976.]
Glencairn Drive, *Pollokshields*	886	67: Baptist (formerly Pollokshields-Glencairn) church. By W. G. Rowan, 1891. Gothic.
	887	72: Pollokshields burgh hall. By H. E. Clifford, 1890. Baronial.
Golspie Street, *Govan*	†888	[Elder Park parish church. By James Smith of Jordanhill, 1826; re-erected here by John Honeyman, 1883–4. Gothick. Destroyed, *c.*1970.]
Gorbals Street, *Gorbals*	889	121–9: Citizens' Theatre. By Campbell Douglas, 1878; columns from Union Bank, Ingram Street (**369**) re-erected as façade by James Sellars. Façade destroyed, *c.*1973. (pp.158, 266)
	890	140–54: Gorbals public baths. By John Carrick, 1884–5. Renaissance.
	891	162–70: former British Linen Bank. By James Salmon, jun., 1900. (pp.222f.)
	†892	[29–81: tenements & shops, *c.*1875. Pilastered. Destroyed 1973.]
	†893	[32–68: tenements & shops. Perhaps by Alexander Thomson, *c.*1875. Destroyed 1973. (pp.142f.)]
	†894	[Palace Theatre. By Bertie Crewe, 1907. Destroyed. 1978. (p.266)]
Govan Road, *Govan*	895	401: Govan burgh buildings. By Thomson & Sandilands, 1897–1901. (p.263, fig.258)
	†896	[485–503: tenement block. Probably by Alexander Thomson, *c.*1872. Destroyed.]

Govan Road, *Govan* (continued)	**897**	635–9: warehouse & shops, *c.*1870. Simple classical, with vertical integration of windows.
	898	640–6: Napier House. By W. J. Anderson, 1898–9. (p.224, fig.213)
	899	816–8: Bank of Scotland (former British Linen Bank). By James Salmon, jun., 1899. (pp.222f.) Sculptors, Derwent Wood, Johan Keller & Richard Ferris.
	900	840: Pearce Institute. By R. R. Anderson, 1903–5. (p.198, fig.178)
	901	868: Govan Old parish church. By R. R. Anderson, 1884–8. 7th- to 11th-century slabs & monuments now inside church. (p.177n)
	902	1048: Glasgow Shipbuilders (formerly Fairfield Shipping Coy.) offices. By John Keppie, 1889; engine works 1874. (p.264n)
	†903	[505: St Columba's church. By James Thomson, 1870. Greek. Destroyed, *c.*1972.]
	†904	[Rutland House. By Bruce & Hay, 1896. Destroyed *c.*1975. (p.259n)]
Grange Road, *Langside*	**905**	Victoria Infirmary. By James Sellars, designed 1882, built 1888–90; extensions by Watson, Salmond & Gray. Renaissance.
Hospital Street, *Hutchesontown*	**906**	[190–2: tenement block. By Alexander Thomson, *c.*1857; design integrated with **853**. Destroyed 1973.]
Jessie Street, *Polmadie*	**907**	Sentinel works. By Archibald Leitch, 1903: multi-storey offices & pattern shops; earliest use of reinforced concrete in Glasgow.
Kilmarnock Road, *Newlands*	**908**	351–5: St Margaret's Episcopal church & hall. By P. M. Chalmers, 1912. (p.180)
Langlands Road, *Govan*	**909**	228a: Elder Library. By J. J. Burnet, 1902–5. (p.210, fig.190)
	910	Elder cottage hospital & nurses' home. By J. J. Burnet, *c.*1902. (p.210, fig.191)
Langside Avenue, *Langside*	**911**	1 (within Queen's Park): Langside public hall (formerly National Bank, Queen Street). By John Gibson, 1847–9; re-erected here by A. B. Macdonald, 1902–3. (pp.72, 122n, fig.98)
	912	122: Langside Hill church. By Alexander Skirving, 1895–6. Disused & dilapidated. (pp.164, 167)
Langside Drive, *Langside*	**913**	2: Newlands South church. By H. E. Clifford, 1902; hall 1899.
Langside Road, *Langside*	**914**	[Queen's Park U.P. church. By Alexander Thomson, 1867. Destroyed 1942. (pp.125–9, 134n, figs.102–4)]
Leslie Street, *Pollokshields*	**†915**	[Pollokshields East church. By W. F. McGibbon, 1883. Normandy Gothic. Destroyed 1983. (p.175n)]
Mansionhouse Road, *Langside*	**916**	25/25a: double villa. By Alexander Thomson, 1856–7. (pp.124, 127, 130, 132, 135f., figs. 100f., 109, 110c)
Mavisbank Road, *Kingston*	**917**	Princes Dock pumping station. By Burnet, Son & Campbell, 1894. Brick; mixed classical & Romanesque.
Maxwell Drive. *Pollokshields*	**†918**	[56: Falkland House, *c.*1859–60. Romanesque, well detailed. Destroyed *c.*1975]
Maxwell Road, *Pollokshields*	**919**	336–62: tenement block, *c.*1865. Free renaissance.
Meiklerigg Crescent, *Pollok*	**920**	165: St James's church (formerly Titwood church, Pollokshields). By H. E. Clifford, *c.*1894; re-erected here by Thomson, McCrea & Sanders, 1953–4. (p.180)
Merrylee Road, *Merrylee*	**921**	80: Holy Trinity parish church. By P. M. Chalmers, completed 1915. Romanesque.
Millbrae Crescent, *Langside*	**922**	2–38: terrace of houses. Probably by R. Turnbull, 1876–7. Thomsonesque.
	923	40–6: terrace of houses. Probably by R. Turnbull, *c.*1877. Thomsonesque.
Millbrae Road, *Langside*	**924**	Corner of Millbrae Crescent: tenement, *c.*1875. Free & attractive window treatment. (p.189)
Moray Place, *Strathbungo*	**925**	1–10: terrace of houses. By Alexander Thomson, *c.*1859–60. (pp.102, 123, 137–40, 251, figs.115f.)
	926	11–17: terrace of houses, *c.*1864–5. Possibly by Alexander Thomson.
	927	19–24: terrace of houses, *c.*1872. Rather crudely classical.
Morrison Street, *Kingston*	**928**	71: warehouse. By James Ferrigan, 1919 & 1933. (p.228n.)
	929	95: warehouse. By Bruce & Hay, 1893–7. Biggest of all Glasgow warehouses (p.262n)
Netherlee Road, *Cathcart*	**930**	Holmwood (now convent of our Lady of the Missions). By Alexander Thomson, 1856–8. (pp.127, 134–6, 145, fig.111)
	931	Netherlee Road bridge (over White Cart Water). Late 18th-century (datestone of 1624 inserted from earlier bridge). Large segmental arch with small side arch.
Newlands Road, *Newlands*	**932**	147: Holm foundry. By Albert Khan, 1913–5. Multi-storey reinforced-concrete workshops.
Nicholson Street, *Laurieston*	**†933**	[216–60: terrace of tenements, *c.*1820. Demolished 1972. (p.73)]
Nithsdale Road, *Strathbungo to Pollokshields*	**934**	161: synagogue (formerly house), 1881. Renaissance.
	935	229: Allerly: mansion by W. F. McGibbon, *c.*1887. Baronial.
	936	18–76: block of tenements. By R. Turnbull, 1877.

Nithsdale Road, *Strathbungo to Pollokshields* (continued)	937	84–112: block of tenements. By Alexander Thomson, begun *c.*1873; completed by R. Turnbull, 1888. (p.140n)
	938	200: Ellisland, villa by Alexander Thomson, 1871. Interior despoiled. (pp.135f., 149, fig.112)
	939	202: villa. By Alexander Thomson, 1870. Interior survives. (p.133, fig.110e)
	940	Sherbrooke St Gilbert's church. By W. F. McGibbon, 1895–9. (p.175n)
Nithsdale Street, *Strathbungo*	941	52–8: Salisbury Quadrant: tenement block. By R. Turnbull, *c.*1880.
Norfolk Street, *Gorbals*	†942	[12–24: tenements & shops. Perhaps by Alexander Thomson, 1860–1. Continuation of **893**. Destroyed 1974.]
Old Castle Road, *Cathcart*	†943	[Cathcart Castle, 15th-century. Keep until recently largely complete. Destroyed *c.*1977. (p.40)]
Oxford Street, *Laurieston*	944	45–65: warehouse, *c.*1865. Much use of glass.
	945	156–60: tenements, *c.*1815. Plain.
Paisley Road West, *Kinning Park to Bellahouston*	946	425: Bellahouston Academy. By Robert Baldie, 1875–6. Symmetrical turreted Gothic with central tower.
	947	252–6: tenements with shops. By James Sellars, 1882.
Plantation Place, *Plantation*	948	Tunnel terminal, *c.*1896. Domed circular lifthouse.
Pleasance Street, *Pollokshaws*	949	Pollokshaws clock tower (relic of old burgh buildings), *c.*1803. Adamesque Scots.
Pollok Street, *Kingston*	†950	[3–5: Pollok Street church. By J. Dick Peddie, sen., 1856. Renaissance. Destroyed 1970.]
	†951	[E. side of street: tenements, *c.*1880. Destroyed 1970. (p.189, fig.168)]
	†952	[36–40: tenement block. By Alexander Thomson, *c.*1873. Destroyed 1970.]
Pollokshaws Road, *Hutchesontown to Pollokshaws*	953	601–5: Strathbungo church. By W. G. Rowan, 1886 (incorporating remains of church by Charles Wilson, 1839). Romanesque. Disused. (p.182n)
	954	939: Camphill House (within Queen's Park), shortly after 1798. Details suggestive of David Hamilton.
	955	2025: Pollokshaws burgh hall. By R. R. Anderson, 1897. Scots renaissance (p.198)
	956	1120: Shawlands Old parish church. By J. A. Campbell, 1888–9. (p.177, fig.157)
	957	2060: Pollok House (within Pollok Grounds). Probably from designs by William Adam, 1747–52; completed by John Adam; plasterwork probably by Thomas Clayton; terraces, wings, pavilions, etc., by R. R. Anderson, 1890 & later. Stable block 18th-century, incorporating parts of 14th-century house, with 17th-century archway. N Lodge (97 Haggs Road) by R. R. Anderson, 1892. S Lodge (300 Barrhead Road) by R. R. Anderson, 1892. Gatepiers 18th-century. Bridge by John Adam (?), 1757–8. Dovecot 17th-century. (pp.65–7, 269, fig.43)
	†958	[2091: Pollok church. By James Brown, 1847–8. Renaissance. Destroyed 1979]
	†959	[2097: Pollock school annexe. By Alexander Thomson, 1856; altered by John Baird no.2, *c.*1875 & John Hamilton, *c.*1910. Rundbogenstil. Destroyed 1968. (pp.132, 134n, fig.110f)]
Polmadie Road, *Polmadie*	960	St Margaret's church & manse. By P. M. Chalmers, 1902. Romanesque.
Prospecthill Road, *Langside*	961	Langside College annexe. By Salmon, Son & Ritchie, 1866–8. Polychrome Franco-Italian gothic. Originally Deaf-&-Dumb Institute.
Queen Square, *Strathbungo*	962	4–50: terrace of houses, *c.*1864–5. Plain classical.
Queen Mary Avenue, *Crosshill*	963	3–9: terrace of houses, *c.*1860. Elaborately decorated.
Queen's Drive, *Crosshill*	964	40: Crosshill-Queen's Park church. By Campbell Douglas, 1872–3. (p.174, fig.156)
	965	174: Seventh Day Adventist church. By J. B. Wilson, 1888. Gothic.
	966	178: Queen's Park Baptist church. By McKissack & Rowan, 1886. Romanesque.
	967	Strathbungo-Queen's Park church. By James Thomson, *c.*1876.
Regent Park Square, *Strathbungo*	968	3–49: terrace of houses, *c.*1861–6. Severe classical.
	969	4–44: terrace of houses, *c.*1861–5. As **968**.
Rowan Road, *Dumbreck*	970	6: Craigie Hall. By John Honeyman, 1872; additions by John Keppie & C. R. Mackintosh, 1892–4 & 1897. Renaissance.
Rutherglen Road, *Hutchesontown to Polmadie*	971	189–203: weaving factory, founded *c.*1822. 4- & 5-storey brick; severe.
	†972	[155–7: Hutchesontown Congregational church (latterly factory). By Salmon, Son & Gillespie, 1902. Destroyed 1972.]
Rutland Cresent, *Plantation*	†973	7–13: terrace of houses, *c.*1850. Classical with Ionic doorpieces.
	†974	[Rutland Crescent public school. By H. & D. Barclay, 1883. Destroyed *c.*1969. (pp.163f.)]
St Andrew's Drive, *Pollokshields*	975	100: Haggs Castle, 1585; reconstructed *c.*1860. (p.40)
	†976	[35–7: double villa. By Boucher & Cousland, 1858–9. Demolished 1968.]

St Kenneth's Drive, *Govan*	†977	[St Kenneth's church. By P. M. Chalmers, 1897–8. Romanesque with fine interior. Destroyed 1981.]
Scotland Street, *Kingston*	978	225: Scotland Street public school. By C. R. Mackintosh, 1904–6. (pp.220f., 272, figs.206f.)
	†979	[471–85: tenements with shops. By Alexander Thomson or R. Turnbull, *c.*1877. Destroyed *c.*1977.]
	†980	[430: St Mark's Episcopal church (latterly Neptune masonic lodge). By R. S. Lorimer, 1910. Destroyed *c.*1975.]
Sherbrooke Avenue, *Pollokshields*	981	11: mansion. By Thomson & Sandilands, 1896. Baronial with tower. (p.264n)
	982	21: villa. By W. J. Anderson, *c.*1893. Renaissance.
Shields Road, *Polloskshields*	983	477–507: terrace of houses, *c.*1850. Classical.
	984	614–20: Christian Brethren meeting house (formerly Pollokshields Free church). By W. G. Rowan, 1877–8. Thomsonesque.
South Portland Street, *Laurieston*	†985	[43: Erskine U.P. church (latterly warehouse). By John Baird no.1, 1842. Gothic. Destroyed 1972.]
Spean Street, *Cathcart*	986	42: S.W. Electricity Board (formerly Wallace Scott factory). By J. J. Burnet, 1913–22. Mutilated & formal gardens despoiled. (pp.209, 266, 271, fig.187)
Springkell Avenue, *Dumbreck*	987	124: Beneffrey. By W. H. McNab, 1910.
Terregles Avenue, *Pollokshields*	988	44–84: terrace of tenements. By H. E. Clifford, 1895. (p.190)
Thistle Street, *Hutchesontown*	†989	[45–7: Cunninghame Free church. By H. & D. Barclay, 1897–8. Gothic. Destroyed 1977.]
Thornliebank Road, *Eastwood*	990	40: Auldhouse, 1631; 18th- & 19th-century additions removed 1983. Crow-stepped.
Tradeston Street, *Tradeston*	991	118: former I.C.I. warehouse. By W. F. McGibbon, 1900. Bargello Gothic. (p.226n, fig.218)
	†992	[13–23: Randolph & Elder engine factory. By William Spence, 1858–60. Destroyed 1970. (p.107, figs.82f.)]
Wallace Street, *Kingston*	†993	[216: Scottish C.W.S. warehouse. By Bruce & Hay, 1888–92. Symmetrical renaissance with central tower. Destroyed *c.*1973.] (p.262n)
	†994	[250: warehouse. By William Spence, 1871–2. Severe classical, the last of Glasgow's classical warehouses. Destroyed *c.*1973.]
Walmer Crescent, *Ibrox*	995	1–18: terrace of houses. By Alexander Thomson, 1857–62. (pp.125f., 139f., 149, fig.117)
West Street, *Tradeston*	†996	[21–3: Kingston grain mills. By James Salmon & Son, 1875–6. Red & white brick rundbogenstil. Destroyed 1978.]

E. West Glasgow

Locating Glasgow's buildings

This sequence of maps, showing West, North, South and Central Glasgow, and the Woodlands Hill area, is intended to enable the reader to establish the location of buildings of historical and architectural interest mentioned in the text. The reference numbers on the maps are keyed to the list of buildings which commences on page 305; and that list provides an index to the textual references and illustrations occurring in the body of the book.

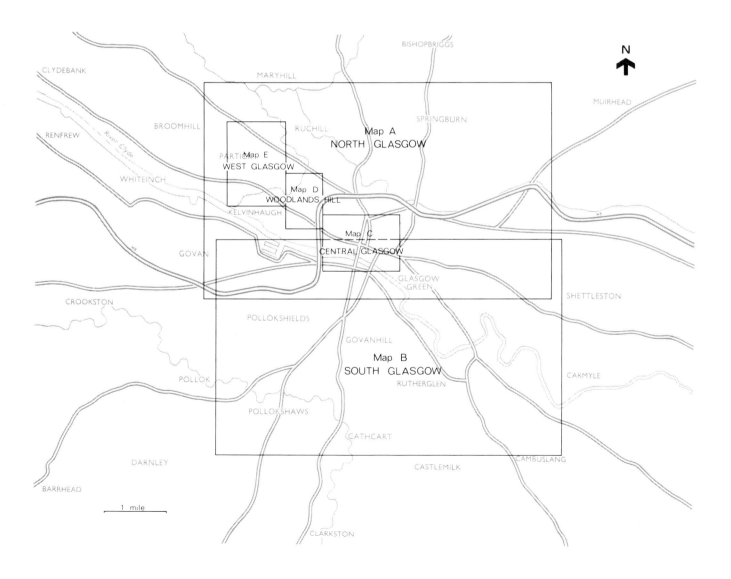

446

31 Lambhill Bridge   32

149

LAMBHILL

666   445   444

MARYHILL

RUCHILL

563   Ruchill Street   Ruchill Park

419

59   Great Western Road   Winton Drive   810

306

KELVINSIDE   Cleveden Gardens   Redlands Road

NORTH KELVIN   530   248

819   HYNDLAND   Westbourne Gardens   Botanical Gdns   404   447*   249*

167   529   BELMONT   816   Raeberry Street   357A

102   DOWANHILL   326   70   71   330

726   For this area see West Glasgow map   310   325   324   69   199   Mount St   817*   581

PARTICKHILL   309   295   HILLHEAD   270   294   WOODSIDE   Windsor Street   580   479

103   University Avenue   Great George   Street   579   443   323   478   ORT DUND

101   PARTICK   Highburgh   KELVINGROVE   533   532   477

667   Dumbarton Road   Kelvingrove Park   795   796   471   472   481*

674   For this area see Woodlands Hill map   794   St GEORGE'S   480*

KELVINGROVE   WOODLANDS HILL   442   COWCADDENS

215*   Esmond St   Dalnair Street   340   341   114   GARNETHILL   790   203*   460*   440   439

KELVINHAUGH   663   339   338   213   148*   204*   352   356

265   12   582   546   551   544   543

584   St Vin   655   653   545

461   CHARING   654

462   463*   22*   178*   474

FINNIESTON   19   329*   BLYTHSWOOD

902   901   899   897   206*   For this area see Central Glasgow

909   900   898   ANDERSTON

910   885*   903*   896*   GOVAN   897   RIVER CLYDE   Docks

888*   895   BROOMIELAW

867   977*   917   948   174*

IBROX   PLANTATION   904   929   928   98

974*   973   992   851   849   856

837   950*   996*   855   718

995   947   952*   993   994   991   850   945   985*   942*   893*   892*

946   KINGSTON   933*   890   889

Paisley Road West   980*   951*   978   LAURIESTON   879   834*   833*   891   894

979*   TRADESTOWN   872*

A. North Glasgow

0 _____ 500 _____ 1000
yards

SPRINGBURN

Springburn Park

33

72

673°

344

239

672

516

562

561

503°

504

561

Royston Road

Alexandra Park

TOWNHEAD

Barony Street

135

Alexandra

158

157   165A°

160°   413A   163

164

7

156   159°

155   165   162

161

413B

221

222   223

752

8

205°

809

67°

703   28

565   27

171 168

173° 169

170

2°   564   172

920   431

267   467   492

70A   681

36

268

99   100 BRIDGETON

Glasgow

Castle Street

Royston

Necropolis

Gartloch Drive

24

DENNISTOUN

Armadale Street

Water Cales

Duke Street

CAMLACHIE

241   242

Wesleyan Street

243

Gallowgate

247°

CALTON

London Road

Glasgow Green

RIVER CLYDE

Cumbernauld Road

Easter Craigs

Alexandra Parade

Edinburgh   Road

CARNTYNE

Carntyne   Road

Carnychhall Road

Shettleston   Road

Westmuir Street

Old Shettleston

244°

231°

488

0 50 100 150 200 250
yards

Bibliography

Official records and collections of
unpublished material

H.M. Register House Edinburgh. Glasgow Sasines.
Scottish National Monuments Record. Photographic collection; drawings.
Mitchell Library Glasgow. Photographic collection; Young's Glasgow Scraps;
 collections of architectural cuttings, including that formed by Professor Gourlay;
 small collection of Alexander Thomson drawings.
University of Glasgow, Department of Fine Art. Hamilton and Mackintosh drawings.
Glasgow School of Art. Mackintosh Collection.
Strathclyde Regional Council Archives. Dean of Guild Plans; Glasgow burgh minutes.
Royal Institute of British Architects. Nomination papers.

Newspapers, periodicals and journals

Architect, The 1869+.
Baillie, The 1872+. Man-you-know series includes several architects.
British Architect 1874–1919.
Builder, The 1842+.
Builders Journal, The 1895–1910. 28 November 1906 of special value.
Building Industries and Scottish Architect 1890+.
Building News, The 1854+.
Civil Engineer and Architects' Journal 1837–1868.
Glasgow Herald 1783+. (As *Glasgow Advertiser* to 1805: no complete set of the
 Advertiser exists.)
Govan Press 1878+.
McWilliam's Glasgow Property Circular ?–1876;
 Glasgow Property Circular 1876–98;
 Glasgow Advertiser and Property Circular 1898+.
Royal Institute of British Architects, Journal of: Obituaries from 1908.
Royal Incorporation of Architects in Scotland Quarterly: Obituaries and articles.
Royalty Club of Glasgow, 1889+.
Charles Rennie Mackintosh Society Newsletter, 1973+.

Annuals

Academy Architecture 1888+.
Studio Year Books of Decorative Art
Transactions of the Glasgow Archaeological Society 1859+.
Royal Glasgow Fine Art Institute Catalogues
Royal Scottish Academy Catalogues 1826+.
Directories: Tait 1783; Jones 1787: McFeat's 1799–1828: Post Office 1828+.

Books

Aikman, J. L. *History of U.P. Congregations* 1875.
Aird, A. *Glimpses of Old Glasgow,* 1894.
Architectural Publication Society's *Dictionary* (Wyatt Papworth, ed., 1848–92).
Billcliffe, Roger. *Charles Rennie Mackintosh. The Complete Furniture, Furniture
 Drawings and Interior Designs,* 1979.
Billings, R. W. *Baronial and Ecclesiastical Antiquities of Scotland,* 1845.
Blackie (pub.) *Villa and Cottage Architecture,* 1868; 2nd edn, 1878.
Blair, G. *Biographic and Descriptive Sketches of Glasgow Necropolis,* 1857.
Bolton, A. T. *The Architecture of R & J Adam,* 1922.
Brotchie, T. C. F. *History of Govan,* 1905.
Brown, A. *History of Glasgow,* 1795.
Burgh of Govanhill, 1891.
Burnet, Sir John and Partners. *The Architectural Work of* (Masters of Architecture
 Series, Geneva).
Cant, R. G., and Lindsay I. G. *Old Glasgow,* 1947.
Chalmers, P. M. *Glasgow Cathedral,* 1914; *The Govan Sarcophagus,* 1920.

Chapman, R. (pub.) *The Picture of Glasgow*, 1st edn, 1806; 2nd edn, 1812; 3rd edn, 1818, 1820, 1822.

Cleland, J. *Annals of Glasgow*, 1816; *Rise and Progress of the City of Glasgow*, 1820; *Former and Present State of Glasgow*, 1840.

Collie, J. *Plans &c. of the Cathedral of Glasgow*, 1833.

Colvin, H. M. *A Biographical Dictionary of British Architects 1600–1840*, 1978.

Cooper, Jackie (ed.) *Mackintosh Architecture* 1978.

Cowan, J. *From Glasgow's Treasure Chest*, 1951.

Denholm, J. *History of the City of Glasgow*, 1st edn, 1797; 2nd edn, 1798; 3rd edn, 1804.

Descriptive Handbook of the Glasgow Corporation Public Libraries, 1907.

Donnelly, Michael. *Glasgow Stained Glass: a preliminary study*, 1981.

Eaton, Leonard K. *American Architecture Comes of Age*, 1972 (contains chapter on Burnet).

Ewing, A. Orr. *View of the Merchants' House of Glasgow*, 1866.

Eyre, Todd G. (ed.) *The Book of Glasgow Cathedral*, 1898 (architectural part by John Honeyman);
and Renwick, R. *History of Glasgow*, 1921–34.

Fiddes, V. & Rowan, A. J. *Mr. David Bryce*, 1976.

Fleming, John. *Robert Adam and his Circle*, 1962.

Fraser, D. *The Making of Buchanan Street*, 1885.

Gemmell, Wm. *Early Views of Glasgow*, 1913.

Gerrard, John, Lindsay, Maurice & Riches, Anne (eds.) *Historic Buildings at Work: a Guide to Historic Buildings in Scotland used by Central Government*, 1984.

Gibb, Andrew. *Glasgow: the Making of a City*, 1983.

Gibson, J. *History of Glasgow*, 1977.

Gildard, T. MS. book on Alexander Thomson (includes Haldane Lectures and 1871 Presidential Address); MS. book on John Carrick; MS. book *Some Old Glasgow Architects* (all in Mitchell Library. See also articles and pamphlets).

Glasgow and its Tributaries, 1901.

Glasstone, Victor. *Victorian and Edwardian Theatres*, 1975.

Gordon, J. (ed.) *Glasghu Facies*, a view of the City of Glasgow, 1872.

Greenhome, W. *History of Partick*, 1928.

Gunnis, R. *Dictionary of British Sculptors*, 1953 (note: the entury 'D. Hamilton and Sons' relates to the architect and the marble business run by his son John).

Hay, G. *Scottish Post-Reformation Churches*, 1957.

Hedderwick. *The Origin and History of Glasgow Streets*.

Hepburn, John. *Charles Wilson* (unpublished thesis).

Hill, L. *Hutcheson's Hospital*, 1855.

Hitchcock, H. R. *Early Victorian Architecture*, 1954; *Architecture 19th and 20th Centuries*, 1958.

Honeyman, John. *The Age of Glasgow Cathedral*, 1854.

Howarth, T. *Charles Rennie Mackintosh and the Modern Movement*, 1953, 2nd edn, 1977.

Hume, John R. *The Industrial Archaeology of Glasgow*, 1974

Johnston, Colin & Hume, J. R. *Glasgow Stations*, 1979.

Kenna, Rudolf. *Glasgow Art Deco*, 1985.

Kenna, Rudolf & Mooney, Anthony. *People's Palaces: Victorian and Edwardian Pubs of Scotland*, 1983.

Lattimer, W. (pub.) *Glasgow Delineated*, 1836.

Laurie, John. *Improvements of Glasgow*, 1810.

Leighton, John. *The Beauties of Clyde*, 1835.

Louden, T. *The Cinemas of a Cinema City*, 1983.

Lugton, T. *The Old Ludgings of Glasgow*, 1901.

Lumsden, H. *Records of The Trades House of Glasgow*, 1910.

Macaulay, James. *The Gothic Revival 1745–1845*, 1975.

McCallum, A. *Pollokshaws, Village and Burgh*, 1925.

McFadzean, Ronald. *The Life and Work of Alexander Thomson*, 1979.

McGeorge, A. *Old Glasgow*, 1880.

MacGibbon, D., and Ross. T. *Castellated and Domestic Architecture of Scotland*, 1887–92; *Ecclesiastical Architecture of Scotland*, 1896–7.

McIntosh, H. *The Origin and History of Glasgow Streets*, 1902.

Mackie, J. D. *The University of Glasgow*, 1954.

MacLellan, A. *Essay on Glasgow Cathedral*, 1833.

Mcleod, R. *Charles Rennie Mackintosh*, 1968, 2nd edn, 1983.

M'Ure, J. *History of Glasgow*, 1736.

Markus, T. A. (ed.) *Order in Space and Society*, 1982.

Marwick, J. D. *Early Glasgow*, 1911.

Marwick, J. D. and Renwick, R. *Extracts from the Records of the Burgh of Glasgow*, 1876–1911.

Millar, A. H. *Castles and Mansions of Renfrewshire*.

Modern Architectural Art (ref. J. J. Burnet), Pts I and II (E. & J. Burrows & Co. London).

Muir, J. *Glasgow Streets and Places*, 1899.

Municipal Glasgow, its evolution and enterprises, 1914 (Glasgow Corporation).

Murray, D. *Memories of the Old College of Glasgow*, 1927.

Muthesius, H. *Das Englische Haus*, 1911; English translation, 1979.

Oakley, Charles. *The Second City*, 1946; revised edn, 1967.

Ord, J. *The Barony of Gorbals*, 1919.

Pagan, J. *Sketch of the History of Glasgow*, 1847.

Pevsner, N. B. L. *C. R. Mackintosh* (Italian: Il Balcone, Milan 1950).

Primrose, J. *Mediaeval Glasgow*, 1913.

Rae, J. S. *The Ministers of Glasgow and their Churches*.

Rait, R. S. *History of the Union Bank of Scotland*, 1930.

Read, Benedict. *Victorian Sculpture* (1982).

Reid, J. M. *History of the Clydesdale Bank*, 1938; *Glasgow*, 1956.

Reid, Robert. *Old Glasgow and its Environs*, 1864.

Renwick, R. C. *Memorials of Glasgow*, 1895.

Richardson, A. E. *Monumental Architecture in Great Britain*, 1914.

Rogerson, R. W. K. C. *Jack Coia: his life and work*, 1986.

Scottish Development Department. List of Buildings of Architectural and Historic Interest (prepared by A. G. Lochhead. Revised with additional material, 1965). Contains references to some of the news items in contemporary building journals.

Senex (R. Reid). *Glasgow Past and Present*, 1851; revised edition with much additional material 1884.

Service, Alastair (ed.) *Edwardian Architecture and its Origins*, 1975 (essays on Burnet, Mackintosh and Salmon).

Simpson, M. A. & Lloyd, T. H. *Middle-Class Housing in Britain*, 1977.

Simpson, W. *Glasgow in the 'Forties*, 1899.

Sinclair, Fiona. *Scotstyle*, 1984.

Small, D. *Quaint Sketches of Glasgow*, 1885; *By-gone Glasgow*, 1896.

Smith, J. Guthrie. *Old Country Houses of the Old Glasgow Gentry*, 1870.

Stuart, R. *Views and Notices of Glasgow in Former Times*, 1848.

Swan, J. *Select Views of Glasgow and Environs*, 1829.

Wade, W. M. *History of Glasgow Ancient and Modern*, 1821.

Walker, Brian (ed.) *Frank Matcham*, 1980.

Watson, T. L. *The Double Choir of Glasgow Cathedral*, 1901.

Wordsdall, Frank. *The Tenement: A Way of Life*, 1979; *The City that Disappeared*, 1981; *Victorian City*, 1982.

Young, A. M. and Doak, A. (ed.) *Glasgow at a glance*, latest edn., 1983.

Young, Andrew McLaren. *Charles Rennie Mackintosh*, Exhibition Catalogue, 1968.

Young, W. *Municipal Buildings of Glasgow*, 1890.

Young, W. *The Old Closes and Streets of Glasgow*, 1900.

In addition to the above *The Dictionary of National Biography* includes memoirs of the better-known architects: the memoir of Thomson is, however, very unreliable. *Who Was Who* gives some useful particulars of John Honeyman; *Who's Who in Glasgow* is helpful on Bruce and Hay and A. N. Paterson, while *Scottish Biographies* (1938) gives some particulars of McWhannel. *Glasgow Contemporaries* (1901) is informative, though anecdotal. There are a large number of church histories which vary in the amount of architectural information they give. Koch's *British Competitions* contain a number of Glasgow designs.

Articles and Pamphlets

A select list only: for Mackintosh see the bibliography in Howarth.

Barclay, D. 'Alexander Thomson', *The Architectural Review*, May 1904.

Beazley, E. and Lambert, S. 'The Astonishing City', *Architects' Journal*, 6 May 1964.

Brewsher, C. C. *The Glasgow Royal Exchange Centenary 1827–1927* (brochure).

Fawcett, Richard. *Glasgow Cathedral* (official guidebook), 1985

Glasgow Corporation. *Park Circus Area* (brochure), 1967.

Goodfellow, G. L. M. 'Colin Campbell's Shawfield Mansion', *Journal of the Society of Architectural Historians* (of America), October, 1964.

Goodhart Rendel, H. S. 'The Work of Sir John Burnet' *Architects' Journal*, 27 June 1923.

Hitchcock, H. R. 'Early Cast Iron Façades', *Architectural Review*, February 1951.

Honeyman, J. 'Glasgow Cathedral', *Transactions of Glasgow Archaeological Society*, New Series, Vol. I, Pt. I, 1885; 'John Baird', *Maclehose's One Hundred Eminent Glasgow Men*, 1886.

Honeyman, H. L. 'Clerks' Architecture', *Glasgow Herald*, 13 May 1914.

Keppie, John. 'James Sellars', *Scottish Art Review*, 1888; 'Architecture of Glasgow' in *Old Glasgow Club*, 1915.

Law, Graham. 'Greek Thomson', *Architectural Review*, May 1954.

Lochhead, A. G. *Hutcheson's Hospital Hall* (pamphlet), 1961.

McRobert, Monsignor. 'Notes on Glasgow Cathedral', *Innes Review*, vol. xvi, 1965, pp.40–47.

Oakley, Charles. Miscellaneous historical articles in *Chamber of Commerce Journal*.

Radford, C. A. R. *Glasgow Cathedral* (official guidebook), 1970

Radford, C. A. R. and Stones E. L. G. 'The Remains of the Cathedral of Bishop Jocelin at Glasgow', *Antiquaries' Journal*, Vol. xliv, pt. ii, 1964.

Ross, Anne. 'Twenty Five Years– then Gilmorehill', *The College Courant* (of Glasgow University), Vol. 19, No. 34, Whitsun 1965.

Skempton, A. R., and Johnson, H. R. 'The First Iron Frames', *Architectural Review*, March 1962.

Stones, E. L. G. & Hay, George. 'Notes on Glasgow Cathedral', *Innes Review*, vol. xviii, 1967, pp.88–98.

Thomson, D. 'Charles Wilson', *Glasgow Philosophical Society*, 13 March 1882.

Waddell, J. J. 'The Western Towers of Glasgow Cathedral', *Scottish Ecclesiological Society*, vol VI, pt. ii, 1919–20.

Walker, D. 'Salmon Son Grandson and Gillespie', *Scottish Art Review*, Vol. X, No. 3, 1966; 'James Sellars', *Scottish Art Review*, Vol. XI, Nos. 1 and 2, 1967.

Walker, Frank. 'Six Villas by James Salmon', *Architectural History* 25, 1982, pp.115–9.

'Wallace Scott Tailoring Institute Cathcart', *Architectural Review*, 1922, pp.128–34.

Watson, John. 'Architects of the Victoria' in Ian Murray, *Victoria Infirmary*, 1967.

Wordsall, F. 'Greek Thomson', *Scottish Field*, February 1962; 'David Hamilton', *Scottish Field*, May 1968; 'Poor Mr. Smith', *Scottish Field*, December 1963; 'J. T. Rochhead' in *Scottish Field*, September 1964; 'Plans that went Awry', *Scottish Field*, March 1965; 'William Leiper', *Scottish Field*, June 1966 (illustrates Dowanhill for Camphill; an underestimate of Leiper's ability and significance, but contains biographical details not given by McNab in *J.R.I.B.A.*).

Index of architects and craftsmen

This index does not include references to the chronological table on pp.277ff, to the genealogical tree on p.282f, or to the street gazetteer on pp.305ff. Minor references to architects not directly connected with Glasgow are also generally excluded.